Women
BETWEEN

Women
BETWEEN

**Construction of Self
in the Work of**

*Sharon Butala,
Aganetha Dyck,
Mary Meigs and
Mary Pratt*

UNIVERSITY OF
CALGARY
PRESS

Verna Reid

University of Calgary Press
2500 University Drive NW
Calgary, Alberta
Canada T2N 1N4
www.uofcpress.com

LIBRARY AND ARCHIVES CANADA CATALOGUING IN PUBLICATION

Reid, Verna, 1928-
        Women between : construction of self in the work of Sharon Butala, Aganetha
Dyck, Mary Meigs and Mary Pratt / Verna Reid.

Includes bibliographical references and index.
ISBN 978-1-55238-242-4

        1. Butala, Sharon, 1940- –Criticism and interpretation. 2. Dyck, Aganetha, 1937-
–Criticism and interpretation. 3. Meigs, Mary, 1917-2002–Criticism and interpretation. 4. Pratt,
Mary, 1935- –Criticism and interpretation. 5. Self-perception in women. 6. Autobiography.
7. Women authors, Canadian. 8. Women artists–Canada. 9. Middle-aged women–Canada. 10.
Feminist theory. I. Title.

NX513.Z8R43 2008   305.43'700971   C2008-903839-8

The University of Calgary Press acknowledges the support of the Alberta Foundation for the Arts
for our publications. We acknowledge the financial support of the Government of Canada through
the Book Publishing Industry Development Program (BPIDP) for our publishing activities. We
acknowledge the financial support of the Canada Council for the Arts for our publishing program.

Printed and bound in Canada by Marquis.
∞ This book is printed on FSC Silva Edition and Gusto Satin paper

Front Cover
Aganetha Dyck, *Shrunken Clothing on the Rocks*, 1976–1981
felting/shrinking, 12 in. x 12 in. x 2 in. (variable)
Private and public collections in The Netherlands, U.S.A., Canada
Photograph by Peter Dyck. Reproduced courtesy of Aganetha Dyck.

Back Cover
Mary Pratt, *Pomegranates in Glass on Glass*, 1993
oil on board, 40.6 cm x 58.4 cm
Private Collection
Reproduced courtesy of Mary Pratt

Cover design, page design and typesetting by Melina Cusano

To my mother,
Edna Josephine MacKay,
who loved all forms of art, who wrote poetry,
and who, during the Depression,
bought books for me by the boxful.

TABLE OF CONTENTS

LIST OF FIGURES*

*Figures 1–7, 19–24, and 26–27 are courtesy of Mary Pratt. Figures 8–18, 25, and the cover image are courtesy of Aganetha Dyck.

ACKNOWLEDGMENTS

Many people helped in the research and preparation of this book. In particular, I wish to thank the University of Calgary and Dr. Beverly Rasporich for starting it all by accepting me, a member of that liminal generation, as a PhD candidate; Dr. Helen Buss, for blazing the trail for my investigation of autobiographical practices; Dr. Ann Beer, for her encouragement and enthusiasm along the way; and Joy Gugeler for her valuable editorial assistance and advice.

I am very grateful for the loving, steadfast support of my husband, Craig, and for that of our children, John Reid, Lois Reid, and Susan Reid Billington, Q.C., and their spouses – Nancy Brager, Brian Brunger and Rick Billington, Q.C. – all of whom cheered me on for almost a decade. They, together with our grandchildren and great-grandchildren, are the light of my life.

I am grateful, also, for the rapport offered to me by my students at the Alberta College of Art and Design who, for many years, shared with me the experience of reading, writing, thinking, and talking about women's lives and art. Similarly, I wish to thank Christine Sammon, library director at ACAD who, together with her staff, offered all possible assistance in the preparation of the images. I also wish to acknowledge Dr. Ann Davis and Nancy Townshend and thank them for their ongoing interest and counsel.

I thank the University of Calgary Press for the warm welcome and for the skilled assistance of the Press staff – John King, Peter Enman, Kellie Moynihan, Melina Cusano, Terry Rahbek-Nielson, and Karen Buttner. I send thanks also to Joan Eadie for her careful work in preparing the index.

Finally, I owe a very special debt of gratitude to those four wonderful artists and women – Sharon Butala, Aganetha Dyck, Mary Meigs, and Mary Pratt – whose generosity and friendship made this book possible.

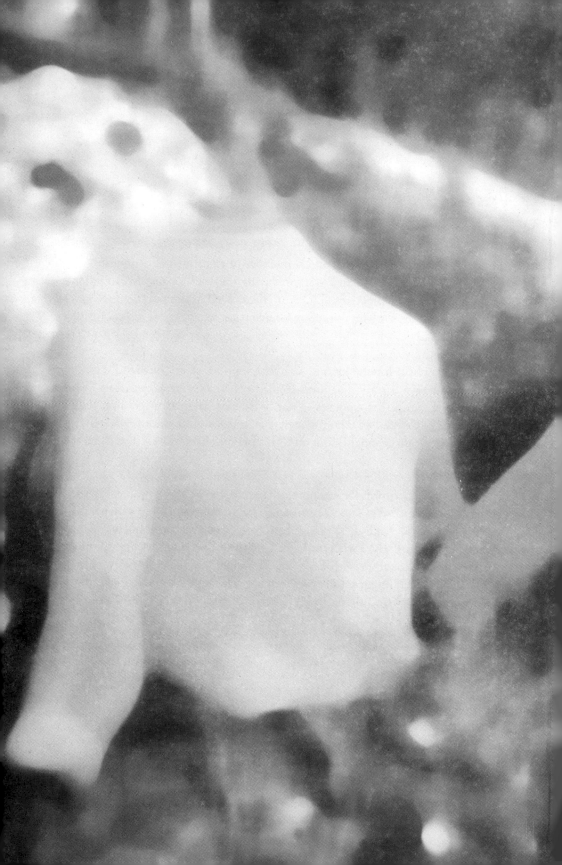

Prologue: "To Teach Is to Learn"

There is an old Latin saying attributed to Seneca, the Roman philosopher: *Discimus docend* – "To teach is to learn." And I can attest to that. It was my experience as a teacher at the Alberta College of Art and Design that led to my interest in female autobiography and in the changing patterns in contemporary women's lives. My investigations led me in turn to the study of Sharon Butala and Mary Meigs,[1] two writers, and Aganetha Dyck and Mary Pratt, two visual artists, whose work is connected on many levels to their experience as women. I began this journey during the 1990s when I first noticed a significant change in the demographics of the student population. I found that, as their children became school-aged, more and more married women in their thirties, forties or older, were enrolling at the College, at times making up as much as a third of the various classes. These women approached the making of art somewhat differently than their younger classmates. With a degree of life experience behind them and searching for their identity both as artists and women, they routinely expressed their personal experience in their art, so that their work had a strong autobiographical content. As their teacher, I began to take a greater interest in female autobiographical art, both literary and visual, in order to learn what such art reveals about female notions of self-identity and to respond appropriately to the students' work. Soon, I was drawn to the work of Butala, Dyck, Meigs, and Pratt because they were women who came into the prime of their careers in middle life, and because their work likewise has a strong autobiographical basis. I wanted to explore further the issues raised in the autobiographical work of my female students by investigating how four prominent Canadian female artists constructed their lives in their art. I wished also to discover the implications of such an investigation for existing traditions of Canadian female autobiographical practice.

Earlier, another experience with female art had shaped my perspective. On December 3, 1982, I attended the opening of Judy Chicago's *The Dinner*

Party at the Glenbow Museum in Calgary. I still remember the excitement of walking into this dramatically lit room; there stood a monumental, triangular table set with thirty-six plates, thirteen on each side. The shapes on the plate were three-dimensional, flowerlike forms suggesting female genitalia, a choice I found both startling and liberating. Under each plate was an embroidered runner with the name of the woman being honoured by a particular plate. I was jubilant, thinking "Finally – a phenomenal work of art by a woman, honouring women." I felt thrillingly at home.

The plates were set out in historical order. Some of the names of the women were new to me, while others I knew well. Strolling around, I was excited to discover the plates for Hildegard of Bingen, Artemisia Gentileschi, Mary Wollstonecraft, Susan B. Anthony, Emily Dickinson, Virginia Woolf, and Georgia O'Keefe, all significant figures for me because of their creative female subjectivity. On the floor were the names of "Nine Hundred and Ninety-nine Women of Achievement," including artists Frida Kahlo of Mexico and our own Emily Carr, two women who have become iconic symbols, representing the cultural identities of their respective countries.[2] That evening stands out in my mind as a kind of epiphany, not only because a female tradition was being fashioned, but also because the work used the image of the dinner table as its organizing motif.[3]

When I was a little girl, I asked my grandmother what heaven was like. She replied that, for her, it was a big dinner table with all her family and friends, including those "loved and lost a while," seated round. It is an image grounded in traditional female experience, including my own. Indeed, as my inquiries proceeded, I often found myself fantasizing that my four subjects were gathered together at a dinner party. Thus, I would place writers Sharon Butala and Mary Meigs across the table from artists Aganetha Dyck and Mary Pratt and listen as the four talked about being women and making art. I usually saw myself as hostess for this occasion, both facilitating and participating in the socialization. Extending the fantasy, I imagined further that this party resulted in the forming of a small community with myself as privileged observer and sometime participant. Each guest would offer the chief motifs of their ongoing work to the others as a contribution to the conversational exchange, a sort of artistic potluck supper where each sampled tentatively the favourite recipes of the others. Knowing these four artists as I now do, it could have been a revealing association, one which would produce in each woman a heightened sense of the significance of the autobiographical content of her own work and its connection to that element in the work of three other women of roughly the same generation.

Such events have never happened nor are they likely to. Sadly, Mary Meigs died on November 15, 2002. I interviewed her at length in April of 1997 at her home in Montreal and came to know her as a wise and gracious woman. Even before she died, the most one could say about any interaction among the four was that each had been familiar with the others' work, and that at least two of these artists, Mary Pratt and Aganetha Dyck, had met. Located as they were all across Canada, they perhaps felt no specific need for association, even if it were possible. However, as I became increasingly familiar with their lives and their practice of art, I recognized the potential in such an association, and so I devised an effective counterpart – a dinner party on the page – that is, a textual community formed through the juxtaposition of their bodies of work, and enhanced by personal interviews with each artist in turn. Taking on the role of instigator, I, like Judy Chicago with her plates, connected the life and work of these four senior Canadian female artists, chosen because they are members of roughly the same generation, and because they have sought and created, through their practice of art, a different space for themselves than that initially assigned to them by society. Their perceptions of self, so well expressed in their art, act as guideposts for Canadian women who, increasingly, are re-inventing themselves after the age of fifty. However, while born approximately during the same era – that is, between World War I and World War II – Butala, Dyck, Meigs, and Pratt come from varied backgrounds and regions, factors also that shape their art.

ARTISTS' BACKGROUND

Sharon Butala

Sharon Butala's father was French-Canadian, her mother English-speaking of Scots/Irish descent. She was born Sharon Le Blanc in Nipawin, Saskatchewan, in 1940, went to school in small-town Saskatchewan, and graduated from the University of Saskatchewan. She was married in 1961 and has one son, Sean, from this first marriage, which ended in divorce in 1975. She worked as a teacher in Special Education and then as an instructor at the University of Saskatchewan before she married Peter Butala,

Photographer: Todd Korol

a rancher, and went in 1976 to live on a ranch near Eastend, Saskatchewan. Inspired by the short-grass prairie landscape and its solitude, she became a writer of autobiographical non-fiction, novels, and short stories, as well as journalistic and critical articles. Almost all of her writing reflects her personal experience of the prairie culture of Saskatchewan. The specific books under discussion in this study are as follows: in non-fiction, *The Perfection of the Morning* (1994), *Coyote's Morning Cry* (1995), *Wild Stone Heart* (2000), and briefly, *Lilac Moon* (2005) and *The Girl in Saskatoon* (2008); in fiction, *Country of the Heart* (1984), *The Gates of the Sun* (1986), *Luna* (1988), *The Fourth Archangel* (1992), and *The Garden of Eden* (1998), as well as the short story collections *Queen of the Headaches* (1985), *Fever* (1990), and *Real Life* (2002). Butala was short-listed for the Governor General's Award for *The Perfection of the Morning* and for *Queen of the Headaches*. In 2001, she was made an Officer in the Order of Canada.

Aganetha Dyck

Aganetha Dyck was born in 1937 in Marquette, Manitoba. Her parents, Jacob and Susan Rempel, were first-generation Mennonite immigrants who operated the family grain farm where Aganetha grew up. She moved to Winnipeg to work as a bookkeeper and payroll clerk until her marriage in 1958 to Peter Dyck, also from a first-generation Mennonite family. By 1966, they had three children, Richard, Deborah, and Michael. Peter accepted a promotion and transfer

to Prince Albert in 1972, where Aganetha began her study and practice of art at the Prince Albert Community College. In 1976, Peter's career as a department store manager led to a move back to Winnipeg. On arrival, Aganetha immediately looked for studio space; by this time, she had become a professional artist focusing on multimedia gallery installations involving drawing, sculpture, and the transformation of found objects. Since 1991, she has concentrated chiefly on working with honeybees and beekeepers, that is, inserting art objects into beehives to be embellished by the bees with honeycomb. Her most ambitious bee project is *The Extended Wedding Party*, first shown at the Winnipeg Art Gallery in 1995. Other series of works to be discussed include *Canned Buttons* (1985), *Hand Held: Between Index and Middle Finger* (1988), *The Library: Inner/Outer* (1991), *Sports Night in Canada* (1995), and *Inter Species Communication Attempt* (2001–03).

Dyck's work is in many public collections, including the National Art Gallery of Canada, the Winnipeg Art Galley, the York Sculpture Gallery in Britain, and the Passages centre d'art in Troyes, France. On July 23, 2006, David Suzuki featured the art of Aganetha Dyck on his *Nature of Things* television series in a program entitled "Bee Talker: The Secret World of Bees." During the program, Suzuki documented the research of Dr. Mark Winston of Simon Fraser University, a leading authority of the science of the bees, and his ongoing association with Dyck in her work with the bees. In 2007, Dyck won two major awards; on February 1, she was given the Manitoba Arts Council Award of Distinction, and on March 23, she received the Governor General's Award in Visual and Media Arts.

Mary Meigs

Mary Meigs was a transplanted American from a notable New England family, one of her forebears having signed the Constitution of the United States of America. Together with her fraternal twin, Sarah, Mary was born in 1917 in Philadelphia to Edward and Margaret Meigs. Her father was an agricultural scientist with the federal government so that Mary spent her childhood in Washington, D.C., moving back to Philadelphia to attend Bryn Mawr College. She graduated in 1939 and during World

© Alicia Johnson, photographer

War II joined the WAVES, a women's volunteer emergency military service formed to release male personnel for sea duty. After the war, she began her lifelong career as a painter, studying first at the Arts Students' league in New York, and then with artist Henry Poor and his stepdaughter Annie. Through them she met Barbara Deming and moved with her to Wellfleet, Massachusetts. In Wellfleet, she came under the influence of literary critic Edmund Wilson and became part of his circle of friends. He introduced her to Quebec writer Marie-Claire Blais, and after her relationship with Deming crumbled, Blais and Meigs formed a strong attachment. After a sojourn in France, Blais and Meigs moved to Montreal in 1975, where Meigs lived until her death in 2002. Although their romantic connection abated, Blais remained Meigs' closest friend.

However, it was the example of Barbara Deming, who had written about her lesbianism, that inspired sixty-year-old Meigs to turn to writing autobiographical books, "and when I started writing it, it just all poured out" (Reid 1997, 2). She followed her first book, *Lily Briscoe: A Self-Portrait* (1981) with *The Medusa Head* (1983), *The Box Closet* (1987), and *The Time Being* (1997). In 1990, she appeared in a National Film Board film *The Company of Strangers* and wrote of the experience in *In the Company of Strangers* (1991). *Beyond Recall* (2005), a collection of her diary entries and her faxes to Marie-Claire Blais during her last years, was published posthumously.

Although the Canadian public knows her best as a writer, Meigs saw herself first of all as a painter.[4] She pursued the career of visual artist for most of her life, producing landscapes, portraits, wood sculpture, drawings, and illustrations, all of which show Meigs to be a versatile and accomplished artist. However, after shows in Wellfleet, Boston, and New York during the 1950s and 1960s, Meigs never again chose to exhibit her work publicly, making it available in Canada only to her wide circle of friends and associates. However, in 2005, a retrospective of her work, assembled from private collections, was shown at the Yvonne Bombardier Cultural Centre in Valcourt, Quebec.[5] This provided a record of her career as an artist. While no catalogue was issued, I have seen photographs of the work shown there and the accompanying pamphlet. These allow me to visualize the range of her work and to refer to it when appropriate.

However, Mary Meigs shines as an autobiographer in her books and articles, and it is these that are the focus of this study.

Mary Pratt

Mary Pratt, a confirmed Maritimer, was born Mary Frances West in 1935 in Fredericton, New Brunswick, to Katherine Eleanor West and William John West, a lawyer. Her father served as Attorney General for that province. Mary and her sister, Barbara, grew up in Fredericton and had, as Mary reports "an idyllic childhood." She showed an aptitude for painting and drawing early on and, accordingly, enrolled to study art at Mount Allison University. There she  met artist Christopher Pratt; they married in 1957 and both graduated with bachelor degrees in Fine Arts in 1961. They settled in Salmonier, where Mary put her painting career on hold to raise their four children – John, Anne, Barbara, and Ned. As the children grew older, Mary Pratt began to paint again, turning for subject matter to the domestic images of daily life: dinner tables, dishes, fish and meat, fruit, and vegetables. At husband Christopher's urging, she began to use photography as a resource to capture the fleeting effects of light and colour. She began to show her work in 1975, having been included in a prestigious show for seven women painters at the National Gallery of Canada. Her reputation as a photo-realist painter has grown ever since, and in 1995 she was honoured by a retrospective show, *The Substance of Light*, organized by the Beaverbrook Art Gallery. This show toured Canada and came to the Glenbow Museum in Calgary in the fall of 1995, where I initially saw Pratt's work first-hand.

In my analysis of her work, I will deal with the major still life pieces such as *Red Currant Jelly*, *Supper Table*, and *The Service Station*, figurative works from the *Donna* series, paintings in the *Fire* series, as well as paintings of house interiors. I will refer as well to *A Personal Calligraphy* (2000), Mary Pratt's only literary text, a collection of selected journal entries and public addresses illustrated by reproductions of some current work.

Pratt continues to live in St. John's, Newfoundland, where she is an active member of the arts community. She and Christopher Pratt are now divorced after some years of separation, and both have remarried – Mary in June 2006 to American artist James Rosen. She has received many accolades, including the Canada Council Molson Prize in the Fine Arts. She has received eight honorary degrees and was named Companion of the Order of Canada in 1996. Pratt was very pleased to be asked to paint the official portrait of former Governor General Adrienne Clarkson; the portrait was installed at Rideau Hall in Ottawa on February 15, 2007. On March 25, 2007, Canada Post issued two stamps in her honour, featuring two of her paintings, *Jelly Shelf* and *Iceberg in the North Atlantic*.

NAMING COMMONALITIES

Despite these disparate backgrounds, I was able to discover commonalities in their lives and patterns of work that struck me as significant. First of all, they pursue art practices in which they represent their subjectivities as women as well as artists. That is, their work has a strong autobiographical basis. Secondly, all four at the time of my writing were well into their mature years, having been born between 1917 and 1940, so that their various constructions of self reflect many decades of experience. Finally, in their careers they exemplify a phenomenon occurring with increasing frequency in North American society, that of women reaching their professional peak during their post-menopausal years.[6] I was anxious to see if a detailed perusal of their work revealed other similarities in how they perceive the world and their place in it.

I am a part of that generation and I see in their stories, my own. As with Butala, Dyck, and Pratt, I came to my career after marrying and raising a family and, like all four, I had my greatest successes (in my case, as a teacher and academic) when I was well over fifty. (Indeed, I was seventy-five and retired when I received my PhD in 2003.) In exploring their art practices, and the way these express their particular experience as women, I found reflections of the trajectory of my own life. Seeing this trajectory expressed through art has given it new meaning.

Introduction: Working Close to the Bone

> "One's research should always involve some element of therapy," he said smiling.
> "It only counts if it's really close to the bone."
> – Jill Ker Conway, *True North*.

Jill Ker Conway, the noted Australian-American academic, is a leading woman of my generation whose life story embodies a redefinition of the possibilities open to women. Born in Australia in 1934, she moved to the United States for her university education and to pursue an academic career. Her reputation as autobiographer and senior university administrator peaked in later middle age. Earlier, she, like myself, chose a graduate research subject that had an intimate connection to her own experience. In her case, the relevant experience was that of undertaking post-graduate education in the face of the anti-intellectualism and gender discrimination that she had encountered as a native of Australia. Accordingly, once ensconced at Radcliffe College in the United States, she chose Jane Adams as her graduate research subject, Adams being one of the first American woman reformers to fight for higher education for women. Her academic supervisor, the noted historian Donald Fleming, whole-heartedly endorsed her choice, urging her always to work "close to the bone."

In conceiving of research as working "close to the bone," I was able to identify the basis of my own *modus operandi*, having been drawn to work with my four subjects, not only as a result of my teaching experience, but also because of the similarity in our life patterns. In this way, I came to see myself as part of the textual community of Sharon Butala, Aganetha Dyck, Mary Meigs, and Mary Pratt, who, by the powerful use of the personal in their art making, similarly work "close to the bone." Essentially, however, my goal has been to gain a greater understanding of the connection between their lives and their art, and of the ways in which both have been affected by the artists' generational placement as "women between." However, this understanding has inevitably been shaped by my own personal life view; I feel that it is appropriate, then, to share this with you.

USING THE PERSONAL: AUTHOR'S LIFE VIEW

Being well into my senior years, and having had many career and cultural opportunities (while filling the roles of wife, mother, grandmother and now great-grandmother), I hold a view of life that is both complex and contradictory, three aspects of which have particular application to this present study: my experience of visual art, both as a critic and a practitioner; my experience as a student and teacher of literature; and my gradual espousal of feminism.

Discovering Art

As a child, I had no experience of art-making other than embellishing my prized colouring books. Similarly, I saw no significant visual art until February of 1944 when, as luck would have it, the Navy League of Canada sponsored an art show in Toronto called *Loan Exhibition of Great Painting in Aid of the Navy League of Canada*. Because it was in aid of the war effort, the curators were able to draw from the great galleries of North America as well as from public and private collections. It was much advertised and, with a girl friend in tow, I set off for what was then the Art Gallery of Toronto. I wandered through a succession of galleries to see paintings by Rembrandt, Goya, El Greco, and Picasso, as well as representatives of the French Impressionists and of Canada's Group of Seven. Seeing this art was truly an epiphany. It was the beginning of my lifelong love affair with looking at paintings, a love which expanded, as my education proceeded, to include all forms of visual art.

My subsequent ability to look at visual art with some degree of critical assurance derived from my association as liberal arts instructor and supervisor at the Alberta College of Art and Design from 1971 to 1995. I was surrounded by visual art and artists and became immersed in modernist and postmodernist theories, some of which challenged the carefully drawn lines between art and life. I was accustomed to engaging with a work of art on its own merits, letting the work of art speak for itself. I had studied art history in my undergraduate years, and I audited many such courses at ACAD in the course of developing liberal arts curricula. As a result, I learned also to place artists and their work in an historical framework, tracking movements and trends. However, art does bring life to the viewer, usually in a metaphoric way. After responding to the clearly autobiographic work of my female students, I began to look at women's art in a different way, still appreciating the aesthetics, but more aware of what such art revealed about the artists and how they saw themselves. I studied the work of Dyck and Pratt from this perspective.

In such a setting, it was perhaps inevitable that I came to test my own limits as a painter. One particular ACAD graduate, Laurel Cormack, played a special role in my development as a landscape artist. I had introduced her to the work of Emily Carr and she, after graduation, introduced me to painting out of doors in the Canadian wilderness, as Carr did. In a paper delivered to the School of Visual Arts in New York, I recount how a teacher and student can trade roles to the mutual benefit of both.[1] My membership in the painting community, which followed upon Cormack's tutelage, has influenced my notions of the role of community, and my construction of myself as painter, both of which I bring to this study.

Discovering Literature

The shaping of my literary imagination occurred long ago in the literature classes taught by Northrop Frye, Canada's renowned literary critic, who influenced such notables as writer Margaret Atwood, actor Don Harron, and playwright James Reaney. In the fall of 1946, I enrolled at Victoria College, University of Toronto, in a carefully designed honours course called *Philosophy (English or History)*. I did not know at the time that it was counted as one of the most enriched liberal arts offerings in North America. In second year, I opted for *English* as my secondary major and so came under Frye's tutelage for the next three years. Frye taught me not only how to read the many forms of literature and to see them as part of a coherent, imaginative whole, but also to find my own voice in writing.

Beyond that, I learned from him the primacy of the notion of freedom and the function of myth as an organizing principle for the human imagination. In his course, *The Bible as Literature*, I came to understand the imaginative centrality of the Bible as a poetic vision of human possibilities, offering a perspective on the significance of the here-and-now as nothing else does. As Frye explained to a 1967 Victoria College graduating class, "Perhaps that is what the New Testament means by faith; knowing what one is experiencing." In the same address, he talked about the function of vision, a kind of practical wisdom that Frye saw both as the product of the educated imagination and the goal of a university education. He explained to the students that the objective upon graduation "is not that you should achieve something but that you should manifest something." For Frye, of course, this is one of the functions of art. He continues:

> And perhaps as we struggle to apply our education and practical wisdom to society, we may occasionally feel a sense of a presence which is ourselves yet infinitely bigger than ourselves, which lives with us but which will not disappear into death when we do. (N. Frye 1967a, 10)

It seems to me that all four – Butala, Dyck, Meigs, and Pratt – whatever their degree of discomfort with Christian doctrine, engage in this struggle to manifest through their art, what Frye would call "vision."

Certain of my academic colleagues have argued that this aspect of my education, grounded as it was in the canon, was antithetical to establishing a feminist tradition and have looked upon Northrop Frye as a forbidding patriarchal figure. In his class, as in others, I found my undergraduate experience to be uniformly gender neutral. Far from being patriarchal, Frye seemed to me to be a revolutionary, recasting the canon in a way that challenged many set ideas.

Nevertheless, I came to my subsequent feminist convictions as a result of forces outside the classroom. They were as influential in determining my present point of view, as was my time with Frye.

As it happened, I was to return to academe once more, this time as a very much older student. Upon retirement, I had the opportunity to resume my doctoral studies and found myself, during the 1990s, sitting in classes on literary theory with energy-filled younger women (and a few men) and enjoying a much changed intellectual climate, one which challenged assumptions about both authorial presence and readership practices. Consequently, I was able to look at my life experience through new theoretical eyes. I was influenced most importantly by theories of life writing and by my encounters with the various feminisms, both of which inform the present study.

Embracing Feminism

Another aspect of my present perspective is, therefore, an avowedly feminist one; it draws upon my resolve to oppose the subordination of women in whatever guise it assumes. I began my feminist enquiries as a liberal humanist, working towards the equality of women in the workplace[2] and in the arena of public affairs. After many successful but conflicted sojourns in academia, the latest being in the mid-1990s, I now see that achieving these rights, important as they are, treats only symptoms. Like others of my generation, I became aware that it is women's internalization of patriarchal myths that engender the continuing power of these myths. As a teacher, I have noticed that many young female students, despite their disclaimers, still defer to the opinions of their male classmates, value their sexual attractiveness as crucial, or cast themselves as romantic heroines awaiting male deliverers or as maternal "earth mothers," the caregivers of society. Stereotyped gender roles such as these can bring comfort to women, but they also can keep women from claiming their full humanity (Conway 1998, 40–45). Radical feminism, the view that female oppression is the most fundamental and widespread of all forms of oppression, has put in place an agenda of female bonding and consciousness-raising that allows women to challenge myth and to learn to act on their own behalf. I have been a part of this agenda.

For example, touring *The Dinner Party*, and meeting Judy Chicago alerted me to feminist issues in the art world. I was also inspired by serving on a 50th Anniversary subcommittee formed in Calgary in 1979 to honour the "Famous Five," led by Emily Murphy, who pressured the Supreme Court to declare women as officially "persons in their own right." *Women Studies* courses in which I have participated, both as teacher and student,[3] acted also to challenge the myths about women in Western society. I have observed the liberating effects of such courses both on others and on myself. However, like many other feminists, I have in later years moved away from radical feminism, feeling that putting too much emphasis on women as being biologically different tends to deny them their full humanity.

The theoretical investigation that has most expanded my knowledge has been drawn from psychoanalytic feminism (as opposed to liberal humanism, which echoed my early inclinations, and radical feminism, which corresponded to my experience in the workplace). The former traces the source of gender positioning and myths constructed about women to unconscious conditioning early in life. I was intrigued because, in studying art and literature produced by women, I had discovered that unconscious forces are indeed at work, especially in art-making about the female body. From Nancy Chodorow, I have gained theoretical insight into women's maternal experience. From the French feminists – Julia Kristeva, Hélène Cixous, and their followers – I have learned to recognize the profound patriarchal nuances in the use of language, to extend definitions of the female erotic, and to view with suspicion even the notion of "woman" as a fixed category. Perhaps, after all, the androgynous perspective is the healthy one, freeing one from seeing gender as a key determinant.

Finally, upon reading art critic Lucy Lippard, I returned with fresh understanding to my earlier view that one's gender, class, race, and ethnic and national origins are all artificial signifiers, magnified as either positive or negative determinants by those who wish to keep power. Paradoxically, however, I honour all personal experience as the valid crucible of what is real, and so I recognize that women are experientially different from men because of their socialization and their ability to bear children, and that accidents of birth are inescapably differential factors, shaping one's experience of the world. I affirm, however, that it is critical not to write these experiential differences in theoretical stone.

These feminist ideas and experience are part of what I bring to the present investigation and, indeed, are what prompted it. That is not to say, however, that my four subjects were chosen because of their ideological allegiances. The construction of self in their work is, and was, a complex and ongoing project. Butala, Dyck, Meigs, and Pratt have evolved towards being autonomous and self-directed, and each has sought to express this actualization through, and in, their art. This was an observation to be discovered, not assumed.

THEMATIC ORGANIZATION

When I began to compare literary and visual works of my four subjects, I discovered early on that a specific area of experience dominated each of the bodies of work. For example, as a painter, Mary Pratt has focused chiefly on still-life subjects drawn from her immediate domestic environment. In the course of her career, she has branched out into other areas – figurative painting, landscapes, interiors – but she always returns to depicting the effects of light reflecting on the familiar objects found around the home. Through this device, her work could be said to valorize the domestic female world.

Mary Meigs, long a visual artist, was prompted late in life to turn to writing in order come to terms with her lesbian identity and to exorcise the resultant shame she felt. While lesbianism can be considered a political choice or an experiential result, for Meigs it was a biological proclivity determined from birth; her sexual orientation was in effect a bodily issue. Consequently, her autobiographical texts tend to centre on body, and on her decision to "come out."

Like Pratt, Aganetha Dyck used her domestic skills as a homemaker as the initial source of her art. However, once Dyck discovered the possibilities of honeycomb as a material for her art, she became focused entirely on working with the bees and beekeepers. It is now the distinguishing feature of her art. In order to further her collaborative work with the bees, Dyck has become an ardent researcher into the realm and science of the bee and thereby into the underlying principles of the larger world of nature; in her work, the bee world becomes a metonymous stand-in for this wider world. Moreover, through her intimate contact with honeybee colonies, Dyck has felt herself privileged to encounter what she calls the basic natural "life force." Even as she ponders issues in her own life and the intricacies of human society, she finds that contact with physical nature provides the "language" through which she expresses herself as an artist.

On the surface, the characteristic feature of Sharon Butala's body of work appears also to centre on the relationship of human beings to the world of nature. When she married Peter Butala and moved to the sweeping prairie grasslands of the Butala ranch, Sharon had to adjust to a whole new environment and come to know the natural world afresh. She tells of the ups and downs of this adjustment in *The Perfection of the Morning* – the joys of being alone in nature as well as of the stress of psychological isolation. Her novels and short stories treat the same themes; one of the goals of her fiction is to give an unvarnished portrayal of ranching life, a life lived close to nature. However, this new life had unforeseen effects on Butala; she became increasingly more spiritually aware, a dimension that is the true centre of her autobiographical body of work. It is, as she says, an account of a spiritual journey.

The notions of domesticity, body, nature, and spirituality emerged, then, as the focal points in art practices of Mary Pratt, Mary Meigs, Aganetha Dyck, and Sharon Butala, respectively. Moreover, by juxtaposing these bodies of work – that is, by creating my "dinner party" on the page – I was able to identify many significant crossovers. Also, I surmised that many female readers who, like myself, are of that same generation, would similarly find crossovers into their own life experience. At any rate, both Pratt and Dyck, for example, found their initial inspiration in the feminine domestic world of the home. And, while it is Meigs who locates the experience of the body at the heart of her life writing, Pratt, too, becomes involved in depicting female bodily experience through the figurative painting of her *Donna* series. For her part, Butala describes her intimate relationship with the awesome prairie landscape also as a function of body. Similarly, aspects of the natural world not only influence the work of Dyck and Butala but also play a part in Meigs' life narrative through her imaginative description of birds; as for Pratt, her bond with nature comes through her love of light and through her connection, via Christopher Pratt, with the rugged Newfoundland wilderness. As for spirituality, only Butala describes her life narrative as the account of a spiritual journey, but, upon examination, the autobiographical practices of Pratt, Meigs, and Dyck also reveal strong spiritual overtones, ones that became more pronounced as these women aged.

As I compared these four bodies of work in some detail, I found myself often "reading against the text" – that is, attaching importance to details presented at the periphery of the artists' main focus. To cite one example, both Butala and Meigs refer to their ongoing housewifery quite casually: it is certainly not at the centre of their life narratives. Nevertheless, as I shall argue, this aspect of selfhood and many other "peripheral" narrative details emerge as basic to their constructions of self.

Each of these artists, then, found a central focus for their particular body of work. It is my method to investigate the degree to which each focusing point illuminates not only construction of self in the work of the artist concerned, but also in that of the other three artists. Accordingly, I divide my text into four chapters, based on each of the experiential areas. Each area has its own set of controversial issues, the significance of which can be best appreciated within the appropriate theoretical context. At this point, a brief outline of the relevant issues and theories in each of the four chapters would, I believe, be useful.

Chapter One. House, Home, and Mother: Fulfilling Expectations

Because of their generational positioning, Mary Pratt, Mary Meigs, Aga-netha Dyck, and Sharon Butala had, of necessity, to conjure with the traditional societal expectations that the realm of house and home would be a female responsibility, and that the role of homemaker would be a women's primary source of identity. I was curious to see how four artists with burgeoning careers, three of whom were married with children, dealt with these expectations. I anticipated that they would be an inevitable source of conflict, the kind of conflict that today's young women experience every day. I was surprised to discover, however, the degree to which these artists' sense of self was bound up with the image of the house, and I was pleased to learn how much they honoured the domestic tasks that long have been seen as "women's work." This is particularly true of Pratt and Dyck, both of whom valorize the notion of female domesticity in their art.

In the work of all four, however, there is an undercurrent of unease and ambivalence with these traditional role assignments, nuances that often escalate to produce images of victimization. Certainly, all four quarrel with the narrow perimeters assigned to women's lives by making the home the inevitable female realm. They observed how such perimeters constricted the opportunities available to their mothers, all of whom modelled traditional home-centred lives for their daughters. Consequently, while the relationship with mother is depicted as one of the most powerful in these artist daughters' lives, it, too, is characterized as conflicted – fraught with ambivalent feelings.

Certain theoretical contexts allowed me to locate these perceptions of valorization, ambivalence, conflict, and victimization within a larger perspective. For example, feminist art critic Mary Kelly analyzes the dynamics of female visual art that attempts to express a feminine sensibility, including art honouring domestic labour in the home. She explains, in psychoanalytic terms, why the latter must inevitably contain an "iconography of victimization." Similarly Nancy Chodorow's study of the powerful mother-daughter relationship reveals that the latter has been based, to a large extent, on mothers taking on the responsibility for teaching daughters what society expects of them. Chodorow's analysis helped me to understand why so many women, including our four artists, find themselves turning into their mothers (or grandmothers) while lamenting, all the while, the narrowness of the mothers' lives.

Chapter Two. Alive as a Woman: Empowering the Body

In *Chapter Two*, I continue the investigation into the manifestation of femininity in the work of Butala, Dyck, Meigs, and Pratt by inquiring into the ways that bodily experience, sexual and otherwise, affect these artists' notions of self. Bodily experiences are defining ones for all four artists, but especially for Mary Meigs, whose realization of her lesbian identity was crucial in her construction of self. She concluded, through retracing her early and persistent discomfort with heterosexuality, that her sexual orientation was constitutional – determined at birth. She thereby accepted a form of essentialism, the theory that gendering is inborn, not socially constructed. Theories of lesbianism argue for and against the notion of gendering as socially constructed, and I review these briefly for the reader. I found Andrea Liss' notion of "essentialism with a difference" helpful in placing Meigs' construction of self, as was Diana Fuss' historical perspective on lesbianism.

I take up the discussion of essentialism also as it applies to the fundamental importance assigned to women's biological roles as mothers, an attitude apparent in the work of Butala, Dyck, and Pratt. I discuss essentialism also as part of the Freudian/Lacanian theories of female sexuality; here, I access the concept of *jouissance*, the notion of female eroticism as involving all of the body, being more global and therefore essentially different than that of the male. I detected elements of *jouissance* in the art of all four women.

Meigs explained that she early on "turned into a little girl who was very boyish – like knives and boys' toys and was a bully to her sister" (Reid 1997, 18). However, on further reflection she acknowledged that, contrary to general opinion, not all masculine women are lesbian, and that some lesbians are very feminine. Meigs, herself, intermittently displayed bodily traits that society generally regards to be "feminine," especially in matters of deportment and appearance. Sometimes, she was merely trying to "pass" as heterosexual and, at other times, it appears to me that she was unconsciously responding to her cultural milieu.

Susan Brownmiller is an important theorist in matters of "feminine" behaviour. She has assembled a comprehensive catalogue of society's signifiers of femininity that she calls "the code of femininity." This code is not about how women, as *subjects*, experience sex, but rather how women can cultivate attributes that make them sexually attractive *objects*. While often resisting the demands of this code, all four artists embody aspects of it in their art. Aganetha Dyck, for example, is able to celebrate and deconstruct this code simultaneously in her large installation, *The Extended Wedding*

Party. Mary Pratt examines woman as sexual object in the *Donna* series. On the other hand, the luscious modelling of her fruit and meat paintings can be seen as a metaphor for female sexual experience – woman as sexual subject. For their part, Sharon Butala and her fictional heroines are doing hard physical work that is called for on the ranches and farms of Saskatchewan. They sometimes long for the rare occasions that call for pretty dresses and high-heeled shoes.

On the darker side, the work of all four artists explores the vulnerability of the female body through descriptions and images suggesting illness, aging, and sexual vulnerability. For example, Meigs explained to me how the effects of an attack of shingles lingered on for years. More poignantly, in the last two years of her life, she kept a diary of the everyday effects of a stroke (published subsequently in 2005 in *Beyond Recall*). Through images of decay and regeneration, Dyck makes metaphoric reference to an auto-immune disorder. Pratt's arthritis has affected in recent years both the subject and method of her art-making. It is Sharon Butala, however, who, in her autobiographically based novels and short stories, makes the most direct reference to women's biological experiences of menstruation, menopause, and the bodily act of giving birth.

Chapter Three. Alive in the World: Connecting to Nature

Theories of essentialism enter as well into my discussion of the ways in which contact with nature affects the sense of self in the work of these four artists. As an extension of the issues of body in Chapter Two, the question arises of whether, because of their biological makeup, women are intrinsically more in tune with the rhythms of the natural world than are men. While interaction with, and knowledge of, the natural world is crucial for Dyck's bee-centred art practice, she sees it as a gender-neutral connection, as does Mary Meigs. On the other hand, Butala and Pratt see the biological rhythms of womanhood as aligning women more closely with the forces of the natural world. Feminists present arguments on both sides; Sherry Ortner is particularly vehement in pointing out the dangers of this kind of essentialism, one that she sees as placing women in opposition to culture.

While Butala and Meigs emerge as the more outspoken ecological advocates, all four artists unite in expressing their concern for the environment. Because this concern takes several forms, I found it useful to examine the kinds of discussion presented in the relatively new field of ecocriticism.

I refer in particular to the theories of Gary Alan Fine, who classifies the current ways human beings view nature. For example, businessmen, rural farmers, urban dwellers, and tourists all relate to nature in different ways, seeing themselves either as natural beings, or as being apart from or as in charge of the natural world. These differing views produce, of course, different environmental policies. Of the four, Aganetha Dyck, in particular, sees human beings as one species among many, and, therefore, in accessing a privileged window into the world of the bee, finds a greater understanding of the human world of which she is a part.

Chapter Four. Alive in the Spirit: Growing Old

In their autobiographical practices, Sharon Butala, Mary Pratt, Mary Meigs, and Aganetha Dyck confront aging and mortality forthrightly as a fact of life. Similarly, they display considerable honesty in assessing the various ethical dilemmas faced in the course of their lives. Theological writers such as Scott Peck and Elisabeth Kübler-Ross count such honesty as the prerequisite of spiritual growth. These two factors alerted me to the spiritual dimensions in these artists' constructions of self.

All four artists find this dimension enhanced through contact with nature. For Sharon Butala, however, walking the prairie grasslands brought about a dramatic spiritual awakening. Consequently, she describes her life narrative as a spiritual journey, marked throughout by a series of mystical experiences that she described as "soul building." The realm of the mystical is a controversial area because hardheaded realists often call into question its objective reality. In discussing such controversy, I rely on the analysis and commentary of psychologist William James and religious writer Evelyn Underhill. Professor Belden Lane, who has studied the connection between spiritual experience and geographical locations in North America, offered me another important perspective on Butala's profound relationship to the prairie landscape. His description of the salient features of such locations is useful in evaluating Butala's experience of the same landscape.

Another useful idea in this discussion is the notion of creativity *per se* as having a spiritual component. For critics such as Georg Misch, Deborah Haynes, and John Berger, the work of the true artist, whether visual or literary, is distinguishable by the presence of such components. I will apply these theories to the work of all four artists, but especially to that of Aganetha Dyck, who finds resonance with Joseph Beuys' notion of the artist as shaman. All four women, however, view their vocation as artist as central to their constructions of self. It becomes the main resource upon which they draw in dealing with the bodily indignities of aging.

METHODOLOGY

Interviewing

My critical method, then, consists of reading or viewing each body of work within the context of both the other three and of pertinent theory. Also, because my subjects were contemporaries and living in Canada, they were accessible for interviewing. I wanted to interact with them, both to test my conclusions, and to gain the objective perspective typical of good biography; I needed to rely, not only on their representations of themselves in their work, but also to be in their presence – to meet, to see them for myself, and to talk to them face to face in order to draw my own conclusions. In fact, it was meeting each in person that convinced me to finalize their choice as subjects. The exception was Mary Meigs whom I first "met" as the white-haired, gentle-voiced Mary in the National Film Board film, *The Company of Strangers*. For me, as for many other viewers, she was the emotional centre of the film. Of course, I chose each subject initially because of the quality and autobiographical nature of her work, her status as a mature artist, and her positioning as to age. I persisted in these choices because of the subject's openness and willingness to be interviewed.[4]

While my text contains strategic quotations from all four, I undertook these interviews, not so much to reproduce the conversations in print, but rather to gain an additional sense of them as persons. A central reason for interviewing them was certainly to have a fruitful dialogue; nevertheless, a most powerful consequence is that they are physically present to me in my mind. My experience of them as living people informs my writing. I discovered, for example, that Sharon Butala is sincere and serious, small, dark-haired and plain-speaking when the need arises. She is all of a piece. Aganetha Dyck is a potent combination of Mennonite "down home" prac-ticality, feminist conviction, and artistic risk-taking. She is a comfortable woman whose flashes of insight are somewhat breathtaking. Mary Meigs was shaped by a background of privilege and did all things with grace. Meeting her in person, I found her to have a kind, maternal quality that made one want to confide. Mary Pratt is calm and deliberate with a bright and alert personality. Her articulate and precise use of language was refreshing, for such is not always the case with visual artists. This gift made interviewing her a challenge and a joy.

Having a few general goals in mind, I conducted all interviews in a spirit of exploration. I hoped to gain insight into what art-making[5] meant to them personally and to discuss the possible significance of their art. I did not, however, take it for granted that these artists were able, or wished to, act as critics of their own work. As Northrop Frye has explained, the creative act and the critical act are two different orders of imaginative investigation and what any given artist might have to say about his or her work could very possibly be irrelevant or misleading (N. Frye 1967b, 1–6). Moreover, while some artists wish to act as interpreters of their own work and have self-consciously produced work that puts forth an ideological position, many operate more intuitively. As Aganetha Dyck remarked, when asked about critical response to her work, "sometimes those aren't the things I think about. I usually don't know what I have done until years after. I'm not going in there [the studio] prepare to make work. I just make work" (Reid 1996c, 1).

On the other hand, I have discovered that, while artists and writers often insist that their art speaks for itself, the majority do wish to talk about it – that is, to enter into a critical dialogue. Such exchanges allow them to speculate about how and what a particular work communicates. These kinds of dialogues can qualify as a species of brainstorming. Occasionally, a breakthrough occurs in which the ideas come, not from one participant or the other, but what phenomenologist Peter Spader calls a "co-acting, a co-discovery, a co-thinking – a thinking together" (1983, 10).

Such "co-discoveries" are more likely to occur during freewheeling dialogues than in structured question and answer sessions. Communication theorists define the former as "interpretive" interviewing, the aim of which is to deconstruct hierarchical and androcentric practices, ones that position the interviewee as a subject to be interrogated and the interviewer as interrogator. Instead, it acknowledges the interview as a give and take process in which both participants have an equal investment.[6] On the whole, I believe that this kind of investment characterizes the four sets of interviews.

I had, first of all, to achieve a "horizontal," more or less equal, relationship, the precondition of successful interpretive interviewing. Because of the many social and political differences among women, such a relationship is easier to imagine that to achieve. These include differences in ideology, race, colour, class, education, marital status, age, sexual identification, language, and so on. My first task as interviewer was to achieve a fully engaging "horizontal" dialogue, one that would foster a new awareness in both parties. To do this, I prepared myself to acknowledge, and to compensate for, differences in outlook and background.

Also, I knew that, if the interview were to achieve its goals, accomplished women such as Butala, Dyck, Meigs, and Pratt must perceive the interviewer to be competent. My status as an academic and my age were both advantages in this regard. Because of the latter, both Meigs and Pratt felt they could share generational knowledge. As Pratt explained,

> I'm not accustomed to speaking with somebody who is more or less my own age. Either somebody is very much older – that's the way it used to be – or now they are very much younger. You know the time. And you are also aware of the problems that I have had without us having to discuss them because we understand that, and so we go beneath the surface (Reid 1996a, 14).

Dyck also found my age reassuring, as was my association with a studio-based art college. Although most often it is part of Dyck's personal credo to talk about art with anyone who shows an interest, my close association with the art world supplied the impetus for an extended interview.

While my art background, age, and academic standing were advantageous, I had several sources of constraint yet to handle. As a painter, Pratt, for example, was not quite as comfortable with my status as an academic because she feared, perhaps, that I would offer overly theoretical postulations about her art practice. Pratt and I had lunch in Vancouver before our interview; she seemed reassured, as I say, by my age, but also by my status as a mother and grandmother, and by my knowledge of her work. We also enjoyed exploring together my extensive family connections in the Maritimes, and the possibility of sharing mutual acquaintances. I interviewed Dyck in Winnipeg and, at her invitation, stayed with her at her home for the weekend. While we talked freely about the sources her art, I found that considerable constraint arose when I questioned her about the effects of her Mennonite background. While her feminist inclinations have perhaps diminished her association with the Mennonite church, she was not about to share criticisms with someone outside the church. In any case, as I discovered during our conversations together, she was uncomfortable with most instances of generalization.

Meigs' privileged background and her sexual orientation were potentially the largest barriers to our communicating on an equal footing. Both in her writing and in our conversations I found her to be somewhat apologetic for her long-standing economic independence. I interviewed her in her Montreal home and, as we warmed up to each other, she was able to share happily her love of her beautiful home and of the memorabilia she had collected, and to talk, with some reserve, about the responsibilities and dangers of privilege. In discussing her sexual orientation, she acknowledged that most of her friends were lesbian. When I asked her why that was, she said:

> I do feel more comfortable with them. I think I have – we all have a deep-seated suspicion of straight women. They may betray us. They may betray you when you are not with them. By talking lightly about lesbians. Ridicule I mean. (Reid 1997, 8)

My initial letter to her had removed this suspicion to a great extent, as did my professional qualifications and the directness of our opening dialogue.

I achieved a comfortably horizontal relationship most easily with Butala. She and I are both prairie people. We had met previously as co-jurors on the board of the Alberta Foundation for the Literary Arts; she knew, therefore, of my commitment to literature and was appreciative of my interest in her work. I interviewed her at the Butala ranch and so became acquainted as well with her husband, Peter.[7] Seeing the ranch firsthand allowed me later to visualize them precisely in the landscape that plays such an important role in Butala's writing.

Because the interpretive interviewing of women includes the mutual sharing of experiences, it was imperative, then, that I be able handle the sources of constraint in a reassuring manner. The sharing seemed mutual but, in transcribing these interviews, I was frequently embarrassed by the number of times I felt prompted to tell personal stories and to offer tentative conclusions about female experience, instead of allowing my subject to talk uninterruptedly in response to strategic questions. I was reassured partly by the quality of the overall interviews, but mostly by the tenets of communication theory that view this kind of interviewer participation as essential: "Heuristic storytelling [that is, storytelling that makes a point] allows meanings to be explored, discovered, even changed in dialogue, rather than assumed, sedimented and reified" (Langellier and Hall 1989, 214). In the practice of trading stories, as well as in mutual questioning, the interviews became an important source of meanings, ones all the more valuable for being joint discoveries.

Coping with Two Disciplines

Having chosen my subjects, I was committed to a study involving the areas of both literature and art. I confess I had difficulty in discovering what degree of synthesis was possible between the two disciplines. The question was "Could this study be truly interdisciplinary, or was it inherently cross-disciplinary?" William H. Newell of Miami University in Ohio guided me here. He defines "cross-disciplinary" as a method in which "One discipline is applied to the characteristic subject matter of another, yielding new insights but not an integration of the insights of both disciplines, and providing a new but not larger perspective" (1990, 75). On the other hand, he defines interdisciplinary methodology as one in which "the insights of the disciplines are integrated into a larger and more holistic perspective."

I would like to have achieved the integration inherent in interdisciplinary study in order to gain "a holistic perspective." However, I have been limited by a particular imbalance in the way autobiographical practice is viewed in the two disciplines of literature and visual art. While life writing, an umbrella category, is now the encompassing literary genre of which autobiography, biography, memoir, confession, and so on are sub-genres,[8] and while female autobiographical texts are an established part of all varieties of life writing, there are no corresponding categories of visual art, much less recognition of a female component. That is not to say, however, that there are not a multitude of visual art practitioners, male and female, whose work has clear autobiographical references.[9] However, even self-portraiture, the most obvious use of the personal in art, has traditionally been examined more as a vehicle of artistic experimentation than as an expression of self-perception (Jansen 1977, passim).

Correspondingly, while there is an established body of critical theory, both for life writing in general and for female autobiographical texts in particular, there is no such coherent body of theory about autobiographical practice in visual art.[10] Because a theoretical context was often desirable in order to highlight the significance of the various features of these artists' work, I most usually turned to literary theory and extrapolated from that when necessary. Consequently, I would characterize my method as cross-disciplinary, taking place in the liminal space at the margins of visual art practice where it intersects with research into the expression of the self in language.

This view of cross-disciplinarity as taking place at the boundaries between theory-based and practice-based disciplines is a frequent one in developing a rationale for the social sciences. Mattei Dogan and Robert Pahre, for example, refer to the cross-disciplinary researcher as a "hybrid" scholar and describe him/her as follows:

> The hybrid scholar is a border crosser who penetrates territory held by another discipline or who establishes a province carved out of the territory of two or more disciplines. The hybrid scholar's research takes place at the periphery of two or more formal disciplines, not their core. It also occurs along a specific part of the periphery, not the entire frontier. The hybrid scholar does not work in a no-man's land. He borrows from his neighbours and what he creates may be borrowed by both parents' disciplines in turn... Hybridization is not a combination of two equal dependencies Usually one component dominates; hybridization does not exclude dependency (1990, 173–74)

This definition of the hybrid scholar as one who carves out new territory is congenial with my aspirations, habits of thought, and manner of working. As such, I draw on many sources of critical theory, chief among which are theories drawn, as I have said, from feminist and life-writing criticism. Some of this theoretical material has particular application to one of the various chapter divisions of the text; other critical theories apply to my analysis as a whole. The latter are concerned chiefly with theories about women's notions of self.

THEORIES CONCERNING THE NOTIONS OF SELF

While claiming that an artistic identity emerged as the prime factor in these artists' notions of self, and while I sensed a strong female artistic presence in each body of work, I did not find their art to be the expression of a unitary, unified subject – unchanging over time and isolated from all other selves. On the contrary, I encountered many other self-perceptions, which either co-existed or were made known sequentially. New aspects of self emerged in their work whenever they reacted to cultural influences, assumed different roles, entered into a variety of relationships, or changed allegiances. Often these various subjectivities were in conflict, emerging off-and-on as part of their search to find their "true" or "essential" selves.[11] In analyzing their many ways of constructing the self, I will apply five concepts: Carolyn Heilbrun's application of the theory of liminality; Simone de Beauvoir's identification of the female as "other"; Sidonie Smith's concept of "performativity"; Mary Mason's theory of "alterity"; and Doris Sommer's concept of "testimonio."

Being "women between" – Locating the Self in a Liminal Space

The concept of liminality has its origins in modern anthropology and, in particular, the work of anthropologist Victor Turner. Turner uses the term to designate a particular stage in the rites of passage typical of tribal societies (1978, 249). Such transitional rituals signify changes of "place, state, social position and age in a culture." Midway through the ritual reassignment, the participant is in the "limen" stage, is called a "liminar," and is said to be in a "liminal" condition.

As the 1997 Alexander lecturer at the University of Toronto, feminist scholar Carolyn Heilbrun talked about the concept of liminality as formulated by Turner and by theologian Tom Driver. In the wider application made by Heilbrun, she calls these liminars "threshold people." Their condition is seen to be ambiguous because such people cannot be pigeon-holed into the normal classifications of the culture. They are "betwixt and between." As she continues, Heilbrun makes it clear that she is applying the notion of "threshold people" primarily to women in contemporary society:

> The essence of liminality is revealed in women's experience once they are willing to move from convention to another form of self-expression. And to do this, they must, of course, have conquered ... the difficulty of individual dissent and that female oppression is always masked as a women's choice – what women want. (1997, 38)

In their work, Butala, Dyck, Meigs, and Pratt reveal that they are among those women propelled by "individual dissent" into that midway liminal position. As artists, they occupy a liminal space between the modernist world of their mothers and the postmodern world of their female descendants, a world they inhabit but do not fully accept. They remain modernist in their elevation of the place of the artist in society, while questioning, at the same time, modernism's "art for art's sake" philosophy. They are postmodernists in their blurring of both the lines between the various literary and visual art genres and of those between art and life.

In their personal life, they similarly occupy a liminal space between the home-centred, traditional positioning of their mothers' generation and that of their daughters, women who are busy trying to "have it all" – the joys of a career and the satisfactions of being a wife and mother. In their roles as artists, Butala, Dyck, and Pratt gradually moved away from centring their lives on the home. Meigs adhered for most of her life to upper-class conventional code of behaviour, only to step outside that code by revealing her sexual orientation. Nevertheless, all four reveal in their work that they move only partially away from the life modelled by their mothers. Their ages of birth bind them to an earlier time when convention had a firmer hold on Canadian and American women. All the more meaningful, then, are their acts of "individual dissent," all begun but never quite completed. To be in a liminal state is to be unsure, and, as one might therefore expect, all four artists waver in their notions of self and in their view of the world. Therapists such as Scott Peck and Elisabeth Kübler-Ross regard this state of uncertainty as a necessary and desirable state on the journey to emotional and spiritual maturity.

Defining the Female as "Other"

Feminist Simone de Beauvoir was the first one to identify and name a powerful cultural source of female self-identity. Her concept of the female as "other" is key to understanding the position of women in patriarchal societies, ones in which the norm is seen to be male. Beauvoir published *The Second Sex* in 1949, but, despite the many cultural inroads into the positioning of women, the perception of female otherness still occurs in every field: law, medicine, history, politics, science, business, and the arts (Tavris 1992, 17). This marginalizing of female identity and experience has been doubly damaging to the female artist because, not only, as in other fields, is the normal practitioner seen as male, but also the experience she is communicating is seen as outside the norm for society. This experience can be the result of cultural shaping or perhaps seen as essential to being female; in any case, it has been judged in the past to be inferior, that is, outside the norm, because it is not male experience. Moreover, as feminist theorists, from Virginia

Woolf, Adrienne Rich, and Carolyn Heilbrun in literature to Mary Kelly, Griselda Pollock, and Lucy Lippard in art criticism have pointed out, the very forms of expression assume a male practitioner.

This assumption is borne out when we observe how Butala and Meigs use and adapt the autobiographical form, a form that was shaped to suit the male story of winning through to success in the public arena. This particular concept of autobiography has its roots in Rousseau's *Confessions* in which the autobiographer represents himself as a unified and unique subject who perceives "a meaningful pattern in the flux of past experience" (Neuman 1992a, 214). As Neuman says, such an understanding of autobiography does not accommodate writing subjects such as Meigs and Butala who construct themselves in terms of a more unstable or marginal subjectivity. In their case, an adaptation of autobiographical form must be sought.

Similarly, Mary Pratt, a realist painter of domestic themes, must re-shape a still-life tradition going back centuries in which domesticity is routinely depicted by male painters as a lesser subject, often "masculinized" or trivialized (Bryson 1990, 161–66). Moreover, as Mary Kelly has pointed out, the painting genre itself has been co-opted over the centuries as territory for "heroic" masculine expression. Pratt uses advertising art devices, among others, to disrupt painting tradition. Dyck, a three-dimensional visual artist, also uses the domestic as subject matter, a practice which, until recently was unheard of in sculpture, traditionally a large scale, heroic art form (Jansen 1977, 681–99). Like Pratt, Dyck also must find ways of subverting a male-generated genre in order to do her work. She consequently turns to assemblage and installation. Like their literary sisters, female visual artists have been seen as "other," not only professionally and in gender positioning, but also within the artistic forms they inherit.

I now turn to theories of life writing to identify three other factors that influence the ways in which women present their selves in autobiographically based art. As outlined earlier, these are the notions of "performativity," "alterity," and "testimonio."

Defining the Self through "Performativity"

Judith Butler originated the notion of "performativity" as part of her theory of gender-positioning. Butler sees gender-positioning as the result of acts repeated consistently in response to one's social environment, rather than as the expression of an inborn tendency. For Butler, "feminine" behaviour is a result of such conditioning:

> Performativity is thus not a singular "act" for it is always a reiteration of a norm or set of norms, and to the extent that it acquires an act-like status in the present, it conceals or dissimulates the conventions of which it is a repetition. (Butler 1993, 12)

In applying Butler's notion to the writing of autobiography, Sidonie Smith argues that the interior "self," which autobiography presumes to express, is actually "an effect of autobiographical storytelling" (Smith 1995, 18). The "self" is a construction formed in the telling, and the story told is the story formed in response to a specific kind of storytelling occasion. In autobiographical writing, Smith contends that one suits one's role-playing to one's audience, the audience constituted in public discourse. One is compelled to repeat the stories one's audience finds intelligible and acceptable; reiteration produces a narrative of identity. That is, if playing a particular role becomes habitual, that role becomes incorporated into one's understanding of oneself. Furthermore, if the art reflects the life, the former will express this performed version of the self.

Smith's contends further that any performance of identity takes place, not before a single homogeneous audience, but before a series of "heterogeneous collectives," and, as these collectives or audiences change, so do the performances of self (1995, 20). Consequently, any attempt to present a unified, coherent self is undermined by the presence of a series of self-perceptions that are often in conflict with each other. The unstable and multiple subjectivities that are characteristic of the work of all four artists can be understood, then, to be the result of multiple performances. As Smith says, "it is as if the autobiographical subject finds him/herself on multiple stages simultaneously called to heterogeneous recitations of identity." It is a phenomenon with which we are all familiar: most often, for example, we perform one aspect of "self" at work or in public, another when we are alone or with family. Smith would see this, not as hypocrisy, but rather as an inevitable response to one's social environment.

The notion of performativity will be particularly useful in detecting enactments of the code of femininity in the work of the four artists. The audience for their potentially "feminine" performances is a patriarchal one; sometimes, they acquiesce to the male gaze; other times, they resist it. More often that not, however, the performance women deliver is the performance expected by the audience. Perhaps, as Gloria Steinem has said, "We are all female impersonators." Of course, all four present themselves to other audiences: small town, urban, cosmopolitan, politically committed, lesbian, class-oriented, and so on, assuming as they go, the roles of citizen and colleague or those of daughter, mother, wife, lover, artist, selves called into being by a particular context in time and space. And yet, as Smith says, there are silences: "These multiple calls never align perfectly. Rather they create spaces or gaps, ruptures, unstable boundaries, incursions, excursions; limits and their transgressions" (1995, 20). Not all aspects of self can find a suitable audience or an outlet in conventional modes of expression.

These are "disruptive spaces," ones that Smith believes find expression in the unconscious. Borrowing from Teresa de Lauretis, she sees the Freudian-Jungian unconscious as the repository of "surplus, of unbidden and forbidden performativity – a repository of that which is not speakable" (ibid.). The bodies of work by Butala, Dyck, Meigs, and Pratt, and the critical discussions of this work, contain many references to the unconscious self. Butala and Meigs include references in their literary and visual texts to psychic material, which Jungians[12] would regard as archetypal – dreams, visions, myth, ritual, unconscious embodiments, and associations. In my analysis of these, I consider the female unconsciousness to be a space of "disidentification," the domain of the excluded, the realm of the unspoken and unspeakable. Bringing this material into consciousness is part of the construction of self undertaken by all four. To achieve this, each had to experiment with existing genres in order to express what was conventionally "unspeakable." As Meigs said when exploring the implications of being a lesbian and a writer, one must enlarge "*the spaces-in-between*, including the space between the cracks" (Meigs 2001, 114).

I also detect an element of dramatic shaping in the art practices of all four. Critic Evelyn Hinz locates this as another aspect of "performativity." Hinz perceives all instances of autobiographical "telling" as the staging of a life, and therefore to be allied more with the field of drama rather than that of the novel. To support her case, she cites the features these allied forms have in common: "an element of conflict and dialogue, a sense of performance and/or spectatorship, and a mimetic or referential quality" (1992, 195), ingredients all of which can be found in the work of Meigs, Pratt, Butala, and Dyck. Essentially, they narrate dramas about their various journeys towards autonomy and freedom. These artists employ several means to dramatize this story, valorize it, and give it ritual significance. Butala incorporates mythic imagery through dream narration and through reference to the drama of the Greek mysteries. Dyck dramatizes her three-dimensional, autobiographical art through installation "staging" in art galleries. She also makes direct reference to ritual through the co-joining of the activity of the ritualized bee society with wedding imagery. The notion of the individual in community is an ongoing theme of Dyck's work. In *The Company of Strangers*, a NFB semi-documentary, Meigs introduces her autobiographical self through the medium of film, a dramatic art form. Meigs' literary texts embody the conflict/dialogue feature of drama, both moving away from other people through conflict and moving towards them through dialogue. Pratt dramatizes her domestic journey through her use of heightened realism, employing compositional devices and a dramatic use of light to communicate her spiritual dimension. Hence, the work of all four includes readers and viewers by reaching out to them through performance. Such work does not serve "to reinforce a sense of the unique individual," but rather "appeals because it counters such 'loneliness'" (Hinz 1992, 209).

Hinz recognizes loneliness as a dominant feature of contemporary life, and she links the role of auto/biography in our society with that played by ritual in primitive or alternate societies. Both supply "a sense of the communal that we lack" (ibid., 208). She argues that, in the absence of ritual in the contemporary world, we are able to join together when we read each other's lives, hereby gaining both a sense of intimacy and of community. Certainly, the writing and art of Butala, Dyck, Meigs, and Pratt afford their female reader-viewers this sense of closeness, belonging, and shared experience.

Defining the Self through "Alterity"

Mary Mason theorizes that this tendency to define the self in relationship, that is, through "alterity," is an enduring paradigm in female autobiography. Analyzing four of the earliest female autobiographical texts,[13] she observes that, from the beginning, women autobiographers tend to depict the self in relationship: "The self discovery of female identity seems to acknowledge the real presence and recognition of another consciousness and the disclosure of a female self is linked to the identification of some 'other'" (Mason 1988, 22). Usually this "other" is another person, but sometimes, as in spiritual autobiography, the "other" is God. Mason explains that these relationships culminate in a heightened recognition of the other person. I observed, however, that, with these four artists, all four formed relationships in which deference was the initial positioning.

In Sharon Butala's life writing, Nature is depicted as the most powerful Presence, one with which she develops this heightened awareness. Husband Peter Butala was her teacher here, and she deferred to him as the authority in the out-of-door world of ranching. He was also the person around whom the domestic schedule of the home necessarily revolved. Similarly husband Christopher Pratt was a powerful if implied presence in the art of Mary Pratt. In our conversations together, it was clear that, for many years, Mary regarded Christopher as the artistic authority in her life, as well as being her husband. As wife and painter, she, too, deferred to him. In the art practice of Aganetha Dyck, the honeybee provides the presence to which Dyck responds with heightened awareness. Otherwise, Aganetha Dyck's art is communally based; her instinct is always to involve others as co-creators in what she is doing. Consequently, when she incorporated art-making into her home-based life with husband Peter, she recruited him as photographer and helper, so that, on his retirement, he became a working colleague. Mary Meigs writes also about her relationships with male colleagues; literary critic Edmund Wilson and artist Henry Poor are significant influences. However, most of her texts are devoted to her relationships with women – her female lovers and friends, her twin sister, and her mother. It is these that shape her sense of self.

The mother figure often emerges as the powerful "other" in these artists' struggle for self-identity. Certainly the mother is central in the autobiographical writing of Mary Meigs, so much so that her second book, *The Box Closet*, is wholly devoted to an account of her relationship with her parents, especially her mother. In the visual art of Pratt and Dyck, the presence of the mother is invoked through association. The vision of the domestic life they valorize in their art is the vision they received as their mothers' daughters and, as our investigation will show, they both honour and undermine this vision in their representation of it. In the work of Butala, however, the figure of the mother is the most ambiguous by virtue of her mother's psychic absence. In *The Perfection of the Morning*, her central autobiographical text, this absence is recorded only in passing but is, nonetheless, a source of poignancy at the heart of the book. Nevertheless, Butala's construction of self is strongly influenced by her mother's modelling of the domestic role.

Defining the Self through "Testimonio"

Mary Mason, then, examines the role of the "other" [person] in the ongoing depiction of female self-perception in women's autobiographies. Connection to and relationship with other people can also be expressed autobiographically by assuming an advocate position for a particular group. One's personal story thus becomes a narrative that speaks not only for oneself but also for a particular section of the community. This kind of autobiographical text is called *testimonio*.[14] The term refers to forms of life writing identified by Doris Sommer as narratives "written neither for individual growth nor for glory but are offered through the scribe to a broad public as one part of a general strategy to win political ground" (Sommer 1988, 109). As Bella Brodzki points out, *testimonio*, of all the autobiographical forms, is the most dependent on the presence of an audience, actual or projected (Brodzki 2001, 871).

The autobiographical writings of both Mary Meigs and Sharon Butala have elements of *testimonio*; both writers are motivated in part by the desire to speak for a marginalized group and to win political ground. In giving testimony, these artists, to a greater or lesser extent, are viewing the dominant culture from a particular standpoint (one which privileges a vision at variance from that of the mainstream) so that the theorizing of "standpoint" feminists such as Sara Ruddick (1999) will likewise be useful in the discussion of the various causes these artists represent through their constructions of self.

Meigs, as an "old" lesbian, aimed to end the marginalization and oppression of homosexuals and to oppose patriarchy. She spoke of the lesbian's right "to be a witness to life" (Reid 1997, 7). In "coming out" herself, an artist and a woman of intelligence, education, and breeding, she sought to legitimize and normalize society's perception of the lesbian community. In a comparable way, Sharon Butala took on the role of spokesperson for the threatened way of life as existing on the family farm. Both her first autobiographical text, *The Perfection of the Morning*, and her 1999 novel, *The Garden of Eden*, end with a plea, aimed directly at the reader, for the preservation of the traditional rural way of life, giving, as it does, an intimate knowledge of the natural world. Similarly, Pratt has revealed herself as a spokesperson for the middle class. In her CBC radio interview (May 24, 1998) after receiving the Molson Prize, she said that it is the members of the middle class who have always been the preservers and appreciators of art and high culture. She suggested that, as the prime taxpayers, their cultural interests should be taken into account by the government they finance.

The work of Aganetha Dyck, characterized as it is by a creative and playful manipulation of material, seems on the surface to contain little of the testimonial. However, in her *Sports Night in Canada* series, she champions funding for the arts; in *Hand Held*, she issues an alert to the dangers of smoking and addiction in general; and in *Close Knit*, she alludes to the horrors of the Mennonite holocaust (Reid 1996c, 28).

It could be said that, in all autobiographical enterprises, the subject defines itself through or speaks on behalf of a wider group, whether it be shared race, class, gender, or some other trait or activity that characterizes the group. The difference comes from creating the perception that one is *standing in* for the group as opposed to *standing up* in the group. Standing up is a political act, rather than a personal and private act; one is a witness, whether for the lesbian community, the Mennonite community, the middle class, the rural community, or some other constituency. This act of giving testimony, while having a political motive, is also a way of establishing one's autonomy as a person and of claiming personal power through public affirmation. In the 1970s' language of female liberation, it is a way of raising one's consciousness.

Summary

I argue, then, that many factors influence how these four artists construct themselves in their work. They manifest the characteristics Sidonie Smith attributes to all autobiographical subjects: they are "amnesiac, incoherent, heterogeneous and interactive" (1995, 20), performing different selves in varying circumstances and for a variety of purposes. And yet, there is evidence in their literary and visual texts (and also in their dialogues with me) that they would resist this reading and its deconstruction of the "deep, autonomous, coherent and unified self" in order to insist on the identity of artist as being at the core of their subjectivity.

Shirley Neuman explains that, on the one hand, the post-structuralist decentring of the subject allows space for expression of difference, female gendering being one of those "differences" and that, on the other hand, the humanist notion of the unified self, when enacted by women, gives them "a visibility and a position from which to act, a position only just beginning to be available" (1992b, 217). Again, these four artists are positioned liminally between the post-structuralist and the humanist notions of self. For women of this transitional generation, both positions are possible. As Mary Pratt has said, "I think women of our generation have been constantly surprised at our abilities ... my life has been a series of surprises" (Reid 1996a, 11). Thus, liminality has fostered optimistic expectations of art and of life for these four women so that they can move beyond the predictions of the androcentric society in which they were raised.

WAYS OF READING

My approach as reader is the final variable in my study of the work of Butala, Dyck, Meigs, and Pratt. I have ways of connecting to the work of these artists that are, as I have said, reflections of my own experience, so that my reading goes beneath or beyond the text's apparent direction into the spaces between, to produce insights not directly suggested by the artist. Conversely, I am often the student, the beneficiary of new perspectives that shake up and redirect my established constructions of the self and of the world.

These ways of reading have been seen as a species of lyrical joining, a romantic union between author and reader. In the reading of autobiographical texts authored by women, Buss suggests a more familial metaphor for the merging of female author with female reader and speaks of "mothering," "sistering," or "daughtering" a text (1993, 26). In this context, she sees the "mothering" of a text "the most profoundly radical intersubjectivity": it is the most risky but the most worthwhile in that it deals with a subject who, in her construction, "is not absent but yet is not fully formed" (ibid.). To identify such potential in subjectivity requires a high degree of sensitivity and perception while still respecting the resolute "other-ness" of the subject.

It is much easier to act as sister to a woman's text since this consists of identifying commonalities in female experience and subjectivity. Buss makes the point that female autobiographical texts reveal these commonalities despite seeming differences "in time, cultures and personal histories" (ibid.). To be "daughtered" by a text is in some ways the most exciting because one is then instructed by the text, as one would be by a wise mother. Hinz locates the appeal of auto/biography in just this way when she sees it as answering spiritual needs, supplying role models, facing mortality, and providing a "living connection to the past" (Hinz 1992, 209).

In the basic organization of my investigation – that is, in proceeding with an intertextual and cross-disciplinary inquiry – I find myself in the position of mother to these texts, involved in the act of bringing to light new commonalities in the work of these four artists. In terms of content of each woman's work, I locate myself most often in a sisterly relationship, while benefiting at other times as a daughter would, being instructed by the ways in which these talented artists locate their female selves in their work.

So, in truth, there are five subjects in this study, inasmuch as I share both my sisterly, daughterly, and motherly responses and the life experiences to which they refer. This impulse to share comes from my love of dialogue and of relationship. My hope is that you yourself will create your own personal narrative as you trace the many intersections between art, life, and ideas that are contained in the co-joined autobiographical practices of Sharon Butala, Aganetha Dyck, Mary Meigs, and Mary Pratt.

1

House, Home, and Mother: Fulfilling Expectations

I think that in fact the whole thing is me. I understood the making of jelly from the time I was a child. We made jelly at home, always made jelly. I picked those berries. I had grown those berries. They were so familiar to me. The making of jelly was part of my life. The skin on the jelly as it begins to form and it reflects the blue of the sky down. All of this stuff I've observed since I was old enough to see. I loved that stuff so much that when my mother put it in the cellar to keep it, I used to put glass bottles in my bedroom full of red liquid so that I could look at it. I just loved the look. – Mary Pratt, speaking of *Red Currant Jelly* (1996)

Red Currant Jelly (Fig. 1) is one of Mary Pratt's most iconic works, recognizable to many Canadians because of widespread reproduction. For example, the image even made temporary inroads into popular culture when it appeared for a time on the lid of a national airline's box lunches, thereby upgrading the appeal of these perfunctory meal offerings. In claiming that "the making of jelly was part of my life," Pratt points both to the autobiographical source of her art and to the particular domestic traditions that have shaped her life. These traditions are likely peculiar to the middle class, their source being traceable to the elevation of the private home during Victorian times. Of course, as Judy Chicago and similar scholars have pointed out, the domestic arts and the keeping of the hearth have been the realm of the female since the beginning of time.[1]

Not many men or women share Pratt's lifelong visual acuity ("I just loved the look"). However, in my experience, women in particular come to share Pratt's vision so that they respond to her work with a startled shock of recognition, surprised to see the elements of their daily lives portrayed lovingly as subjects of gallery art. This female reaction was uniformly apparent in the student response both in my *Women and Art* courses at the University of Calgary and in my habitual eavesdropping at gallery showings of Pratt's work. I, too, respond to Pratt's work, not only as aesthetically pleasing, thrilling me with its colour and light, but also as a reflection of my life as a woman, married with children, immersed in domestic chores, and taken up by the task of making house a home, whatever my other vocational or recreational preoccupations.

Sharon Butala, Aganetha Dyck, and Mary Meigs also become involved necessarily in the domestic positioning of the self and in the resulting issues of femininity and questions of gender. That is, much of the presentations of self in and through their work are determined by how these four artists have seen themselves as women. And, how they have seen themselves has been, of course, a work in progress, a work affected not only by the passage of time and their particular experiences but also by the act of representation itself. Jeanne Perreault employs the term "autography" to indicate this function of autobiographical practice:

> One way in which autography differs from autobiography is that it is not necessarily concerned with the process or unfolding of world events, but rather makes the writing itself an aspect of the selfhood the writer experiences and brings into being. (1995, 3–4)

Thus, I argue that the mere act of working autobiographically brings into being new aspects of selfhood and serves as a vehicle for initiating change. Nevertheless, as women who were born between 1917 and 1940, these artists have been shaped markedly by outside forces as well, especially by a culture that accepted routinely the traditional patriarchal vision of the female. Such a vision places women firmly in the home and sees their natural destiny chiefly as wives and mothers seeking fulfillment in service to husband and children. Before they actively pursued professional careers as artists, Butala, Dyck, and Pratt lived their adult lives as wives and mothers, roles that they then saw as primary. Mary Meigs firmly rejected the possibility of traditional marriage and sought the role and life of the artist from the beginning. Nevertheless, for Meigs, as for the other three, the private domestic female world – the world of the house – played a powerful role in shaping both the sense of self and the art that explores and expresses that sense. As Mary Pratt told me, "When I dream, I dream of houses. And I dream of halls" (Reid 1996a, 18).

Domestic sensibility is particularly evident in Mary Pratt's extensive series of still lifes that take as their subject female domestic activity in and around the house. Pratt, the painter, chose as her initial subject matter the everyday activities and domestic environment of Pratt, the wife and mother. In so doing, she began what has remained an essentially autobiographical visual art practice. Early on, Pratt insisted that what she was interested in was merely the effect of light on surfaces of the domestic objects easily at hand: "I simply copy his superficial coating because I like the look of it" (Smart 1995, 76), and the effects of light remain a lifelong artistic preoccupation. Later, however, she confirmed publicly (*Life and Times*, CBC-TV, 1997) that her art is, in fact, not a series of random images but a form of personal autobiography so that her body of work follows chronologically, and expresses emotionally, the stages and issues in her life experience. From her comments on *Red Currant Jelly*, it is clear that many of her still lifes not only deal with her adult life but also resonate as well with childhood observations of an earlier house, her mother's house. In many cases, they act as memoirs of an earlier time and place, expressing a value system drawn, not only from her own female domestic sphere, but also from that of her mother, Katherine West. As such, Pratt's still lifes are shaped by perceptions determined by class as well as gender. In the upper-middle-class home from which she came, the house revolved around the comings and goings of the undisputed head of the home, the husband. This was certainly true also for many years in the home of Mary and Christopher Pratt (Reid 1996a, 1) so that Christopher's presence is marked in a variety of ways in Mary Pratt's paintings.

In seeking to discover and express the shaping of her own subjectivity, Mary Meigs was also drawn back into the past to trace, in literary memoir and autobiography, her career as visual artist and, more significantly, the road leading to her eventual acceptance of her sexual identity as a lesbian. For Meigs, as for Pratt, notions of gender are shaped by ideas of class. Meigs said of herself and her early mentor, Edmund Wilson, "We both had authentic good manners and impressive pedigrees" (Meigs 1981, 10). A Puritan view of sexuality accompanied that pedigree which, in Meigs' case, delayed both her sexual awareness and expression. While Meigs discarded any thought of marriage and children in favour of pursuing a life of art, the concept of the house emerges, nevertheless, as a persistent focus in her autobiographical practice. As with Pratt, much of her memory of childhood is informed by images of houses, notably those of her mother and her two grandmothers; consequently, description of interiors and objects is a constant in her autobiographical writing. Meigs' mother is not, however, an implied presence, as with Pratt's work, but is a fully described character, the chief one in Meigs' third book, *The Box Closet*. And, while Meigs' sexual companions are shown, with few exceptions, to be female, Meigs does not escape the feminine habit, instilled in her by her mother, of deferring to men.

In examining the role of domesticity, house, and mother in the work of Aganetha Dyck, an interdisciplinary artist, one becomes immersed in the three-dimensional art forms characteristic of installation art or assemblage. Typically, installation art assembles objects from everyday life and reconstitutes them within the gallery, so that the signification of the objects is brought into question (de Oliviera et al. 1993, 4). Accordingly, Dyck incorporates found objects and sculptural elements in her assemblages; thus, the actual domestic object is not so much represented by painted or verbal image but is appropriated or incorporated bodily into the work. Canning jars, shoulder pads, radiators, and refrigerators are examples of objects so appropriated. Much of Dyck's art consists of manipulating and transforming found objects by putting them into an unfamiliar context within the gallery space. This allows Dyck to comment obliquely on the fact of domesticity and the traditional life of the female, and to involve the viewer in a space both familiar and strange. Shirley Madill, curator of the Dyck retrospective (WAG, 1995), makes the point that, while historically the use of the ready-made represents a rupture between art and life, "in Dyck's hands the rupture ... is being bridged" (Madill 1995, 9).

Dyck's initial *modus operandi* had its source in her Mennonite upbringing as well as her traditional life as a wife and mother. As a housewife, she continued the thrifty and accomplished housewifery learned from her Mennonite mother; as an artist she began by extrapolating in both method and material from this housewifery while employing the ingenuity she observed as a child watching her inventor-farmer father "make up" and "make do." As with Pratt, the male presence is discernible but Dyck transforms the habit of female deferral into colleagueship.

Like Dyck, Sharon Butala also experiments with form in that, as a writer, she switches with regularity between fiction and non-fiction. Butala wrote fiction first, novels based on her observations of life in rural Saskatchewan. The writing of short stories was interspersed with novel writing, and these stories have a wider range, examining all of contemporary female experience, including rural life. She is best known, however, for three auto-biographical texts: *The Perfection of the Morning* (1994); *Coyote's Morning Cry* (1995); *Wild Stone Heart* (2000), and the non-fiction *Lilac Moon* (2005), a commentary on myths of western Canada. In 2008, she published *The Girl in Saskatoon* (non-fiction) after a lengthy period of research and reflection on the 1962 unsolved murder of a female classmate. Fiction and non-fiction are, for Butala, simply two ways of investigating her self and her world.[2] She makes this plain when she discusses the sources of her fictional practice:

> I know what goes into my stories. They come from incidents
> in my life and in the lives of women I know because there was
> a moment that was like a sort of epiphany in my life when I
> realized that I didn't have to make it up. (Reid 1996b, 7)[3]

Taken as a whole, then, Butala's writing practice is a way of her making sense of female experience – her own and, by extension, that of other women. As with Pratt, Meigs, and Dyck, this experience has as its starting point the private world of the home. While in her non-fiction she is drawn out of the house into nature, in her autobiographically based fiction, she investigates the domestic world of rural women. It is a world into which she was intro-duced through her marriage to Peter Butala and which revolved during their life together, even more than that of her city counterpart, around the needs and work of the husband.[4] All four of these artists are influenced in their construction of themselves as female by the dicta of the code of femininity,[5] which sees women's place as being firmly in the domestic realm of house, home, and mother.

To sum up, then, one of the values found consistently in the work of all four is the valorization of both female labour in the home and of the prod-ucts of that labour. This is particularly meaningful inasmuch as they come to seek self-definition through careers as artists, either literary or visual, and must come eventually to delegate at least part of the necessary domestic labour in their homes to others. On the one hand, they all decry the limiting in previous generations of female aspiration and activity to the domestic arena, and so come to criticize or lament the lives of their mothers. On the other hand, all four claim for themselves, even in the midst of a busy artis-tic career, a share of the feminine domestic life and, to this degree, *become* their mothers. In this, they reflect the ambivalence of many contemporary women (see Heilbrun 1997, 1). Among that of the four artists, the work of Mary Pratt mirrors this ambivalence most precisely.

MARY PRATT

While Pratt's total *oeuvre* includes figure paintings, landscapes, and interiors, valorization of the work and products of domesticity is most marked in Pratt's still lifes of domestic subjects, paintings that form the bulk of her output. As her art practice has progressed, however, this elevation of the domestic has become subtly subverted. Art critic Mary Kelly identifies this progression from valorization to subversion as characteristic of women's art practices that seek to convey distinctive female experience (Kelly 1987, 303–12). Kelly identifies four stages in this progression: *female culture (mother art)* – "identification with the woman who tends"; *female anatomy (body art)* – "identification with herself" rather than her mother; *female experience (ego art)* –identification with "an image of what she would like to be"; and *feminine discourse* –"identification with herself as female *subject.*" Each stage features particular artistic devices, what Kelly calls "the forms/means of signification" (ibid., 305). It is the first stage, *female culture (mother art)*, which is pertinent here. Kelly says of this stage:

> It valorizes the products of her labours of love: food preparation, washing, ironing, quilt making and other handicrafts. There also is a darker side to this art having its source in the working out of the Oedipus complex. "Women's work" becomes an iconography of victimization. Routine activities assume an obsessive quality, and preparing food becomes a signification of cannibalism. (ibid.)

My reading of Pratt's still lifes finds them to possess both the valorization and the iconography of victimization that Kelly describes.

Kelly takes the Freudian-Lacanian psychoanalytic position that the unconscious is a construction of language that emerges with one's entry into language. According to Lacan, language is shown to mark the separation from the mother and the creation of a separate identity; one therefore is always striving to overcome a perception of loss. In seeking to overcome this loss, the child identifies with the father, hence the patriarchal nuance in symbolic language and, if one extrapolates, in the language of visual art.[6]

The consequence of this for a female artist seeking to pursue a feminist art practice (i.e., one expressing female experience) is that the artist becomes involved in what Kelly terms "the female problematic" (ibid., 303). I take this to mean that what is presented as feminine is the product, not of unconditioned experience (the "essentially" female), but of a set of social conditions interacting with the female unconscious as constituted by the entry into language. Kelly reasons that what is typical of this "problematic" is a heightening of the Lacanian sense of "lack." She continues:

> It is precisely in trying to make sense of this threatening symbolic "lack" that she carves out the characteristic features of feminine narcissism i.e. the need to be loved and the fear of losing her love objects, in particular her children. (ibid.)

Female art that affirms the value and beauty of the domestic realm addresses this "lack," and contains, inevitably, elements of the narcissistic.

I find Kelly's analysis to be persuasive and a useful tool in viewing the art of Pratt. Indeed, one can hear echoes of Kelly in Pratt's own comments about the sources of her art practice:

> ... I want to make paintings that are accessible, I want to make paintings that are so beautiful that people can't help but love them. I think that is how I feel about myself too. I want to be accessible. I don't want people to say, "There is an arty human being, I can't reach her." I want to look like the girl next door. I want to have an apron fresh each morning. (Reid 1996a, 18)

Here, Pratt links together her art practice and her sense of self. They are both bound up with the desire for an accessible beauty that asks to be admired but is still insistently down-to-earth. It is a wonderfully feminine and narcissistic combination, one which women in particular recognize and to which they respond because, as Pratt puts it, her art is concerned with celebrating "women's stuff" (Gwyn and Moray 1989, 19).

Sandra Gwyn identifies this "stuff" as "the female muse ... the energy which accrues to women out of the small things around them" (ibid., 9). These "small things" are associated both with the domestic tasks that fall to women and the household objects that, to a feminine sensibility, go to make a house a home. In discussing Alice Munro as a symbolic writer, critic Beverly Rasporich refers to Munro's "profound attachment to objects and the wonder and pleasure with which she presents them" (1990, 167). "Wonder and pleasure" also describe the way with which Mary Pratt represents objects. Rasporich concurs but goes on to discover many other parallels in the ways in which the code of femininity informs both the work of Alice Munro and that of Mary Pratt (1993). Rasporich notes further that feminist critic Hélène Cixous sees this attachment to objects as "a demonstration of an id-liberated female discourse in contemporary female authors" and that such authors represent objects "in a nurturing rather than dominating way" (ibid., 167). Rasporich is contending that Munro's use of objects in her writing is a form of *écriture féminine* through which the author conveys a purely feminine sensibility. It is my view that Pratt's work and her representation of household objects is similarly a species of feminine iconography that speaks particularly powerfully of feminine experience. Some of these subjects are intrinsically "homely": broken eggs in a crate, dead fish on the sink, clothes on the line, remnants of dinner on the table. Other subjects are more traditionally eye-worthy: fruit in a bowl, flowers in the window, a favourite tea service or wedding present, a decorated birthday cake. By her act of choice and then through her artistic treatment, Pratt bestows importance on both classifications of household objects and hence upon the private domestic realm, which is the arena of the traditional middle-class female. She insists that the essence of reality is in the everyday and that women are the closest to this everyday reality (Reid 1996a, 41).

By Pratt's own account, her initial choice of a domestic subject was not premeditated; her attention was caught by the way the light hit an unmade bed and she hastened to catch the scene before the light faded (Gwyn and Moray 1989, 12). In trying subsequently to catch the visual effects of light on ordinary objects, she was led at Christopher's suggestion to use slide photography to freeze the moment. The first subject so photographed was "leftover hot dogs and dirty dishes" (Lind 1989, 21), the image of which was subsequently transformed into *Supper Table*, 1969 (Fig. 2). This painting achieves the effect that time somehow has stopped so that ordinary family life has been caught in mid-act. That is essentially what photography is able to do – catch life in the act.

With the aid of the slide photograph, a light table, and a slide projector, Pratt is able to achieve a remarkable realism. Pratt's photo-realism focuses the viewer's attention on what is being portrayed in a way that a more expressionistic style would not. Pratt does not want the viewer to be aware of the artist's handling of paint and considers an expressive brush stroke distorting to the subject matter:

I didn't want the brush strokes to get between me and the people who are looking. I didn't want people to look at it and say: "What a wonderful technique." I wanted them to get right to the image. I didn't want them to think about paint. (Reid 1996a, 8).

Therefore, she uses very tiny brushes and a careful layering technique, which together produce a surface as smooth as that of a photograph. Consequently, while Pratt draws on her own experience in her choice of subject matter, there is little painterly indication of the artist's presence.

Pratt does, however, emphasize the lighting effects captured in the photograph so as to heighten the sense of drama and lend importance to subjects drawn from the everyday. These are techniques borrowed from advertising art, an early influence on Pratt (Smart 1995, 52). Her use of them in her depiction of the domestic allows her to avoid the sentimental overtones that are sometimes part of genre paintings. Similarly, the obvious female familiarity with domesticity that is conveyed in her still lifes allows her to avoid the condescension characteristic of much traditional still life painting, a condescension produced by lavishing artistic skill on the mundane domestic scene (Bryson 1990, 164, 178). Pratt maintains a truthful realism lit by a celebratory sparkle, the latter lending to her subjects the seductive beauty she so desires.

Another technique used to impart a sense of importance and even reverence to Pratt's still life paintings is her use of compositional centring. A roast of beef, a bowl of fruit, a casserole, freshly caught fish – all are dead centre in the middle of the canvas (for example, *Salmon on Saran*, Fig. 3). Moreover, the sense of space is foreshortened so that the object is both front as well as centre, confronting the viewer. This is a formal, somewhat ceremonial compositional method that produces tension when treating mundane subject matter, as if to say, "You didn't think this was important, did you?" Consequently, the technique of centring acts as an antidote to the trivialization and devaluing of domestic work typical of our patriarchal society. It is also expressive of Pratt's preference in her personal life for a certain decorum and simplicity.

Similarly, Pratt presents objects set out in rows or carefully placed in containers. Fish are lined up side by side on the salt bag, the preserves are shoulder to shoulder on the shelf, the apples carefully lined up in the pan. Alternatively, she displays the fruit tastefully in a bowl, the turkey and the steamed pudding hidden under foil, the jam in tightly lidded jars (Gwyn and Moray 1989, 111, 108, 88, 90). Even the baby in *Child with Two Adults* (1983), one of her most beloved paintings, is tucked into its bath (Fig. 4). What is being communicated here is a sense of containment and decorum, the valorizing of feminine domestic control, and even more, of a class value. When I asked Pratt what was the source of her compositional method, she replied:

PRATT: I was taught that by my mother. My mother insisted on a house with a door in the middle, with a staircase in the middle. And when we had our pictures taken, we had to be looking straight at the camera, or a definite profile. She couldn't stand the three-quarter view.

REID: Why not?

PRATT: Well it was baroque. The other was Plain-Jane; it was simple. It was not putting on airs. It was not wearing taffeta. It was not frivolous. You didn't look over your shoulder. You either looked at a person or you looked away from a person but you didn't give someone a sideways glance. I remember her actually saying things like that. It's Presbyterian. My daughter-in-law's father was Presbyterian and I remember him saying similar things to the children. When you have your picture taken, don't smile. We don't want to see your teeth. This kind of thing. My mother was very much like that. My mother was the one who was the moral and ethical centre. My father was a lot more fun. He really was. (Reid 1996a, 42)

This exchange is expressive of the cultural, moral, and religious traditions with which Mary Pratt was raised and of her mother's powerful role in transmitting these traditions. The mother's emphasis was on decorum and restraint, but in the daughter's work these show as images of enclosure and strict geometric balance. Such images communicate more constraint than restraint. They suggest the emotions provoked by trying to deal with the limiting code of femininity, a code passed from mother to daughter. Emblematic of this transmission is Mary Pratt's memory of posing, while still a little girl, for a formal portrait. Her mother wanted photographs resembling the ones being taken of the little princesses, Elizabeth and Margaret, those models of upper-class British femininity. To keep her from squirming, Mary was hoisted onto a piano stool so that she would stand still, not moving for fear of falling off. Surviving photographs show, according to Pratt, a fixed smile of endurance (Reid/Pratt, phone interview, March 23, 1996).

Her mother-in-law's style was less restrained and more flamboyant so that early in her marriage Pratt experienced, through her mother-in-law's example, a challenge to her own mother's social and cultural standards, those of the British Protestant aristocracy in Fredericton. She was torn, but "of course, I had to choose my mother," she said (Reid 1996a, 43). The act of "choosing her mother" reverberates throughout Pratt's work, from still lifes such as *The Florentine*, 1971 (Gwyn and Moray 1989, 49), to her 1998 series on the buildings of Fredericton, familiar since childhood (M. Pratt 1998, C12).

The life-long power Pratt gives to her mother emerges as significant in Pratt's constructing her adult sense of self and discovering/expressing a sense of this power through her art. Post-structural feminists such as Chodorow (1978) see the strong mother-daughter bond as resulting from the fact that it has been largely women who have undertaken the care of children in infancy. Consequently, the boy, being mothered by a person of the opposite sex, has a difficult time establishing himself as male and must separate himself from a female-dominated environment in order to establish his sexual identity. Women have no such corresponding task; their female identity comes from a connection with, not a separation from, the mother (Grimshaw, citing Chodorow, 1992, 19). As Grimshaw puts it, "Typical psychological problems for the male ... will tend to revolve around questions of connectedness and intimacy, whereas those for the female will revolve around questions of separation and individuation" (ibid.). Autobiographical acts by female artists are, *ipso facto*, defiant gestures of individuation committed in the face of an instinct for connectedness. As a result, the female artist in an autobiographical practice often, in an act of compensation, turns the centre of the narrative stage over to another, either through words or images. As Mary Mason points out (1988, 23–24), female autobiographers historically have gone so far as to construct their subjectivity solely in relation to others, defining themselves essentially as wives of important men or as servants of God.

In mapping patterns of subjectivity in Canadian women's autobiography, Helen Buss also identifies patterns of alterity and, having reference to Bella Brodzki, goes on to contend that the mother-daughter relationship is a primary manifestation of the female need to define oneself through relationship (Buss 1993, 16–17). Consequently, the reader is cautioned by Buss to be watchful for maternal pretexts; that is, internal scripts inherited from the mother that the writer unconsciously enacts in the text (ibid., 17). Women's autobiographical art, whether in written word or (as I contend) in visual image, consequently displays an ambivalence in creating a life's narrative: women want to assure an ongoing connectedness with the mother (present or absent), while longing, at the same time, for a mature, independent subjectivity.

In autobiographical texts, this ambivalence often results in a split subjectivity, a sense of having or performing two selves. Carolyn Heilbrun characterizes this split or ambivalence as indicative of a liminal state, a condition of being on the threshold, and identifies liminality as typical of the female memoirs written in the 1990s (Heilbrun 1999, 45). In such memoirs, the writer takes her place on a public stage, moving out of the home through the act of creating a public subjectivity in words or images. Moving into the public arena, and hence away from the patriarchal control of the husband, is precisely the step that their mothers refused to take, "preferring to suffer and· strive without affronting society's conventions or expectations of women" (ibid., 8). Daughters, Heilbrun maintains, have watched their mothers struggle with the marriage plot, and, while they pity them, they don't forgive their mothers for remaining in stasis: "The key to liberation is an act of denial of the mother's life" (ibid., 7). But because of the persisting mother-daughter psychological bond, the denial is never absolute and the pattern is one of separation and reconnection. The daughters move tentatively into public life, entering a state of liminality. As Heilbrun says, they are "on the threshold," half in their mother's world and half in the one they have made for themselves. Again, they are "women between." They may not act out the maternal pre-text consciously but they carry it still in their heads. The memoir form allows a way out, placing as it does the narrative of self in a social or historical context: "Memoirs of childhood and leaving mother ... allow one to be in two places at once; living now, remembering then" (ibid., 7).

"Living now, remembering then" has characterized much of Pratt's art practice in the 1990s and particularly since 1995 when *The House Within My Mother's House* show opened, featuring images of her doll's house shown inside Pratt's childhood home (Smart 1995, 22). These paintings are overtly about the persistence of the mother-daughter bond, but they are not celebratory, nor are they nostalgic in mood. There is throughout the series a sense of enclosure and alienation in the placing of the doll's house, shown as it is in empty halls with walls and shadows pressing in. In a television interview (Smith-Strom 1996), Pratt talked about these paintings (at the time of taping a work in progress), saying that these were very personal works, tentative explorations, involving walls and shadows around the little house. "I am looking for the life in those shadows," she explained, a comment that could be taken both as a metaphorical and a technical description of her practice at that time. One senses that she is trying to come to terms with altered perceptions of her childhood home and to re-evaluate her mother's life.

While not as overt as in the doll house series, an ambivalence about this maternal pre-text can be detected in Pratt's work dated as early as the 1980s, and therefore produced before the advent in North America of the age of the memoir to which Heilbrun refers. Underneath the characteristic valorization of the domestic scene and the surface of decorum prized by both Pratt and her mother, there exists a continuous subtext of constraint and confinement, the dark side of the insistence on order and restraint. Pratt is quoted as having chosen the traditional life of wife and mother and is therefore not to be commiserated with (Cheeseman 1981, 19), yet there are clear intimations of the victimization to which Kelly alludes. For example, the foil-covered turkey, the covered and tied pudding bowl, the casserole about to be irradiated in the microwave (Gwyn and Moray 1989, 109, 89, 141) are all images in which the contents are constrained and hidden from view. The celebratory light and compositional techniques in such paintings are at variance with the subject matter. These are domestic images in which the real subjects (the turkey, the pudding, the casserole contents) are hidden, secreted, tied down, contained. The suggestion is to read these paintings as metaphors for the submerged artist self. As Gaston Bachelard says in describing objects that contain hidden spaces, "The action of the secret passes continually from the hider of things to the hider of self" (Bachelard 1994, 88). Pratt's artist subjectivity was hidden for many years in her performance of domesticity, a life style she avowedly chose, but also one required by the culture inherited from her mother. Her desire to break loose is communicated in these still lifes and in her subsequent fire paintings in which the flames finally escape from the burn barrel and rage across the canvas.

Reservations about women's role in the traditional marriage plot are revealed most specifically in a series called *Aspects of a Ceremony* (1986). Here Pratt comes to reverse the mother-daughter positioning, the mother taking her lead from her daughters. Centring on the wedding, that crucial event in the feminine life, this enterprise started out to be a celebration of the emerging womanhood of her two daughters. Her artistic choice and conscious intent can be understood, in Chodorow's terms, as the "reproduction of mothering," that is, the act of transferring to and constructing in her daughters the cultural expectation that they too, as females, centre their lives around a man and marriage, the making of a home and the nurturing of children. The fulfilling of this expectation is the subject of the aforementioned baby painting, *Child with Two Adults* (Fig. 4), showing Pratt's female grandchild in the bath supported by mother and grandmother. The paintings in the *Aspects* series were similarly to pay tribute to a happy event and to centre on the image in Pratt's mind of a wedding dress blowing in the wind. Daughters Barby and Anne had been married some little time before, so, at their mother's request, they resurrected their wedding dresses and posed for slide shots on the lawn. Pratt had trouble getting the "wedding dress in the wind" shot, and finally hung the dress on a tree to take a break and, voilà, there was shot that inspired *Wedding Dress* (Fig. 5).

Three paintings, produced from the slides of that day's photography, formed the nucleus of the *Aspects of a Ceremony* show. These were *Anne in My Garden* (Smart 1995, 113), *Barby in the Dress She Made Herself* (ibid., 114), and the aforementioned *Wedding Dress*. Of the three, however, only *Anne in My Garden* turned out as Pratt intended. It is a beautiful, romantic painting, a tribute to the lovely femininity of her daughter, Anne, and an elevation of the wedding ceremony about to be enacted. The other two paintings have a different subtext. In *Barby in the Dress She Made Herself*, the making of which is in itself a display of feminine accomplishment, the dress is shown in exquisite detail, but its effect is undercut by the anxious questioning look on Barby's face. In this representation of her daughter, Pratt, the mother/painter, is similarly displaying her ambivalence. Nor did *The Wedding Dress* turn out the way Pratt intended. Pratt came to the realization, half-way through the painting of it, that she was subverting her subject:

> It was not the wonderful image I had imagined it would be; it did not float. It [the dress] hung there, sacrificial. It was like Christ on the Tree as far as I was concerned. And I was forced to look at that. But it wasn't something I planned. (Reid 1996a, 48)

This unintentional subversion is an example of how Pratt, consciously or not, uses her work to express and work out personal issues and emotions, in this case her disillusionment with traditional marriage. At the time of her preparation for this show, the Pratt marriage had been experiencing difficulties, and, as Pratt says, "I realized that we were not after all going to 'walk hand in hand into the sunset'" (Reid 1996a, 45). Nevertheless, when Christopher announced that he was leaving just as she started to prepare for *Aspects of a Ceremony*, she was devastated. She did not, however, realize the depth of her pain and anger until she saw the painting and realized how she had transformed what was intended as a celebratory image into a metaphor for female crucifixion. Pratt said further that she accentuated "the angst" in the other painting, the one of Barby, and that it was in fact a comment, not on Barby's marriage, but on her own (Reid 1996a, 49).

Pratt goes through a similar process in producing paintings of the interiors of her childhood home on Waterloo Road in Fredericton. At that time (1989), the house was still the same as in her childhood; the furniture was the same and in the same position. Therefore, Pratt could revisit it literally as well as figuratively. It was a house built specifically to Mrs. West's taste as a gift from her husband, and it exists as an extension of Mrs. West and her preferences, an upper-middle-class home full of comfort and good wood. Mary insists, "It is my *mother's* house" (Reid 1996a, 55) [emphasis added]. When I asked her why she returned to this house in her paintings, she said, "Because I long to be there" (ibid., 59). In this sentiment she reinforces Bachelard's analysis (1994, 14–15) of the imaginative and reverberative power of one's childhood house in memory and in daydream. It is a maternal space, intimate, enclosing, and protective. Amid the emotional upheaval Pratt experienced at the breakup of her own marriage, her returning in her art practice to the doubly maternal spaces of Waterloo Road was undoubtedly both an escape and a comfort – a validation, despite her reservations about marriage, of her mother's value system. This validation is the subtext of one of her rare landscapes, *On Waterloo Street* (Smart 1995, 18), showing the street as viewed from the West house. The long rays of an afternoon sun lend a golden haze to the scene, much like the aura memory bestows on one's childhood.

Pratt has written a memoir article about her experience of Fredericton as a child (*The Globe and Mail*, August 19, 1998). It contains the same idyllic, light-filled sensibility. One senses that she is again longing for that time and that place and the maternal protection these afforded. Darkness does, however, threaten twice, both times from outside the home. Pratt tells how she was confined in the backyard because of a polio epidemic and later in the article she describes her memory of straying from home, getting lost, and being frightened by a shadowy male figure, to be finally rescued by her father and taken safely home. In the paintings of these house interiors, Pratt once again flees to her childhood home in order to escape the psychic darkness of marriage breakup only to find that some of the rooms are filled with similar shadows. In this she enacts the sense of victimization that Mary Kelly postulates as an essential component of "female culture/mother art."

One of the earlier interiors, *The Hall in My Mother's House* (Gwyn and Moray 1989, 181), contains the darkest shadows. In the accompanying text, Pratt explains that this painting is of the front hall in summer when the drapes are drawn to keep out the heat. The contrast is between the light coming through the door and the darkness in the hall. It is a threshold painting and brings to mind Heilbrun's concept of the threshold as the place of liminality. Certainly, Pratt has been a liminal figure for all of her career. In 1989, this condition was intensified as she acknowledged that her marriage had ended and as she began to define herself principally as artist, moving metaphorically out of the hall of her mother's house into the light of the outside world. In the painting's composition, one's eye is led out of the painting by the flight of stairs slanting up to the left to the bedroom floor, perhaps imaginatively "the dark at the top of the stairs."

The darkness of the bedroom is apparent again in a later painting *My Parent's Bedroom*, 1985 (Smart 1995, 23),[7] and, as in her creation of *The Wedding Dress*, the finished product came out differently than she intended. Here again, her art practice became the vehicle for exploration of personal issues and emotions. In talking with me, she explained that the darkness in that painting caused her to re-examine remembered observations of her parents' marriage and to compare these with aspects of her own marriage so as to see both with greater clarity (Reid 1996a, 61). The feminine positioning in traditional marriage becomes problematic for one constructing an identity as an artist and Pratt comes to realize that it was, in all likelihood, also problematic for her mother. Pratt is expressing through her art a response to the maternal bond in which she "seeks variously to reject, reconstruct and reclaim – to locate and retextualize – the mother's message" (Brodzki and Schenck 1988, 245–46).

The sense of an unseen presence gives power to these paintings. It is as if the woman whose house it is has just left the room, being only lately absent. There is, however, another unseen presence in the work of Mary Pratt, that of her first husband, Christopher. His is the place at the other end of the table in *Supper Table*, 1969 (Fig. 2); his is one of the two places in *Breakfast Last Summer*, 1994 (Fig. 6) and the absent one in *Dinner for One*, 1994 (Smart 1995, 133). As husband, Christopher provides most of the fish one sees so carefully arranged in Mary's still lifes. And in the Donna series (as will be discussed in chapter 2), Christopher is the one who first provided the photographs of Donna and the one to whom the model's challenging gaze is directed.

In these painterly gestures towards Christopher, Mary Pratt displays again the autobiographical sources of her art practice. In this case, she enacts in her work the time-honoured feminine script that directed her attitudes for most of her life, the one reproduced in her by her mother, in which the wife puts the husband at the centre of her life. It is part of her choice of the domestic as subject. As was inevitable, once Mary gained a measure of success in her painting (a success that advice from Christopher had fostered), she allowed her practice of art to gain a place in her life at least equal with that given to the husband, a situation which caused Christopher increasing discomfort. One senses again that Mary envisioned a different marriage script, one that integrated the careers of both into the marriage. That likely was the significance of building two studios in their homes in St. John's. However, Christopher could not work there, choosing to go back to Salmonier to build a new studio; they separated shortly thereafter. Mary reflects her pain and anger at this decision in her *Fire* series (See *Burning the Rhododendron*, Fig. 7), the pictorial version of "It all went to hell" (Reid/Pratt phone call, Feb. 1996).

One might expect Christopher to be psychologically banished, but it is apparent that Christopher remained emotionally significant to Mary for some time after their separation. In 1989 Mary is still painting their shared bed (Gwyn and Moray 1989, 173), albeit encompassed by shadows. Mary's powerful *Fire* series was a vehicle for working through her pain and anger so that in the 1990s Christopher's implied presence in the work is lessening. Nevertheless, in Mary's paintings of domestic still lifes during that period, one can still detect remnants of a shared life. Moreover, as late as 1997, Mary cooperated with CBC-TV to produce a segment for *Life and Times* about the two Pratts as artists and as a couple and, on film, Mary again appeared to concede centre stage to Christopher.

After their divorce, however, Mary was remarried in 2006 to American painter and art historian, James Rosen,[8] so that Christopher, also remarried, is now off the scene except as father of their joint children. Besides offering Mary companionship and affection ("Jim made me feel like sixteen again"),[9] Rosen has prompted Mary to see life and art from a fresh perspective by initiating travels to Europe and visits to its famous art galleries and architectural sites, which he knows well. Back home, Mary and Jim are working at developing a new life pattern that accommodates two artists who still pursue active painting careers. At this point in her life, Mary again has to resist the temptation to assume that the domestic side of their life together is her responsibility. The habits and performances of femininity die hard.

It would seem that the marriage plot, once reproduced by a mother in her daughter, can be difficult to displace.

To this day, Pratt's mother, with her model of femininity, remains the chief unseen presence in her work. However, in the early 1990s, Pratt's work entered a new phase. She still revisited the still life genre and the feminine world of objects "with wonder and pleasure" but turned her attention away from the kitchen and more to images of fruit and surfaces. Pratt explains that still life painting in the 1990s was a way of pausing and gathering herself before starting in a new direction (Smith-Strom 1996). She found this new direction in 1994 through a continuing association with printmaker Masato Arikushi, who translates her specially created paintings of fruit into meticulous woodcuts.[10] Nevertheless, Pratt is still drawn back to the scenes of her childhood. She again depicts it as a time of safety and protection with an edge of menace, a time epitomized through images of the rooms of Waterloo Road and the streets and buildings of Fredericton. To borrow from literary autobiographical practice, it is akin to moving from the diary and journal forms to the memoir. In fact, with the publication of *A Personal Calligraphy* (2000), a collection of her journal entries and public addresses, Pratt does, through the juxtaposition of the personal and the historical, move into a literary memoir mode that matches in mood the painting of Waterloo Road interiors. In any case, the implied presence of her mother and the upper-middle-class values she represents are an enduring feature of her art practices, whether visual or literary: "I always come back to Fredericton. Hauled back like a yo-yo on a string – reeled back to my mother, to the old order, to the rituals" (2000, 39). Defining one's subjectivity in terms of that of one's mother is a particularly persistent form of alterity in the autobiographical texts (both literary and visual) of all four artists.

MARY MEIGS

Accordingly, maternal presence and class values, this time of the upper class, are notable characteristics of the literary practice of Mary Meigs. Meigs, however, positions herself differently in that she rejected early and emphatically the heterosexual marriage plot. She was, as she says, "never tempted to marry" (1981, 7). Instead, after much hesitation and self-doubt, she embarked on a career as a visual artist. It is this identity she presents in her autobiography, *Lily Briscoe: A Self-Portrait*, taking as her model the artist figure, Lily, a character in Woolf's *To the Lighthouse*. Only in later life did she turn to writing in order to trace her artist's journey and to acknowledge publicly her sexual identity as lesbian: "The two chief tasks of my life have been to become an artist and to overcome my shame" (1981, 8).[11]

In undertaking these tasks, she has rebelled against the path set out for her, the expectations of her respectable, conservative, and moneyed upper-class family. She admits that this rebellion, while necessary to her character, is feasible only because of an independent income (1981, 7). In fact, the rebellion is only partial, with Meigs actually occupying a liminal social positioning. In this, she constructs her subjectivity as Pratt does, expressing the traditions of her family and their class values as part of the "self-por-trait." These traditions shape Meigs' feminine domestic self, a subjectivity shown in *Lily Briscoe* to be at odds with the artist self. As with Pratt, the domestic self is one who values order and has no patience with messiness and dust, and who loves small things, the little objects of utility or beauty that personalize one's surroundings. Consequently, it is a self for whom the image of the house has a primary imaginative power.

One of the results of this desire for domestic order has been that Meigs found herself playing the role of wife in her two principal relationships with women. That is, she took the main responsibility for domestic arrange-ments: planning ahead, cleaning the house, making the meals, and so on (1981, 85). I found it significant that, in her description of even lesbian relationships, one partner assumed the primary feminine domestic role of nurturing, rather than these tasks being shared equally. While it infuriated Meigs that she fell into this role, her explanation was that she cared about domestic order and practicalities of daily life and her partners did not. Both of her long-term lovers were artists like Meigs, but, unlike Meigs, the art-ist identity did not coexist with feminine domestic proclivities. It would seem for a woman to choose a female sexual partner does not guarantee her escape from the traditional trope of female domesticity so entrenched in the marriage plot. Lesbian theorist Marilyn Frye defines the true feminist as "a willful virgin" – an "undomesticated woman" – and therefore not any form of a patriarchal wife (1992, 136). Frye is of the view that this is possible only if one is lesbian. Meigs' experience suggests that being lesbian is no guarantee of being "an undomesticated woman."

As she was wont to do, Meigs conveys this aspect of her perception of self through reference to literary characters, this time to the sisters Mary and Martha in the New Testament (Meigs 1981, 86). Meigs is convinced that she is destined to play Martha, the practical one, and to fall in love with Mary characters who choose the "one thing [that] is needful,"[12] that is, tending to spiritual matters. Meigs professes to admire the ability of Marie-Claire and Barbara, the two Marys in her life, to be indifferent "to messiness and dust, to what to eat and wear" (ibid., 87), but the reader notices that in this respect she is quite unwilling and unable to change. Like Pratt, she remains true to her upbringing and, like Pratt, who is meticulous in her handling of paint, she extends her instinct for orderliness into her visual art studio:

> Habits. What do they mean? How much light do they cast on a person's character? I have the idea that even the humblest object should be treated with respect. A toothpaste tube, for instance, should be rolled from the bottom... My palette, orderly like everything I touch, is a half circle of logical colours, enclosing an oiled area of smooth brown wood, which I clean after every day's work. (Meigs 1981, 110)

However, Meigs expresses uneasiness about her instinct for order because she suspects that "carelessness seems to go with greatness of spirit" (ibid., 110). To be an artist is to be a person of the spirit like the Biblical Mary, able to choose the "one thing that is needful," not heeding material considerations. It is in the writing of the autobiographical text, *Lily Briscoe*, that she finally accepts the Martha self as being necessary to her artist Mary self, the self she strives to be:

> Is it possible that the Martha-me with all her fusspot order and irritability has been a kind of wife to the Mary-me, has tended the little flame of spirit, such as it is, taken out the ashes and blown life into the somnolent embers? (ibid., 86)

This is an example of the kind of epiphanies that come to Meigs through the act of writing the self. Meigs demonstrates in the form of *Lily Briscoe* that a sense of mere orderliness is not her criteria for the textual examination of her life. If it were, she would have adopted a birth to old-age linear narrative form of traditional autobiography. Instead, in *Lily Briscoe*, there is continual play between the self she remembers and the older self who is creating the text, which results in a running commentary or dialogue between the two selves.[13] She calls the form an "inscape," a term borrowed from Gerard Manley Hopkins, meaning an outer pattern or design by which the writer arrives at an epiphany, an outer representation of an inner reality. And it is the inner reality that Meigs explores in *Lily Briscoe* and that she conveys to the reader in a series of stream of consciousness paragraphs interspersed in the text to establish the psychological significance of the narrative. Her reconciliation in the text of her Martha with her Mary is an example of such an epiphany.

Nevertheless, in *Lily Briscoe*, Meigs presents herself as a woman shaped by the material surroundings of an affluent childhood and, as with Pratt, the image of a childhood house persists into adulthood and remains as a standard for all the homes of adult life. Like Pratt, Meigs dreams of houses: "My happy dreams have all been visions of sunlit rooms ..." (1981, 40). And again, as with Pratt, the house is imbued with a maternal presence. For both, the archetypal image of the house is as a feminine space, one built for, organized by, and belonging to a woman. Perhaps, as Gaston Bachelard observes in his *Poetics of Space*, most houses owe their essence to women:

> The housewife awakes furniture that was asleep...In the intimate harmony of walls and furniture, it may be said that we become conscious of a house that is built by women, since men only know how to build a house from the outside. (1994, 68)

In Meigs case, this female presence is that of a grandmother, not a mother; the house in question is "The Peak," the one in which she spent her summers as a young child and which she tries to re-create in subsequent houses: "There is something of The Peak in every house I have chosen for myself" (1981, 40). The picture she presents of this early home is one of emotional and physical comfort where children are watched over by a loving nurse or governess and where the peace of a beautiful garden seeps into all the rooms.

In contrast, the house of her other grandmother in Philadelphia was not a welcoming place, being instead one "where thousands of objects spoke in a large stage whisper of money and only the plants in the bathroom spoke of love" (ibid., 198). In retrospect, Meigs tries to analyze why neither the Philadelphia house nor Meigs' childhood home in Washington were welcoming places. She concludes that it was because of "the rules of properness: proper conversation, proper behavior" (ibid., 47), and the enforcing of this propriety was a female task. In the world of pre-World War II Washington to which the Meigs family moved in 1921, the family found themselves in exalted social circles, and Meigs remembers enjoying the excitement of high society, even though she came to rebel against the constraint of society's decrees. Again, Meigs emphasizes that it was her mother, not her father, who was socially ambitious and who enforced the socially correct standards. But, as Meigs observes, some grandmothers can exempt themselves from the enforcement role (1987, 147), hence the more loving atmosphere at "The Peak."

The enforcement of restrictive social norms by her mother is only one factor that led to a problematic relationship between Meigs and her mother, Margaret. As with Pratt, Meigs in autobiographical practice assigns to her mother a lifelong, if troubling, power. As Chodorow and Grimshaw have observed, the female need for separation and individuation is crucial, but it co-exists with an enduring desire for reconnection to the maternal. In Meigs' case, maternal absence during childhood heightened the adult desire for this reconnection. As was usual for women in her social position, Margaret Meigs turned much of her nurturing duties over to a series of nurses and governesses, chief among whom was one Miss Balfour. Moreover, Mary was one of twins and had to share whatever maternal attention was available. It was her mother's absence in childhood that elicited the adult Mary's reproach:

> ... you had forfeited eleven crucial years of our growing up [ages 5–16], had handed over your mother-power to Miss Balfour. The development of your twins' hearts was slowed because we were separated from our real mother by the presence and authority of Miss Balfour. (1987, 162)

Sixty years later, Meigs still was, as she says, "hashing over" the mystery of her mother's relinquishment of her two daughters. Meigs wants her mother back. On the other hand, Meigs' lesbian positioning and her espousal of an artist identity intensifies her rejection of the marriage plot, the pattern that dominated her mother's socially conventional life. Heilbrun's dictum that "the key to liberation is an act of denial of the mother's life" (1999, 53) is particularly apt for Meigs because such a denial is a prerequisite on many levels to her identification as a lesbian and as an artist. It is a complex situation for Meigs as daughter, one with which she comes to terms in the text of *The Box Closet*.

The Box Closet is a combination memoir and biography in which Meigs interacts, after her mother's death, with the collection of her mother's letters found in the attic of the Washington family home. This "intercourse with the mother's text" (Buss 1993, 195), a ground-breaking textual construction, serves two purposes for the daughter. Firstly, it allows Mary an intimacy of contact with Margaret that was not risked in life by either party. Secondly, Meigs is able to explore in detail the pernicious effects on her mother's subjectivity of society's iron-bound strictures in general and the marriage plot in particular. The emotion in this text varies between an intense longing for the connection that never was and anger at the institution of marriage and the social context of that marriage, both of which made a prisoner of her father as well as her mother.

To indicate the restrictive power of society in the lives of her parents, Meigs uses an image that is found extensively in the work of Aganetha Dyck – the beehive: "Society is like an immense queen bee, faithfully tended by swarms of drones who do exactly what they must to ensure the next generation" (1987, 25). Meigs laments this mindless drone-like reproduction by women of a system that constricts the potentiality of men and women alike, especially when she sees this reproduction enacted in the life of her own mother:

> Always law-abiding, she (Margaret) obeyed the law that turns
> daughters into their mother, generation after generation as soon
> as they marry and become mothers themselves. (ibid.)

Meigs devotes an entire chapter in *Lily Briscoe* to examining images of restriction and to understanding the resultant sensations of claustrophobia that have punctuated her own experience. As she explains, enclosure of any sort, whether physical or psychic, causes her emotional discomfort of varying degrees. She mentions in particular certain kinds of room interiors, "cut glass ... on dark buffets" (1987, 178), ones whose furnishings have been dictated by convention or by the impersonal taste of a professional decorator. She traces back her claustrophobia occasioned by these environments to a reaction against the social milieu of which they are an expression. Her family, and in particular her mother, became inextricably a victim and prisoner of the rules and taboos of convention and came to rely on the indicators of class and respectability as an essential environment: "I see as a tragedy the warping and shrinking of my mother into a person who cared so fiercely about her position in society" (1981, 79). Similarly, it is likely that the shadows in Pratt's paintings of the rooms in her mother's house are expressive not only of Pratt's reservations about marriage but also of the way social expectations constricted the life of her mother, Katherine West.

Meigs' chapter on imprisonment reveals how necessary it is for her to reject the upper-class feminine role as exemplified in her mother's life in order to find the freedom to discover aspects of her own subjectivity. She says, "It is the work of a lifetime to recognize life's prisons" (1987, 180) and Meigs' prison has been the same one as her mother's: class and respectability. Equally significant, however, are the feminine terms in which she speaks of personal freedom. Just as the image of convention is presented in terms of compulsory clichéd house interiors, so the freedom from convention is seen in terms of the ability to choose one's physical surroundings, the outward and visible signs of an inner psychological state (1981, 179). Meigs' autobiographical expression exemplifies, as does Pratt's, the feminine love of objects and their use as an iconography of self. For Meigs, objects provide a means, not only of her own personal expression, but also of the discovery of Margaret, the woman and mother she lost to respectability and convention. She writes of the memory of her mother's personal collection of treasures in tones of tenderness. They are kept in an upstairs closet, far from the impersonality and formality of the downstairs rooms:

> ... little tortoise-shell fans and Chinese bottles, cats made of lead glass, ivory and wood carvings, ancient Greek toys and Egyptian scarabs and fragments of statuettes. There, hidden away in the dark behind the painted door, was the hidden fantasy life of my mother, like buried treasure. (1981, 51)

While Meigs does not spell out the exact message of this "buried treasure," it is clear that these objects represent an aspect of her mother's psyche not usually expressed and speak of a hidden Margaret Meigs, more imaginative and lovable than the convention-ridden mother she knew. As with Pratt and Alice Munro, whom Rasporich compares (1993), Meigs regards the objects with which a woman chooses to surround herself as a form of personal expression, a feminine language again reminiscent of Hélène Cixous' "id-liberated female discourse" to be found in the work of contemporary authors. Such a discourse allows expression of female experience not expressible through the male-dominated nuances of common language.

Furthermore, the image of these treasures in a closet echoes the organizing image of her memoir about her mother – the box closet – in which Margaret's boxes of letters were kept. These letters, like the treasured objects, reveal to Meigs another and earlier Margaret, not discernible in the maternal persona. In his phenomenological examination of the poetic imagination, Gaston Bachelard reinforces the notion of these enclosed and hidden places in the house as the imaginatively proper repositories for the intimate representations of self, the secret and the hidden parts of the psyche (Bachelard 1994, 74–88). Meigs' incorporation of the box/closet imagery in her writings about herself and her mother, while originating in fact, has the further virtue of communicating on a symbolic and subliminal level the imaginative power of her investigations.

Throughout her writing, Meigs consistently displays the feminine tendency to define herself through alterity, beginning, as we have seen, with her mother. She explores in equal depth her relationships with women she has lived with – women who became her lovers, chief amongst whom was Marie-Claire Blais. An entire book, *The Medusa Head* (1983), is devoted to the examination of a lesbian love triangle and the patterns of domination and submission that caused Meigs considerable anguish. *The Time Being* (1997) describes another love affair, a long-distance one having its beginnings in a lengthy exchange of letters. In such examinations, Meigs explores areas of experience outside the boundaries of conventional feminine experience, at least as constructed in patriarchal culture. The dynamics of lesbian relationship are also outside, at least directly, the behavioural code of femininity, which places a man at the centre of a woman's life. And while the struggle for dominance might have been part of the relationship dynamics, the ideal that Meigs and her chief partners had in mind was one of equality, neither deferring habitually to the other, each being a person "in her own right" (1981, 16).

Relationships with men have, however, been an important part of her life, but here she tends not to position herself as equal. As coached by her mother, Meigs shows herself as habitually taking a feminine position of deferral when in the company of men. As late as 1988, when Meigs was involved in the filming of *The Company of Strangers*, she reports that, between takes, the appearance of a male member of the filming crew would cause a flurry of response, a shift of attention among the female cast, herself included (1991, 42). She describes her own actions as "negative flirting" and the general flurry of the group of women as "cooing." She comments, "It made me reflect on the silly helplessness of women in the presence of men" (ibid.), and she does not exclude herself from this group. Her reflection on this "silliness" takes her back to her mother's admonitions on how to act in male company, and Meigs devotes a mocking paragraph to analyzing the feminine skill of being a good listener and making the man the centre of attention, an attentiveness seldom reciprocated.

In her accounts of her relationships with Edmund Wilson, the literary critic, and Henry Poor, an America painter, Meigs analyzes another manifestation of this feminine positioning: that of satellite to a powerful man. Assuredly, her relationships with both men have other dimensions. Edmund Wilson professed to be in love with Mary Meigs (1981, 14), and Henry Poor inspired love, as Meigs tells it, in a bevy of lesbian women, including herself (ibid., 195). The secret of their power over Meigs, however, is not so much sexual as intellectual. Both men were at the centre of traditional male modernist literary and art circles in America. Meigs acknowledges their ascendancy in her cultural life, and her willingness to learn from them and to become a satellite, but at the same time she makes it clear that this yielding of agency was, in part at least, a performance, one exacted as the price of belonging:

> We were like mice who were brought up with cats and not eaten.... We old time lesbians occupied a very strange position; we were able to infiltrate the patriarchy and become an honoured part of it. We took our nourishment from the masters of literature, painting, music – all men. The art of becoming an honorary cat was to mimic a cat's behavior and eat cat food.... I still live with these ideas of speaking, painting and writing which I have taken in and give out automatically. (1983, 31)

Meigs is making two points here: firstly, that the arenas of painting and literature where her interests lay, were, in that age of modernism, securely controlled by the patriarchal culture and, secondly, that in order to enter these arenas a female must adopt a male perspective. To adopt a male perspective meant to accede to the patriarchal form of culture. For a woman that meant to write or paint as a man would while, at the same time, acting in a feminine manner by deferring to male power. In describing metaphorically how to survive as a woman in a male environment, Meigs shows the enactment of femininity to be a form of hostile infiltration of the male world and has identified the actions of the intellectual or artistic woman in patriarchal culture as a performance, intended to protect and allow one to "pass" in patriarchal culture. However, imitation becomes habitual and that is dangerous if one is a woman, whether lesbian or not. One comes to believe that being a satellite of a man is at the same time natural and feminine. Meigs' reference to this habitual or reiterated performance (in this case, the enactment of being a "cat" when you are really a "mouse") echoes Judith Butler's notion of "performativity," whereby each repetition acquires "an act-like status in the present" so that "it conceals or dissimulates the conventions of which it is a repetition" (cited in Smith 1995, 17). In terms of Meigs' metaphor, then, the mouse comes to believe it is really a cat. And women come to believe both that masculine art forms are the norm and that femininity and the consequent positioning of the female as satellite to a man is intrinsically expressive of being a woman. Meigs becomes aware of these dangers but states that it is possible to turn men's thought and learning to their own uses if women recognize the performance for what it is (1983, 31). Accordingly, in her autobiographical writing, Meigs turns the male genre of autobiography to her own use. In her radical act of writing her lesbian subjectivity, she moves out of the feminine position of satellite to the influential men in her artistic life. Similarly, in the "inscape" form of presentation in *Lily Briscoe*, she moves away from the linear, narrative form of traditional, male-centred autobiography.

In writing her life, then, Mary Meigs revealed her determination to live freely. For her, this meant breaking out of the prison of convention and propriety that stunted the development of her mother's personal subjectivity. It also meant avoiding traditional marriage, pursuing a career as an artist and overcoming her shame about her sexual identity. The actual writing of the life was not merely a reproduction of the freedom process, but part of the way to freedom. The search for freedom does not mean, however, that Meigs constructs herself as unfeminine. She emerges both as Martha, the practical domestic woman, and as Mary, the spiritual artist, and she comes to see that Martha's penchant for order and discipline makes possible Mary's artistic expression.

AGANETHA DYCK

The urge for freedom is similarly a crucial impetus in both the art practice and life experience of Aganetha Dyck; she made this clear in our discussions together. Here is one example:

REID: I wrote something while I was sitting here. "Aganetha Dyck – she is an open person who dislikes being tagged because it sets her apart. Or to put it another way, it subjects her to stereotypes that are false."

DYCK: Or correct. It doesn't matter. I just think to be free you can't be stereotyped. (Reid 1996c, 35)

In rejecting "correct" stereotyping as well as that which is incorrect, Dyck is reacting against any attempt to fix her subjectivity or to fit it into an unchanging mold. She rejected generalizations about herself, about women as a class or about Mennonites, the religious-communal culture from which she sprang. She insisted at every juncture on her right to grow and change. At one point she challenged me: "Are you putting me back into my old community?" (ibid., 25). It is my view that Dyck's emergence as an artist in the period from 1972 to 1976 (Madill 1995, 63) resulted in an extensive re-evaluation of self and a changed world view. It was clear that she expects such changes to continue as she works, reads, and extends her investigations through her art practice. In this, she exemplifies the function of life narrative that Jeanne Perreault terms "autography" (Perreault 1995, 3–4).

In this process of change, Dyck has come to refigure the patriarchal view of women that once shaped her life as a wife and mother. In so doing, she rejects society's undervaluing of the domestic work traditionally done by women: "I thought my job was very important as a mother and a housekeeper" (Reid 1996c, 20). Dyck went on to explain she did not see this job as gender specific nor that the woman must necessarily be the person at home. Dyck appears to sanction social experimentation in which a variety of domestic arrangements would be seen to be valid and workable. In this and in her opposition to stereotyping, Dyck shares what Rosemarie Tong describes as a postmodernist feminist desire to "think non-binary, non-oppositional thoughts" (Tong 1989, 233).

In any case, Dyck regards nurturing, home-making, and raising children as a serious undertaking to which attention must be paid by society. Accordingly, as with Pratt and Meigs, images and objects from the feminine domestic world form an important part of her body of work. However, as with Pratt, Dyck both celebrates the work of women in the home and points to the female victimization inherent in the patriarchal system. The coexistence of celebration and victimization can, in this regard, be seen as another example of what Mary Kelly has called "female culture/mother art" referred to earlier.

In our discussions, Dyck's reactions against stereotyping were prompted by my enquiries as to how her Mennonite background affected her work. First of all, she corrected many of my preconceived notions of the Mennonite culture, ones that included a moratorium on dancing, the practising of shunning, uniform dressing, and an understanding of the community as strongly patriarchal. Dyck explained that there are many substrands in the Mennonite church, that her birth family belonged to the General Assembly, the most liberal wing of the Mennonite faith, one which sanctioned dancing, did not practice shunning, and was more liberal in matters of dress (Reid 1996c, 23). She appeared to know little of the practices of the more conservative wing of the Mennonite faith (ibid., 1). When I talked to her in 1996, she had been an established artist since the late 1970s and had come to define the essence of her subjectivity as artist, a part of the artistic community in Winnipeg. Allegiance to the Mennonite community remained, but she could no longer accept its patriarchal agenda. In any case, she would not want to be stereotyped as a Mennonite artist, whatever that might be.

Nevertheless, her background as the child of Mennonite parents has profoundly influenced her art. As a child, Dyck did not know there was such a thing as "art" *per se*: Mennonite culture judged art-making as frivolous, if not downright sinful. On the other hand, examples of handiwork were plentiful. Her mother was a skilled seamstress, quilter, and gardener, while her father, Jacob Rempel, was a farmer and inventor who used ingenuity instead of money to transform what was available into what was needed. Aganetha remembers her father buying a World War II bomber for parts, the stripped down skeleton of which was given to the Rempel children to play with. That was probably Dyck's first experience of sculpture. Material was imaginatively transformed, an enduring feature of Dyck's own body of work. The Mennonite skill of making do and using what is at hand has stood Dyck in good stead; no wonder she began with the transformation of found objects and materials. Moreover, the farm environment nourished her artistic sensibility: "the shapes and forms and textures at the farm were natural and organic and I work with them today" (Yeo 1987, 38).

Marrying young and never going to art school, Dyck was initiated into the life of an artist as an adult in Prince Albert when she was doing volunteer work with the Art Centre there. She subsequently took classes with Margaret van Walshem, a fabric artist, and with George Glenn, a painter. In due course, she came to share a studio with them. She was lavish in her praise of both of them as teachers and mentors who taught her about what it meant to have an art practice and to create a body of work. They also taught her much about the history of art and discussed the issues that emerged from its study. Dyck was lavish in her praise of Glenn's teaching technique; it enabled her, finally, to trust herself as an artist. "[He was] an amazing man. He gave me, in the end, total freedom" (Reid 1996c, 17).

Dyck then proceeded to describe the four years she spent with Walshem and Glenn. In many ways, hers is an example of the ideal education of a female artist. In the first place, it was studio-based so that theory and practice were integrated continuously, a goal of modern art education for both men and women. Secondly, as Dyck told it, the space that she shared with Glenn and Walshem was a gender-neutral place; the male was not assumed to be the universal artist, and work based on a female sensibility was accepted on its own merits. If there were ideologies, they were "owned" by the individual and not part of the entrance requirements into the studio community. Finally, in her interactions with Walshem, Glenn, and their colleagues, Dyck became aware that art-making takes place in, and contributes to, a community that includes fellow artists but reaches beyond them to include the larger society.

When Dyck left Prince Albert in 1976 to move to Winnipeg, she knew herself to be an artist. She signalled this new identity by taking a radical act: the opening of her own studio. In so doing she stepped into a liminal space beyond the world of the private and domestic and into the threshold of the public. Dyck's own description of this act makes it clear that, with this step, she began to redefine her subjectivity and to temper her proclivity for fulfilling traditional patriarchal expectations:

> The day I opened my studio I stopped all connections to what was expected of me. Every single bit, and my whole family probably thought I had gone over some edge. And I had really. I was frustrated because I didn't know what the break was but that was the start of my trying to find out who I was, what was important in life, and what the world was all about besides doing what was expected of you. (Pike 1989, 16)

Dyck continued to fill the roles of wife and mother but, from that time on, her life had two centres: her studio and her home.

It is typical of Dyck that, initially, she was able to reconcile these two subjectivities by using her domestic experience directly in her art practice. It is also a tribute to the mentorship of Glenn and Walshem that she came to do so. They urged her to "Do what you know" (Reid 1996c, 19). What she knew as a wife and mother for fifteen years was "how to wash and iron, cook the meals and look after the children" (ibid.). Dyck took her teachers at their word, using her domestic experience, not only as a subject of her work, but also as a source of materials and methods. Her first successful integration of domestic methods into the studio came about by accident. She began to search for shortcuts to bypass the tedious process of weaving and felting and began instead to shrink woolen sweaters in the washing machine in order to produce the necessary basic material. However, the shrunken products attracted Dyck in their own right: "those sweaters spoke to me" and she entered upon an orgy of washing and shrinking: "I just wanted to shrink these clothes forever" (ibid., 18).

Close Knit (Fig. 8) emerged out of Dyck's exploration of the possibilities of these shrunken woolen garments; it was featured in the 1995 retrospective. In this work, sixty-five shrunken white wool sweaters are displayed in a long row with each sweater piled onto, and thus connected to, the next. As curator Bruce Grenville explains, the various sweaters might be assembled and reassembled, so that the exact constituents of any particular work, including *Close Knit* varied:

> The elements of this and other shrunken clothing works were often interchangeable so that a work took on a concrete form only when it was photographed, exhibited or sold. Time is here measured against the body moving through various spaces; the spaces of the domestic, the spaces of the studio, the spaces of feminism, the spaces of the family. (Grenville 1995, 30)

Interpreted this way, *Close Knit* reflects the "spaces" through which Aganetha Dyck herself has moved.

When I first viewed it as part of Dyck's retrospective show (Vancouver, 1996), *Close Knit* made me laugh out loud; it was a reminder of the once common domestic mishap of washing a wool sweater and having it shrink. The idea of having it presented as art came across as a witty incongruity. Further contemplation of the piece revealed the complexity of content that Grenville identifies but, basically, the piece represents the invasion of "lofty" gallery space by the humdrum domestic space, thereby challenging the former and elevating the latter. Moreover, the possibility of the dismantling and reassembling differently the elements of the work recollects the nature of domestic chores, which have to be done daily, over and over again.

Dyck routinely blurs the line between art and life, using a domestic activity to create an art piece. Curator Sigrid Dahle notes that Dyck uses a wide variety of housewifely activities in her art practice: "shopping, canning, cleaning, washing, drying, ironing, sewing, sawing, decaying, dyeing. Collecting, preserving ..." (Dahle 1990, 15). These methods are elevated by alerting the viewer to their creative possibilities. The product being displayed as art is often unsettling to the viewer; it prompts a re-thinking of traditional social attitudes towards this work and the women who do it.

In so doing, Dyck recasts material in a sensuous way that another curator, Timothy Long, sees as "part of a feminist based strategy of recovering subjectivity" (Long 1996, 5).

Aganetha Dyck's and Mary Pratt's retrospectives toured Canada simultaneously. In fact, the Vancouver Art Gallery mounted the two major shows at the same time (December to March, 1995). This prompted one reviewer, noting a similarity in the sources of their art, to wonder whether the conjunction of the two "was serendipity or brilliant planning ... both artists address what it means to be a post-feminist artist with one foot in the house and the other foot out in the world" (Jordan 1995, 20).

Amongst all of her works, Aganetha Dyck's *Canned Buttons* series (Fig. 9) most invites comparison with the still life paintings of Mary Pratt. Both artists feature objects or images of objects set out in rows. These rows often depict containers of one sort or another, and use glass as a material or subject. The *Canned Buttons* series has all three of these features and therefore resembles Pratt's paintings of jars of jam (see *Red Currant Jelly*, Fig. 1). Pratt in particular has spoken of her interest in the transparency of glass and the way it allows the artist to suggest inner workings of the body or mind:

> When you are painting this [a smooth piece of glass], you are given a great many lines. These lines will establish the glass and the wonderful smooth satiny-ness; all the stuff that is underneath will still be there. You will be able to see it all. It is almost like looking at a womb through Saran wrap, as if you had a window in your arm, and you open a window, a little glass window and you could see what was going on underneath there. (From my transcript of Pratt's remarks. See Smith-Strom, *Adrienne Clarkson Presents*, 1996)

Here Pratt goes beyond celebration of the domestic into the examination of a more visceral reality. This description applies equally well to many of the objects set out by Dyck in the *Canned Buttons* and *Canning Jar* series.

Like many of Dyck's projects, the *Canned Buttons* series arose out of a personal situation, a chance happening that presented Dyck with the challenge of making use of found material. As curator Shirley Madill points out, Dyck's aesthetic sensibility finds beauty in the used and the worn objects and material that bears the traces of human contact (1995, 8). The challenge for Dyck is to play with found material and to manipulate it so as to challenge its usual context and force it to yield up unforeseen associations.

In the case of *Canned Buttons*, experimentation was prompted by her purchase of abandoned merchandise from a defunct shoe factory converted into studio space. Dyck gloried in this bonanza of found material that included such things as wooden shoe lasts, hat forms, shoulder pads, and boxes and boxes of buttons, all shapes, sizes, and colours. The question was, what to do with them. The large quantity of buttons was particularly challenging. And, as with *Close Knit*, it was the methods of domesticity that again suggested themselves to Dyck. After experimenting with boiling, baking, and deep-frying them, she tried canning them in the canning jars in which she was already storing them. The results were amazing; the buttons expanded and metamorphosed into an extraordinary range of shapes and colours, qualities that allowed her to produce a series of pieces and installations. She found she was using them as material in the way that a painter uses paint. "I like this [canning buttons] because the rholoplex inside bled, the different metals into different colours. I looked and looked and thought 'I am painting.'" (Reid 1996c, 41). The largest of these, *The Large Cupboard* (Fig. 10), features three hundred jars of buttons set out on pantry shelves. Other installations from this series display the jars on old tables or small cupboards, similar to those found in the summer kitchens remembered from childhood. When positioned in the gallery, these become kitchen furniture transported through time and place. One piece features two tables of jars with bright blue contents and ornamental tops sealed with rholoplex. On one level these jars suggest canned blueberries; on another level they appear as either ornamental relics of a past civilization or exotic chemistry experiments.

The sealing of containers with rholoplex, paraffin, or beeswax has become an enduring feature of Dyck's. In speaking later of her *Hand Held* series, Dyck recalls being struck by the practice of the bronzing of baby shoes (Dahle 1990, 15). The *Canning Jar* series prefigures this notion; here also, the effect of the sealing is to suggest coating something from the past in order to preserve it. By coating as well as canning, the *Canning Jar* series is able to suggest that the female domestic practices of her mother's generation are being honoured but are also being consigned to the past. Like Pratt and Meigs, Dyck connects herself to her maternal antecedents (her mother, grandmother, great-grandmother) but Dyck, by becoming an artist, builds on this legacy rather than emulating it. Nevertheless, in our conversations together, she valorized her maternal inheritance by querying rhetorically, "Who made the path for where I am? For where we are?" (Reid 1996c, 4).

However, the contents of the processed button jars, each of them different, often do not resemble wholesome food products. In some, the contents look like body parts, in others, like fungi of various sorts, or like disintegrating or spoiled contents. Mary Kelly's theory suggests that a sense of victimization is an inevitable part of female culture/mother art, so this more gruesome material in the "motherly" canning jars suggests that the domestic world to which this series refers has a darker, more threatening side, poisoning or annihilating those who come into contact with it. Dyck, like Pratt, valorizes the traditional work of women while, at the same time, pointing to the victimization inherent in the social practice of delegating such work exclusively to women. In this, Mary Kelly's analysis of female culture/mother art (1987, 303–12) as containing both a valorization of domesticity and an iconography of victimization, is borne out.

This questioning of her maternal legacy and of the feminine identification with the domestic is heightened in the *Canned Buttons* series, as elsewhere in Dyck's *oeuvre*, by the moving of household objects out of the house into the gallery. The use of old furniture, cabinets, tables, chairs provokes a curious sense of absence in these installations as if their owners had died or had abandoned the furnishings. One can perceive a similar atmosphere of absence in Pratt's painting of empty rooms from the Waterloo house. Again the suggestion is that we are looking at and evaluating the past, the vanished world of one's mother, not the present world of one's female self.

The art practices of Dyck and Pratt show the maternal influence in another way. As was noted in the discussion of Pratt's paintings, the cultural values of Pratt's mother were reflected in these paintings through the compositional techniques of setting objects out in rows and the centring of subjects on the canvas. As Pratt explained, her preference for these devices came from her childhood training, from her mother's insistence on a simplicity and forthrightness that came from a Presbyterian value system (Smart 1995, 21). Dyck's work also favours setting objects out in rows and in the repetition of form that characterizes her practice to the present day. The forms used in repetition include sweaters, hats, shoulder pads, suitcases, shoe lasts, canning jars, buttons, zipper pulls, briefcases, purses, cigarettes, Braille tablets, and, more recently, coat hangers. The repetition of each of these forms, many of which have a domestic purpose, result in differing visual effects and consequently communicate in differing ways. Nevertheless, as with Pratt, it can be argued that Dyck's use of the repetition of form is a legacy of her upbringing, speaking this time of the experience of community that comes from her Mennonite roots.

Implicit in the Mennonite perception of community is the notion of collaboration, an activity found consistently in Aganetha Dyck's art practice. It appears to be almost instinctive with Dyck to involve others in what she is doing, whether it be through enlisting family in installation chores, getting neighbours to collect material for her, asking friends to undertake sewing projects for a big installation ("sister acts"), or undertaking to mentor younger artists. The most extraordinary application of this drive to collaborate is found in Dyck's work with bees.

Since 1992, working with bees has been the distinguishing characteristic of Dyck's art. This work requires her to recruit the help of beekeepers and to enlist the honeycomb-making talents of honey bees. Her method involves the introduction of a variety of found objects and personally created sculptures into the hive and, using techniques learned from beekeepers, inducing the bees to construct honeycomb on these objects. This way of working came about as a result of her search for a source of beeswax to use as a coating-encrusting material in such series as *Canned Buttons* and *Hand Held*, which, in turn, led her to visit the apiary outside of Winnipeg and to a meeting with beekeepers Gary Hooper and Phil Veldhuis. She became entranced by what she calls the "life force" of the bees, and this passionate interest led to in-depth research into what is scientifically known about these creatures.

So far, her most ambitious "bee" piece is *The Glass Dress* (Fig. 11). It was the centrepiece of a large installation, *The Extended Wedding Party* (Fig. 12) and is now in the collection of the National Gallery of Canada in Ottawa. In the subtexts of this and of Dyck's subsequent "bee work," one can detect a wide range of content, including speculation about such issues as the relationship of the individual to society, the social uses of ritual, the institutionalizing of female reproductivity, the mystery of instinctive animal behaviour, and, most recently, the phenomenon of communication in the natural world. In the exploration of how the domestic feminine world informs the construction of self as revealed in the work of all four artists, what is particularly relevant is the way in which Dyck's bee work directs the viewer's attention to an alternate hive-centred domestic world revolving around the production of honey and the nurture of another female creature, the queen bee. The hive is devoid of light, literally a dark world, which the queen bee, once she completes a "bridal" flight, never leaves, remaining entombed within the hive to fulfill the sole function of laying eggs.

This alternate world is invoked in *The Extended Wedding Party* through Dyck's use of the honey-making skills of swarms of honeybees as well as bee screens to create enclosures and bee blankets to fashion heavy ceremonial robes for the wedding "guests." The result is both beautiful and eerie. In the original installation in Winnipeg, Dyck was able to import actual honeybees into the gallery to continue work on the glass bridal dress that was kept coated with dripping honey. The effect was to enhance the idea of the bride's fertility. In all of the subsequent installations, bees and honey had to be omitted, but the stunning beauty of the bride's honeycombed glass dress served nevertheless to valorize and elevate the bridal notion of femininity in a way comparable to Pratt's bridal paintings of her daughters.

As has been suggested, in at least one painting (*Wedding Dress*, Fig. 5), Pratt points to the existence of a darker side of weddings and marriage: "It [the dress] hung there, sacrificial. It was like Christ on the Tree as far as I was concerned" (Reid 1996a, 48). This notion of the bride as a sacrificial figure is, despite its valorization, also the underlying concept in *The Extended Wedding Party* because, through conceptually invoking the world of the hive, Dyck is able to suggest parallels between the bride's domestic future in a patriarchal society and that of the queen bee in the hive. Dyck says of the hive: "I find the bee hive very black, very dark" (Reid 1996c, 24), and in her installation there is a reiteration of this darkness in the way the wedding guests are presented.

There are no actual figures, only empty costumes, a device that suggests a ghostly gathering (See *The Groom and Groomsmen*, Fig. 13). The male guests in particular are forbidding figures. Their costumes are fashioned out of heavy hive blankets and many of these guests occupy niches constructed out of hive screens. The effect of this is to show these male guests as priest-like figures who instigate and oversee the wedding ceremony. While the bride is the one being celebrated, the viewer can sense that the power is with these priestly male figures, who act as the enforcers of social tradition and as the controllers of female reproduction. Dyck comments thereby on traditional patriarchal societies, depicting them as having confined women to a hive-like domestic world because of their reproductive capabilities.

According to Dyck herself (Reid 1996c, 72), the subtext of *The Extended Wedding Party* bears a strong resemblance to that of *The Handmaid's Tale* by Margaret Atwood, a cautionary narrative that depicts women being valued and enslaved solely for their reproductive power. In her novel, Atwood looks ahead to a fictional future, the seeds of which are contained in the historic present. Dyck, on the other hand, is suggesting, in her use of a ghostly, archaeological scene, that the ceremony of the wedding, the ritual action that consolidates the subordination of women, should rightfully be consigned to the past. Dyck stops short of declaring herself a feminist because of her reluctance to stereotype either men or women (Reid 1996c, 26). She is an advocate of freedom for both sexes. Nevertheless, in the critique of the tradition of female domesticity implicit in *The Extended Wedding Party*, Dyck projects a subjectivity that has much in common with that of radical feminists: "For radical feminists sexual relations are political acts, emblematic of male/female power relationships" (Mandell 1998, 12). It is apparent that it is these power relationships that Dyck here is confronting.

Aganetha Dyck in her personal life has accordingly reordered her domestic existence to accommodate her work in the studio. Symbolically, she has banished those "garbed ghostly ceremonial male figures" from her own life. Her home no longer revolves around her husband, an expectation she apparently laid on herself; she recounts her surprise when, for the first time, she expressed unwillingness to cook dinner for his business associates, her husband shrugged and said that he would take them out (Tousley 1992, 60). Similarly, she once explained to me that in her house, everyone now does the laundry. As one can observe from catalogue notes, her husband, currently retired, collaborates in her art practice by helping with the actual installation and by taking photographs of her work. (Madill 1995, 1, 14, 64). When I met Peter Dyck in Leeds, England, where Aganetha was visiting artist at the York Sculpture Gardens (1997), he was very much in evidence at the Gardens, welcoming visitors and showing them around the installations. When I questioned her about the seemingly liberated character of both her father and her husband, Peter, she accounted for this by saying: "They both loved their mothers ... who were strong women" (Reid 1996c, 12), the identical answer given by Sharon Butala to a similar question (ibid., 23). One could muse over the power of mothers to shape their sons' expectations in future heterosexual relationships.

Consequently, while Aganetha Dyck's art practice honours women's domestic work and the feminine accomplishments of her female progenitors, she has moved away from the view that this work is inherently gender specific (ibid., 20). What has freed Dyck to question most gender stereotyping, whether it be about women or about men, has been her construction of herself as a thinking person. This is partly an inheritance from her maternal grandmother who would discuss anything and who tended to judge controversial issues on the basis of rationality. For example, when the young Aganetha brought up the subject of birth control to her grandmother, it brought this response:

GRANDMOTHER: I don't understand why there's a fuss about this because why did God give you a brain?

DYCK: Why did God give me a brain? Well, to think.

GRANDMOTHER: Well then – How many children can you bring into the world, how many children can people afford to have? Once they know that they don't have to have them. (Reid 1996c, 21)

It appears that both her grandmother and her innovative, inventor father modelled rational thought and innovative problem-solving for Dyck in her pre-artist life (Dahle 1990, 37–38).

In speaking of her decision to open a studio upon her move to Winnipeg, Dyck similarly makes it clear that this action marked a radical change in direction. This directional change resulted from a decision to take herself seriously both as an artist and as an intellect, to become autonomous and to forego acting in response to the expectations of others. Dyck's making a commitment to art necessarily involved a similar commitment to intellectual investigation; this in turn led to questioning many beliefs about herself and the world, ones that previously she had taken for granted. The connection between self-exploration, the making of art, and the act of thinking is clear. Rational investigation can be seen as a precondition for her art-making. That does not mean, however, that for Dyck the making of art is an altogether rational activity. Rather, work in the studio seems to be an investigative process in which the possibilities of material are explored and through which important personal ideas and concerns come to be expressed. Research and reading proceed parallel to, and feed intuitively into, art-making.

A similar *modus operandi* can be observed in the art practice of Mary Scott, a colleague of Dyck's in the MAWA mentoring project. Dyck's meeting with Scott in 1987 is cited by Sigrid Dahle as a significant one: "[Dyck] meets Mary Scott who exhibits/lectures in Winnipeg. Impressed by Mary's deep understanding of feminism and by her approach to reading" (Dahle 1990, 51). Scott herself describes her art practice as follows:

I read more than I make paintings, especially since late 1981, when my paintings began coming from my reading. I would literally read for a month or so – and mark out that information. I would collect images in my mind, going through the ones that I would need, but the writing in the paintings came from that repository of reading. My interest lies within the call to arms of the French feminists whose writings have addressed the question of how one finally does write, how finally one does construct something in opposition to the patriarchal. (Scott 1986, 132–34)

Scott's use of text in her work and her directly feminist content are characteristics of her body of work. Over time, these also have become evident in Dyck's art practice. Initially, however, it is the role assigned to reading in Scott's art-making that has influenced Dyck. Dyck's methodology differs from that of Scott in that the connection between reading and studio practice is less direct. Nevertheless, Dyck does credit Scott with heightening her awareness of reading as a tool in her own art-making by introducing her to an intense research process and by making her personal library, with its emphasis on feminist investigation, freely available to Dyck (Dahle 1995, 21).

The concept of "library" and the image of the book are organizing principles in Dyck's 1991 installation, *The Library: Inner/Outer* (Fig. 14) and reflect Dyck's renewed interest in reading. Here, she concerns herself with the existence of various bodies of knowledge, how these are produced, and how disseminated. The installation consists of book-like found objects – briefcases, record jackets, women's pocketbooks, and so on – coated with wax or rholoplex and displayed on a series of tables and shelves. The various titles are enigmatic (*About Prayer, Inside Iron, George Littlechild*), suggesting Dyck's personal associations. The work points to domains of experience not available in conventional public discourse in order to elevate these personal and marginalized areas. She does so by representing the domains metaphorically as "books," that is, sources of knowledge. For example, one of the tables all in black is dedicated to her Mennonite grandmother and grandfather while the *George Littlechild* book alludes to the experience of aboriginal people. The women's pocketbooks, mostly small evening bags, are filled with feminine trivia such as curlers, makeup, and jewellery, as well as queen bee images, objects that point to feminine experience as an area of hidden knowledge. Because of the large number of "pocketbooks" in the various installations, Dyck apparently gives more weight to knowledge to be derived from the propagation of female and feminine experience than the other marginalized sources. In so doing, she points to the idea that such knowledge is particularly worth positioning at the centre of the culture. In any case, *The Library Inner/Outer* and the related *Pocket Books for the Queen Bee* (Figs. 15 and 16) provide "texts" seldom found in the annals of our dominant culture.

In the case of private feminine knowledge, Dyck suggests, by the variety of objects included, that this knowledge has its source partly in experience specific to bodily female experience and partly in experience based on the enactment by women of the code of femininity. This aspect of Dyck's work will be discussed more fully subsequently. Of note here is Dyck's placing of *Pocket Books for the Queen Bee* in the context of an installation about sources of knowledge. In doing this, she continues to honour female experience in her work even as she exhibits a primary interest in matters of epistemology. Private experience, including her own, is considered a legitimate source of cultural wisdom. By joining of this elevation of female experience (including that in the domestic arena) to the construction of herself as a thinking subject, Dyck is able to claim an understanding of all women as autonomous individuals. It is a feminist gesture.

This act of claiming is more radical than one might suspect. As recently as 1997, Carolyn Heilbrun, has voiced the view that, despite the successes of the feminist movement, there have been only a few women of genuine intellectual authority in the United States since World War II, and she cites Hannah Arendt, Mary McCarthy, Susan Sontag, Helen Vendler, and Diana Trilling. Heilbrun finds it lamentable that, not only are there so few, but that these few "are not only not feminists, but are explicitly against feminism" (Heilbrun 1999, 42). (It is probably safe to conjecture that, during this period and since, the same has been true of Canada.) The reason Heilbrun gives for this is that to achieve this authority in a society dominated by men, women must become "honorary men." They represent themselves as "sports," as a kind of third sex. They are pretend men or, as Mary Meigs has said, "like mice brought up like cats and not eaten" (1983, 31). Dyck is very conscious of her lack of academic training and would be the last one to claim intellectual authority for herself. Nevertheless, what she does, unlike the female authorities such as Arendt to whom Heilbrun refers, is to make genuine intellectual authority possible and valid for women by presenting the intellectual component as an integral part of the subjectivity of ordinary women.

Consequently, Dyck's is a paradoxical position, one that honours expressions of feminine domesticity while, at the same time, claiming for herself and all women an intellectual autonomy and a freedom to think, a construction of subjectivity not in keeping with the subordinate and marginal position traditionally assigned to women in patriarchal society and culture. Claiming the studio as her rightful workplace as artist goes hand-in-hand for Dyck with the assertion of intellectual autonomy, both being manifestations of agency. At the same time, she asserts in her work the validity of the feminine domestic function and maintains an emotional connection to "house, home and mother."

Dyck's positioning of herself would be seen by Carolyn Heilbrun as an example of the state of liminality, a case of a woman being "on the threshold": part way still in her mother's world, the private domestic world, and venturing part way into the world she seeks for herself, a public arena where agency and self-determination are feasible. She is a "woman between." This liminal positioning certainly has been characteristic of Dyck during most of her career.

However, post-structural theorists in feminism conceive of this contradictory or liminal positioning rather differently. They see the contradictions arising inevitably from the subject position assigned to "woman" in a world in which "humanist discourses are hegemonic" (Davies 1992, 55). Rational humanism takes as universal the male self that is conceived of as unified and solitary. Clearly, then, the gender positioning of women determines that female experience cannot be accurately represented through male-oriented humanist discourse. Post-structuralist theory, recognizing the inevitability of contradictory elements, represents female experience as being constituted through a variety of discourses that are taken up through the speaking of the self and which thereby become part of the subjectivity of that person. Bronwyn Davies puts it this way:

> Post-structuralist theory thus opens up the possibility of seeing the self as continually constituted through multiple and contradictory discourses that one takes up as one's own in becoming a *speaking subject*. One can develop strategies for maintaining an illusion of a coherent unitary self through such strategies as talking of roles or through denial of a contradiction, or one can examine the very processes and discourses through which the constitution of self takes place. (Davies 1992, 57)

While the examination of these processes and discourses is perhaps not consciously taken up by Dyck, the various discourses are apparent in an art practice through which she communicates a multiple selfhood, a practice that allows her to represent herself variously as an artist, a thinker, a wife and mother, a community-aware citizen, and a Mennonite woman. Nevertheless, Dyck is still a woman in a patriarchal society, and the stance she takes as a thinking artist and a domestic woman is one that critiques and contests the dominant way of thinking in the patriarchy. This is apparent, as we have seen, in the way she privileges woman's work in the two series *Shrunken Sweaters* and *Canned Buttons* and the way she critiques the institution of marriage in her *Bee Work* series. In so doing, she can best be understood in terms of "standpoint" feminism. Sara Ruddick defines this theoretical position:

> A standpoint is an engaged vision of the world opposed and superior to dominant ways of thinking. As a proletarian standpoint is a superior vision produced by the experience and oppressive conditions of labour, a feminist standpoint is a superior vision produced by the political conditions and distinctive work of women. (1999, 406)

A case could be made (although not likely by Pratt herself) that Pratt expresses a standpoint inasmuch as hers is a superior vision produced by the "distinctive work of women." Meigs certainly writes from a declared "standpoint" by virtue of her lesbian "vision," a position that will also be discussed further in terms of *testimonio*. Furthermore, Dyck, privileging the ideal of the practice of art as an exercise in creative and intellectual freedom, can be seen as undertaking, among other things, the struggle to overturn the subordination of women, a stated goal of standpoint feminism (ibid.).

SHARON BUTALA

One of the articulated goals of Sharon Butala's autobiographical practice is to examine the truths about women's lives (Reid 1996b, 7), her own and others, and, in presenting her perception of these truths, Butala seeks (as do Pratt, Meigs, and Dyck) both to honour women's traditional domestic lives and to contest the subordination of women inherent in such lives. One could not, however, represent her work as proceeding on the basis of a feminist standpoint principally because another standpoint has shaped much more powerfully the vision that gives impetus to her writing. This standpoint results from support of the institution of the family farm of the prairies and of farmers marginalized in the post-war world by the mechanization and industrialization of farming in Western Canada. In standpoint terms, she presents another "vision ... opposed and superior to the dominant ways of thinking," a vision coming from the observation of lives lived close to nature and opposing the urbanization of our culture, the "dominant way(s) of thinking." This standpoint is apparent in her writing as early as 1988:

> But today, in the 1980s, farm people are fighting a battle as bad as or worse than that fought during the Great Depression, not so much against the elements this time as against the world economic order, and the giant multi-nationals which know no allegiances other than to money and power, and against governments that are helpless in the face of them, or are in league with them while paying lip service to the ideal of the family farm, have little desire to save it and no real understanding of why it should be saved. (*NeWest Review*, 1988, 4)

Ranch and farm life provide the setting for the majority of her fiction, while a life in nature is the focal point of most of her life writing. She came to this setting as a woman and an outsider; her entry into this predominately male world, and the source of this standpoint was through her husband, third-generation rancher Peter Butala and she, like traditionally married women everywhere, found herself positioned as wife in a setting that centres around the person and needs of the husband. As with Dyck, Butala consequently manifests in her work multiple selfhoods that point to the various discourses operative in her experience. Butala, however, is forthright in stating that by the 1980s she had come to privilege her vocation as writer as the primary source of self-definition, as at least equal to that of wife. Even when Peter was alive, she told me unequivocally, that, when she was writing, "It means that I give my life psychologically to that project. I don't give it over to Peter. I don't give it over to this ranch." (Reid 1996b, 23). Paradoxically, it was her move to the Butala ranch that made possible this re-shaping of subjectivity.

At the age of forty-two, Sharon Butala embarked on a new life with rancher Peter Butala and moved to a ranch thirty miles from Eastend. While not regretting this marriage, Sharon found that the solitude of her situation as a rancher's wife and her position as an outsider in that rural community caused her much distress. Her main consolation came from nature and she took to roaming the prairie. As a result, she developed an insight into the power of nature and gained a new vision, one prompted by her experience of the natural world and by her conviction that a life lived close to nature brings a wisdom to human beings that is not available any other way.

The story of the Eastend years and the spiritual journey it prompted form the narrative line of *The Perfection of the Morning* (1994). Her account of her contact with the "ancestral voices" of the aboriginal people who lived on the land that was subsequently the Butala ranch is the subject of *Wild Stone Heart* (2000). These two autobiographical works will likely come to be regarded as the cornerstones of Butala's *oeuvre*, and in their emphasis on a life in nature, they do not present much opportunity to investigate Butala's perceptions of "domesticity, home and mother." Nor does *Coyote's Morning Cry* (1995), a set of meditations prompted by a variety of personal experiences concerning "matters of spirituality." If, however, one reads against the text (that is, taking a point of view as reader that is not precisely in keeping with the direction indicated by the author), one can see that the traditional positioning of the "feminine" holds here as well. Opportunity for reading against the text in this way presents itself in the opening of *Coyote's Morning Cry*:

> I believe as firmly in the reality of my mental life, including dreams and visions as I do in the reality of the dishes I wash every day, the beds I make, the husband I cook for and sit beside evenings, watching television or reading. Neither is possible without the other. (1995, 1)

It is obviously the "mental life" not the domestic reality that forms the subject of Butala's meditations; what is significant in the present context is the degree to which Butala takes for granted that a feminine, domestic positioning is the foundation upon which her everyday life and subjectivity is based.

Only in a magazine article for *Western Living* does Butala deliberately give the reader an intimate, if casual, glimpse of her personal domestic feminine life. Here, she delivers a lighthearted spoof on her attempts at interior decorating, trying to impose "urban rustic interior design on Peter's bunkhouse-inspired taste, the quality motel aesthetic of the community at large, our country lifestyle" (1996b, 13). As she tells it, she is compromised in her remodelling by the emotional associations attached to several Butala living room fixtures and she lists a television inherited from her deceased mother-law; "Peter's much-loved leather armchair," another chair dating back to her first marriage (now the afghan-covered cat's chair), an overly framed pencil drawing of a chuckwagon race and a cloth elephant mailed by her son while he was trekking in Nepal. The final remodelling incorporates a new rug and some quality furniture but leaves the much-loved old objects in place. Butala concludes, "Looks like home to me" (ibid., 21).

Butala's article is significant because in it the notion of the house and its arrangements emerges clearly as a female domain and concern. Redecorating the living room, a project long postponed, is tackled by Butala not only in the interests of good housekeeping but also as an outlet for artistic expression, an opportunity to show off "the owners' [read wife's] good taste" (ibid., 15). What serves to thwart the aesthetic goal are the strong emotional associations that cling to Butala's world of objects. As has been discussed, forming such associations is characteristic of a feminine sensibility. In fact, in *The Perfection of the Morning*, one discovers that, when city girl Sharon first visits Peter Butala's ranch, it is the domestic objects in bachelor Peter's ranch kitchen – "the can of evaporated milk on the table we used for our coffee … the orange offered for dessert" (1994, 7) – that speak to Sharon and give her a sense of homecoming. These objects serve to summon up her life as a child in the houses of her mother and grandmother, rural farmhouses she, as an urban woman and a university academic, had ostensibly outgrown and forgotten. As with Pratt, Meigs, and Dyck, it is the memory of maternal houses that has shaped Butala's domestic feminine identity, represented to her by the "small log house" of childhood – memories of paddles churning butter, of eating porridge from "blue willow bowls till the sad lovers and the weeping willow between them were revealed" (1994, 8). As Butala remarks, it is these objects from the past and their associations with a rural world close to nature that give the weight of meaning to the dessert orange and to the can of milk. It is as if the rural past sheds a paradisal light, lending an aura to those simple objects comparable to the celebratory sparkle of Pratt's still lifes.

While Butala is primarily concerned in *The Perfection of the Morning* with telling the story of her spiritual journey, her "apprenticeship in nature," in so doing she unavoidably sets out the terms in which she defines her subjectivity. In this autobiographical telling, Butala, like the other three artists, displays the feminine proclivity to define herself in relation to others. The most powerful "other" in the text is this "nature," the unspoiled natural world, which becomes for the reader, as for Butala, a palpable spiritual presence. Next in terms of frequency of mention is Peter Butala, who, during his lifetime, acted as her conduit into and interpreter of this world, as well as being her husband and chief companion. He is shown to be both her teacher and the centre around which her feminine domestic existence as a country woman revolves. However, even more fundamental than these two is Butala's positioning of her mother as the touchstone for her own life as a woman, a view that bears witness to Butala's essential embrace of a femininity.

Arriving at this positive positioning of their relationship appears to be one result of Butala's spiritual journey because Butala's relationship with her mother is shown to be even more fraught with ambivalence than those of our other three artists. As with Meigs, Butala endures a childhood in which the mother is absent emotionally, if not physically. In the case of both Meigs and Butala, this absence has an economic cause. In keeping with her affluence and social position, Meigs' mother delegated maternal responsibilities to servants. In contrast, Butala's mother endured "shameful" poverty (Butala 1994a, 12). The result for Butala was, however, the same as for Meigs. Mrs. Le Blanc, with little money and five children (one disabled by polio), apparently could not be a nurturing maternal presence for Sharon. Butala indicated clearly to me that she had not felt loved as a child (Reid 1996b, 15) and in *The Perfection of the Morning* the desolation that she remembers feeling as a very young girl is apparent. She describes being sat down under a tree with her toys:

> I recall the scene from inside that two or three-year old's psyche: everything gray and colourless, myself crying hard and loud but most of all I remember how the world seemed utterly without hope or joy or love. (1994a, 81)

In the same passage, she tells of being in a room with her mother and father "where the scene might have been carved of ice" (ibid., 82). She says in another passage that she was "the daughter of a strict and rather formidable mother" (ibid., 29) and concludes that her relationship with her mother was "never very satisfactory" (ibid., 81).

This mother seems to stand condemned as unloving by her daughter but other comments in the text temper this. For one thing, Amy Le Blanc was an avid reader and passed this passion on to her daughter. Similarly, she encouraged Sharon's very first teen-age attempts at writing by reading her "novel" and by carefully binding and keeping it (1994a, 75). Furthermore, as the mature Butala comes to affirm the intuitive potential of older women, she remembers a mother who had strange powers over the Ouija board constructed to amuse a sick ten-year-old ("Seeing," 2001). Butala pays tribute to her intuitive mother, now deceased, "who knew so much she never said, whose wisdom lit up her eyes as she gazed at me" (ibid., 13).

While having its source, no doubt, in Butala's personal mother-daughter relationship, this contradictory portrait of the mother figure is one which we have come to expect – the daughter seeking on the one hand to deny the mother's life and experience and, on the other hand, maintaining the connectedness so psychologically necessary for women. The urban Butala enacted such a denial and entered a period during which she identified with her father and his family (1994a, 11). The rural Butala, the one who becomes the writer, spirals back to her mother and the life the mother led. Brodzki suggests that the female autobiographical project "is generated out of compelling need to enter into discourse with the absent or distant mother" (Brodzki and Schenck 1988, 245–46).

Consequently, if one accepts with Butala that the natural world possesses a nurturing maternal and spiritual presence, one could argue that her whole autobiographical body of work could be considered as constituting a maternal re-figuring. Even aside from such an extrapolation, Butala in *The Perfection of the Morning* demonstrates what Buss calls "re-emerging … a continuing act of separation/merging" (1993, 17) with her mother. The defining moment of separation for Butala comes when, as with the other three subjects, she names herself as artist (i.e., writer), a naming that supersedes previous assumptions by Butala of the traditional roles of wife and mother.

Nevertheless, even as she writes, Butala second-guesses her own history as an independent urban woman and career-holding mother. She remembers that "I had been raised expecting to be supported by a man and had been trained to be a good wife and mother" (1994a, 30), and Butala, by marrying Peter and becoming a "country wife," still in part responds to these expectations and comes to re-evaluate her former feminist convictions, "merging" once more with her mother and her mother's world:

> As I lived this new way part of me was beginning to feel all that the life of the modern, urban woman had been a mistake and not the improvement on my mother's life I thought it had been. (1994a, 52)

Butala goes on to describe her early domestic life with Peter in a old cabin on the Butala ranch, a life in which one hauled the water, used an outdoor toilet, and for which the cook stove was the only source of heat. It was a life based on physical labour and lived more through the body than the mind. It was also a life attuned to the rhythms of nature, and Butala learned to pay attention to the weather and to the movements of the sun and moon.

The Butalas built a new house with modern conveniences three years into their marriage, but the awareness developed in those early years remains with Butala and feeds her art. This awareness has a spiritual component and comes directly out of her connection to her maternal antecedents:

> I was experiencing firsthand what I knew from their stories and from my earliest memories had been the lives of my mother, my aunts and my grandmothers. That was deeply gratifying, despite those very real physical hardships, in a way I don't feel able to articulate other than to say that it had to do with some primal sense of womanhood stemming both from what I knew of their lives, and from an unconscious tribal memory, much more basic than mere family history, and which I had not even known existed. (1994a, 54)

This basic domesticity leads Butala back to a feminine identification with these maternal predecessors. In the process of self-discovery, which Butala describes in *The Perfection of the Morning*, she comes to know that this identification shapes her subjectivity as powerfully as the relationship with nature.

In coming into this relationship with nature, she did not proceed on her own, even though most of her days were spent in solitude. It was her husband Peter who fostered her knowledge of nature and who therefore emerges in the text as teacher and mentor as well as domestic partner. Feminine positioning in a traditional patriarchal society requires that a married woman put the husband at the centre of her life. This is doubly the case in a ranching community where the work setting is indisputably male and where the rancher's wife and her kitchen are seen as an adjunct of the ranching operation (Korol and Butala 1992, 2). By marrying Peter, Sharon accepted initially the ranch wife's traditional role and the domestic work associated with that role. Moreover, as an urban woman, she was strange to this society and had to depend on her husband to show her what she needed to know in order to be a rancher's wife, able to help with the outside work when appropriate. It is no wonder, then, that Peter figures strongly in the account of this time in her life.

Mary Mason's notion of alterity has application here. The concept of a "real presence and recognition of another consciousness" (Mason 1988, 22) is particularly descriptive of Butala's disclosure and location of self. Peter and his example are constantly in Sharon's mind as she re-lives a multilevel experience in the text of *The Perfection of the Morning*. She explains further in *Coyote's Morning Cry* (1995a, 1) that she lived her life on the ranch in two realities, the down to earth one of an everyday domestic existence and the mental realm incorporating the world of dreams and visions, having its source both in a spiritual realm and in the subconscious.

Peter figures in both realities even though the mental realm is most powerfully experienced in solitude. In the everyday reality, Peter is the dominant force. Throughout *The Perfection of the Morning*, Peter is shown as the one to whose authority she appeals. The text is peppered with affirmations such as, "I had faith in Peter," "Peter taught me," "Peter said ... In such matters Peter was always right on," "Peter came and got me." This husband appears to wife Sharon as a source of strength, a man living a "real" life who sees his role traditionally as the protector and breadwinner in the family. As wife and writer, Sharon also accesses Peter's experienced perception of the natural world, rural culture and ranching life, all sources for the content of her art:

> And I had Peter, an unconventional thinker if there ever was one, clever, patient, and in whose long silences a lot of cogitation had gone on over the years. He had some clear ideas about what had gone wrong [on the land] and more, what really mattered, what losses counted in the ongoing stream of life, and what didn't, out of which I might discern what the essence of rural life really is. (1994a.199)

Peter here is the authority in the everyday reality of ranch life, and, in the text, Butala is comfortable in this area of her life in accepting a feminine, wifely positioning as an admiring acolyte.

Sharon Butala's mental life, however, is shown to be essentially a private realm. Nevertheless, here too Peter is revealed as a strong presence because Butala's imagination fixes on an image of Peter that becomes a talisman for her spiritual journey. She tells of how she was taking her usual prairie walk and came to the brow of a hill. She looked down into the dry coulee bed below to see "twenty or so cows grazing," Peter's saddle horse also browsing, and at the edge of the cattle a couple of antelopes stood, "noses down in the grass." She is struck by the peace of the scene and the animals seeming ease with each other. She continues:

About a hundred feet out from the foot of the hill, in the midst of his animals, lying face down in the grass, head on one bent arm but shielding his eyes, Peter lay sound asleep. I stopped dead in my tracks, overcome with an emotion I couldn't identify; that I had caught him in a moment so private I felt I had no right to be there; that something was happening here beyond my experience and understanding – something significant. (1994a, 27)

Butala later remarks that this image of Peter asleep among the animals becomes the "benchmark" against which she measures her experiences of her new outdoors environment, the indigenous grasslands of Saskatchewan. This image ranks in her mind on a par with the dreams and visions that are such a powerful part of her spiritual journey. It seems evident that, for a woman such as Sharon who feels strongly the womanliness of her identity, it must be satisfying to have as her primary "other," a mate who is not only a man among men: ("I saw in him what I thought was a real man" (Reid 1996b, 18) but who also has achieved the mystical union with the natural world that she herself seeks. In a way it parallels Mary Pratt's view of Christopher as the consummate artist, an identity she coveted for herself and a reason for finding satisfaction in close association (Reid 1996a, 1).

Unfortunately, Mary Pratt's achieving of her artistic goal proved to be one of the disrupting factors in the Pratt marriage (ibid., 2, 45–48). The Butalas' marriage followed a somewhat different course. Peter Butala's identity as rancher was securely fixed. Consequently his wife's successful career as a writer posed no threat and he was able to support it without reservation. As Butala explained to me: "… he recognizes the value of my work which is writing, not housekeeping, not driving trucks, and he's in complete control of his kingdom" (Reid 1996b, 28). This no doubt changed in the short period of Peter's retirement before his death in 2007. However, in her directly autobiographical writings, Butala presents little critique of her second marriage or of marriage in general. It is in her fiction, which has an avowedly autobiographical source, that Butala queries the institution of marriage, and the positioning of women in the rural farming and ranching culture Butala has said that it is her intent in the fiction set in rural Saskatchewan to "demythologize" the romancing of the West:

I think it was partly the woman in me who objects very strenuously to the way the myth of the West is a male myth and a macho myth. I had begun to see, first of all, that I had a great respect for the men and the physical courage they had to have to do the normal, ordinary things in ranching. I wanted to respect that. But I wanted to say how the life was, in fact, mostly extremely hard labour. The only reward was feeling like a man on a horse. (Reid 1996b, 24)

Later, in the non-fiction *Lilac Moon*, another work of "de-mythologizing," she discusses directly what it means to be a Westerner, putting this in an historical and political context, and in the chapter "*Tough Stock*," she comments on "our profoundly patriarchal world and our gritty resolute women" (2005, 147). The trilogy of novels – *The Gates of the Sun* (1986), *Luna* (1988), and *The Fourth Archangel* (1992) – treats the same theme in a fictional fashion so that *Lilac Moon* addresses the readers' minds while the novels address their imagination.

The Gates of the Sun has a male protagonist, Andrew Samson, who serves a harsh apprenticeship on the way to taking his place as a man of the land. *Luna* is the novel in which Butala depicts the feminine perception of rural life, that of the "modern day women who still lived a traditional life" (Butala 1994a, 182). *Luna* features four different female characters, Rhea, the old woman, Phoebe, the teen-age daughter, Diana, the rebel who strikes out on her own leaving farm, husband, and children behind, and Selena, the traditional wife and mother with whom Butala feels the strongest identification (Reid 1996b, 6). *The Fourth Archangel* is the most political of the three novels, treating as it does the trauma of a Saskatchewan farming community, swept by economic changes that result in the loss of one family farm after another. The mood of the novel is apocalyptic, the "fourth archangel" being the one among the archangel hierarchy who foretells doom.

Butala's method in these novels is somewhat paradoxical. On the one hand, her goal is to show the harsh reality of farming and ranching life as she has observed it; on the other hand, the whole structure of the novels is informed by Greek mythology (ibid., 36). And it is in her use of these myths that she makes her point about the difference between male and female experience in this male-dominated culture. The men, and in particular Andrew Samson in *The Gates of the Sun*, are depicted as being embarked on a heroic undertaking, a kind of Odyssey, in which they are seeking to preserve a paradisal way of life, a life in "the sun." Accordingly, Andrew Samson is shown as undertaking a Herculean task (hence "Samson").

The informing myth for *Luna*, the novel that treats female experience, is the story of Persephone, the woman who is stolen from her mother and taken to the underworld, the underworld here being a metaphor for the patriarchal culture in which marriage is the inevitable female fate. The subject matter of *Luna* is the various degrees of victimization that women in the male culture endure. Selena enjoys the womanly satisfaction of fulfilling the nurturing role of the feminine but has to endure being undervalued and dominated. Phoebe's victimization is more marked and poignant. She becomes pregnant after being forced to have intercourse, and the men in the community sympathize with the exigencies of the male nature that result in rape. Diana is the rebel who undertakes the heroic male Odyssean quest but must pay the price of losing her children. Rhea, the old woman, emerges as the least victimized; she is shown to be the wise one of the community, the mother to whom all Persephones return. In *The Fourth Archangel*, men and women experience equally the great sense of loss that comes with the extinction of the family farm as a viable way of life.

These three novels put into fictional form Butala's feelings concerning the rural life of which she has become a part. She honours the incredible talent and work that is part of being a rural woman, but she decries the fact that this work is not honoured more fully by the community and that women have very little share in the decision-making that determines the shape of their lives. In this blending of elevating the work of women, and acknowledging the victimization inherent in their lives under the patriarchal system, Butala demonstrates, as did Pratt, Meigs, and Dyck, the characteristics of female culture/mother art as set out by Mary Kelly.

The victimization is even more dramatically drawn in the short story collections, *Queen of the Headaches* (1985), and *Fever* (1990). The economy of the form heightens the sense of enclosure and imprisonment issuing from a feminine sense of powerlessness. In these stories, the woman's life is determined by her husband's situation, decisions, and character. Temporary relief is obtained in fleeting affairs but in only two stories – "Where the Red Hibiscus Flares" (1985, 119–30) and "A Tropical Holiday" (1985, 131–45) – does the female protagonist take matters into her own hands by physically removing herself from the scene. It is in these short stories that Butala most clearly reveals her ambivalence about the institution of marriage. There are none of the affirmations that are found in *Luna*. Marriage is shown rather as an institution where men have the power and do not hesitate to use it, often in a brutal fashion. As does Pratt, Butala, through these stories, makes a plea for a new form of marriage, one that allows for the personal fulfillment of women as well as of men.

Only in a fourth novel, *The Garden of Eden*, does Butala depict a female character, Iris, who lives on the land and takes charge of her own destiny; Iris, however, is empowered to do that only after the death of her husband. She inherits her husband's farm and, despite community expectations, refuses to relinquish control whether to greedy economic interests or by means of a second marriage. She thereby seizes agency for the first time and uses her power to plan the restoration of the land by returning it to its original grassland, the Eden that has become lost. In *The Garden of Eden*, the theme of conservation of precious land resources is combined with an examination of the power of a three-generation mother-daughter relationship and the Persephone motif becomes overt. Lanny, the daughter, recounts the myth for Iris, her mother. It is Iris who responds: "Oh, I see…. It's another kind of fall – the fall of maidens stolen from the safety and innocence of their mothers' world into the world of men." (1998, 369). In this novel Butala connects the affirmation of feminine power with the healing power of the land, a connection that is at the centre of the Butala *oeuvre*.

Towards the close of *The Perfection of the Morning*, Butala muses over the nature of femininity and, while she accepts that the traditional domestic life of women allows them to fulfill what she sees as their innate need to nurture, she rejects the subordination of women and asserts the claim of all women to be persons in their own right. As before, one finds that Butala's attitude towards "House, home and mother" is ambivalent. She finds the domestic role alone to be too limiting for herself, but, extrapolating from her mother's life, she concludes that most women yearn for more personal fulfillment without sacrificing their roles as wives and mothers. On the whole, Butala displays an essentialist view of femininity. That is, she believes that men and women are innately different because of all that comes from women giving birth and men not. However, Butala wishes for a more complete expression of the fullness and uniqueness of femininity and sees that as part of her task as a writer. She puts it this way:

> Women experience the world differently than men do. Experiencing it differently, and if left alone to try it, we would live it differently…. We haven't yet told the truth about our lives. Until we tell the truth out loud, no matter how humiliating or painful or at variance with society's version, we will not come to know what we are, what is truly our world of experience, and through that, what our roles should be or could be. (1994a, 187)

SUMMARY

Certainly, Dyck, Pratt, and Meigs would agree with the necessity of "telling the truth out loud" about their personal experience as women, but, from my observation, only Pratt would agree with Butala that men and women are innately different. Meigs as a lesbian has expressed the view that gender can be most clearly understood as a continuum. Dyck, in her rejection of all stereotyping, tends to deny differences between people as being innate, whether these differences are based on gender, race, religion, or any other observed variation. What all four do agree on is the necessity of viewing women as autonomous persons and therefore all four oppose the subordination of women in patriarchal culture.

Nevertheless, all four embrace domesticity as part of the enduring structure of their daily lives, investing great emotional significance in the houses they have inhabited and the objects in these houses. All four display this penchant for domesticity as part of their maternal inheritance, and all four witness to the power of the mother figure in their lives and the ambivalent but strong emotions inspired by maternal antecedents. All four have in the past habitually constructed their subjectivity through relationship to significant men in their lives, whether husbands or mentors. As their identity as artists becomes securely affirmed, the relationship to these men has, to varying degrees, been put on a more equitable basis. The habits and associations of domesticity and the power of the mother remain.

These women are all born between 1917 and 1940 and are, therefore, well past middle life. They are members of a liminal generation, the mothers of whom were traditional women; unlike their mothers, they have come increasingly to define themselves through their chosen careers. It would appear, nevertheless, that, in this liminal generation, the power of the traditional model for feminine life persists.

READING AS DAUGHTER AND SISTER TO THE TEXT

My investigation into the power of house, home, and mother in the work of these four artists has alerted me to the significance of similar aspects of my own identity, shaped in the same liminal space. One could say that I have served as a daughter to these literary and visual texts, having been mothered by them into a sharpened awareness of my own experience of conflict as regards domesticity. The image that expresses this ambivalence most clearly comes from the passages in *Lily Briscoe* in which Mary Meigs applies the Biblical references to Mary and Martha to her own domestic obsession for order and neatness. In this regard, Meigs emerges as a definite Martha, concerned inevitably with the practicalities of domestic orderliness. My own inclination for keeping order in my home is distinctly a "sometime thing" and if a messy painter's palette indicates, as Meigs says, one's identity as a Mary, then I must plead guilty. However, like Meigs in reverse, I now realize that my Mary self, while probably dominant, has come to be balanced, in the years as wife and mother, by a Martha side which keeps my "nose to the grindstone," allowing me both to arrange for domestic order and to expedite movement towards the personal and professional goals in my life.

I have long been aware of the power of my own mother in my life so I felt a profound sisterhood for these four women artists who similarly acceded to their mother's power in their construction of self, all the while holding firm to their mental vision of the female artist. My learning of the notion of alterity, so fundamental in the female construction of self, permitted me merely to put into theoretical context an enduring facet of personal experience. As a young woman, however, the act of getting married at the age of twenty in a burst of love and romance contained something of the hope of escape from my mother's influence by moving out from under her roof. I smile now at my naiveté; this influence was so internalized that change in status and domicile made surprisingly little difference.

It would take a book like *The Box Closet* to do justice to my relationship with my mother. As a child, I often found her to be an embarrassment because she was not like other people's mothers. For one thing, she was conspicuously beautiful with her wavy mahogany red hair, blue eyes, and flawless complexion, looking something like Jeanette McDonald, a favourite 1930s movie star. Also, Mom had a collection of what seemed to me then to be eccentric friends, women who ran little poetry magazines and whose marital partners seemed to come and go, women who had long red nails and gypsy-like jewellery, women who told fortunes in teacups and subscribed to numerology. Mom struggled all her life to "fit in" to a domestic, wifely role, both loving the various homes she ran and longing to escape from them. She could have claimed an artist's identity with her flair for the dramatic, her passionate love of music and her truly wonderful mezzo-soprano voice. She loved to write verse and was thrilled when a long-vanished Canadian periodical called *The National* published three or four of her poems. It was one of my mother's "eccentric" female friends who, through a simple phone call, changed my life by inspiring my last-minute decision to enroll at university.

What I realize at this distance is that I am my mother's daughter: I share in that complex mix of Mary and Martha that in time came to be elements in both our subjectivities. For its part, *The Dinner Party* plays tribute to the Marys of female history, such as Virginia Woolf and Georgia O'Keefe, while honouring the Marthas over the centuries who perfected the domestic arts. It is a liminal positioning on Chicago's part, and my mother likewise was truly ahead of her time in occupying a liminal space between filling the traditional wife-mother role and casting about for artistic expression. When my father's construction business became involved in a long lawsuit because of partner disagreements, my mother, then fifty years old, went to work in a marketing job, selling maps of the new Toronto subdivisions to various businesses. As it turned out, at least one of her colleagues used this occupation as his day job, pursuing musical "gigs" as a pianist at night. My mother, a born sales woman and music lover, found herself in a very congenial atmosphere and, despite her heartache for her husband, experienced one of the most satisfying periods of her life. She worked until she was almost seventy when she retired to look after my ailing father. When he died a short time later, she was devastated. She had married at the age of seventeen, and despite her joy at working for more than a decade outside the home, her primary self-definition was as her husband's wife. I am not sure that his death changed that.

When I announced after the second year of university that Craig and I, against all common sense, had decided to get married, my mother and father were visibly upset. Craig was two years out of the RCAF, having served five years overseas. He was still sorting out his career direction after getting the two-year Bachelor of Arts degree then available to veterans. Curiously, I had no worries about our financial future. Moreover, married or not, I had no intention of quitting university.

Nevertheless, my mother's first act after our announcement was to buy me a cedar chest and a little supply of linens, a belated attempt to give her daughter the conventional "hope chest" that she decided my new "engaged" status required. I was bemused by this, not realizing fully the domestic implications of what I was undertaking. I still have that cedar chest. It is not ten feet from me as I write, one of the many objects in our home that speaks of "women's stuff." It serves to honour my mother's unqualified support for me no matter what, the prized family life that I have subsequently enjoyed and my primary construction of self as wife to my husband of over fifty years and mother/grandmother/great-grandmother in our extended family.

I see more clearly how the relationship with my mother has shaped me than how my subjectivity has been formed through relationship with my husband, because, even after our lengthy time together, our marriage is still a work in progress. We are now coping with semi-retirement and the various health issues that old age brings. What I can say is that a large degree of symbiosis has developed. As a World War II veteran, a longtime social worker in the criminal justice system, and then a local politician, he has a knowledge of the world and an unerring sense of values that I trust. I am the one who assists in matters of language and communication.

Further than that, our relationship is not unlike Sharon and Peter Butala's or that of Aganetha and Peter Dyck in that the house remains the female domain no matter to what degree the husband ventures into domesticity. Similarly, the wife respects the masculine domain, relying on the husband for a particular kind of wisdom and support. We have spent some time with both couples and their modelling of marriage is one with which we both felt comfortable. It is a model that occupies the liminal space between a two-career family, now so common, and the traditional one in which the husband was the primary breadwinner. In the liminal model, the wife/mother is in the home in the early years of child-raising, postponing the pursuit of professional interests until the middle years. I, for example, stayed home until our youngest child was in kindergarten, and then dabbled in a series of part-time jobs until finally settling in middle age into a career as a literature instructor in various post-secondary institutions. Over the years, the politics operative in educational institutions has often distressed me, but I always felt supremely and happily at home when walking into a classroom to share with students my love of the literary and visual arts.

In the opening paragraph of *Coyote's Morning Cry*, Butala pauses briefly to make reference to the solid underpinning reality of her domestic existence, positioning it as running parallel to the mental life that occupies her professionally. She says, "Neither of them is possible without the other." Dyck, Pratt, and even Meigs would unquestionably agree, and that, too, is how it is with me. Sitting around any dinner table, we would, in this, as is many matters, be women together.

2

Alive as a Woman:
Empowering the Body

> In my case, my upbringing prevented me from accepting my
> sexual nature by making me ashamed, doubly ashamed because
> I belong to a despised sexual minority. The two chief tasks of my
> life have been to become an artist and to overcome my shame,
> and, at the age of sixty-one, I am only just beginning to feel
> that I have accomplished them.   – Mary Meigs, *Lily Briscoe: A*
> *Self-Portrait*

While enjoying many aspects of their femininity, most women in our society
have often felt ill at ease with their bodies and bodily desires. Women's connection to their physical selves has historically been a site of conflict, bound
as they are by biological rhythms, trained often to deny their sexual nature
while, at the same time, being valued for the degree of their feminine attractiveness. As a lesbian, Mary Meigs has been particularly conflicted about
bodily experience. In *Lily Briscoe: A Self-Portrait* (1981), she documents her
memory of the long-standing alienation of her mind and spirit from the
"shameful" physical body because, as she says, "part of my inheritance was
a belief in the life of the mind and the Christian soul at the expense of
the body. In my family the body was unmentionable" (8). It was not until
the writing of *Lily Briscoe*, tracing as it does her early sexual attitudes and
experience, that Meigs came to a full acceptance of her sexual identity; it
both released her from a sense of shame and led her to express her artist
subjectivity in a new form. However, the sexual body does not become fully
"mentionable" until sixteen years later with the publication of *The Time Be-*
ing, a description of her love affair with an Australian woman. Here, Meigs
writes lyrically and graphically of the body's desires:

Will they look at each other differently now? ... Now that they know how the hands, the mouth can greet and take possession of uprising nipples, and move confidently down, deep into a widening valley and bathe in a warm flood of welcome (1997, 34).

Meigs experienced this bodily awakening late in life, and it affected both her life and her art, providing a kind of epiphany. As she explained in an article: "the cells of my body seemed to voice themselves as words, corporeal words like 'hands,' 'mouths,' 'nipples'" (2000, 99).

Until the last two years of her life, the act of "coming out"[1] – that is, her acknowledgment of a crucial bodily issue – was the central fact of her life narrative. In those two years, Meigs accomplishes another radical break-through when she documents the effects on the aging body and mind of a debilitating stroke in a series of diary entries, faxes, and pieces of freewrit-ing,[2] entitled *Beyond Recall*, edited by Lisa Weil and published posthumously in 2005. Here, Meigs tells of the bodily minutia of her everyday life as well as her thought processes during her last two years when she was confined indoors and forced to cope with a multitude of physical losses. Fortunately, hers was a right brain stroke so her speech and her ability to write and draw were not affected. With the encouragement of Weil and other friends, Meigs kept writing until the very end. Her last entry came on the morning of November 15, 2002; Meigs died in the afternoon. In *Beyond Recall*, Meigs demonstrates how a creative mind turns bodily affliction and the knowledge of approaching death into what Weil calls "a time of abundance" (2005, xi). The diaries in particular offer the reader an intimate physical and spiritual connection, tracing as they do her daily challenges and consolations.

Issues of body are located differently in the work of Aganetha Dyck, Sharon Butala, and Mary Pratt. Unlike Mary Meigs, their female lives fol-lowed the more traditional pattern of getting married and having children. Accordingly, the physical act of childbirth directly affects their sense of the possibilities and vulnerabilities of their female bodily selves. Inevitably, how-ever, as women in a patriarchal society and as artists with autobiographical practices, all four artists conjure with, not only bodily experience, but also with a whole range of attitudes and beliefs that govern how the female body is construed both in life and in art. In both their life and their work, they are necessarily conditioned to a significant degree by social convention. As one traces the development of their art practices, it becomes apparent that they are dominated by society's perceptions of the female body and, at the same time, moved to contest these perceptions.

Meigs' medium of communication in her autobiographical texts is, of course, written language, and she invokes the body through an imaginative and vivid use of words. Aganetha Dyck, however, working visually as a sculptor and installation artist, invokes the body with even greater immediacy by moving the body of the viewer through space and by the exploration and exploitation of material. Material, with its appeal to touch and smell as well as sight, is the source of her visual art vocabulary and it communicates emotion by association. That is her artistic method. Dyck also invokes the body in her art practice by the incorporation of actual clothing, costume, and accessories, either found or constructed. She thereby makes a variety of experiential bodily references in order to suggest feminine domestic work, to allude to bodily ways of enacting femininity, to convey the dynamics of the body situated and controlled within a community, and to suggest dominance or violation of the female body by the constructs of patriarchal society, all factors in the symbolic representation of her own subjectivity in her art.

I argue that Dyck's is largely an autobiographical practice, having its source in issues arising from her personal experience and her desire to contest patriarchal expectations and constructions of women. As with Meigs, part of Dyck's personal bodily experience has involved learning to deal with chronic health problems. These health issues surface in her work through the devices of metonymy and metaphor, so that a variety of images serve to suggest physical illness, poisoning, bodily contamination, decay, and regeneration. At other times, her art is life-affirming, especially in her investigative work with *apis mellifera*, the honeybee. Dyck sees in bee culture an expression of an energy-filled life force, a force that influences her notions of her relationship to nature and to which she responds by using the bees' bodily activity and their material products in her work.

Sharon Butala fashions her life narrative as a spiritual journey. It is significant, then, the degree to which she privileges bodily experience in her female construction of self. Butala sees women's reproductive capacity as a basic determinant in the character of women's experience and asserts therefore that women are "grounded in their body" (Butala 1994a, 82) and "go through body to spirit in a way that men do not" (Reid 1996b, 12). Certainly that is the case for Butala personally. For example, in *The Perfection of the Morning* and *Wild Stone Heart*, it is the simple act of walking the prairie that allows her to connect with nature and prompts her spiritual journey. In this, Butala reveals her experience of the connection between psyche and body. The interplay of the two is shown further in her detailing of physical illnesses that she comes to understand as symptoms of spiritual unease or acute mental distress.

However, it is in her autobiographically based fiction rather than in her life writing that Butala conjures with the biological life of the female body: the implacable rhythms of childbirth, the urgency of desire, and the ongoing female monthly signalling of blood. In both fiction and non-fiction, Butala depicts the physical labour that is part of the farming and ranching life for both men and women. Her novel, *Luna*, portrays this life from a female point of view, showing what is involved in the injunction that ranch and farm wives should "pull their weight" (1988b, 40). For rural women, "pulling one's weight," in bodily terms, means not only doing the physical domestic work necessary to provide meals and run a house but also performing physical work out of doors. Butala reveals, moreover, that for rural women opportunities for purely feminine expression – clothes, makeup, parties – can be limited or non-existent, depending on degree of prosperity in the rural economy.

As a visual artist, Mary Pratt privileges bodily expression in a different way. It is the perception of light, a bodily function that informs her still life painting, a kind of painting that Burnett and Schiff identify as "pictorial phenomenalism" (1983, 167), drawing attention thereby to the importance given by Pratt to the experiential moment. In this way, Pratt does share with Butala this sense of the eternal "now," a perception initiated by personal sensory experience and leading to a celebration of spirit, a concept to be explored subsequently. Additionally, allusion to her female bodily experience exists as a subtext in a large proportion of Pratt's still lifes, both in terms of the shapes used and in the choice of organic or animal subject matter. In general, Pratt's use of food as subject can be read in several ways: as suggesting directly the sensual experience of eating; as representing, through metonymy or metaphor, maternal nurturing and female sexuality; to signify social convention; and, finally, to represent the whole culture of killing animals for food. The social code of table manners and the social regulation of personal bodily functions are ways of containing the personal body, Pratt's included, of rendering it "docile," a notion communicated by Pratt through rigid compositional strategies and through the use of containers as subject matter.

As in life, the body is also frequently invoked through its absence: a dress left hanging, a table revealing the remnants of a meal. In such works, the body exists as a ghostly presence, all the more evocative through visual suggestion rather than outright statement. In somewhat the same way, Pratt herself as a physical presence is evoked for the viewer in those paintings, notably the *Fire* series, in which she employs, instead of her carefully blended tiny brush strokes, expressive marks created by full arm movement. In such works, Pratt throws off her customary restraint and uses bodily movement to release and communicate strong emotion.

The human form as overt subject matter, however, is found chiefly in a group of paintings known as the *Donna* series. In this series she undertakes depiction of the female figure, a painting genre traditionally reserved for the male artist, in which representation of the female body serves variously "as muse, an object of beauty and the source of erotic male pleasure" (Berger 1997, 47, 64). Pratt's painterly inquiry consequently raises issues of female narcissism, surrogacy, and voyeurism, and the degree to which women can shape their bodily subjectivity and can contest their objectification in the gaze of men. These are personal issues for Pratt, ones that have a powerful effect on her constructions of self.

THEORETICAL CONTEXTS

Sociopolitical determinations, as well as the sensations and perceptions in and of their own bodies, govern how these four artists experience their female bodies. To come to some understanding of the underlying dynamics, it is helpful to view these determinations within a variety of theoretical contexts. Most relevant here is the assumption of difference, which lies at the heart of the construction of gender. To be named "woman," as Simone de Beauvoir pointed out (1952), is to be viewed in almost all cultural traditions as a variant from the normal, a "second sex," lesser than, and derivative from, the primary designation of "man." This privileging of the male in the social construction of gender has become a matter of resistance for a wide variety of feminisms that have developed over the past fifty years; echoes of these positions mark the work of all four. However, in one area at least, feminist resistance to male privileging has made few inroads in our society and that is in the enactment of the code of femininity. Even though partially contested by these four artists, these powerful notions of the feminine nevertheless inform their notions of body just as they informed their concepts of female domesticity.

The Code of Femininity

In her book, *Femininity* (1984), Susan Brownmiller analyzes the paradoxical attitudes of women towards the code of femininity, a code that objectifies the female by putting a premium on physical beauty, dictates the accepted standards of this beauty, and subordinates the feminine to the masculine as regards physical power and mental competence. Brownmiller points out that it is women who endorse this code and validate its claim by internalizing these demands.

This internalizing is more understandable if one accepts Michel Foucault's notion of power as a "network of practices, institutions and technologies," a "network" into which women are born and therefore accept as normal or as "a given." Foucault calls the body in containment by society the "docile body" and points to a kind of automatic self-policing by the individual in order to conform to the proliferation of bodily mandates in contemporary society (cited in Jaggar and Bordo 1989, 14). In this construction of society, the code of femininity can be seen as one element in Foucault's network of practices. The practising of the code exemplifies also the Smith/Butler notion of performativity (Smith 1995, 20) in which the repetition of certain conventional actions are best seen as role-playing prompted by the repeated presence of a particular audience, the audience in this case being the male majority in patriarchal Western society.

Brownmiller offers a further reason for the acceptance by women of a code that objectifies them and positions them as subordinate in power to men. She points out that the performance of femininity, while involving conformity to a rigid code of appearance and behaviour that is "bafflingly inconsistent," at the same time offers women "a brilliant, subtle esthetic" (1984, 14).

> We are talking, admittedly about an exquisite esthetic. Enormous pleasure can be extracted from feminine pursuits as a creative outlet or purely as relaxation; indeed indulgence for the sake of fun or art, or attention, is among femininity's greatest joys. (ibid., 15)

Then she adds another inducement for the practice of femininity:

> But the chief attraction (and the central paradox, as well) is the competitive edge that femininity seems to promise in the unending struggle to survive. (ibid.)

The competition is for male attention and approval and therein lies the paradox; in achieving this approval, one accedes to one's own trivialization and loss of power. Yet, there is a narcissistic "payoff" that for many women is an addictive substitute for real power and for authentic subjectivity. A fixation on the bodily performance of femininity (a performance encouraged by mass media and commercial advertising) can represent a form of autoeroticism consisting of the admiration of one's own adorned body presented as a desirable sexual object. Such autoeroticism can interfere with the notion and experience of oneself as a desiring sexual subject (Kelly 1987, 310). In investigating the work of Mary Pratt and Alice Munro, Rasporich comments similarly on the strangling effects of another manifestation of femininity, the "veneer" of "gentility and superficiality which does not even allow for the physical realities of the female life or the physical actualities of the female body" (Rasporich 1993, 134). It is this veneer of gentility that Meigs referred to as her "inheritance."

While all four of the artists under study accede in varying degrees to the code of femininity, all reflect some understanding of this code as contingent, a middle-class social construction of a male-dominated society. Further, the work of all four describes female bodily actuality unmediated by this code. If the nature of this bodily actuality is as constant in female experience as, for example, the rhythm of the menses or the experience of giving birth, the question is raised as to what degree gender difference is the result of male/female biology and to what extent the assigning of gender is an act of social construction. In seeking to free women from a subordinate position in society, feminist theory has had to come to terms with essentialism, the notion that female experience necessarily differs from that of the male because of biological difference.

Psychoanalytic Theory and the Female Body: Jouissance and Essentialism

Of particular concern is the psychoanalytic myth of lack, as developed by Freud, and revisioned by Jacques Lacan. As was discussed earlier, the Lacanian theory of lack was the source of Mary Kelly's notion of the female problematic in the practice of painting by women. Similarly, the French feminists turn to Lacan when identifying an insufficiency in language for the expression of female sexuality. They point to the possibility of another kind of discourse for women that they term *écriture féminine*, the writing into actuality of the erotic female body. This perception of its potential for female sexual expression finds echoes through portions of the work of all four, ones in which these artists strive to achieve authentic female embodiment. Feminist theorists explain the necessity for such a resource in discourse as follows:

> Gallop and Silverman explicate *écriture féminine* by claiming that through discourse the human body is territorialized into a male or female body. The meanings of the body in discourse actually shape the materiality of the real body. (Cited in Jaggar and Bordo 1989, 59)

According to this conceptualization of *écriture féminine*, what has been unspoken in canonical discourse has been female pleasure, and feminist theorist Luce Irigaray appropriates from Lacan the term *jouissance*, a designation for female sexuality beyond the phallus.[3] Irigaray describes female sexual pleasure as follows:

> Woman has sex organs everywhere. She experiences pleasure almost everywhere; even without speaking of the hysterization of her entire body, one can say that the geography of her pleasure is much more diversified, more multiple in its differences, more subtle than is imagined…. Woman finds pleasure more in *touch* than in sight and her entrance into a dominant scoptic economy signifies, once again, her relegation to passivity. (Irigaray 1981, 101, 103)

This description of female sexual pleasure and the notion of *jouissance* is one that I find particularly germane in a more detailed examination of how Meigs and Pratt, in particular, represent female eroticism and so are able to "speak the unspoken" in their autobiographical practice. Female eroticism has traditionally been the "unspoken" in the arts because both in literary text and in the visual art genre of painting, artists such as Meigs and Pratt, operate in male-dominated discourses.[4] They have to use, as Meigs says, the space between the genres in which to express their female sexual experience and thus to accomplish *écriture féminine* (Warland 1995, 47). Meigs does this by finding space between autobiography and memoir, between biography and autobiography, and between fiction and non-fiction. Similarly,

Pratt reinvents both the male traditions of still life painting through the use of photographic techniques and that of the painterly representation of the female figure through the strategy of female voyeuristic intervention.

While psychoanalytic theorists and their inheritors see gender as something to be explained, and therefore a matter of social construction operating at the unconscious level, *écriture féminine* feminists Irigaray and Cixous nevertheless have been charged with essentialism (Dallery 1989, 63), the view that the female is to be defined as constitutionally, rather than culturally, a woman. The essentialist view, whatever its form, seems to consign the female again to "second sex" gendering. The charge against Irigaray and Cixous comes from representatives of other brands of feminism, those rejecting limitations to females that come from accepting any universal description of womanhood. As Dallery points out, one defence against the charge is that *écriture feminine* is primarily a function of discourse. Nevertheless, some insist that to write the body in its specificity is to risk affirming universalism. For, while *écriture féminine* theory acknowledges that forms of female desire are undoubtedly culturally taught, it still affirms an eroticism beyond phallic construction or control, a phenomenon observable in the work of Meigs and Pratt.

This opposition between essentialist and social construction theories is played out in the ways these artists represent body in their autobiographical art practices. The work of Mary Pratt and Sharon Butala is more likely to express essentialist positioning as concerns gendering because both locate their womanhood as holistic, affecting many levels of experience. In eschewing any form of stereotyping, Aganetha Dyck is more likely to question traditional attributions of gender despite her penchant for honouring all forms of female experience. Consequently, Dyck's work reflects a more investigative attitude towards gendering even as she extends the notion of feminine domestic production into a means of art-making. Similarly, as a lesbian who came to accept her personal sexuality only after considerable emotional conflict, Mary Meigs expresses, through various autobiographical stances, a concept of gendering that challenges the binary assumptions of male/female and heterosexual/homosexual at the heart of mainstream social organization. In her self-gendering, Meigs comes to resist any charge of transgression or marginalization and seeks a definition of her sexual selfhood that permits a claim of social legitimacy. This is a task addressed by a wide variety of feminist, lesbian theorists, ranging from, among others, Adrienne Rich in the early 1980s to Marilyn Frye, Teresa de Lauretis, Judith Butler and Diana Fuss in the 1990s.

Theories of Lesbianism

The main inheritance from Adrienne Rich is her claim that lesbianism is neither an inborn proclivity nor a set of deviant practices but is rather a political choice motivated by resistance to patriarchal oppression (Mandell 1998, 61). Rich thereby initiates an anti-essentialist view of lesbianism that is taken up in various ways by postmodern, social construction theorists of the 1990s. Judith Butler, for example, characterizes all sexual behaviour or claims of sexual identity as a series of "performances" induced by particular social discourses (Mandell 1998, 72). Both de Lauretis and Butler see gendering as a function of language and are concerned with the differences obliterated by universalist terms such as "woman" or "lesbian." De Lauretis coined the term "queer theory" in order to contain a wide range of cultural differences within gay-lesbian designations (Mandell 1998, 72). The danger being subverted here arises from a species of oppression called "planned authenticity" by Neuman (1992a, 224, citing Trinh Minh-ha), by which political coherence within a marginalized group is enforced by requiring specific allegiances and behaviours. In the upcoming investigation into how Mary Meigs presents her experience of love and desire between women, essentialism, social constructionism, and the issues of difference within the lesbian community emerge as factors that impinge on Meigs' sense of her bodily self. Still, the central task she sets herself is to overcome her sense of shame.

Diana Fuss can offer Meigs an historical perspective. In her definitive book, *Essentially Speaking*, Fuss examines in some detail the controversy between the essentialists and social constructionists as concerns sexuality and gender. She credits the social constructionists with the refiguring of homosexuality as follows:

> Perhaps the greatest contribution social constructionists have made to the theory of homosexuality is their collective subversion of the traditional medical, legal, and sociological approaches to gay identities, which inevitably begin with the question: is homosexuality innate or acquired? ... It is pointless to investigate the root causes of homosexuality if we realize that homosexuality is not a transhistorical, transcultural, eternal category but a socially contingent and variant construction ... the point all social constructionists agree on is that homosexuality is a comparatively late phenomenon in Western culture. This claim

is asserted on the grounds that there is an important distinction to be made between "homosexual behavior which is universal and a homosexual identity which is historically specific." (Citing Weeks 1977, 3 – in Fuss 1989, 107–8)

In other words, if Meigs had been born in a different era or culture, her sexual behaviour would not have determined her identity: that is, it would not have been given a marginalizing label, such as "lesbian." While put forth by constructionists, this figuring of homosexuality through a distinction between behaviour and identity still seems to give considerable ground to the essentialist position. In her extended investigation, Fuss repeatedly returns to the idea that, paradoxically, essentialism, in one version or another, seems to form a substrata in most constructionist arguments (ibid., 12–15). Another theorist, Andrea Liss, who seeks to reconcile or refigure the two positions, recognizes this paradox. In so doing, Liss seeks to find a psychic space in which a specific woman can acknowledge her personal female body as a site of legitimate knowledge, despite its existence in a politicized, social environment. Liss calls this refiguring "essentialism with a difference" (Liss 1994, 89). It is likely that this is the psychic space that Meigs finally occupied in coming to terms with her sexual orientation.

MARY MEIGS

Meigs travelled a long journey to arrive at that psychic space. She had to learn to cope both with that veneer of gentility that is her inheritance and with a sexual orientation she found difficult to name. Her life writing finally brought Meigs into full bodily consciousness, but it is not until she completed *The Time Being* (at age eighty) that her sexual being received a remarkably fulsome expression, which, in its vitality, recalls Irigaray's *jouissance*. She explained to me what she had to overcome:

> My feeling about my body I think was completely erased when I was a child by all the ideas disseminated by our mother. Forbidden to look, forbidden to touch, explore, all those things were forbidden so from the very beginning I felt horribly awkward with my body – not "bien dans ma peau" – and I never thought it was a desirable thing. (Reid 1997, 24)

The positive side of her family inheritance was an unvarying "niceness" consisting of "a guileless goodwill and willingness to help our fellow man" (Meigs 1981, 32). The negative side was a denial of the body such as she describes, with absolutely no acknowledgment of sexual realities. Meigs searched for virtually a lifetime for an appropriate context for her sexual experience. While a reversal of bodily denial is heartily wished for, her initial refusal was so acute that the issue of "niceness," sexual squeamishness, and a puritan sensibility remain as lifelong sources of conflict. The squeamishness diminished only somewhat despite the moments of *jouissance*; the "niceness" and puritan sensibility remained along with a "bluestocking" dedication to the life of the mind, another part of her inheritance

Two of her books seemingly shift the focus from the issue of her sexual orientation, that is, from the "coming out" narrative. *The Box Closet* (1987) concentrates on the life of her parents, especially her mother. Through pondering her mother's letters in writing, Meigs arrives at a deeper understanding of the strong influence that notions of propriety had on her parents and, consequently, on Meigs and her siblings. *In the Company of Strangers* (1991) centres on her "actor" companions and their adventures together in the making of the film; nevertheless, Meigs shows herself as steadily conscious of being chosen for the film because she was lesbian. On this basis, she accepts this role but she does so with trepidation, fearing to be used. In this text, her acceptance emerges mostly a political act, a *testimonio*, to use Sommer's term (Sommer 1988, 107), and she undertakes it partly because of the eagerness of Gloria, an assistant director, a lesbian who realizes that Meigs, with her upper-class charm and respectability, will elevate the public's notion of lesbian identity. As it turns out, however, Meigs' lesbianism is shown in *The Company of Strangers* film to be just one of the several varieties of difference existing among the female cast. Of the other three books, two – *The Medusa Head* and *The Time Being* – deal specifically with lesbian experience in the context of two love affairs. In *Lily Briscoe* (her earliest book), Meigs traces her career as visual artist and her growth of sexual awareness, but she places the telling in the context of a childhood to old age narration.

Reading these books in the order of publication, one is able to identify that Meigs becomes increasingly more comfortable in the telling of her sexuality and with explicit sexual description. It is my view that, starting with the publication of *Lily Briscoe*, Mary Meigs increasingly was made aware of, and found her place in, a larger lesbian community of writers, a community which, on the whole, made her welcome and validated not only her bodily experience but also the political necessity of writing about it. The worldwide showing of the film, *The Company of Strangers*, enhanced her celebrity both outside and within lesbian circles and she came to consolidate her view of herself not only as a writer but also as a lesbian writer. Meigs' joy at finding a community, the lesbian writing community, in which she felt accepted and celebrated, is recounted in *The Time Being*. She recalls her attendance at a woman's book fair in Amsterdam, where a lesbian presence is a foregone conclusion. She contrasts it with her feeling of awkwardness at a mixed-gender arts festival back in British Columbia:

> ... she feels homesick for the familiar faces.... the swirling of women happy to see each other, spontaneous embraces and their ease of communication.... Hundreds of women were talking and listening to each other there, with a sense that they could set the world on fire. (1997, 120)

This integration into the lesbian writing community finally frees her to bring the sexuality of her body into language and, in so doing, to depict female sexual response as a kind of dance involving the whole body. The eroticism of the experience comes as a surprise to Meigs; thinking as she did that old age would diminish desire:

> "... I didn't know." Know the strange magnetism of a body accepted.... Nor the tug toward the strong, knowing uninsistent hands that draw their bodies together. Together they seem like flocking birds, or fish who know when to turn in unison, to rise or wheel or sink to earth or water. (1997, 33)

This passage is significant in several ways. First, it recalls Irigaray's description of *jouissance*, the quality of sexual experience that is peculiarly female, by characterizing her sexual response as tactile and global, involving the body as a whole. Secondly, it acts to combat ageist stereotyping by depicting old women as sexual beings, as capable as anyone else of being sexually active. Thirdly, through the use of simile, it connects the women's experience to the natural world, a use of language typical of Meigs' writing. Finally, Meigs uses language in such a way that the lyricism of the text reiterates the original experience. Arleen Dallery, in describing the necessity of representing the body in language in order to give it reality, asserts that

... writing the body is both *constative* and performative. It signifies those bodily territories that have been kept under seal; it figures the body. But writing the body is also a performative utterance; the feminine libidinal economy inscribes itself in language. (1989, 59)

Dallery then goes on to quote Silverman: "Just as women's sexuality is bound up with touch, so too women use words as a form of touching" (ibid.). The comment is particularly applicable to Meigs, for whom letter writing was a lifelong way of touching when bodily touching seemed too risky. Indeed, as she tells in *The Time Being*, she and Ruth fell in love through letters. In a more recent article, Meigs corroborates that her use of language in *The Time Being* represents a breakthrough into freedom, an escape from writing "self-censored lesbian books" (2000, 100). In this breakthrough, she joins a community of lesbian writers in Canada who speak the language of lesbian eroticism "a song of physical immediacy and oneness" that, Meigs adds, "lesbians have always sung" (ibid.). In keeping with her celebration in print of her ability to write the lesbian body, she declared her intention to strip from the description of lesbian experience any connotation of deviancy (Reid 1997, 26). As one reader, I am struck by the way Meigs locates the sexual desire of one aging female for another as a species of normal human eroticism. As Meigs describes it and, indeed, as one might expect, lesbian falling in love is psychologically much the same experience as heterosexual physical entrancement.

That having been said, Meigs' identification with a worldwide lesbian community was firm. She entered permanently into a different community from the one into which she was born and it further reshaped her subjectivity, partly by association and partly by exposing her to unfamiliar ideas in gender theory and lesbian politics. Similarly, she became more aware of the lesbian press, referring to reading such books as *S/he*, a book on the nature of transsexual experience and the implications such experience has for the understanding of gendering (Griggs 1998). *S/he* stressed, for example, the importance of an individual arranging to match his/her public appearance with the inner sexual orientation. Meigs also told me about her experiences of being chastised by sections of the lesbian community for her non-working-class origins and cited a review in a Canadian periodical that took her to task for the privileged upper-class milieu which formed the setting of *The Medusa's Head* (Reid 1997, 26). It is this kind of militant categorization or "planned authenticity" on the part of existing lesbian communities that Neuman describes as mitigating against a complex and hence bona fide autobiographical representation of the lesbian self (1992a, 224).

When I asked Meigs, "What variety of lesbian are you?" she replied, "I haven't the slightest idea of what category I belong to" (Reid 1997, 1). She had been telling me that she had attended a conference for "Old Lesbians," where she had discovered that there were other lesbian categories such as "fem" and "stone butch," homosexual variations such as transsexual, trans-gender, bisexual, and so on, and that sometimes these were the result of a political choice. It became clear, however, that Meigs viewed her own sexual orientation as "essential" – that is, as not to be explained as politically or socially constructed. As a fraternal twin, she perceived herself as inherently different from her heterosexual sister, possessing the supposedly masculine trait of aggressiveness that from the beginning allowed her to dominate her more submissive, vulnerable and "feminine" twin. She found it significant, or perhaps prophetic that, at the birth of Mary and Sarah, her father bought blue baby clothes for Mary alone and that, in the baby photograph of the twins (1981, 127), her sister Sarah is crying while Mary presents a cross face to the camera, disgusted as Meigs says, with her sister's feminine fussing. "I am the one who is mad. My idea is that our struggles began in the womb." She continues:

> I have always been terribly irritated by noise and crying babies. But it wasn't only that. I turned into a little girl who was very boyish. Liked knives and boys' toys and was bully to my sister. I felt superior to her, and I didn't like anything female. (Reid 1997, 16)

Meigs positioned her sexual orientation, then, not as a matter of social conditioning, but as constitutional – a "given" at birth. Still, in her allegiance to the larger lesbian community, she can be seen as constructing her lesbian identity in a politicized, social environment finding thereby the space which Liss calls "essentialism with a difference" (1994, 89).

In terms of the binary construction of gender, male being at one pole and female at the other, Meigs spoke and wrote of gender construction as a continuum, seeing femininity and masculinity as matters of degree. In this vein she described herself as not a "real" woman and her father as not a "real" man (1987, 214). Similarly, she perceived degrees of lesbianism, defined as a love for women, as present in a large percentage of females. For example, she describes rather enviously the experience of artist Käthe Kollwitz, an "almost" lesbian who lived in Europe in a privileged and cosmopolitan milieu that countenanced her expression of a physical love of women without requiring the disruption of her conventional heterosexual marriage (1981, 10–11)

Meigs reveals that her emotional response to masculinity and the bodies of individual men took a variety of forms. She experimented as a young woman with heterosexual sexual activity but in a perfunctory way. The male body up close repels her but the generalized male form in Greek or Egyptian art has more aesthetic appeal than the "curvaceous" bodies of Venus de Milo or Rubens' women (1981, 13). Here is her description of maleness up close:

> Men turned into the sum of their details: their huge feet, the hair that often covered their arms, legs, chests, or even sprouted from their ears, emphasizing their close cousinship with the apes, their mouths, their chins, like rough sandpaper, the friction of which in those days of dancing up close made one's face sore for days. (ibid., 12)

Over the course of their long friendship, Edmund Wilson experienced a strong sexual attraction for Meigs, but Meigs, alarmed, definitely saw Wilson in terms of close-up physical revulsion, despite her high regard for him in other ways. Only twice did she confess to sexual attraction to a male; neither time was physical intimacy involved. One such attraction involved her sister-in-law's brother Caleb, who felt for Meigs only brotherly regard (1981, 215). Meigs for her part was infatuated with his physical perfection, which seems to have been cast in the Greek mode "like Praxiteles Hermes." Similarly, she recounts feeling a kind of sexual love for artist Henry Poor and, as she says, "was obsessed for the first time in my life to have a child – ours – a beautiful child, of course, that would combine the best features of both" (1981, 195). It is difficult to tell whether Meigs' habitual squeamishness concerning non-Greek male bodies is similar to that felt by many women[5] about the coarseness of male physicality, or if it is to be taken solely as an indication of lesbian preference.

In contrast, throughout all five books, Meigs describes in detail, up close and with delight, the physical characteristics of her female lovers and friends. Here the reader becomes aware of a painterly eye used to observing and translating details of appearance. In particular Meigs is wont to linger over the descriptions of longtime lover Marie-Claire Blais. As both lover and artist, she studied Blais closely and made her the subject of many painted portraits. One such portrait is reproduced for the cover of the retrospective pamphlet for the 2005 show at the Bombardier gallery. It shows Blais seated with her hand raised thoughtfully to her face. Her hair is a heavy brown helmet and dark eyebrows shadow rather dreamy eyes. She seems young, almost girlish. In *Lily Briscoe*, Marie-Claire is described as emerging from a swim with shy smile, pale shoulders and arms, and a body tapering from heavy breasts to narrow feet "like Egyptian feet found in tombs" (1981, 112). Similarly, but without quite the same emotional investment, Meigs describes the physical presence of a multitude of friends and lovers, including Barbara Deming, her Australian friend Ruth, and her companions in the making of *The Company of Strangers*. In a class by herself, however, is the French woman Andrée who, in *The Medusa Head*, undergoes at Meigs' hands a physical transformation from an elegant, silver-haired gamin in white tennis shoes into the monstrous figure of the Medusa, whose gaze turned hapless victims to stone.

Aside from its depiction of the dynamics of a power struggle, *The Medusa Head* is significant in the present context because of its exploration of the interdependency of mind and body, particularly the effect of emotion on the body. It is rage that transforms Andrée's visage into "the head of an angry ram with baleful, protuberant eyes" (1983, 8) and terrorizes Marie-Claire and Mary. In *The Time Being*, the conflict is about control. The heated struggle between Marj and Kate (i.e., Mary and Ruth) eventually dominates the relationship so that the body can no longer feel desire: "… alone again, they are unable to move towards each other, the magnetic waves which connected them in Australia are jammed" (1997, 116). The erotic bodily love between the two is permanently dampened by mutual irritation. Sexual attraction becomes a memory, leaving behind only a wary friendship.

Part of the conflict between Marj and Kate is due to the fact that Kate is still very much concerned with "passing" while, at this point in her life, Marj is not. Interestingly enough, it is Andrée in *The Medusa Head* who is nonchalant about the issue because she understands that societal class in some cultures makes sexual orientation irrelevant. If one is a rich American in Europe, one is taken at one's own evaluation, at least in the circles to which Andrée aspires. Andrée is thereby witnessing to a variation on Fuss' notion that lesbian identity is historically (or in Andrée's case, culturally) specific (Fuss 1989, 107–8). In her relationship with Andrée, Mary's concern for society's censure of one's sexual orientation is replaced by the tyranny of taste, the badge of the very rich, and Andrée's substitute for the dictates of morality.

At first Meigs does not understand that Andrée is pursuing her because of her money, money needed by Andrée to bring into being an elegant lifestyle. Andrée perceives the decoration of the female body, the preparation of food, and the arrangement of living quarters to be as exacting as the production of an object of art, to be judged similarly by the canons of exquisite taste. In her devotion to enacting this canon, Andrée succumbs to what Brownmiller identifies as one of the chief attractions of femininity, the presentation to women of "a brilliant, subtle esthetic" (1984, 14). Meigs feels the attraction, too; her instincts as an artist guarantee a positive response to such an appeal, and she confesses to "enjoying my education in food and clothes and exquisite objects" (1983, 29).

The aesthetic satisfaction that comes from feminine "dressing up" is evident also in Meigs' description of dinnertime at Chateau Borghese in Quebec, when the female participants of *The Company of Strangers* shed their drab film attire in favour of a variety of "stripes and spots," sequins, velvet, and satin (1991b, 26). Dressing in fashion served another purpose for Meigs; conforming through dress protected her from easy public identification as lesbian, a possibility she dreaded for most of her life. Non-conformity would be like wearing the symbolic pink triangle on her chest: "Expensive clothes drew looks which obliterated the pink triangle; they contained the magic which enabled me to pass" (1983, 30).[6]

Here Meigs writes of a past self and reveals a shifting subjectivity from an earlier construction to a later one. It is a case of the writing self not being completely identifiable with the written self, an enduring characteristic of autobiography. The 1983 self who wrote those words about an earlier Meigs was able to say, "I no longer care if I'm recognized" (1983, 32), a liberation due to representing her lesbian self in text. Yet, even the earlier self tended to be ambivalent about the exigencies of fashion; accordingly, in the same part of the text, she presents another aspect of her subjectivity, one that endures to the present time. She says of her encounters with Andrée's devotion to taste, "our natures fatally clashed; my puritanism ran into her worldliness" and Meigs persisted in cutting her hair herself and in presenting naked feet and unvarnished toenails encased in "big men's sandals" (1983, 29).

A certain puritanism governs her bodily behaviour in other ways. In *The Company of Strangers*, Meigs laments the lack of bodily ease that prevents her from any consideration of appearing nude in a frolicsome swimming scene. In *The Time Being*, this same puritanism causes real friction between

Marj (Mary) and Kate (Ruth) and, as with Andrée, brings about a real clash in value systems. For example, Marj's abstemious habits make her dubious about "drinkie time," Kate's beloved cocktail hour, and, when pressed, lead her to insist on only "fourteen drops of brandy." When Kate visits Canada, she is disturbed that Marj has not in any way modified her Spartan regime and that she is expected to live "according to Marj's habits, to her indifference to real comfort, her carelessness about food, planned menus, and shopping" (1997, 133).

There is another cause for the disintegration of the Marj/Kate, Mary/Ruth love affair, one more irrevocable than Meigs' puritan sensibilities, and that is Meigs' fear of any infringement on her sense of self. The need for autonomy is primary for Meigs, confounding her almost equal drive for alterity, and this need translates into bodily habits. The intimacy, which is concomitant to sexual bonding, does not, for Meigs, extend to shared bed or bedroom space. Therefore, Marj and Kate's relationship is further strained when, at a conference, they have to share a bedroom, used as they are (probably at Marj's instigation) to dressing and undressing privately. Moreover, it became clear earlier that the proposal to co-author a book about their relationship was doomed from the start. After the initial enthusiasm, it appeared that their version of events did not match, and each proceeded to begin her own book. Meigs notes that "Marj's self is reclaiming its perceived rights and taking back its precious autonomy" (1997, 89).

Meigs was in her mid-seventies when she began her love affair with Ruth and, by that time, she had acquired a long history of carefully protecting her autonomy. She translated this into the need for a physical space stamped firmly with her own individuality. Accordingly, Meigs' personal history revolved around the houses she bought, furnished, and lived in, from the beloved Red and Yellow houses of Wellfleet, to the Breton farmhouse she filled with Wellfleet furniture and to *La Sucerie*, her longtime rural Quebec retreat. It is clear from her writing and from our interview together that she traced this need for both psychic and physical space to her experience of being born a fraternal twin, of having to share even the womb. Had the twins been identical, Meigs' reaction might have been different; as fraternal twins, theirs was not evidently the "one soul in two bodies" relationship that identical twins sometimes describe. Reportedly, in the early years, their sisterly bond was marked by discord and competition.

Their competitive baby life is the source of one of the more evocative references by Meigs to the physical reality of the female body. Their mother is nursing them and reporting to her husband in a series of letters quoted by their daughter, Mary, in *The Box Closet*. The nursing of twins is a happy challenge for Margaret and she is jubilant about producing enough milk to feed her thriving babies. Meigs quotes from her mother's letters:

> Sarah [gained] 10 ounces and Mary 11 ounces. I am speechless and breathless.... And I had so much that I had to cut down a little on food.... I have been lying down before each feeding.... the babies noticed each other for the first time today. (1987, 119)

Margaret's letters of this period reveal to Meigs a capacity for physical devotion in her mother that Meigs did not realize existed; she sees it as the source of her own capacity for love "which finally bubbled up after its long life underground" (160). However, the mood of the letters changes. The demand for breast milk gets too much for the mother and she supplements it with bottles: "will keep up with breast milk as long as possible" (120). Margaret's euphoria fades a little: "It is rather like a life sentence in a treadmill" (121).

The twins' competition here is of the most elemental and physical kind. Mary Meigs herself felt that it was characteristic of her relationship with her sister. She admitted: "We were bitter rivals" (Reid 1997, 17). One can scarcely wonder at the adult Mary wanting a space, whether house or room, that was clearly her own. Bachelard equates the role of the house in the human imagination, and physical protection it gives, with maternality. He quotes a line of poetry: "I say Mother. And my thoughts are of you, oh, House" (1994, 45). Meigs made this equation too. Certainly as an artist and writer, Meigs subscribed to all women needing Woolf's "room of one's own." She lamented to me the fact that her sister Sarah, in designing and building a house with her husband, did so without specifying a space that was indisputably Sarah's (Reid 1997, 21). The implication was that this was another example of the loss of autonomy implicit in the institution of marriage, whether heterosexual or homosexual.

Besides the loss of autonomy, another of Meigs' fears in her relationship with her Australian lover was that the spectacle of two old women in love would appear ridiculous. The absurdity would reside partly in the fact that the lovers were both female. The prospect of ridicule by heterosexual acquaintances was, as Meigs explained, the reason why she preferred to draw most of her friends from lesbian circles: "We all have a deep-seated suspicion of straight women. They may betray us [by ridicule]" (ibid., 10).

Meigs realized also that her age increased the likelihood of her love affair being laughed at. In *The Time Being*, she, as Marj, is reluctant to divulge to Canadian friends that she and Kate had made physical love:

> 'It's under discussion,' she said. Post facto she will smile – a smile tinged with the old ineradicable guilt and, because she is seventy-five, a small new fear – that she will provoke smiles herself. (Meigs 1997, 35)

Here, Meigs is aware that the spectacle of old women in love physically, offends the sensibilities of our culture because of the identification in the code of femininity of sexual attractiveness with youth. Lesbians are victims of ageism both within and outside of the lesbian community, this variety of ageism (i.e., old bodies seen as unattractive) being a function of gender rather than sexual orientation (Nussbaum et al., 2000, 50).

The experience of female old age is the subject of the film *The Company of Strangers*. The making of the film and the final product are remarkable because both offer to the old women involved a refuge from ageism. Audience, cast, and production crew are given, in Meigs' words, an opportunity to "step out of time and logic into a magic space where old women are given room to exist" (1991b, 10). In her account of this process, Meigs pays fellow cast members the profound compliment of giving her full attention to their bodily presence and to the personality that the bodily presence expresses. For example, Beth has "the tidy, trim look of a white-throated sparrow" (ibid., 49), Cissy has "eyes as blue as a Siamese kitten's" (ibid., 109), and Catherine becomes an octopus, her totem animal, "waving her many arms around to explore the world" (ibid., 135). Such focusing on one's physical idiosyncrasies serves, in the case of these old women, to restore themselves to themselves.

One of the penalties of old age, particularly for women, is that one becomes socially invisible, given no "room to exist," resulting in an immense loss of self-esteem. Nussbaum et al. report that the "disengagement" theory of aging actually validates this invisibility (2000, 7–9). This model of aging takes as appropriate and necessary to social stability the bodily and psychic withdrawal of the elderly from society and vise-versa. While other theories of aging (ibid., 9–16) argue against isolation as conducive to successful aging, Nussbaum et al. (2000) point to the existence and operational practices of nursing homes as proof of the persistence in North American society of the "disengagement" outlook. In Meigs' presentation of the ongoing lives of the other six old women, one can see them accepting a degree of disengagement as inevitable. Being in her eighties and with a weak heart, Constance, for example, comes the closest to disengaging herself from her surroundings. Notwithstanding, all were energized by the extreme level of engagement that came with acting in a film. Their participation in the film and their subsequent emergence as subjects of Meigs' book undeniably gave these women a new lease on life. All redefined the possibilities for women physically aging but still indisputably themselves.

That does not mean that either Meigs or Cynthia Scott, the film's director, played down the physical consequences of aging. In the movie, the old faces are filmed without stage makeup, and the movements of the women are shown to be deliberate, as if to avoid unseen pitfalls. All of the women are shocked by the contrast between their interior bodily self-image formed long ago and what they see on the screen: "'Am I so old?' they ask, like the Masai warrior on television who sees himself for the first time in a mirror" (Meigs 1991b, 75). Constance's partial hearing loss that prevents her from listening any longer to the song of the white-throated sparrow is a symbol in the film of the many bodily losses that aging brings. Still, Meigs reports that, in the filming, the cast is protected from the denigration routinely afforded by the young to the old person "as invisible or perceived as a obstacle or as a doddering idiot.... They want to show that old women don't necessarily dodder, quaver and shuffle" (ibid., 77).

Nevertheless, in her account of the filming, Meigs reports the off-screen physical struggles: "Beth's falls and almost falls downstairs, her sprained ankle, Constance's lurid bruises and high blood pressure, followed by a precipitous trip to the clinic in St. Jovite" (1991b, 25). Meigs shows the group, at the end of their day, "hauling one another up the long steps to the Chateau Borghese," and Meigs herself falls victim to fatigue and insomnia. More disturbing than the bodily changes that age brings, however, is the slow disintegration of the mind/brain, an extension of those changes. It is with great compassion and love that Meigs describes the post-film Cissie, who is in the process of this disintegration. Cissie has succumbed to another stroke, and watches the film from a wheelchair connected to intravenous apparatus and with only partial attentiveness or understanding. Similarly, Constance at eighty-eight, is shown as anticipating her own death and living mostly in memory. The seven old women who become friends are finally "forced apart by death and illness and our relentless aging" (ibid., 69).

Meigs depicted her own relentless aging through her books, in various articles and in a series of self-portraits. Most of the latter, however, show the Mary Meigs of *Lily Briscoe*. At the end of *Lily Briscoe*, Meigs refers to the countless times she has attempted to paint her self-portrait and never succeeding "wanting to show something profound, and succeeding only in painting a face either too pretty or too severe" (1981, 251). Her ideal self-portrait, she explains, would be the "portrait of a Lesbian, my life with its mixture of shame and pride ... visible in my face." She told me that what she wanted, in any self-portrait, was to "look intelligent." Readers of *Lily Briscoe* can assess if she achieved this goal: one of Meigs' favourite self-portraits is reproduced on the cover. Here, Meigs depicts herself as past middle age with her elderly mother smiling in the background. She does look intelligent as well as distinguished. She has a thin face, with deeply shadowed eyes and a drift of white hair. There is something tentative about her expression that could suggest a mixture of shame and pride but nothing that would unequivocally suggest her sexual orientation; this is not Meigs' "portrait of a Lesbian." Instead, she depicts herself as her mother's daughter.

The self-portrait that forms the frontispiece of *Beyond Recall* shows a thoughtful, almost literary Mary, peering out through large glasses, leaning on her elbow. She does, indeed, "look intelligent." In her self-possession and independent bearing, she looks also like the Mary we have come to know in *The Company of Strangers* film. The photograph at the end of the book tells a different story. Mary is sitting is a lift-assist chair with a friend's dog in her lap. The drift of white hair is the same, the glasses almost the same, but her face is thin, her body shrunken, with frail wrists and hands. Meigs' diary chronicles in careful detail the effects of the stroke on her daily routine and the severe limitations these have imposed on her physical activity. Some things, however, emerge as constant: her devotion to friends, her love of animals and nature, and her love of language. Her daily writing stint is kept sacrosanct; this precious activity allows her to retain her sense of herself and to ward off depression. The grace and honesty that marks all of her writing is intensified as she records her unflinching struggle.

Despite her frail health, Meigs seems able to attend equally to the demands and discomforts of her body and to her external environment. Each morning, she records precisely her own physical condition then focuses intently on the weather. Sometimes they seem to mirror each other:

> November 30: Could I feel limper that I do today? No feeling in left foot except heat and difficulty walking – dragging, knee locking. Left hand crumpled up. Post therapy? Dismal Snow still on the ground. (2005, 69)

The diary entries describe in detail the effects of a right-brain stroke – unsteadiness, loss of mobility, loss of muscle control, and a sense of weakness and fatigue, as well as intermittent mental confusion. Older people will recognize other symptoms: the uncertainty of memory, the humiliation of bedpans and soiling, the gradual loss of hearing and sight, all of which culminate finally, in physical confinement indoors. Meigs reacts to all of this with intermittent anger and grief.

Her descriptions of illness and bodily aging would make for grim reading except that each entry is enlivened by her talk of art and books, by her artist's sensitivity to everyday visual beauty and by the portrayal of beloved friends, caretakers, and pets. In addition, the reader is allowed access to a series of humorous faxes purportedly from Meigs' cat, Mike, to Mouser, Blais' cat. These are complete with lively line drawings of Mike's various doings. With the exception of cover art, this is one of the few times that Meigs illustrates her own published writing.[7] Inside the aging body, the artist and writer were alive and well.

AGANETHA DYCK

In *Beyond Recall*, Meigs does grow past being "her mother's daughter." However, as Carolyn Heilbrun has pointed out, a contemporary woman's affirmation of her mother is likely to be intermittent at best, the pattern being one of separation and reconnection (Heilbrun 1997, 7). Such is the case also with Aganetha Dyck. Dyck's defining act of separation from the home-centred world of her mother came in 1976 when she rented a separate artist's studio after her move to Winnipeg. She thereby declared herself to be a professional artist with a whole new focus of attention. However, her instinct for relationship and for functioning in a community carried over into an art practice in which she constantly involved other people – beekeepers, handcrafters, scientists, family, and so on. In this way Dyck reconnected with the Mennonite value system that her mother exemplifies.

However, Dyck displays considerable ambivalence about the relationship of the individual to society. Dyck's preferred method of connection is through voluntary collaboration. Any pressure by society to impose conformity on the individual is one to be resisted. In her work, Dyck communicates this ambivalence through her repetition of form, a repetition emblematic of the containment of both mind and body within a social context. When the forms being repeated have their source in bodily accessories – for example, shoes, shoulder pads, purses, cigarettes, and various articles of apparel – the allusion to the grouping and bodily presence of discrete individuals is reinforced.

Such is the case with the *Close Knit* (Fig. 8). As has been described, the installation consists of sixty-five shrunken sweaters, piled with their woolen arms outstretched in a long row, one upon the other. I explored the possible allusions of the piece during my interview with Dyck in 1996. The reference to the human form was obvious, a reference to be assumed in all of visual art's incorporation of clothing. As I explained to Dyck, my initial response, however, was one of amused delight at her elevating use of a common domestic misadventure familiar to most women – the shrinking of a woolen garment in the washing machine. Dyck laughed along with me; she called it "the displacement of a small disaster" from her home to the gallery.

However, *Close Knit* also reminded me one of humanity's most horrifying catastrophes. I commented that the more I studied the piece the more it reminded me of the photographs of piles of bodies of the World War II holocaust. Dyck accepted this interpretation with alacrity and responded that it was not just the Jews who were the victims of mass extermination – it was the fate also of the members of many Mennonite communities at the hands of the Russians both in the Second World War and earlier in the aftermath of the Russian Revolution. She described that part of Mennonite history and the experiences of her own and her husband's family:

> You see, my whole family has been in concentration camps. And my husband was in lineups where all the people were shot and the gun didn't go off when it hit him.... The holocaust that happened to the Mennonites, hundreds and thousands of non-Jewish people, is equivalent to any other holocaust.... An artist I am mentoring has made a thousand and one black ceramic shoes for the millions and millions of children that have died today because of war. So the holocaust continues for all people. (Reid 1996c, 28)

Dyck then told of her sister-in-law's narrow escape from being raped during World War II after Peter's family was dispossessed from the Ukraine to Siberia. She also related her grandmother's experience with dispossession after the Russian revolution. Dyck compared these stories to the ones documented in the work of Wanda Koop (a fellow Manitoba artist and friend of

Dyck's) of losing a wealthy estate and fleeing for one's life to start over in a new land (Reid 1996c, 22).

In its macabre bodily reference, *Close Knit* can be considered as part of the worldwide body of work that attempts through the arts to accommodate the horror of both Jewish and non-Jewish holocausts. Yet, the artist comments that, in *Close Knit*, the bodies can be seen as supporting each other. Dyck knows that human experience always has more than one dimension: "Humour and disaster seem contradictory and that is just the way the world is" (Reid 1996c, 27). Nevertheless, the immediacy for Dyck of what might be called the Mennonite holocaust has had the effect of sensitizing her to the horror of war as destructive of both the body and the spirit. She said, "The holocaust is brought to us everyday through the black box [TV]" (ibid., 28). This awareness of violence forms part of Dyck's bodily reference and appears as a subtext in much of her work. It is my view that, in making art that has reference to this part of her family's history, Dyck has absorbed the reported experiences of this physical horror and victimization into herself, allowing it to shape her notion of who she is so that is becomes one of her various constructions of self.

Invocation of bodily experience is even more personal and direct in *Hand Held: Between Index and Middle Finger* and *Brain is not Enough* (Figs. 17 and 18), a series of installations that were prompted by Dyck's quitting smoking and encouraging others to do the same. After making a cigarette substitute for friends to hold when trying to quit, Dyck extended the idea and sent out a call, "offering to transform 'the last cigarette' of anyone trying to quit" (Madill 1995, 21). She received a plethora of "last cigarettes," another species of "found objects," which she transformed through various coating substances and decorating devices. The result is an installation of great visual interest, one that invites the viewer's minute examination.

With many of the cigarettes, however, the coating does not conceal the initial connection between the cigarette and the mouth. In these, there exists a definite suggestion of saliva, mastication, or both. The result is a bodily immediacy that brings physical actuality of smoking into the gallery space and communicates Dyck's message that smoking is a "dirty" habit. On the whole, however, that message tends to be obscured by the overall glamour of the embellished cigarettes. For example, thread wrappings with beads, sequins, rhinestones, costume jewellery, tinsel, toy figures, plastic flowers, screws, and safety pins all serve to change them into rather precious "objects d'art." Meeka Walsh makes the point that with Dyck, metonymy is an ever-present tactic and in the case of *Hand Held: Between Index and*

Middle Finger, Walsh comments that "her elaborated, decorative, bound and embalmed cigarettes implied, always, the absent smoker" (Walsh and Enright 2000, 43).

The decorative quality of the cigarettes, then, clearly expresses the seductiveness of bodily addiction and the displacement of the sexual onto to the oral experience of smoking. The nature of some of the decorations extends the territory of addiction to include drug and sexual addiction, while the use of such objects as safety pins and screws add an additional connotation of violence. Dyck explains that at that time there was a particularly violent rape in Winnipeg, one that made her really angry. She recalls buying twelve little ballerina figures and sticking them onto cigars only to discover subsequently that they reminded her of this rape incident, rape and violence being, she says, "something else I'm really concerned about" (Madill 1995, 21).

The whole matter of the contamination of the body by the environment is another cause with which Dyck has become involved. This is another example of her art practice expressing personal issues, which then broaden into general social concern. In recent years, she has become allergic to cigarette smoke and has been experiencing other effects of an auto-immune disorder possibly caused by pernicious environmental substances to which Dyck was exposed in childhood.[8] Even before the onset of this disorder, which incidentally coincided with the production of *Hand Held: Between Index and Middle Finger*, Dyck's work reveals a consciousness of the inevitability of bodily degeneration and decay and a correlative for this notion can be found in the material potential of many of her pieces. That is, some of her work is not environmentally stable, one example being the cigarettes in *Hand Held*. However, Dyck faces the temporality of some of this work with equanimity, seeing it as subject, like all physical matter, to the laws of mutability, of degeneration and disintegration that rule the physical world.

The appearance of the contents of many canning jars in the *Canned Buttons* series of installations (Figs. 9 and 10) communicates an awareness of the processes of decay and disintegration. The canning process changed the buttons in unpredictable ways so that some of the results look like body parts or poisonous flora or fauna. Dyck reports further that the contents of some of these jars are not stable, and the texture and shape of the canned buttons continue to change in much the way that improperly canned food does. This deterioration does not displease Dyck. Firstly, it reinforces a central subtext of the "*Canned*" series, with its focus on change and decay. Secondly, the incorporation of chance happenings into the work is a primary characteristic of Dyck's art practice and another way of connecting the studio with the material world, always a Dyck goal. Again, through the process of metonymy, Dyck establishes the notion of danger to the body and, by extension, to herself, of an unhealthy external environment. She is suggesting through the spoiled food motif both, as has been said, the toxic psychic effects of the solitary domestic life on women (Walsh and Enright 2000, 53) and the toxicity for the body of much of contemporary foodstuffs, air, and water, a toxicity from which Dyck personally has suffered. Perhaps for Dyck, as for Joseph Beuys, the noted German sculptor, the making of art is a way of dealing with bodily trauma, a method of self-healing.[9]

In talking to interviewers, Aganetha Dyck has emphasized that she is always thinking – examining her experience and environment with what amounts to a scientific curiosity (Dahle 1990, 25; Pike 1989, 16). As a result, Dyck routinely extends an expression of the personal into an examination of the environmental and social. Such is the case with Dyck's use of clothing and dress accessories that has marked much of her art practice and that came about because of Dyck's early training as a fabric artist and because of her fascination with the possibilities of material – cloth, wax, purses, shoes, jewellery, and so on. Caroline Tisdall has said that clothing is the tissue between the individual and the social; Dyck employs clothing to emphasize this positioning.

There are many ways that society employs clothing to enforce its mores and to produce what Foucault has termed "docile bodies." For example, dress has a function in social ritual. It can be a signifier of class, status, occupation, or all three. Primarily, however, it is used as an indicator of gender and, as an extension of this, dress is a major way of enforcing the code of femininity and of consolidating the positioning of women as sexual objects. Clothing can also be used as an element in play and as a vehicle of humour. In focusing her investigatory curiosity onto the society in which she lives, Dyck uses clothing and accessories, both constructed and "found," as signifiers of these many social practices and environments.

In doing so, Dyck again concerns herself with the freedom of the individual, a freedom she sees as curtailed by social institutions, ones that, while taken by custom and habit as immutable, are in fact, subject to change. As does Foucault in his notion of the "docile body," Dyck sees the physical body as the locus of social control. This is clear in a comment she makes to Sigrid Dahle:

> Maybe part of the illusion of living in our culture is that we think we have more freedom than we have.... We have these behavioral codes and social structures and rules and systems and we go about our business doing things in a certain way. We think it's "natural" and we think, "It's just the way it is done and will always be done." (Dahle 1995, 26)

In her work, Dyck challenges what is "natural" by her studio/gallery manipulation of cultural artifacts, including clothing. One of her targets is the bodily docility in women induced by the dictates of what Naomi Wolf calls "the beauty myth" (1990), a societal construction that equates the psychic worth of women with their physical appearance. In the contemporary world, this mythic feminine ideal puts a premium on slenderness and youth. In one installation, Dyck draws attention to the discrepancy between this ideal and the realities of women's bodies (including her own) by displaying twenty shrunken evening skirts standing, like human figures, on the floor: "Six skirts are size ten, eight skirts are size twelve, one skirt is size fourteen and five skirts are size eighteen" (Dyck 1982, 12). The implication in the size assortment and placing of the skirts is that the body sizes represented by the skirts are all valid and normal for women, the size ten to be no more privileged that the size eighteen. In another installation Dyck displays the ideal dress to clothe an impossibly slender and child-like body. It is quite tiny and made of beautiful cloth of gold (Baert 1996, 19). There is a hand-drawn image of a heart organ to be seen in a tear at the left breast, and it is coated with a tissue-thin layer of wax. The dress is caged on two sides by bee screens hanging from the ceiling at body height. The piece is entitled *Anorexic Dress*, a reference to the disease induced in young women by their futile attempts to measure up by starving the body. The piece dramatizes the fact that the social code of femininity is as pernicious to the actual human female body as the toxic physical environments cited in *Hand Held* and *Canned Buttons*.

Not all references to the code of femininity are as obviously deconstructing. The *Pocketbooks for the Queen Bee* installations (Figs. 15 and 16) signals a validation of the pleasures of femininity through the alignment of the status of the human female with that of the queen bee, the centre of the hive. As described earlier, it is a collection of evening bags, filled with small feminine accoutrements and preserved with coatings of bees-wax, originally displayed on two semicircular tables as part of *The Library: Inner/Outer* (Fig. 14). As such, and from the pun in the title, one can conclude that Dyck intends the "pocket books" and their contents to be read as compendiums of feminine knowledge, not readily accessible in a patriarchally dominated society.[10] Dyck talks of the collection in a celebratory fashion, citing the feminine occasions where an evening bag might be in use:

> I think of these books as party stories. The stories are about weddings, dates, graduations, Harlequin romances, office parties, female beauty, desire, moral confusion and sexual encounters (Dyck 1993, 12).

In this listing, the corporeal body is suggested only through the mention of "desire" and "sexual encounters." A closer examination of the individual "Pocket Books" reveals a voluptuousness about the wax coating that invokes more immediately both the female body and female desire (Madill 1995, 40). Moreover, the half-open purse suggests female genitalia in a way comparable to the vulva imagery in Judy Chicago's plates in *The Dinner Party* (1979). Similarly, there is a strong suggestion of female genitalia in Dyck's repeated use of coated shoes in many of her other installations. Just as Dyck and Pratt elevate domesticity by making it a subject matter of their work, so Dyck elevates female cultural and bodily experience by making it the subject of *Pocket Books for the Queen Bee*.

In *The Extended Wedding Party* (Fig. 12), the physical body is again invoked through the use of clothing. The installation consists of wedding garments for the bride and groom, the bridal attendants, and the multitude of guests both male and female. It includes also wedding gifts, food for the feast, and a host of shoes, all of which are encrusted with honeycomb deposited by the bees. As with *Close Knit* and the shrunken sweater series, Dyck uses the empty garment to indicate bodily presence: "I thought I could still see the person in it," Dyck says of the sweaters (Reid 1996c, 19). And that no doubt applies to all of the installation garments, especially *The Glass Dress* (Fig. 11), the centrepiece of *The Extended Wedding Party*, and the surrogate for the body of the bride.

The use of live bees and dripping honey in the original installation at the Winnipeg Art Gallery as part of the decoration of the bridal *Glass Dress* emphasized the reproductive potential of the bride. Dyck had used the dripping honey device before; she described for me an impulsive last-minute decision to paint with honey an already installed green dress, the dress representing Eve in a piece entitled *Looking at the Garden Again*. She hesitated and then decided, "I am going to paint this dress – and I didn't think about it again" (ibid., 47). Through her spontaneous addition of the honey, she emphasized the bodily femininity of Eve, the archetypal woman. Similarly, her use of dripping honey reveals her construction of herself as a sensual woman, aware of, and celebrating, the holistic nature of female sexuality. Through her use of honey as a coating for *The Glass Dress*, the figure of Eve, and the *Pocket Book* purses, Dyck reflects the idea of female *jouissance*, the notion of female eroticism as involving the whole body. In *The Extended Wedding Party*, however, the mood of celebration is undercut by the drawing of a parallel between the body of the bride and the body of the queen bee and, to reiterate, the point being made is that the wedding ritual is as deadly to the female autonomous sense of self as the organization of the hive is to the queen bee.

Again, Dyck uses the material to invoke the immaterial; that is, Dyck uses the wedding garments as surrogate bodies to invoke the complex social mythology enacted in the formal wedding. Earlier, I described the troupe of wedding guests as a ghostly gathering of priest-like figures surrounding the dazzling glass and honeycombed bride figure at the centre. The installation with its careful lighting and arranged shadows has, however, more dramatic overtones than this description conveys. It is almost operatic in its staged effect, and as with grand opera, the physical setting dramatizes the powerful and tragic emotions being enacted, through the medium of the body of the actors. One is reminded here of the critical views of Evelyn Hinz. As noted earlier, Hinz suggested that as a genre, auto/biography, with its mimetic referential quality, is more properly allied with drama than with the novel (1992, 196). Dyck's use of installation art, especially in *The Extended Wedding Party*, bears this out; it is a dramatic extension of the autobiographical, reflecting Dyck's personal processing of the social environment. To put it another way, Dyck can be seen as "staging," through bodily representation, her personal concerns as a woman and an artist in contemporary society much as Meigs does by acting in *The Company of Strangers*. Furthermore, while *The Extended Wedding Party* is about failed expectations, there is also a sense of the corporeal magic of the stage and of the artist as the shaman director who conjures up alternate visions of the ordinary.

With *The Extended Wedding Party*, Aganetha Dyck establishes that working with colonies of honey bees will be the major characteristic of her art practice, and, in the work done subsequently, she continues to investigate the nature of their society and the various methods of mutual collaboration. Over the course of her practice, she has come to access the beehives herself, donning the protective beekeeper's costume in order to place her own carefully constructed objects within the bee boxes. In this way, Dyck becomes engaged bodily with the bees and their crawling, flying, buzzing, and stinging reality: "They are so warm and so tenacious" (Walsh and Enright 2000, 55). It is significant that in more recent projects, she has turned to drawing as a primary means of tracing the bees' physical qualities. Because of the precise connection needed between the hand and the eye, drawing is a much more physically intimate medium than installation art. Therefore, it allows Dyck a surrogate for bodily contact in the winter when the bees are dormant. I do not think it is too much of an exaggeration to say that Dyck has fallen in love with the bees, and with her bent towards intellectual curiosity, she sets out to research them thoroughly. Always though, it is their physical presence that calls to her as a "life force." She explained: "I am just very interested in life forces. So the bees were an investigation and still are. I think the jars and all that stuff are all about life forces" (Reid 1996c, 8). Here, she constructs herself as a corporeal being responding to a material world. She also extends her construction of herself as artist to include aspects of the role of beekeeper and of scientific technician.

As for her presenting her own body in her work, Dyck does so only metaphorically and as a subtext. In interview, she notes the bodily changes over the years and remembers her younger self, just coming into marriage as a "Barbie doll," slim and blond with a bubble hair-do (Reid/Dyck conversation, 1996, Glenbow Museum, Calgary). In person she has a comforting matronly build and favours dressing in black. When I asked her, "Why black?" she replied, "I don't know; the clothes just call to me" (Reid 1996c, 22). She suggested further that they call to her because of her memory of her grandmother's Mennonite manner of dress. I sensed also that, for Dyck, the black clothing is emblematic of her subjectivity as a creative artist: "I feel strong in it" (ibid.).

SHARON BUTALA

During her marriage to Peter, Sharon Butala's normal dress at home was that of a ranch wife – jeans, shirt, sweater, or jacket – and likely still is when she is on the ranch.[11] She occasionally lamented being "out of fit with my own feminine nature" by having no reason or impetus "to dress up, paint my fingernails and curl my hair" (1994, 51). She enjoyed these bodily expressions of femininity and counted their loss as part of the price to be paid for marrying a rancher. Having been a rancher's wife, and therefore immersed in an environment that takes male physical strength and prowess for granted, served also to heighten Butala's awareness of her small, feminine stature. Butala has perceived her height or lack of it – "barely five feet tall" – as a lifelong disadvantage, one that often caused her to be overlooked or underestimated in social situations (Reid 1996b, 35). In accustoming herself to life in the country, she confessed to having been initially in awe of the amount of work rural women accomplish both inside and outside the house: "I would drop down dead after one day like every one of theirs" (Butala 1994a, 33). Butala showed herself, nonetheless, to be a physically resolute woman who, despite her size, was able to load steers onto a truck, to drive the same truck competently through snow storms, to handle large horses, to keep the house going and the meals on time in primitive conditions, and to demonstrate her stamina by walking mile after mile across the prairie regardless of the weather. Butala evidently shaped herself into an active, rural woman to a greater extent than she realized.

Butala, herself, has enormous regard for physical labour as having phenomenological value, that is, as giving one a realistic perception of the world. Her initiation into rural life, based as it is on interaction with the natural world, has made her very bodily aware and has led her to puzzle over the meaning of life in the body in a way she never did when she lived the life of an urban academic. Her urgent need to understand this new awareness led her into an extensive reading program, starting, as she says, with the Christian mystics (Butala 1995a, 51). Their denial of the body, their "separation of the spirit and the flesh," went against what she was experiencing in her new life, and it was with relief that she discovered Simone Weil who insisted that "physical work is a specific contact with the beauty of the world and can be, in its best moment, a contact so full that no equivalent can be found elsewhere" (cited in Butala 1995a, 53). Weil confirms for Butala the notion of the primacy of the body in perceiving the real world:

> It is with our bodies that we engage in the physical world, through our bodies we learn physical ecstasy and physical suffering and all the gradations between and this knowledge which enters us through the muscles and bone – through the flesh – then tutors the spirit and the soul in feeling empathy for our fellow humans, whether suffering or joyous. It is through our bodies that we feel love. (ibid., 55)

Some people are more bodily aware than others; Mary Meigs, for example, had to learn to receive the messages her body was sending. In the course of her reading, Butala cites an unpublished thesis (2000a, 215) which introduces, among other concepts, the idea that women past child-bearing years have "softer personal boundaries" that allow them "to open wider, without fear, to the universe" (ibid., 217). Critic Shirley Neuman makes much the same point in connection with the work of writer Daphne Marlatt, when she quotes Marlatt as raising the question of whether one's subjectivity must be seen "as crossroads of recognition of things/personae briefly transparent in all their interconnectedness and then disappear into individual and unknowable opacity again" (Neuman 1990, 333). I take both citations to mean that there can exist a personal permeability that overcomes, however briefly, the perceived separation of the self from its environment.

As a result of her experience in nature, Butala sees herself as one who possesses this permeable or "softer" personal boundary. This permeability allows her to be both acutely aware physically of the natural world and to register through her body a variety of psychic phenomena. In her descriptions of her contact with the grasslands of southwestern Saskatchewan, Butala makes much of the physical act of walking, of moving the body through space in much the way an animal would, that is, suspending thought so as to be fully present in the here-and-now. Butala consciously develops this ability over time so that she becomes open to a variety of experiences. The most basic of these is her profound awareness of the land on which she walks: "It is through my body that I make the connection with the earth" (1995a, 55), and, for Butala, the earth contains a life force to which she becomes attuned. This awareness sparked both of her major autobiographical works, *The Perfection of the Morning* and *Wild Stone Heart*.

The act of getting out of the house to walk the ranchlands, a territory traditionally the scene of male enterprise, may, however, have more significance and be more liberating than one would initially suppose. In an article on mobility and gendering, Sidonie Smith (1999) makes the point that in the realm of socially instituted norms, travel and adventuring have been seen traditionally as a masculine prerogative while feminine subjectivity "has been tethered at home." Smith theorizes that the technologies of modern travel, utilized as much or more by women as by men, are agents of change. As women travel, the accepted norms of feminine activity become more ambiguous. Earlier figures such as Amelia Earhart, for example, are seen by Smith as enlarging the repertoire of femininity in the popular imagination by claiming air space for women as well as men and, in so doing, de-mythologizing it. Smith concludes:

> The mode of motion, whether locomotion, automobility or foot, is itself defining of the logic of mobility. Thus technologies of motion have everything to do with the ways in which traveling women use mobility to achieve un/defining identity effects. (1999, 17)

Following this line of reasoning, it can be argued that Butala's act of walking out of the house to roam the prairie not only supplied her with subject matter but allowed her to un-define herself as a ranch wife and assume the adventuring identity of a writer.

Thus, Butala's walking allowed her to interact with the physical world and to redefine her notion of self. Butala's autobiographical writings are full of examples of the interaction of mind/spirit and body (another kind of "soft boundary").[12] Sometimes, her body acts as a kind of spiritual barometer. For example, when she tells of the childhood spiritual epiphany that accompanied her First Communion, she locates it in her body: "a cloud of white light lit inside my chest, swelling till it filled it" (1994a, 20). When finding a stone scraper, a remnant of the ancient aboriginal settlement formerly on the Butala land, there is an accompanying physical sensation: "I felt something strong in my chest" (ibid., 107). Similarly, when curiosity leads her to enter an earth dwelling of the Anasazi Indians of New Mexico, her body signals to her that this was a place filled with spirit.

> I knew at once that my whole body felt different. I felt, not exactly heavier, but more substantial in a physical way; I felt more solid and the air around me seemed more real, more intense, more personal. Perhaps I should say that I felt more connected to the air, more connected to the earth and that both of these were physical sensations which I felt with my whole body and were not merely psychic phenomena. (1994a, 135)

Additionally, she cites a long-lasting physical exhaustion that she was convinced had no medical cause and seemed to be heightened when she walked outdoors (2000a, 33). Eventually, the exhaustion became dissipated as her personal integration with the prairie grassland proceeded. Conversely, once she becomes habituated to the out-of-doors, she reports experiencing acute physical discomfort when enclosed in big buildings (such as high schools or airports) for any length of time:

> Inside them I felt a disruption of my normal way of experiencing the external environment; I felt disconnected with my physical self. It was as if my body didn't end after all with the surface of my skin, and that some invisible, exterior part was being subtly disrupted by the machinery running the building.... I couldn't help but think of all the young people who were growing up mainly inside of them [large schools] not even knowing that the buildings were warping, perhaps destroying a dimension of their humanity. (1994a, 133)

Here, Butala is again describing her perception of the continuity between mind and body. She is also suggesting her major thesis – that is, that physical contact with the natural world is part of our birthright as human beings. In the present context, the phrase "not even knowing" is significant; at this point in her spiritual journey, Butala does "know." Her bodily sensitivity to nuances in environment has been shaped by long periods of solitude on the plains of Saskatchewan. Butala firmly believes in a world fully imbued with spirit (1994a, 108), but, whatever explanation for these bodily sensations one might give, their significance here lies in Butala's construction of body as capable of response not only to physical stimuli but also to mysterious forces not perceivable by the five senses. Indeed, for those such as herself possessing what I now term "soft boundaries," she conceives of the body as having an additional somatic faculty located variously in the chest, the solar plexus, the abdomen, or the uterus, bodily areas which can apprehend directly without mental intervention or interpretation (1994a, 125, 137). Moreover, Butala depicts the body as being as expressive of, and responsive to, various emotional and mental states. This kind of mind-body interrelatedness is a phenomenon that is more widely accepted in our society than the somatic ability just described because it has a basis in neural physiology. One takes for granted, for example, that an emotion such as extreme fear will cause one's heart to beat faster and one's mouth to become dry.

The Perfection of the Morning is replete with Butala's descriptions of the effect emotions have on her body. For example, she locates her disappointment physically when, because of an emergency, she is required to leave the annual cattle drive: "I had an actual pain in my chest as I drove away and that stayed with me until I went to bed that night" (ibid., 93). She devotes an entire chapter entitled "Anomie" to an analysis of the long-lasting depression brought on by her sense of alienation and dislocation when first moving to the Butala ranch. One can feel it reach into her body: "I was in constant pain; tumult roared inside of me … only dying made sense" (ibid., 85).

However, Butala conveys the effects of depression most graphically, not in her life writing, but in her autobiographically based fiction, most specifically in a short story called *Mermaid in the Watery Deep*. *Mermaid* is in the collection of short stories called *Fever* (1990), which, according to the author, contains her most personally based fiction (Butala 1994a, 104). In this story, Butala uses one of her own dreams as the source of the imagery. As she describes this dream in *The Perfection of the Morning* (177), she is thrashing about in the water, terrified, while far below the shape of a giant man-o'-war can be seen. When fictionalized, the man-o'-war becomes a huge sea creature and is presented clearly as a metaphor for the urge to self-destruction. The story is a graphic representation of a life-threatening depression that finds bodily expression for the female protagonist in a debilitating weakness and in a six-week menstrual flow. In our discussion of the story (phone call, March 23, 2001), Butala explained that, while this had not happened personally to her, she had listened to similar accounts of a woman's female menses being activated through emotional stress; one such acquaintance was indeed told, like the woman in the story, that she could just as well bleed at home as in the hospital.

This is but one example of how Butala in her fiction graphically represents women's experience of the reproductive functioning of the female body and of how indelibly this functioning marks women's perceptions of self. In *Country of the Heart* (1984), a woman's endurance of painful menstruation is a major element in the narrative, while both *The Gates of the Sun* (1986) and *Luna* (1988) contain careful and complete descriptions of childbirth. In *The Garden of Eden* (1998), she shows Iris, newly widowed, experiencing the hot flushes of menopause and calculating how many years she menstruated, "something like forty years, month after month after month" (1998, 201). In both her novels and short stories, Butala depicts women as conflicted sexual subjects as well as being the objects of male desire, and she holds women accountable in claiming the status of sexual subjects for themselves. In *Luna*, for example, she has Rhea, the grandmother "crone," ask Phoebe, who has been raped: "Why did you change from wanting his caresses to fighting them?" (1986, 144), implying that, while not condoning the rape, Rhea saw Phoebe as denying her womanhood through fear of social convention. *Luna* contains also a description of a miscarriage remembered by Rhea in old age and prompting this musing:

> There is no woman without the knowledge of blood. Trickling down your legs, smearing it on all the things you own, your hands, reminding you of yourself, the self you don't talk about. The self that seems most real to you, no matter how you try to pretend it isn't. (1988b, 79)

This then is Butala's central point about the female body, that bodily experience is phenomenologically the most real. It is the determining element in female subjectivity and is irredeemably different from male experience. In my interviews with Butala, she reinforced this position. I pointed out to her that her views represent a form of essentialism, a position frowned upon by most contemporary feminist critics (Mandell 1998, 13) as being confining to women while ignoring the individual, racial, cultural, and class differences that are the significant cultural determinants. Butala replied that viewing womanhood as a cultural construction is a position

> ... which I happen to think is convenient for them because if you decide that is how things are then of course you can change things to any way you want. And I'm saying the world wasn't all that screwed up. Of course, women have been basely mistreated and continue to be – I told you that story at lunch about Ethiopia. I am very, very well aware of the mistreatment of women institution-wise. What I concluded, though, is that the only way to explain what a woman is, is to understand that she created the world. That it wasn't a male god. And I mean that in the metaphoric and the literal sense. Both. Those women in their sphere are more powerful than men are. I say in that essay, "Telling the Truth," that if you are able to give birth to children you are different than men. This is *not* a culturally determined difference although there are also culturally determined differences. And you will never conceive of the world as the male of the species does because you are still going to be different (Reid 1996b, 10–12).

In this way, Butala rejects anti-essentialist feminisms; however, her assertions here have much in common with the tenets of a less recent form of feminism, that of the radical feminists who elevate "the power and the spirit of the female body" so as to facilitate "the development of women's reproductive and sexual powers in new ways" (Mandell 1998, 12). They hold, as does Butala, that the oppression of women is the most fundamental form of oppression, that women have innate, if unrealized, power by virtue of their reproductive capabilities and that a fundamental re-sorting of social practices is needed in order to restore the feminine principle to its rightful place (Mandell 1998, 10–14). Accordingly, Butala does not dismiss summarily the lifestyle of her female progenitors, rural women who were able to raise a family close to the land, in harmony with nature. She observes that, while contemporary urban women

> ... gained a measure of personal freedom and self-determination ... they lost some valuable things too, the chief one being a stable support system in which to raise their children in peace and security, a terrible loss from which society, I believe, has not yet begun to feel the full and awful effects. (1994a, 183)

In *Luna*, there is a long description of Rhea making bread – setting the bread to rise and baking it in a cook stove – that reads like an evocation of the fulfilled traditional feminine life, one lived in the body and giving life to others. Rhea comments ruefully, "Women don't know anymore, don't know what bread making is for, what it means to make your own bread" (1988b, 71).

MARY PRATT

Mary Pratt's description of bread making also verges also on the symbolic but is unabashedly more erotic in its imagery. For example, in *A Personal Calligraphy*, Pratt describes her memory of the making of Easter breads when her children were small:

> ... hot cross buns – high butting loaves of erotic Easter breads baked in clay pots – and rising like phallic towers of golden ecstasy – I filled them with cardamom, cloves, anise and cinnamon, frosted them with icing so pure and white that the crusts look dark underneath the lines of frosting. (Pratt 2000, 28)

Pratt re-creates these breads of decades ago, not in the sacramental way of Rhea, but more as source of exquisite sensual pleasure. Pratt has explained in many interviews that her art had its genesis in her holistic physical response to her surroundings and she again refers in her published journals to the epiphany that occurred when seeing sunshine pouring onto an unmade bed: "The sight of this familiar part of my life stopped me in my tracks. Sent such shivers of pleasure through me that I recognized it as the beginning of a new life for me" (ibid., 125). This experience launched Pratt into a painting career, the mainstay of which is her still lifes of domestic subjects, especially containers of various kinds of food. Thus, Pratt's still life paintings invoke the body on at least two levels: first, as a visceral response to the visual appeal of her surroundings; and second, as referring to the body through the choice of food as subject matter. Pratt's treatment of the latter produces her most erotically suggestive work.

Pratt is perfectly aware that images of food and references to the body intersect symbolically. This is clear in her description of agreeing to create a piece for the *Survivors* show (1995), dedicated to breast cancer victims. As Pratt's description demonstrates, the image of bread again becomes a surrogate for the body, but not this time in a celebratory fashion:

> The bowl full of rapidly rising dough – the dough cresting the rim with a lumpy over-proofed surface – does look like a breast that has a transparent skin, the rapidly growing yeast making large and irregular pockets pressing against the surface of the glass. (2000, 116)

Margaret Visser suggests that the association of bread with the female breast is universal. In *The Rituals of Dinner*, she asserts: "Bread is, for us, a kind of successor to the motherly breast" (1991, 3). Pratt's awareness of food images as referents for the female body is evident also in earlier comments about a painting of broken eggshells in an egg crate. As she says, she intended to throw them away:

> However, the textures and colours combined to create an image of life and abandoned life. I, who had recently failed to bring twin sons to term, felt the importance of the image. (Pratt commenting on *Eggs in an Egg Crate*, 1976: Gwyn and Moray 1989, 70)

It is one of the most clear-cut examples of food images intersecting metaphorically with Pratt's feminine bodily awareness and experience.

Susan Sceats similarly identifies the association between broken eggs and sexuality and childbirth in the fiction of Michele Roberts (2000, 127–28). She does so in the course of her investigation into the portrayal of food in fiction written by women, making the point that "the essential and necessary qualities of eating invest its surrounding activities with value, whether psychological, moral or affective" (ibid., 1). For Sceats, a description of food carries with it a multiplicity of associations and functions that include viewing food as an instrument of nurturing and as a connector with sexuality through metaphor or metonymy. Further, she identifies that food is a social signifier (123) with food consumption being therefore an arena of social convention and manners, both of which are mechanisms for social bonding, maintaining the status quo, and assuring bodily propriety (ibid., 141). In a similar vein, Visser insists that modern manners take the form of

> ... unspoken almost subconscious guidelines and constraints.... Eating behavior is still – and, I would argue must always remain – guarded, enculturated, ritualized, and even taboo-laden. (1991, 341)

Here one can detect echoes of Foucault's notions of "habitual practice" and the "docile body" although, unlike Foucault, Visser is content to describe rather than challenge cultural techniques of social control.

Pratt's portrayal of food and the paraphernalia of food preparation and eating reveal the operation of Visser's "guidelines and constraints" as well as the various food associations that Sceats describes. These "guidelines and constraints" are especially apparent in Pratt's depictions of her personal meal times in the dinner table paintings, these being at least nine in number, ranging from the 1969 *Supper Table* (Fig. 2) to the 1994 *Breakfast Last Summer* (Fig. 6), and, most recently, to the 1999 *Ginger Ale and Tomato Sandwich #1* (2000, 57). On the most obvious level, these paintings document the passage of time and with it the inevitable changes in domestic arrangements and eating habits. *Supper Table* depicts the remains of the Pratt family's evening meal when the children were still at home; *Breakfast Last Summer* shows a table set for two, while the remainder of the paintings, all completed in the 1990s, depict food and table settings set out for a solitary eater. In her 1990s journals, Pratt refers often to presently living alone, a lifestyle documented in these paintings. Moreover, they demonstrate again Pratt's ability to catch the fleeting moment. They convey a sense of arrested time – of a bodily act interrupted and frozen in mid-air – by showing leftover food or a meal just begun. For example, *Supper Time* documents the remnants of a family meal awaiting clearing; in *Ginger Ale and Tomato Sandwich*, the tomato sandwich has one bite out of it and the ginger ale still has its bubbles. Often fruit is shown half-peeled and ice cream dishes half full. The absent eater, the bodily Pratt herself, is obviously not long gone and Pratt, the artist, is just off-stage. It is as close as Pratt comes to self-portraiture.

These mealtime paintings demonstrate how thoroughly Pratt has been "encultured" and "ritualized," to use Visser's terms. For Pratt, eating is a ceremonial act, even when eating alone. It is undertaken with decorum, as indeed, are her manner of dress and her lifestyle. Even in the after-meal shambles of *Supper Table*, one can detect delicate teacups for the two adults and place mats set out for everyone. Pratt's careful observance of the niceties is the most impressive, however, in the paintings of solitary lunches. There are, for example, always cloth table napkins and pretty glassware with cutlery and place mats arranged symmetrically. In *Picnic with Pineapple* (Smart 1995, 135), the array of fruit, seemingly for one, is set out of doors on an exquisite eyelet tablecloth. Some of this insistence on carefully tasteful presentation can be attributed to Pratt's love of beauty and her search, as artist, for particular visual effects. Her characteristic aesthetic mode finds its source, as Gerta Moray says, in an affinity for the painting tradition of Northern Europe as well as the devices of North American advertising art (Gwyn and Moray 1989, 28–29).

Nonetheless, her aesthetic owes much to more personal sources, especially her childhood inculcation into Fredericton culture in which propriety, order, and discipline were primary values. In her published journals, Pratt makes frequent mention of her inherited proclivity for ritual, order, and propriety, and each time it is in the context of the social containment of impulses for pleasure and abandonment. For example, the rituals demanded of bedtime compel her to leave a magic nighttime view of her garden, denying her "the unexpected beauty I might have allowed myself" (Pratt 2000, 59). Conversely, she writes of her "dark preference for the exotic ... driving the blood," and again, of "being like a ribbon of fire that flares and glows and calms and flares again" (ibid., 40). Yet, Pratt perceives danger in "dark preference" and surmises "only in oases of detachment ... do I see the base of order which has kept me from self-destruction" (ibid.).

Here Pratt presents a construction of the self in conflict. In Freudian terms, the conflict would be seen to be between socially behavioural demands of the "super ego" and the instinctual impulses of the "id." The containment of sensual impulse and bodily pleasure by this "base of order" is the subtext and organizing principle of a great proportion of her still lifes and most particularly in her portrayals of bowls overflowing with fruit and jelly shining through glass containers. Particularly evocative are the many images of cut fruit with the seeds spilling out, the plates and bowls barely accommodating them. They are highly suggestive of the female erotic, the holistic *jouissance*. These images suggest female sexual energy, but energy being controlled.

For the most part, the fruit still lifes function as a kind of contained celebration both of the body and of a way of life. It is only those of sliced fruit with the knife still nearby or inserted that emphasize the suggestion of female bodily violation. More recent examples are *Preparation for Plum Jam* (Pratt 2000, 72) and *Pomegranates and a Knife* (ibid., 39), the latter being quite graphically suggestive. It is a theme that is more startlingly obvious in the earlier paintings of meat, poultry, and fish. Pratt tells of accompanying her grandmother on her ritual visits to the butcher shop where she surveyed the hanging carcasses of meat "hind legs splayed with wooden sticks" in order to pick out the Sunday roast (ibid., 73); consequently, Pratt knew from an early age that slaughter was a precondition of meat for the table. This awareness has informed her art practice from the beginning and compelled her to balance the bright still lifes of foodstuffs with the darker subject matter of dead animal flesh. Pratt has commented often that the darks and lights, literally and metaphorically, are essential to produce the necessary balance both in life and in art.[13]

Her first raw meat painting was *Eviscerated Chickens* (Fig. 19); it is interesting to compare it with *Self-Trussed Turkey* (Pratt 2000, 122), painted twenty-three years later. *Eviscerated Chickens* is lovingly and lusciously modelled, with yellow fat glistening under the skin. As with her bursting fruit paintings, there is a clear reference to the female body as subtext; this reading was a subject of discussion during our interview. In speaking of *Eviscerated Chickens*, she said, "I think it is the shapes of the fat that hang down. Interior globular shapes that women are aware of" and she proceeded to elaborate:

It has an awful lot to do with sexuality. You know what it is to put your hand inside a chicken. I know what that's all about; I've cleaned chickens. I've stuffed chickens. I've done it all. I've watched my mother and my grandmother pulling the guts out of chickens and stuff like that. The painting is all about that. (Reid 1996a, 18)

It is my view that, through the luscious modelling of this animal form, Pratt is expressing her experience of female sexuality as holistic; she is, in fact, expressing *jouissance*. But Pratt's feelings about her sexual experience are contradictory. I confirmed with Pratt that the image carried an implied reference to the female body and questioned further:

REID: Is there a dark side to this?

PRATT: Of course. There is the interior of the chicken.

When I pressed her on this cryptic answer, she inferred that the conclusion should be obvious. I took this to mean that as a woman who had borne four children in quick succession and lost twin sons in a miscarriage, Pratt viewed her reproductive and sexual experience as including a sense of physical violation and victimization. Evidently, the passage of time has done nothing to soften her perception; her later painting of *Self-Trussed Turkey* through its harsh lighting and choice of subject (*self*-trussing?) conveys a palpable sense of confinement and violation.

This sense is most pronounced, however, in the two paintings that are based on the male hunting and fishing culture of Newfoundland: *The Service Station* (Fig. 20), a painting of a splayed moose carcass reminiscent of Pratt's visit to the butcher shop; and *Another Province of Canada* (Fig. 21), showing two men – one younger, one older – holding up an enormous gutted fish. In his book on Pratt's retrospective exhibition, *The Substance of Light*, Tom Smart locates the image of the moose carcass as a statement of feminine rejection of the violence of male culture, a culture in which Pratt, a transplant to Newfoundland, was immersed. He quotes Pratt's description of her initial reaction to the seeing the moose in her neighbour's garage: "'To me it screamed 'murder, rape, clinical dissection, torture'" (Smart 1995, 82). It was, as Smart comments, "a female statement about a male world," a world of physical violence to which Pratt could not help but be exposed, if only from a distance. According to Smart, sexual violence is the unmistakable theme of *Another Province of Canada*. The gutted fish is an intended allusion "to a vagina and labia into which a young man has thrust his hand and, by inference, a knife" (ibid., 81). While Pratt's subtext is likely more ambiguous than that, the sense of slaughter and victimization is clear. Certainly the images in both paintings are likely to make mature female viewers, such as myself, wince, recalling as they do, through *The Service Station*, the stirrups of male-organized gynecological and childbirth procedures, and through *Another Province of Canada*, the vulnerability of the female sexual organs.

The passage from celebration of the female body in the fruit paintings to the notion of its victimization in the meat and fish paintings recalls the theorization of Mary Kelly and her analysis of women's practice in art which she calls "problematic" in that it is "socially constituted" and manifests itself in four forms of signification (1987, 305–10). Of interest here is the first stage, which, to reiterate, Kelly calls "female culture/mother art" and which is specifically descriptive of domestic-based art. In this context, it applies to the female body in its tending/nurturing mode. In this mode, a dark side inevitably emerges out of celebration, by which routine activities assume an obsessive quality so that preparing food becomes a signification of cannibalistic relationships (Kelly 1987, 305). Some such notions are discernible in Pratt's description of a photograph of a bowl of trifle she is in the process of painting:

> This doesn't look like a dessert at all. It looks an awful lot more like a sacrifice that has confection on the top of it to mask it and I found all the photography I did of this trifle somewhat alarming. This looks like the reality of life; this looks like blood and something we prefer not to think about. (Smith-Strom 1996)

Moreover, if, as Smart does, one perceives an equivalency between Pratt's imaging of gutted fish and the laying bare of the female body, the notion of metaphorically devouring or being devoured becomes a conceivable subtext, perhaps "the something we prefer not to think about" that had its imagic source in Pratt's long-ago visits to the Fredericton butcher shop.

Awareness of the body, then, appears in various guises in the majority of Pratt's still life paintings and through these paintings, based as they are on personal experience, Pratt constructs her subjectivity as being rooted in the body. However, it is through her figure paintings of Donna Meany – Mary Pratt's household helper and subsequently Christopher's studio model – that the female body makes an overt appearance in her art practice. Earlier, she had been reluctant to paint the female figure, identifying correctly that the painting of the female nude was historically male territory. Kelly, extrapolating from this historical fact and what she sees as the resultant inescapable positioning, locates the woman artist's entry into the representation of the female body as the second and third stages of the "feminist problematic" (1987, 308–9). In these stages, the art practice is in turn narcissistic, and then objectifying, of the very subject (i.e., the female body) it is seeking to express directly. I argue, then, that the *Donna* paintings are characterized by both narcissism and objectification under the male gaze.

However, Pratt's comments on the importance of the female body to both men and women proceed from a somewhat different perspective, albeit a degree of narcissism can be observed:

> I have come to the conclusion that everybody understands the woman's body because men are born from women. And everybody loves a woman's body, because women love their own bodies and men love women's bodies. A man's body is very uninteresting. It is not worthy of painting, not worthy of discussion. It is just there; it is a useful thing. It is rather a machine. It's useful. But it is not beautiful. And it doesn't give you this sensual thing … to be honest is to know we all love women's bodies. It doesn't matter if you are a woman or if you are a man. You are born of woman. (Reid 1996a, 43)

In a somewhat similar vein, Pratt explained that the female role is as muse to man:

PRATT: Eve engages Adam erotically in the world. She says, "This is what the world is all about. It is about sensuality, about eating; it is about being in touch with the world."

REID: Women are more sensitive to that. Their bodies are different.

PRATT: They understand that. They know it and so that is what they give to men. They are receptors; men are not. (Ibid.)

In these exchanges Pratt reveals, first of all, her essentialist position, an assertion that gendering comes about because of bodily difference. As with Butala, woman's reproductive power is seen as a radical element, forever marking female experience as different from that of the male. Beyond that, however, is Pratt's denotation of erotic pleasure as a female attribute, an endowment to enjoy as part of being a woman and to share with men. One is reminded of Irigaray's dictum that "women have sex organs everywhere"

(1981, 101), and it is my view that, even as she privileges the visual in her sensual delight in the effects of light, Pratt's aesthetic, as well as her understanding of herself as a woman, is best understood as expressions of *jouissance*, "a designation for female sexuality beyond the phallus ... the unspoken in canonical discourse" (cited in Jaggar and Bordo 1989, 59).[14]

Pratt likely has little knowledge of, or interest in, French feminists.[15] Nevertheless, one can extrapolate from their work to place Pratt's widespread use of the female body as subtext as a form of *écriture féminine*. I pointed out to Pratt that many would construe sentiments such as "we all love women's bodies" as an indication of a lesbian tendency. She replied impatiently that this had been brought to her attention before but that she "was a normal woman who had enjoyed fully that side of her married life" and that "there was more to be said" about female sexuality (Reid 1996a, 43). Pratt did not elaborate, but I now interpret that "more to be said" as expressive of *jouissance*, and that, consequently, she sees women's sexual nature as involving their bodies holistically, and presents her still lifes, especially of fruit, as expressions of that global eroticism. This eroticism is not expressed satisfactorily, however, in her paintings of the female nude.

Pratt comes to the painting of the female figure in a complex position, entering a genre in which the female nude is by established tradition objectified as an source of male pleasure (Berger 1997, 55) but which, to Pratt, acts also as a reminder of her pleasure in her own body. She attempts to express both perceptions, showing a woman displaying herself for a man and then showing a woman taking pleasure in her own body. The first Pratt does easily; the second is more difficult simply because the traditional signification of the female nude does not facilitate construction and presentation of the female as experiencing subject.

Mary Kelly theorizes that female painters can only do so through changing the discourse – that is, through some distancing technique such as the use of text (1987, 308–9). However, in reading Pratt's work from a feminist perspective, Wendy Schissel argues that "Mary Pratt is producing a different kind of nude" and that she "tries to give subjectivity back to traditionally objectified woman" (1991, 158). Accordingly, Schissel identifies several techniques that Pratt uses to endow her female nudes with individuality. These include naming the figure as "Donna," bestowing small bodily imperfections on the model to establish her specificity, and using techniques of portraiture to individualize the model's subjectivity.

In response, I would agree that Pratt endows Donna with individuality. I would argue, however, that Pratt does not achieve any real suggestion of woman as experiencing sexual subject. Schissel affirms that Pratt establishes the female painter's right to "look all she wants and paint what she knows" (ibid., 158, citing Anne Collins). I would agree that Pratt "looks all she wants." In keeping with Mary Kelly, however, it is my view that, within the *oeuvre* of the female nude, Mary Pratt knows more of female sexual experience than she can possibly paint.

One, then, can divide Pratt's figure paintings, consisting mostly of the *Donna* series, into two classifications, those overtly posed and those purportedly of "caught in the act" private moments. The first classification consists of large, life size paintings that present the figure rather starkly and are placed against a blank wall facing forward, with Donna, the model, self-conscious but gazing directly at the viewer (Smart 1995, 89, 93, 111, 117; Gwyn and Moray 1989, 159). Because of the size and the confrontational positioning, the effect of these particular Donna paintings is rather heroic, as if the model were daring a judgmental examination.

As Pratt became well aware, this gaze was directed in the first instance at the male photographer, Christopher Pratt, and it is as if Mary Pratt, by painting from these photographs, has intercepted and usurped the gaze, becoming simultaneously its source and object, voyeur and surrogate. She told me in interview, "I have always tried to be what I paint.… It has to be so much a part of me that I am what that is" (Reid 1996a, 13); her positioning in this series of paintings is a rather poignant extension of this need to integrate her subject into herself. The erotic nuances of the reciprocal gaze thus become the subtext of the painting, and Pratt through the act of painting is able to look with her husband's eyes in order to examine the challenges of a seductive third party in the constructs of intimacy in the Pratt household. The painterly subject thus becomes not merely the female body but rather the bodily dictates of the code of femininity by which women become objects to be scrutinized.

The triangular subtext of the Donna paintings is most clearly discernible in *Girl in My Dressing Gown* (Fig. 22). In this painting, Donna is shown garbed in a beautiful negligee borrowed from Mary, a garment clearly too large for her. Pratt denies any intent of denigration (Reid 1996a, 30), but the iconography of the work points clearly to feminine rivalry and an attempted usurpation of the wifely position. Nevertheless, in other Donna paintings, Pratt shows appreciation for Donna's vulnerability as her body is subjected to the viewer's gaze and scrutinized for its beauty and femininity. For example, in two of the paintings, *Girl in a Wicker Chair* (Smart 1995, 89) and *Donna* (Fig. 23), Donna is shown with her knees drawn up to her chest, in a protective, even defensive pose. In *Girl in Glitz* (Gwyn and Moray 1989, 159), Donna's seductive expression is undercut by the same sense of vulnerability, communicated visually by the markings on the unclothed body caused by the zipper and belt of her discarded jeans. Pratt seems to waver between constructing Donna as a rival and viewing her as part of a sisterhood trapped into enacting the code of femininity.

Of all Pratt's paintings, *Cold Cream* (Fig. 24) communicates most clearly the self-destructive, victimizing effects of trying to measure up to society's arbitrary standards of female physical beauty. Donna looks out from the canvas as if into a mirror, surveying the finger gouges inscribed into the cold cream that covers her face. Rasporich comments on the self-reflexive nature of the image, linking it to the difficulty female visual artists have in finding a facilitating tradition through which to express their bodily experience:

> On one level, Mary Pratt's *Cold Cream* can be read as a … visual enquiry into the dilemma of the female artist who attempts to *engender* art from her own feminine experience and, in the process, becomes her own self-reflexive, self-limiting muse (1993, 122).

The painting *Cold Cream* can thus be read as reflecting a problematic aspect of Pratt's subjectivity as artist.

Mary Kelly makes much the same point when she locates the use of the mirror concept, whether in video or on canvas, as being a narcissistic structure by which the female artist attempts to return the image of herself to herself and negate the demands of the code of femininity. She sees this as characteristic of feminine "ego art," where the artist is trying to affirm female experience. As is usual with Kelly, she identifies the negative manifestation as inevitable, again because of the alienation women artists feel in the male-dominated tradition of painting. Therefore she asserts that the use of the mirror device is "often carried out in conjunction with attacks, visible or verbal on her own person, a kind of exorcism of her own negative signification" (Kelly 1987, 309–10). The gouges and mirror-like positioning of the female countenance show that *Cold Cream* belongs to that species of exorcism.[16]

The second classification of Pratt's figure paintings is one in which the subject is not overtly posing as artist's model but is presented as if caught by a candid camera. Pratt confirms the spontaneity of the pose in *Nude on a Kitchen Chair* (Gwyn and Moray 1989, 99). It portrays the model, Donna, at rest, being "preoccupied," Pratt says, "with some minor [bodily] problem or defect" (ibid., 98). The viewer/artist is again in the position of voyeur. Meanwhile, Donna, the subject, is depicted as involved (as in *Cold Cream*) in the self-scrutiny prompted by the anticipation of being judged on the appearance of one's body. *In the Bathroom Mirror* (ibid., 123) is more complex in that Donna seems, in her mirror gaze, to have caught and challenged the artist, Pratt, in the act of voyeurism. The painting records an intimate exchange, likely best read as documenting again the complex relationship, involving both rivalry and empathy that exists between these women – artist and subject, wife and model.

In the paintings of candid moments, Pratt is faced with a difficult task – the depiction of the female as an experiencing sexual subject, beautiful both to herself and to others because of the *jouissance* that is fundamental to female bodily experience. It is my view that, even in such seemingly personal bodily experiences as enjoying the bath (*Blue Bath Water*, Smart 1995, 96), Pratt, the artist, cannot overcome the narcissistic/voyeur positioning. Perhaps the closest Pratt comes to expressing *jouissance* in her figure paintings is in *Child with Two Adults* (Fig. 4), a portrait of Katherine, Pratt's first grandchild, who is shown at one week old as unmistakably female and completely present to her body and its sensations. At a more visceral level, the redness and the slipperiness of the baby's body and the clear delineation of the female labia refer to the central event in the life of the female body, the act of giving birth, an event of blood and mucous, and of basic animality. At one time Pratt said that, of all her work, *Child with Two Adults* is her favourite piece and by this designation, she placed maternality and the reproductive function as a key element in her subjectivity to be surpassed only by her sense of identity as artist. She said publicly in 1998: "creativity and the spark that ignites it have been the most powerful forces in my life" (2000, 123).

While aging has consolidated Pratt's subjectivity as artist, it has also affected the character of Pratt's artistic method, in that bouts of arthritis have from time to time dictated her choice of media and mark-making. Her preferred method, necessary for the accomplishment of her painstaking realism, has involved the careful use of tiny brushes and delicate hand-eye coordination. The result has been that no trace of the artist's mark (and therefore of the artist's bodily involvement) is discernible. In later years, surgery and drugs have controlled the arthritis and have enabled Pratt to continue with her customary painting method, but there have been times in the past decade or so that Pratt has used oil pastels and other media to draw rather than paint, thus allowing for a freer and less painful art-making technique.

Pratt explained to me that this freer technique reached a climax in the huge paintings that comprise the *Fire* series. These were produced during the period of her grieving and rage at the fate of her first marriage. For paintings such as *Burning the Rhododendron* (Fig. 7), she abandoned the careful hand movements of painting and used her whole body to produce the vibrant patterns of fire. "I was making all this frenzy and I got right into my painting as I had never done before. I was as frenzied as those paintings" (Reid 1996a, 9). The Pratts had a tradition at year's end of burning the Christmas boxes and paper, and Pratt remembers it as a ritual of renewal. Her three fire paintings of this period (1988–90) are about expressing rage, burning the past and turning the art-making into a frenzy that became like a freeing dance (Smart 1995, 124, 125, 126).

In viewing her retrospective show, I came upon the *Fire* paintings unaware and was astonished at the contrast between them and her still lifes. The still lifes are about control and decorum, at least on the surface. The fire paintings, on the other hand, raged across the gallery walls, control at a minimum, with the physical bodily energy that went into the making of them clearly visible. The result has been that the movements of Pratt's arm and hand are discernible in the final image and the artist's bodily presence is communicated. The *Fire* paintings, especially *Burning the Rhododendron*, allow emotions, body, and image to come together in an explosive combination. As with *Aspects of a Ceremony* and the *Donna* series, these paintings constitute another example of Pratt both expressing and constructing her subjectivity through the act of painting.

SUMMARY

The pervasive presence of bodily representation in the work all four artists is again indicative of a liminal cultural positioning. Being born approximately between the two world wars, these artists were of the generation in North America in which patriarchal views of the female body were dominant and in which standards of proper "lady-like" behaviour prohibited public reference to female bodily experience, whether sexual or reproductive.

Nevertheless, Mary Meigs, whose upbringing was the most sexually repressive of the four, comes to write graphically not just about female sexual experience but about specifically lesbian sexual experience in a demonstration of both *testimonio* and *jouissance*. Similarly, Mary Pratt imbues her visual art, predominantly still lifes, with a celebratory *jouissance*, albeit contained within a rigid compositional structure. Her feminine "ego art" reflects accurately the psychological struggle between preserving a feminine decorum while pursuing the freedom necessary to express visually her bodily *joie de vivre*.

Aganetha Dyck comes to her art practice from a liberal Mennonite background. It is an enormous leap from the domestic bound traditional life of the Mennonite woman, however liberal, to the practice of art as an installation artist. The strength and imagination to do so came, paradoxically enough, from the modelling of creativity by her mother and father. Her seminal work, *The Extended Wedding Party*, like most of her other major installations, is grounded in bodily experience and bodily reference, examining, in this case, society's attempts to regulate and control women's reproductive power. Sharon Butala's bodily awareness came also from a cultural shift, this time from being an urban academic to being a rancher's wife. In her autobiographical texts, Butala displays an acute perceptiveness as to the effects of this shift on her bodily well-being, the curative powers of moving the body into the natural world and in her ability to represent accurately bodily experience of phenomena that lie outside the accepted norm.

Adrienne Rich said that "the great thing older women could do for younger women is to tell the stories of their lives" (Heilbrun 1991, 33). Extrapolating from Rich, I perceive that what these four artists do for younger women, indeed for all women, is to cross a threshold into a liminal space where it is feasible to deny society's dictates concerning perceptions of the female body. They discover that this liminal cultural space allows for the construction of their female bodies as experiencing subjects, although such expression often must take the form of subtext rather than direct representation. In so doing, these artists come to resist many of the dictates of the code of femininity. Theirs is a narrative that goes against the whole thrust of contemporary North American culture, which currently puts such a premium on the display of the female body as object. Such a narrative encourages all women to withstand the pressure exerted by exploitive media role models in order to come personally and subjectively "alive in the body."

READING AS A MOTHER, SISTER, AND DAUGHTER TO THE TEXT

In that liminal time period between the lifes of our mothers and that of our daughters, technology, unlike the media, did much to make women's lives better. The most notable advance came through improved methods of birth control. Chief among these was the advent of the birth control pill, a chemical intervention that gave women both a release from the fear of pregnancy and a resultant sexual freedom not known previously. It came on the Canadian market in the mid- to late 1960s.[17] It is not overstating the case to say that the advent of the "pill" is the one single contribution of science that changed twentieth-century women's bodily lives the most, and the one that separates the experience of those women born before or during World War II from those born after it. Of course, other devices and methods of birth control predated the advent of the pill, some of which depended on the cooperation of one's male partner, others not. None are as reliable as the pill, and many a woman, married or unmarried, filled that first prescription with profound relief.

The issue of birth control is one not dealt with directly in the work of any of these women, although, in acting as mother to these texts, I perceive that it exists as a subtext in Sharon Butala's novel *Luna*, in Aganetha Dyck's *Pocketbooks* series and in her *The Extended Wedding Party* installation. I surmise that it was an issue in the life of these two women as it must have been in that of Mary Pratt, who had four children and a miscarriage in the decade between 1957 and 1967, the miscarriage being avowedly a subtext in her painting, *Eggs in an Egg Crate*. My own children were all born in the 1950s, and what I find missing in the narratives of the body in the work of these four artists is a scarcity of reference to the monthly anxiety of waiting for a show of blood, a feature of my early married life. Similarly, my teenage years were haunted by a fear of pregnancy instilled in me by my mother who, in the previous era, knew first hand the threat of social shame that accompanied such an event. For me, this trepidation translated into a clear image of my mother's horrified distress at such an eventuality and, together, these inhibited any extended premarital sexual exploration on my part, despite the emergence very early of a distinctly healthy libido. Nevertheless, at the age of thirty-six, I was very upset to learn that a hysterectomy was necessary, feeling the existence of my womb was directly connected to my sense of womanhood. At the time, I found it ironic that this surgery occurred in the mid-1960s, just as the pill became freely available in Canada. The silver lining in that cloud was that my libido emerged unscathed and a very much freer sex life emerged, accompanied by a cessation of that monthly watch for the flow of blood.

Still, despite having three children, I grieved not being able to ever have more. After all, the biologically central act of the female body is the act of birthing. However, in the work of these women, the psychological experience of relating to one's mother is treated far more overtly than the fact of being a mother. Nevertheless, in conversation, Sharon Butala and Mary Pratt made it clear that, for them, a woman's reproductive capacity was the defining essence of what it meant to be female. Accordingly, in fiction Butala incorporates this view by making Phoebe's birthing scene the climax of the novel, *Luna*. However, the point of view is largely that of the onlooker/facilitator, Rhea, so that the reader is left to infer the exact quality of what Phoebe is experiencing. In Mary Pratt's *A Child with Two Adults*, the focus is on the newly born child, and the viscous nature of the rendering does cause bodily remembrances in me as it likely does in the majority of viewing mothers. The painting, though, is really about relationship and the powerful way the reproduction of mothering is being passed from one generation of women to another.

Accordingly, I found that the physical experience of bearing children occupies a far more momentous position in my bodily sense of myself than is suggested in these texts or that I myself can convey in language or in painting. The actual birthing of my three children did not always go smoothly. I found the prevailing attitude in maternity wards during the 1950s to be deliberately detached and reluctantly supportive. I remember, for example, being left alone in a dark room as the head of my son crowned and I screamed for attention. Luckily, I have given birth relatively easily and found, once out of the labour room, the act of producing a child to be a supremely physically and emotionally satisfying experience. Moreover, being able to nurse successfully produced a smug physical contentment like no other. I remember and puzzle over the fact that, as a pre-schooler, the younger of two children, I longed to hold and possess the small babies of my mother's friends. Similarly, my family of dolls was a constant in my play world, perhaps the result of a certain reproduction of mothering in me by my mother and grandmother.

The reason, I think, that I find little reflection of the powerful physicality of the birth experience in the work of these four artists[18] is that the traditions both in language and visual art have been male-dominated and the woman artist has to find room in the spaces between the genres to express the experiences of her female body. For me, the piece of art that succeeds best in doing this and that best expresses my single-minded absorption in the physicality of my babies is Mary Kelly's *Post-Partum Document*[19] in which debris of her real-life care of her baby son – soiled diapers, baby shirts with the inevitable ties, and "blankies" – are presented as artifacts.

In the original installation, the bodies of neither mother nor son are depicted. Instead, these fetish-like objects document the moment-to-moment physical interplay between mother and child. These artifacts summon up in a moving way this intimate relationship and serve to remind mothers how difficult it can be when social institutions inevitably supersede this relationship. The *Post-Partum Document* reminds me that hidden away in my cedar chest, a central domestic icon since my marriage, are, among other keepsakes, my collection of infant clothing that are the sole remnants of the mother-infant bond. These include various knitted garments: one surviving Curity diaper; the little hand-sewn flannel nightie I made painstakingly while awaiting the birth of John, my first child; the tiny pink angora-trimmed booties of Susan, my youngest; and the crocheted wool dress that was babyhood's Sunday best for Lois, my middle child. All are marked with the bodily signs of wear of my children's bodies, and, touching them, I again experience the power of the fleeting infant-mother physical and psychological bond.

With an unerring instinct and a Lacanian theorizing rigour, Kelly moves on to deal with these notions of separation and loss that she locates at the intersection of society and feminine experience:

> It [*Post-Partum Document*] is an effort to extricate the mother's fantasies, her desire, her stake in the project called motherhood. In this sense, it is not a traditional narrative; a problem is continually posed but no resolution is reached. There is only a replay of moments of separation and loss, perhaps because desire has no end – resists normalization, ignores biology, disperses the body. (1985, xvii)

In this passage, Kelly articulates for me my intellectual and emotional ambivalence – "a problem continually posed" – concerning the lifelong project of motherhood that issues from the biological event of giving birth. Kelly questions the notion of femininity as an essential concept, preferring instead to investigate it as a social construct. As expressed earlier, I waver between the affirmation of essentialism, based on the centrality of the birthing experience and the intense mother-baby bond, and a common-sense suspicion that nurturing could emerge to be a human function, not merely a female one, and that socialization is, in fact, a far more primary factor in the binary shaping of gendering than I had assumed. It is in these latter issues that these texts, together with the theories that underlie them, have "mothered" me into a conscious awareness of the contingency of gendering. For that and for a greater understanding of the many complexities of human sexuality, I am indebted to my textual "mothers."

Aside from this lack of emphasis on what was for me a crucial bodily issue, I found the embodiment existing in the works of Butala, Dyck, Meigs, and Pratt elicited in me many sisterly shocks of recognition. In particular, the play of light in Pratt's paintings and her conversation about her physical response to visual beauty reminded me of how assiduously from childhood on I have sought exposure to colour and light in my life. In the Depression years in Winnipeg, flowers were a miracle that never failed to amaze me. Lilacs were the neighbourhood staple while Winnipeg parks had ornate flower arrangements and even a conservatory. Like Pratt, I longed to possess and to become what I saw. When I received a gift of a box of fifty crayons containing all shades and hues, even that of my favourite pink, I gloated and hoarded. Later, I came to realize that the road not taken for me was the life of the visual artist and that unexpressed realization was probably what led to my pursuing a teaching career at the Alberta College of Art and Design. The students returned the favour by encouraging me to enter bodily the world of colour and light via applying paint to canvas, an avocation still happily part of my life.

Not so happily, like many women (and men) of the post-World War II's liminal generation, I was for many years a dedicated and unconcerned smoker, thinking the habit to be harmful, but not dangerously so. Regretfully, I, like the majority of my peers, submitted my children to second-hand smoke during much of their childhood. I started to smoke as a teenager and quit when I was forty-one. My story as a smoker is much the same as that of Aganetha Dyck's; I quit for what I thought were medical reasons – in my case, a prickling in my hands and feet that I identified as circulation problems brought on by smoking. The prickling went away, never to return, but it took me fully a year to stop smoking entirely, and so I understand the addictive hold of tobacco use. Consequently, when I encountered Aganetha Dyck's *Hand Held: Between Index and Middle Finger* as part of the retrospective show in Vancouver, I experienced a moment of shock that evoked in me again the self-disgust at the dirtiness of the habit, the repressed fear of health damage, as well as the bodily pleasure of that first morning cigarette and the sense of pseudo-sophistication associated with smoking. All these aspects and more, Dyck was able to communicate through presenting the physical reality and the artistic manipulation of other people's "last cigarettes."

What Dyck remembers, as do I, is the Barbie-doll self that accompanied smoking. That is, smoking, through its substitute for eating and its metabolic speed-up effects, kept us slim. And it is here that I enter the female world as lived according to the code of femininity. Like all four of these artists, I have a very conflicted relationship to the world of clothes. As a slim young woman, clothes were a source of delight, although as a young stay-at-home wife and mother, the economic opportunities of unbridled indulgence were non-existent. Now, semi-retirement has brought with it a secure income for my husband and myself. Alas, for me, it has also brought with it a distinctly matronly figure with the result that the prospect of clothes shopping (or any kind of shopping) looms as a trial of endurance with a degree of comfort being the major goal. In Meigs' situation, I, in firm sisterhood, would likewise cling stubbornly to bare feet in a comfortable pair of sandals and would favour trousers, no matter what Andrée's French sense of style dictated.

Having said that, I admit to the remnants of a passionate interest in clothes and to my life-long perception of garments as an extension of my body, one formed at the age of four when I received a beloved blue dress. Perhaps that is part of my obsession with trying to appropriate visual beauty to myself. Perhaps, too, it comes from an actress's use of costume that facilitates the trying on of roles, a process intricately involved with the construction of subjectivity. It is quite likely also that this concern with dress springs from the demands of what Sidonie Smith terms "perfomativity," the compulsion to conform to the role-playing demands involved in facing repeatedly a series of everyday audiences, the ones which occur in public discourse.

Similarly, I confess freely that with the majority of women, including these four artists, I cannot help but succumb to what Brownmiller calls "the brilliant subtle esthetic," which the code of femininity offers women It surfaces in myself particularly in this love of clothes and I part only reluctantly with old favourites that no longer fit – a pink hunting coat with braided buttons, a Chanel-like suit, and a cashmere tuxedo theatre suit. They recall a younger woman who found a means of expression and a sense of feminine worthiness through the wearing of beautiful clothes. I recognize with a kind of guilty sisterly pleasure the same inclinations in the work of Dyck and Meigs and in my conversations with Butala and Pratt, both of whom love to dress for the occasion. However, as I grow older, most days I am more likely to identify with that classic mystery writer, Dorothy Sayers (Carolyn Heilbrun's idol), whose sense of dress was purely utilitarian and who assuredly did not care what anyone thought about how she looked.

These days my personal bodily issues are more concerned with function or, more precisely, the loss of function that comes with aging. I acknowledge with gratitude that surgery has given me a new right hip and has repaired a lower back damaged by osteoarthritis. These are events that I share in a sisterly way with Mary Pratt, who also copes with arthritis (the knife in the fruit) and is likewise grateful for an artificial hip. Even Sharon Butala, thirteen years my junior, says nowadays that sore knees have cut down on her riding if not on her walking. I remember gratefully Mary Meigs' sweet quavery voice recounting over the phone the bodily losses that accompanied her stroke in 2001, and I wonder whether I could, in those circumstances, keep, as she did, an unwavering sense of self. For her part, Aganetha Dyck offsets the bodily losses of auto-immune problems by her joyous physical contact with the bees, an interaction that provides the transfer of energy observable in her art-making.

All four women retained their ineffable *jouissance* into their mature years, as do I. In my particular reading of the work of these artists, feminine global sexual energy is evident right into the final decades of life. I am grateful to them for exemplifying *jouissance* so that I was led to that theoretical conceptualization of female sexuality. It gave me the ability to recognize and name my personal experience of sexuality, one that so often did not fit any male representation with its emphasis on coitus as the inevitable sexual destination. In this respect, I have learned from them as a textual "daughter." After more than fifty years of marriage, my husband's body seems to have an electrical connection to my own, resembling the life force connection that Dyck feels in the act of art-making with the bees. I am not able to share verbally, as Meigs does, matters of nipples and mouths and "widening valleys down below," although I am grateful for her explicitness. I find it amazing that the touch of a familiar male hand in the middle of the night comes at this time of life as an abundant source of affection, comfort, and energy. This is the most profound reassurance that, like these four artists, I am an experiencing bodily subject, alive as a woman, and able to take pleasure in representing myself as such.

Alive in the World: Connecting to Nature

What I am really interested in is the natural part of the bees, the natural animal. People seem to think that apiary work is natural. They don't think anything at all about the fact that we take the honey or who built the hive boxes. There is a whole artificial thought of what natural is. So as soon as the bees built 'art,' that is not natural anymore and yet it is the most natural thing that they do because they will build in anything. On to anything. They just build anywhere. – Aganetha Dyck, speaking with Sigrid Dahle (1995)

For a few hours in July of 1997, I was privileged to join Aganetha Dyck in observing the local bees "build art" in a bee project she conducted as artist in residence at the York Sculpture Gardens on the outskirts of Leeds, England. The fact that I, too, was in England at that time was a happy coincidence. I had arranged to attend a conference in Leeds some weeks before, unaware that Dyck would be working nearby. On learning of each other's presence, we quickly arranged to meet, and I accepted with alacrity Dyck's subsequent invitation to attend one of the regularly scheduled openings of the hives.

For me, it was an exciting excursion into an unfamiliar world. However, I experienced some trepidation; one of my earliest memories is of my outrage, at the age of four, at being stung on the neck by a wasp. I was relieved, therefore, when Dyck outfitted me from head to toe in a white bee suit, complete with headdress and boots. I felt gloriously invincible as we entered a rather commonplace field, occupied by bee boxes set one on top the other, to await the opening of the hives by the beekeepers. In keeping with Dyck's description, the aviary set-up was indeed a combination of the artificial and the natural. The bee boxes and their supervision were the work of beekeepers (humans), which, at that time, were to feed the bees a sugar and water solution. The bee suit was an indication, however, that the bees were unpredictable and only partially under human control. Part of this unpredictability was expressed through their "art"; that is, Dyck was often surprised where and in what manner they would build on the glistening objects she had inserted into the hives. When Dyck and the beekeepers opened the hives that day, the bees had only begun their work. I remember seeing a myriad of insects crawling over the coated flower bouquet in one of the open hives. I was intrigued by their acceptance of this foreign object in their territory, one that they eventually would make their own by bees-wax embellishment.

That day, however, something about our human presence unexpectedly angered them, and they began to swarm. I was secure in my bee suit but I could feel their energy as they buzzed around and tried to penetrate the tough bee suit material with their stingers. I came away with an overwhelming sense of the bees' power and of the single-mindedness of their communal will. In describing that day in England to Robert Enright, Dyck commented simply "It was amazing" (Walsh and Enright, 2000, 56). She subsequently learned that it was the British practice to capture a whole swarm of bees for a particular aviary, and that the swarming in the bee yard was sometimes the result. Her experience that day allowed Dyck to add to her knowledge of the worldwide interaction of humans and honeybees, those wild creatures with whom she collaborates in her art practice. As for me, I felt privileged to make intimate connection with the bee world, a part of nature heretofore unexplored.

Because of her artistic collaboration with the bees, Dyck bonds physically and psychologically with nature. And, while she sees herself as an integral part of that natural world, she recognizes that cultural attitudes shape that relationship as well. Although their relationship with nature takes different forms, Butala, Meigs, and Pratt similarly view the natural world in much the way that Dyck does. For example, all four artists take up a paradoxical positioning; they experience nature as having a vital connection to the rhythms of femininity – the source of life – and yet they have come to realize that the natural world has been perceived by and large as masculine territory. While all four have wide experience of urban living, they all have sought out aspects of the natural world and profess a love of Canadian landscape. Consequently, they uniformly sound notes of alarm about the current global environmental crisis, a crisis threatening to change the natural world, as they have known it. As a result, all four take positions through their work as ecological and environmental advocates. It has been noted previously that these artists tend to construct themselves in relationship.[1] Accordingly, the natural world, in its various manifestations, emerges in their work as another powerful "other" in the shaping of the subjectivities of all four.

In this context, Aganetha Dyck's work with and study of the bees can be seen as reflecting most directly the character of the physical universe in that, being guided in the actual hive processes by knowledgeable beekeepers, the resultant art has come to reflect a deep, unmediated, and disinterested contact with this aspect of nature. As Robert Enright says

> Dyck's achievement is a rare thing.... Hers seems an almost artless practice that tells us something profound about art's simplicity of form and purity of intention. She is a natural artist and the nature she offers is not red in tooth and claw, but gold in wing and filament. (Enright 2001, V8)

She is "a natural artist," both in her devotion to the honey bee as a part of nature, and in her seemingly "artless practice." The keeping of bees is a worldwide phenomenon that, in its universality, allows her work to resonate with viewers from many cultures. Consequently, she has been invited as visiting artist to countries such as England, France, and Holland. This, coupled with the fact that Dyck comes from an immigrant Mennonite family with connections beyond Canada, that the work of German artist Joseph Beuys has been a seminal influence, and that her bee research has led her to interdisciplinary exploration, serves to explain the increasingly global awareness observable in her art practice and the cosmopolitan sensibility that is part of her construction of self.

As for Sharon Butala, the artistic sensibility awakened in her by the landscape of the Great Plains allows her to connect with readers and critics in the United States, many of whom associate her work with that of such American nature writers as Anne Dillard and Kathleen Norris.[2] Like Dillard and Norris, Butala perceives contact with nature to be spiritually enhancing and, like them, she is shaped in her view of nature and her consequent construction of self by her experience of a very particular region and landscape – in Butala's case, the grasslands of southwestern Saskatchewan. These rolling plains and the impact of the experience of walking them form the central subject of Butala's life writing. In her autobiographically based fiction, on the other hand, Butala is concerned with depicting the perceptions of rural inhabitants who live close to the land and have developed an understanding of nature. The life writing takes as its emphasis her personal journey into nature, a journey that evolves into a psychic and spiritual quest. At the same time, the fiction concerns itself more with rural society and the clash between two ways of relating to nature, as enacted on the family farms and ranches of Saskatchewan. The personal and the social, however, are woven together in all of Butala's writing so that passionate political advocacy is always present to a greater or lesser degree. As Mary Ellen Pitts comments in her analysis of American nature writing, "Life writing has been a crucial genre within which to voice personally felt protest and philosophies of nature" (2001, 641).

Of the four artists, then, it is Dyck and Butala who focus their work most consistently on the investigation of nature; the resulting interaction directly shapes their understanding of the world and their place in it. There is evidence in the work of Pratt and Meigs that experience of the natural world plays its part in shaping individual subjectivity, even though nature is usually referred to peripherally, appearing either as subtext or source of metaphor but seldom targeted directly. Mary Pratt is a life-long Maritimer and, while her work does not focus specifically on the natural world, she, like Butala, can be perceived as a regional artist in that her creative imagination has been shaped both by her Fredericton roots and by the four decades of immersion in a Newfoundland environment. However, what claims Pratt in her later years, and what claimed her as a child in Fredericton, is not nature in a wilderness state, but nature in a garden, nature mediated and domesticated.

Mary Meigs, too, loves gardens and has been shaped by memories of the gardens of her childhood. Moreover, while her various life narratives centre around relationships, these narratives invariably demonstrate an artist's sensitivity to a wide variety of natural landscape – from seaside Cape Cod, to rural Brittany, and from the Quebec lake country, to the Australian beaches and to the coastal islands of British Columbia. (Her 2005 retrospective show at the Yvonne Bombardier Cultural Centre featured several of Meigs' landscape watercolours). However, as with Dyck, Meigs' most consistent conduit into the natural world is via another species, which, in Meigs' case is that of birds. It is her love of birds and her fear for their survival that generates Meigs' whole-hearted advocacy of environmental and ecological causes.

ECOLOGICAL THEORETICAL CONTEXTS

Meigs reflects the growing awareness in Canada that ecological damage on a global scale is approaching crisis proportions. David Suzuki has been the major Canadian voice protesting industry's treatment of nature as a commodity to be accessed at will, and warning of the potentially fatal consequences of this view to the future of life on earth. Sociologist Gary Alan Fine classifies industry's perception of nature as one of three possible ways human beings view nature.

Gary Alan Fine: "What is nature like?"

Fine describes the human perceptions of nature from a phenomenological point of view, asking not "What is nature?" but "What is nature like?" (1992, 157). Accordingly, he identifies three different answers to this question, producing a classification that is useful in the subsequent discussion of the work of the four artists. He calls the first classification, "An Imperial Vision; Nature as Usufruct.[3] He labels the second "A Protectionist Vision; Saving Nature from Ourselves," and the third is called "An Organic Vision; Civil Rights for Trees" (1992, 157–60). The first two of these visions, the "imperial" and the "protectionist," have one thing in common: both are anthropocentric, perceiving the world hierarchically, with conscious human beings ranked as the highest form of life, of a different order and separate from the unconscious natural world. These two visions differ only in the way that they envisage humankind's responsibility for its impact on the natural world. The third vision, the "organic," locates human beings as an integral part of the natural world, one species among many.

The "imperial vision" represents nature as a realm created for man's use, to control as he sees fit. In this case the term "man" is appropriate in its reference to the male gender because it is the human masculine principle that is seen as subduing the natural world and the greater the struggle, the more heroic the victory. In Canadian literature, such victories are rare. Nature in these Canadian portrayals is set off against man as the "other," and, with a pioneer imagination gripped by the vision of vast unpopulated regions and the harsh northern climate, this "other" has often taken on a demonic persona. In the first decade of the twenty-first century, other views of nature have appeared in our literature; nevertheless, there always remains an undercurrent of caution in the artistic depiction of the Canadian wilderness, or even of nature in general. This cautious view emerges consistently in the content and subtexts of the work of these four artists.

In the "imperial vision," there is, however, an apparent contradiction. On the one hand, there is a persistent cultural designation of nature as a feminine entity (as in "Mother Nature," or Susanna Moodie's "Divine Mother"), a perception owing much historically to the romantic Wordsworthian view of nature, and, while Margaret Atwood claims this perception is appropriate only in more felicitous climates (1972), it persists nevertheless – in Canada as elsewhere. At present, the designation is more likely to be "Mother Earth" on the basis that the land/earth is the source of nourishment for all life. The maternal designation does not mean, however, that the natural environment is to be taken as female territory, under the control of women. To the contrary, the out of doors is most often seen to be male territory and herein lies the source of the paradox: in patriarchal cultures – and that includes most cultures – feminine entities, whether Woman or Mother Nature, are seen to be under the control of men.

Formulating this idea in another way, Sherry Ortner (1974, 74–83) observes that, as a result of women's physiology, social roles, and psychic structure, women universally have been perceived as being closer to nature and less involved with culture than men. As culture has simultaneously been valued above nature, the result has been the subordination of women. Ortner has been criticized for claiming universality for her theory, but critics such as Vera Norwood claim that Ortner's conclusions remain unchallenged "if one limits them to Western traditions" (1996, 324). Ortner of course rejects this "naturalization" of women, stating that "woman is not any closer to or further from nature than man – both have consciousness – both are mortal" (1974, 87). Aganetha Dyck and Mary Meigs would agree; Sharon Butala and Mary Pratt would not, believing that the biological capacity for reproduction puts women in touch with a feminine principle existing at the heart of the natural world.

Nevertheless, in their early adult years, all four artists perceived the female domain to be in and around house. Canadian rural life was a part of the experience of Butala, Dyck, and Pratt and, for farmers, ranchers, and fishermen, nature is a formidable adversary, defeated only by unremitting physical labour. While women often "pitched in" to do their share, the basic labour was seen to be clearly men's work. As all four subjects come into their identity as artists, however, they take up a liminal position in relationship to nature, initially ceding the territory of the natural world to masculine power, yet coming to claim through their work and through the various life strategies a subjectivity enlarged and deepened by contact with the natural world. As they gain agency in the natural environment, they come to contest what Fine describes as the imperial vision and move variously towards the protectionist and organic visions of nature.

Both these latter visions result from the environmental movement and are reactions against the imperialist view and the resultant appropriation of natural products as practised by industrialized nations. The difference between the protectionist and organic visions is best understood as reflecting the connotative difference between the terms "environment" and "ecology." Cheryll Glotfelty, a critic in the rapidly emerging field of literary ecology,[4] elaborates on this difference, pointing out that

> ... in its connotation, *enviro* is anthropocentric and dualistic, implying that we humans are at the centre, surrounded by everything that is not us, the environment. *Eco*, in contrast, implies interdependent communities, integrated systems and strong connections between constituent parts. (Glotfelty and Fromm 1996, xx)

Accordingly, in Fine's definition of the protectionist view ("*enviro*"), nature is a "special realm – authentic and uncontaminated – fundamentally distinct from the built environment" (Fine 1992, 158). It privileges wilderness areas as favoured places that confer, on humans, spiritual or psychic benefit. In this, it shares much with the pastoral view of nature in which entry into the natural world is seen as an escape, a source of renewal and refreshment. Consequently, humankind has a duty to keep nature as unspoiled as possible, a resource essential to human well-being. For these and other reasons, Sharon and Peter Butala, for example, demonstrated a protectionist view in their determination to save some of the last of the original prairie grasslands; Mary Meigs similarly is a protectionist in her concern over the loss of bird habitat and in her resultant alarm over the fate of the planet.

On the other hand, the organic perception ("*eco*") insists on the primacy of nature, not as an external resource for human beings, but as the source of all life. Accordingly, human beings exist as part of an organic whole (the *eco* to which Glotfelty refers) and are therefore interconnected to, and interdependent with, all other life forms on the planet earth. Fine points out that the logical conclusion of such a view is to incorporate culture into nature, on the basis that what human beings build and do is as natural to them as building a dam is to a beaver, and no more to be censured. Yet human beings seem to feel instinctively that their built environment is qualitatively different from any feature in the natural environment. Those, however, who take an organic view of nature hold that it is humankind who have by their actions separated themselves from nature, that they are not "naturally" separate, and that human beings need to re-establish a harmonious connection with nature for their own benefit. The organic view gave rise to the animal rights movement that, on the basis of claiming equality for all species, agitates against the widespread practices of animal husbandry and the use of animals for scientific research.

The organic view has also inspired a revival of animism, by which all elements of nature are seen to share the basic life force and are therefore imbued with spirit and possess an expressive faculty (Glotfelty and Fromm 2001, 14). This animism characterizes the cosmological views of indigenous people of North America, and the revival of animism has been coupled with a renewed interest in indigenous traditions very different from those typical of cultures dominated by science and industrialism. Environmentalists, such as David Suzuki, find in indigenous cultures wisdom about how to live harmoniously in nature that is an extension of the most enlightened environmental science (Suzuki 1994, 182–84). In her investigations of the history of the Butala land, Sharon Butala becomes aware of the ranch's previous "Amerindian" inhabitants and comes similarly to honour both the indigenous people's understanding of the natural world and their ability to live in harmony with it. In studying the mythological underpinning of the Canadian psyche, essayist John Ralston Saul figures animism even more prominently, seeing this view of nature as the inevitable result of the Canadian northern experience of place.

> Being in the north is a central factor in our animism. It is not simply a geographic option – one among many in which human beings may choose to live. Nor is it merely a progression beyond what lies further south. It is a condition in and of itself, one which makes it impossible to turn away for more than brief periods from an animistic approach to our existence. (Saul 1997, 190)

His point is that the exigencies of living in a northern country make it impossible to conceive of either dominating or romanticizing nature. One can only take up a position of coalition, a position consistently evident, he submits, in both Canadian literature and Canadian visual art. Dyck, in particular, espouses this view.

Dana Phillips: Theory of the "Post-natural"

Over against the organic view of nature is the new concept of the "post-natural," a species of postmodernism discussed at some length by ecocritic Dana Phillips (1996) and a position that Saul would see as impossible for Canadians to maintain for any length of time. The "post-natural" is the most recent variation on the imperial view, a variation whereby the intrusion of scientific and industrial innovation into regions previously thought to be exclusively "natural" has rendered obsolete the perceived distinction between culture and nature. Intrusive practices cited include the tree-farming methods of the lumber industry, genetic manipulation of plant species to produce uniform production and disease-resistant crops, the obliteration of plant biodiversity in the interests of industrial crop management, fish and game farming so that "Deer have become cows," and the industrialization of the sports of hunting and fishing so that these sports are really exercises in "put and take." In describing this post-natural world, Phillips takes an almost apocalyptic tone, pointing to the end of the natural world as we have known it: "Whatever remains of nature, in its former significance as wilderness, exists as such precisely because it is, if only for the time being, unknown to us" (1996, 217) and as he says further, even this "unknown" wilderness is "smudged with our pollutants."

As with much ecocriticism, Phillips' comments are cautionary, almost elegiac, undergirded with a great sense of loss. This note of loss permeates the perception of the natural world in the work of Butala and Meigs, and to a lesser degree that of Dyck and Pratt. These artists would not be reassured by the comments of scientists who accede to this spectre notion of the post-natural world even though it is scientific discovery that makes possible the intrusion of culture into what were thought of as uncontested territories of nature. For example, geneticist Barry Commoner – who insists on the organic character of the universe, and whose first law of ecology is "Everything is connected to everything else." (1971, 33) – sounds a similar note of warning when he cautions against industrial genetic engineering, in particular the production of transgenetic crops, because the overall consequences are beyond the power of humans to predict. His point is that not only is everything connected to everything else but also that these connections are complex, as yet mysterious, and beyond human understanding. The consequences of scientific innovation are, therefore, difficult to foresee.

Despite the notion that "everything is connected to everything else," human beings, in the act of conscious perception, experience a subject/object split, which sets the natural world off from themselves. Interacting physically or psychologically with the material world is one way of bridging this gulf between the experiencing subject and its object. Perhaps that is the reason why genuine contact with another species (as described, for example, by such field researchers as Jane Goodall and Diane Fossey or even by the ordinary pet owner)[5] gives the person involved so much satisfaction. It is a source of satisfaction experienced and reported on by both Aganetha Dyck and Mary Meigs.

Another method of bridging that gulf is to project emotional meaning onto material phenomena outside of ourselves in order to make the world imaginatively habitable. As Northrop Frye points out (1963, 9), such assignation is part of the religious impulse. What interests Frye in the context of literary criticism, however, is that such extension of meaning from the human to the non-human universe is part of the function of art and is the chief characteristic of what he calls "the educated imagination." However, in literature, writers who depict an emotion in the human world as sparking a correspondence in the natural world are sometimes accused of committing the "pathetic fallacy."[6]

Similarly, those rejoicing over genuine contact with animal species are often tempted to anthropomorphize – that is, to assign human characteristics to the non-human world, personification being the corresponding literary device. Personification and the pathetic fallacy can be employed for humorous or dramatic effect but are sometimes dismissed as expressions of sentimentality or wishful thinking. Frye, on the other hand, sees such devices as being motivated by the desire to humanize an indifferent natural world by imaginative acts of association. However, Frye identifies analogy (simile) and identity (metaphor) as the central poetic devices and, citing a Wallace Stevens poem, he identifies this desire for association as "the motive for metaphor" (Frye 1963, 10). The same desire for connection and the same metaphoric turn of mind is manifested in the use of animal and landscape imagery in the art-making of all four artists.

AGANETHA DYCK

In my conversations with Aganetha Dyck, I discovered that any discussion of a particular work or installation included, as is usual with most multi-disciplinary visual artists, an explanation of the genesis of the piece and a description of the process involved. Such artistic processes can sometimes be expressed as formulas so that method is not as important as subject matter or content in interpreting the art. With Dyck, however, such is not the case. Her art-making method has come increasingly to involve a collaborative and interactive process with honeybees (*apis mellifera*), beekeepers, assistants of various kinds, other artists, and with the unexpected resources of the material. In this interaction the elements of play, and of serendipity and chance, are allowed a part in determining the final product. To understand the role of process in Dyck's art practice is to understand both her art and the nature of her artist subjectivity. She enjoys her artistic agency – connecting, exploring, making, doing – and this agency is usually evident in the final product. Dyck's invitation to the York Sculpture Garden in 1997 allowed me to be a part of this bee world and, on that occasion, it was borne home to me even more clearly how central this collaborative process is to the art practice of Aganetha Dyck and how she facilitates the marking of the product by the process so that process/product emerge as an integrated whole.[7]

Further, I concluded that Dyck's work with the bees has enlarged her bodily life as well as her art. Because of an allergy to sunlight, Dyck must monitor carefully any outside activity. Donning a bee suit gives Dyck protection from the sun so that her collaboration with the bees allows her to be unconcernedly out of doors, thus restoring to her a sense of bodily freedom. Primarily, however, the purpose of the bee suit is to allow her direct interaction with the bees and it is this direct contact with the bees that has enlarged both her knowledge of nature and her view of how nature and culture intersect. These knowledges have led necessarily to her reshaping her personal subjectivity. For example, she now questions cultural positionings that heretofore she may have taken for granted, and she places a much higher priority on her contact with, and information about, the natural world. Dyck's process of art-making and her construction of her own subjectivity have proceeded in tandem. To borrow from Jeanne Perreault's critical analysis of feminist life writing, Dyck's visual art can be seen, by extrapolation, as a project in "autography" whereby the act of writing (art-making) "is itself an aspect of the selfhood the writer [artist] brings into being" (1995, 3–4). To reiterate: the art, then, comes to engender new aspects of the self. For Dyck, these new aspects include a sense of her personal integration as a part of nature.

Consequently, Dyck's bee work functions as an exercise in "alterity" wherein the bees act as the powerful "other" in her construction of self. Contact with the bees has offered Dyck an adventure, an excursion into unfamiliar territory that stimulates her imaginatively, intellectually, and even physically so that the domestic woman/artist self is overlaid with the persona of the explorer/seeker. As she explains to Robert Enright, "When you go to an aviary, you are leaving your space and you're going some place very few people go" (Walsh and Enright 2000, 57) and as the interview continues, she refers repeatedly to her bee research as "exploration." The fact that this place she explores is a world in miniature does not detract from it but adds to the sense of mystery and privilege; it is a world so close and yet so far. And, as with other animal researchers such as Goodall and Fossey, Dyck gets great emotional satisfaction from physically bridging the gulf between herself and another species. As she tells Enright,

> … just to have a massage from the bees is the greatest thing I've ever done. I notice beekeepers will take a bee and put it on their hand. For a couple of years, I thought, I wouldn't do that. But they pick out the drones who can't sting. There's all these little things that you learn about the hive. (ibid., 56)

Dyck talked to Sigrid Dahle five years earlier in much the same vein, explaining that working with the bees made one feel really alive. She made reference then to how absorbing bee work was, so much so that it made "time stand still."

DYCK: I really feel alive when I'm there and the beekeeper says the same thing. That when they work with the bees eight hours a day, every day, 9 to 5, the time is gone, the time stands still, doesn't exist. The bees are so touchy feely. It's really primal – that's why I call it a base.

DAHLE: Just being.

DYCK: Just being, existing there. And knowing that you are there. When you watch a movie or something you lose yourself, but when you go in the apiary and open the hive, you get a real sense *you* are *there*. (Dahle 1995, 22)

Here Dyck is making a distinction between two kinds of pleasurable experience – one passive ("watch[ing] a movie") – and the other active ("go[ing] into the apiary and open[ing] the hive"). She privileges the latter. This distinction is analyzed at some length by Csikszentmihalyi in *Finding Flow*, a book on how to create a life with a heightened sense of well-being. "Flow" is the term he gives to this sense of well-being or state of elevated psychic energy that is to be derived from an active involvement in the present. He defines "flow" experiences as follows:

> These exceptional moments are what I call *flow experiences*. In moments like this what we feel, what we wish and what we think are in harmony.... Flow tends to occur when a person's skills are fully involved in overcoming a challenge that is just about manageable.... When goals are clear, feedback relevant and challenges and skills are balanced, attention becomes ordered and fully invested. Because of the total demand on psychic energy, a person in flow is completely focussed.... The sense of time is distorted: hours seem to pass by in minutes. (1997, 29, 31)

Certainly the way Dyck describes her experience in the apiary corresponds to this definition of flow. Czikszentmihalyi observes also that some people are more prone to flow experiences than other. Those who habitually experience flow as part of daily life possess or have achieved what he calls "autotelic" personalities. They are those who choose to pursue activities for their own sake rather than for any extrinsic reward. On the basis of investigation into Dyck's art practice and into the degree to which it colours and reflects her personal experience, one could conclude that Dyck, like many artists and scientists, possesses an "autotelic" personality, a result of engaging fully in most endeavours at her own choosing and for their own sake.

In the present context, therefore, it is significant the high degree to which Dyck privileges her interaction with the bees in a life already full of energy and accomplishment. She joins, thereby, the legion of human beings who perceive working with animals to have a peculiar satisfaction that is obtainable in no other way. While "flow" experiences come in many guises, including the making of art, engagement with another species allows the human being a sense of having penetrated a barrier and pierced a mystery, the mystery that is at the heart of the world of nature. When I pressed Dyck on this, she concurred, "I am just very interested in life forces" (Reid 1996c, 9).

That is not to say that Dyck considers the beehive world to be a model for a utopian human society. In fact, she has observed that it resembles the dystopia created by Margaret Atwood in *The Handmaid's Tale* (1985) in that "the queen bee [is] there, down there (trapped in the hive), not able to get out of there" (Dahle 1995, 23). It is a place she perceives as "very dark" both literally and figuratively "where they do away with each other as soon as they don't need each other" (ibid.). And while Dyck reiterates that she loves the bees, she takes a cautionary view, being all too aware that the bees' power to sting is a fearsome thing, especially when a swarm of bees is involved. In her interview with Enright (Walsh and Enright 2000, 56), Dyck gives a graphic description of being attacked by a swarm of bees. I was present at that happening, and, although very well protected, received my share of the bees' anger.[8] It is evident in Dyck's account how very aware she is of the power of this aspect of nature. Consequently, she has come to realize that the beekeeper's success depends on his knowledge and his accommodation of bee habits and instincts.

Learning from the beekeeper, Dyck, too, accommodates the bees, adapting as she goes ("I know now what they will do on glass ... they don't like corduroy"[9]) and so surrenders considerable control over the shape of the final product. In the final analysis, this surrendering of control is a necessary element in the relationship of humans to nature and this necessity is, for some, regrettable. For Dyck it has wondrous consequences; the bees' construction constantly surprises and amazes her. After coating a piece here and covering it there, she places it in the hive and leaves the bees to work: "I come back the next time and I find out they have made a decision for me. They've done something much better than I could ever have imagined" (Walsh and Enright 2000, 54). Dyck puzzles over the degree to which the bees can be considered artists, and, conversely, the degree to which the practice of art by humans can be thought of as a 'natural' activity. As a sculptor, she is attracted to the bees as fellow beings who build and construct and whose architecture serves as a model for human architects. Musing over these phenomena, she concludes, "there is a whole artificial thought of what nature is" (Dahle 1995, 24).

Similarly, Dyck questions the drawing of a clear line between the practice of art and the practice of science. One of the personal benefits of her collaboration with the bees has been the development of her drive to amass bee knowledge, partly for its own sake but mostly as a conceptual basis for her studio work. As a result she has become an indefatigable researcher, conferring with a wide variety of bee specialists and compiling a lengthy bibliography of bee literature. In the course of this research, she has been led far afield and she has come to depend on scientific enquiry and on its published results.[10] It is clear that in her art practice she is bringing about collaboration between art and science. In our discussions together, she questioned the difference between the two kinds of enquiry:

Are scientists artists and are artists scientists? It is one discussion I am interested in. Someone said in one of the books I am reading that an artist is not responsible but a scientist is responsible for what they discover. A scientist wants control over and an artist wants to investigate into. A scientist will try and control the environment where artists seem to be fighting against altering the environment. (Reid 1996c, 10)

As often happens in free-ranging investigation, Dyck's bee research has led her into associated fields of enquiry. Accordingly, she has become interested in all minuscule creatures and in particular the world of minute microorganisms – microbes and bacteria – upon whose activity the forces of natural regeneration depend. Dyck's interest in gardens comes from her perception of the garden as an arena filled with unseen minute species all working together in an interdependent biodiversity. Similarly, she has come to recognize that human bodies are not independent organisms but are in truth collections of colonies of microbes and bacteria on whose interaction the life of the body depends. Decay and regeneration appear in her practice both as themes in her work and as factors that affect the actual product. Many of the materials with which she works are unstable. As discussed earlier, Dyck accepts with equanimity the continuing chemical changes in finished works, these changes being one manifestation of the profound connection between her art and the material world. Like the German artist, Joseph Beuys, Dyck shares the perception of the bee as one of nature's magic creatures and of honey as a transformative substance, a mark of nature's bounty. Therefore, any threat to the survival of the bee as a species must be regarded as a threat to human welfare as well.

From Manitoba beekeepers, Dyck learned early that the survival of the bees of that province was under threat because of an infestation of bee mites (Reid 1996c, 9). As a result of free trade agreements with the United States, beekeepers became able to import bees across the border, and the scientific speculation in Manitoba was that the imported bees were the carriers of the mites.[11] Dyck's research told her, further, that 95 per cent of wild bees have died in the world so that any threat to domestic bees is all the more crucial. No wonder, then, that Dyck was devastated to learn in 2007 that a mysterious disease called "TCC" or "total colony collapse disease" is threatening the global honeybees' very existence. Accordingly, she now uses all speaking opportunities (such as her acceptance speech for the Governor General's Award) to advocate even more strongly for the bees, suggesting that widespread planting of flowers and indigenous grasses in vacant lots, road allowances, and so on, might serve to reduce the environmental stress on all pollinators.

For Dyck, the bees serve as "canaries of the earth," indicators of planetary illness. However, the link between the fate of the bees and the fate of humankind is more direct than that. Bees are the major pollinators of the earth and the production of foodstuff depends on pollination. As Dyck told me, "We are so connected to them that if they go, we go." (Reid 1996C, 8) In our conversations, she gives a particular application to Commoner's dictum "everything is connected to everything else" while recognizing, as does Commoner, that these connections are complex and mysterious. Like Commoner, she acknowledges that, considered in the context of geological time, life on the planet would continue regardless of mankind's fate:

> The flowers and these creatures could evolve so that we really didn't need the bees anymore. Over time. Now what happens to the life force of a human during that time I don't know. But we don't need dinosaurs any more. So far as we know, we don't need them. (ibid., 10.)

Environmental awareness has marked Dyck's art practice from the beginning. It has been a factor in her recycling of found materials and in the emergence in her work of the themes of violation, decay, disintegration, and regeneration. For Dyck, the recognition of the extreme vulnerability of the honeybee is just a part of an overall recognition of the vulnerability of life on this planet as we know it. To apply Gary Fine's classifications, Dyck takes the *eco* view, perceiving nature as an organic whole of which human beings are an integral part. Furthermore, by virtue of her extraordinary collaboration with the bees, she demonstrates her acceptance of them as equals in aesthetic capability as well as fellow species. In this, she has come to equate their "natural" building with her own "cultural" art-making in a way the appears to incorporate culture into nature, a position which Fine says is the logical conclusion to the organic view of nature.

That is not to say, however, that Dyck takes an anthropomorphic view of the bees; although Dyck draws parallels in her work between bee society and human society, she insisted to Enright that the bees belong to "a totally different order of things" (Walsh and Enright 2000, 55). That does not mean that she elevates the human species above other species, as do the imperialist and protectionist views of nature. She can be seen as taking a protectionist view only in regard to her determination to protest practices damaging to the environment. In fact, Dyck displays an almost maternal subjectivity in her protectionist attitude towards the bees.

As for the post-natural world described by Phillips, Dyck emanates mixed signals. While much of her work honours the hand-made, she is a keen observer of our consumer society, being enough of an innovator to want to make use of modern technology. Son Richard Dyck is a computer artist and creates a virtual world in his art. His technological expertise was requisitioned by Dyck to produce a sound tape, "Sounds from the Hive," for the installation *Inter Species Communication Attempt* (1999–2000). As might be expected, technology has been put to the service of the bees; what Richard Dyck has recorded is the sound of the honeybees at work on the installation.

In choosing to collaborate with the bees and to use the products of the bees' industry as well as beekeeper paraphernalia, Dyck inherits and re-creates an age-old symbology. Those, like Dyck, who are familiar with Biblical imagery, know that in the Old Testament honey is the food symbolizing nature's nurturing abundance. Moses' Promised Land is "the land of milk and honey"; prophets in the wilderness survive on what is available from nature – "locusts and wild honey." Similarly, German artist Joseph Beuys privileges honey as the quintessential source of life-giving warmth. In fact, he views the bees' manufacture of honey and bees-wax as a prototype for the whole of nature's warm, life-preserving proclivities. In the ancient world, honey had mythological significance. In this connection, Beuys refers to an Apis cult, described as "a culture of Venus that concerned itself specially with bees" (Stachelhaus 1987). Beuys sees this ancient bee mythology as signifying a socialist society; accordingly he refigures the concept as a way of reading his work: "My sculptures too are a kind of Apis cult." Dyck does not embrace all the ways in which Beuys superimposes apian nature on human nature, but Beuys is an acknowledged influence (Pagés 2001, 82), and, in at least the first stage of her work with the bees, the world of the bee is invoked, as it is in Beuys' work, as a form of comment on human culture and society. At the same time, Dyck uses bee materials (honey, honeycomb, and bees-wax) in a paradoxical way: to give sculptures both a life-giving aura and to suggest objects in a reliquary.

In most gallery installations outside of Winnipeg, Dyck has reluctantly omitted the use of the actual honey, as it is impractical. Fortunately, the honey presence lingers through the odour of bees-wax and honeycomb, lending a ameliorating sweetness and a whiff of the natural world to all of

Dyck's bee installations. The employment of honeycomb deposits, bees-wax, or both, is now routine in almost all of her sculptures and installations. The effect of the use of honeycomb is to juxtapose disparate elements: the natural overlaid on the cultural; bee society superimposed on human society.

Many of Dyck's works since the late 1990s revolve around an installation entitled *Working in the Dark* (Fig. 25). The title is a play on words, a pun, and while the installation is not humorous, it is characterized by an experimental approach that is akin to play. This approach is apparent in the choice of both material and method. Dyck commissioned writer Di Brandt to respond to the bees in poetry, then transcribed the poem onto tablets using Braille notation. Dyck then inserted these tablets into the hive, thus surrendering the Brandt text to the machinations of the bee. The bees, thereby, were given the power not only over the shape of the finished piece but also over the final version of Brandt's poem, a version in which the original text became fragmented and its meaning changed or lost.

In the gallery pamphlet issued for the opening of *Working in the Dark*, Dyck explains, "This project deals with translation, transcription, transformation and transmutation" (Dyck 1999, 4), all of which could be taken as a description of the preoccupations of her art practice. However, she makes it clear that *Working in the Dark* is to be read as a contemplation of the mystery of bee communication. She has learned that bees "use a communication system which includes dance, vibration, sound and scent" working for the most part "in the dark." And so she speculates: "What is it that *apis mellifera* (honeybees) know because of the unique way that they are constructed and socialized that we can't access because of our species limitations, our uniquely *homo sapiens* (human) subjectivity?"

I find it significant that Dyck does not accept "our species limitations" as irreparable. She yearns to know how to communicate with the bees and asks rhetorically: "how does one translate and transcribe from one [our] sign system to another?" (ibid.). It is this yearning, coupled with intellectual curiosity, that galvanizes this stage of her practice and shapes her subjectivity. Her work with the bees and the art engendered by this collaboration is bringing Aganetha Dyck ever closer to a personal understanding of "what natural is." Such an understanding is crucial to her construction of self in that, as a human being, she believes herself to be a part of the integrated whole that is nature.

SHARON BUTALA

Coming to an understanding of nature is as important an issue in the work of Sharon Butala as it is in the art practice of Aganetha Dyck. While, however, Butala's experience of nature includes contact with animals, both domestic and wild, it is the land itself that speaks most continuously and deeply to Butala's psyche and shapes her idea of nature. She credits her twenty-odd years of "living in the landscape" (2000a, 176) – specifically the grasslands of southwestern Saskatchewan – with shaping her subjectivity, building her soul, and inspiring her art: "It is the best thing in my new life" (1994a, 61).

Consequently, the land is afforded a place front and centre in Butala's narratives about her quest for self. Cheryll Glotfelty has a similar comment on how environmental historians (a new breed, surely) position the land in their accounts of any particular region. She observes that "[In] studying the reciprocal relationships between humans and the land, [they are] considering nature not just as the stage upon which the human story is acted out, but as an actor in the drama" (Glotfelty and Fromm 1996, xxi). John Ralston Saul expresses the same notion from a Canadian perspective, making the point that this is particularly apparent in art from a northern country: "The place is never the background. It is a leading character and the humans unfold in images which include the whole" (Saul 1997, 189). Saul cites the Butala *oeuvre* as one example of this use of place (ibid., 195).

The Butala prairie land – including the hay farm, the ranch proper, the Frenchman River running through, the plants, the rocks, the wide skies, the golden light, together with the animals residing there – are what Butala thinks of as "nature" and what she constitutes as "place." This non-human world is an integrated system imbued with a life force that she experiences as "presence" (Butala 2000a, 65) and that appears distinctly as an actor in her personal drama. Earlier, it was established that Butala, like our other three artists, displays a penchant for "alterity," the proclivity to construct herself in relation to others. In that earlier discussion, the significant "others" were identified as Butala's mother and her husband Peter. The landscape of the Butala ranch, situated as part of the Great Plains, emerges also as a significant "other," its palpable presence a powerful force in the shaping of Butala's sense of self.

It is a force both benign and mysterious. In a chapter in *Wild Stone Heart* entitled "The Wild," Butala recounts a dream about a curious figure called "the Lord of the Wild." She connects this figure to a strong sense of presence she experiences some years later in the special area of the Butala land she calls "the field." The two events prompt her to muse over the character of this spirit, marvelling over the masculine power of "the Lord of the Wild" and contrasting it with the standard characterization of the land as Mother Earth. She theorizes in a Jungian vein that perhaps men and women conceive of nature in terms of the opposite gender: "What one does not truly understand is the essence of the other gender and so one projects that onto the other unknown – the essence of nature" (2000a, 85).

Against this, however, Butala insists that nature is an objective reality and that our perceptions of it are more than projections. However, it is apparent in both *The Perfection of the Morning* and *Wild Stone Heart* that her perceptions of nature's reality are at odds with her portrait of the rural society in which she finds herself. For Butala, nature presents a feminine face, one that is predominantly nurturing and therapeutic. On the other hand, the masculine-dominated ranching society is forbidding; she is an outsider who never really wins acceptance. In the chapter "Anomie" in *The Perfection of the Morning*, Butala describes the alienation and psychological malaise that afflicted her after her move to the ranch, and, while her writing offers her escape and consolation, it is her contact with the landscape that ultimately heals her.

Butala feels the beneficent and maternal quality of this contact most acutely on an occasion when the land is seemingly hostile. Sharon and Peter are driving home after a winter holiday to find that the road into the hay farm has been flooded. On impulse, Sharon decides to walk home across the fields. She gets into trouble crossing an icy ditch but struggles on. Nearing home, she is still very aware of being alone in the bright darkness under the moon when the whole emotional atmosphere changes:

> I began to feel – and this is not easy to describe – a kind of warmth, as one feels when someone loving is near, like a child basking in the warmth of a mother's love or a much loved wife held in the arms of her husband. I looked up and to the right and knew it was coming from the moon. (2000a, 167)

And, while she equates the love she felt as comparable to the love from a mother or a husband, it is the maternal quality of it that she stresses in retrospect "I felt a much loved child again" (171). She acknowledges that the experience was a kind of enchantment, but, as with all her numinous contacts with nature, she insists on the objective reality of the happening.

Nonetheless, Butala rejects any sentimental, romanticized writing about nature as "New Age trash, or just trash" (Reid 1996b, 1). However, in reviewing *The Perfection of the Morning*, one critic finds something of the romantic in the way she shapes her narrative:

> The careful arrangement of her book reflects the shape of one kind of Romantic plot: regaining psychic health guided by natural powers, as in Wordsworth's *Prelude*, which celebrates a similar return to nature in restoring health. (Taylor 1995, 202)[12]

Butala's "Romantic plot" reaches its climax in her story of the moon's beneficence. In the Roman world, the moon was associated with the goddess Diana, and it is the female power in nature that Butala is describing here, a power that somehow confirms the worthiness of her own feminine subjectivity. Perhaps that is why she says: "Most miraculously of all, I could understand my womanhood in the light of the rhythms of nature, as part of nature" (2002, 71). As a writer, however, Butala is equally a product of culture and asserts, "Of all the things in life, I love books best and writing" (2000, 183). She would agree with Sherry Ortner that women should be as closely identified with the production of culture as men (Ortner 1974, 87). In the face of feminists such as Ortner, however, who warn that any special identification of the female with nature is inimical to the social positioning of women, Butala insists that the spirit of the land resonates in a particular way with the female psyche and that contact with the land has special psychic benefits for women.

On the other hand, Butala realizes fully that making a living off the land is traditionally a masculine enterprise demanding hard physical work and that farming and ranching land is therefore generally acknowledged to be male territory. She remarks ruefully, "It seems all land belongs to men" (2000a, 113). However, such appropriation is clearly seen as a product of patriarchal tradition rather than as the result of a quality inherent in nature. In her description of Peter's job as a rancher in *The Perfection of the Morning* and in such fiction as *The Gates of the Sun* and various stories in *Queen of the Headaches* Butala nevertheless pays tribute to the male physical courage such work demands, because of the hard labour involved and the necessity of being out of doors in all weather. Winter visits the most hardships; freezing to death, for example, is always a real possibility. In these descriptions, nature seems neither male nor female but resembles instead Margaret Atwood's hostile "Nature as Monster" (Atwood 1972, chap. 2).

Where Butala positions nature as intrinsically masculine is in her discussion of the concept of the "wild." The wild is presented as a manifestation of those forces of the natural world that are untouched by humankind and are unconcerned with beneficence towards humans. It is beyond human understanding – unknowing and unknowable. Butala's sees her dream figure, "The Lord of the Wild," as an embodiment of those forces. This male figure has a persona to be feared, not because it is hostile, but because it has "great vigour and strength ... unstoppable and unequivocal" (2000a, 83). And yet, as Butala observes, one yearns to be close to the wild (ibid., 87) as allowing access to an unseen presence or essence that lays at the heart of the mystery that is nature.

Eventually, Butala discovers that one undisturbed and uncultivated hundred-acre field on the Butala property is still an expression of the wild, even though civilization surrounds it. She devotes herself to walking this field and, in a low-key way, walking the field becomes for Butala an adventure, just as exploring the world of the honeybee becomes Aganetha Dyck's adventure. Both artists' conceptions of self are enlarged imaginatively and psychically through contact with these worlds and, as with Dyck, it is animals that provide Butala with a magical breakthrough, this form of contact with the wild bringing with it a sense of privilege. One experience in particular comes to epitomize the enchantment of the wild – the "perfection" of a life lived close to nature:

> One day I stood across the river on a high bank picking chokecherries while on the other, lower side a white-tailed doe, unaware she was being watched, fed at a tree and talked steadily to her fawn. The sound was somewhere between a whinny and a whisper. I had never heard it before and never have since. (1994a, 155)

Another sighting gives Butala a sense of triumph. After years of walking her field and thinking it held no more surprises, she is astonished to see "the largest snake I have ever seen in the flesh, perhaps six feet long, four inches in diameter ... beautifully striped" (2000a, 36). It was a bull snake, "so shy or rare or both" that even Peter Butala, who lived his entire life on the ranch, had never seen one. She again feels privileged at the rare sighting, but it is a feeling edged with uneasiness. The field reveals itself once more as a place of hidden presences and, as with Barry Commoner, nature again is shown as complex and mysterious even after long acquaintance.

While Peter Butala may never have seen a bull snake, Sharon represents him as being fully familiar with the wild and completely at home in the prairie landscape. Again, nature is perceived as having an affinity with the masculine because of the fact that it has been largely men who have made their living off the land. Whether, however, the worker on the land is male or female, Butala makes the point that their experience yields knowledge of the natural world that cannot be duplicated any other way, even by science. It is this conviction that leads her to lament publicly the demise of the family farm and to devote the second last chapter of *The Perfection of the Morning* to an analysis of the changes in agricultural practices in Saskatchewan and of the damage large-scale industrialized farming has done to both the land and the knowledge base of rural society.

The primary object of ecological concern for Sharon and Peter Butala was the preservation of the "wild" as represented by the virgin shortgrass prairie. As a rancher, Peter Butala was very aware of the ecological value of his holdings and kept most of his land unbroken, allowing only selective grazing so that wildlife ecologists were able to determine that the Butala ranch is still one of the best tracts of shortgrass remaining in Canada. When Peter was nearing retirement, he became concerned as to how to preserve the shortgrass for future generations, a cause to which he devoted his life. Consequently, after much negotiation and in conjunction with many Saskatchewan government agencies, in 1996 "The Old Man on his Back Shortgrass and Prairie Preserve" was formed, a conservancy dedicated to the protection of this important natural asset. His achievement won Peter Butala many conservation awards, including an award in 2002 from Agriculture and Food, Canada, a Government of Canada agency.[13] In addition, the Canadian edition of *Time* magazine named both Peter and Sharon Butala as among "Canada's Heroes" for "restoring their corner of southwest Saskatchewan to its natural state" (July, 2004).

The significance of the Butala conservancy in the present context is as a testament to the view of nature to which Sharon Butala, in conjunction with Peter Butala, is committed. In taking a stand against the agricultural practices of the dominant business culture in Canada and elsewhere, Butala practices a form of *testimonio* as outlined by Doris Sommer (1988) and John Beverley (1992), whereby the individual, in testifying to her experience, goes against the dominant culture. As Sommer puts it, "To save the culture, she must violate it" (Sommer 1988, 123). In the case of the Butala testimony, it is the rural community who ultimately benefits from land conservancy (the culture being saved). Nevertheless, many in the rural community see themselves as "violated" and are therefore, as Butala reports, the most implacably hostile at the prospect of so much land becoming unavailable for purchase and cultivation (2000a, 104–5).

Similarly, Butala can be seen as taking up a standpoint positioning. From an environmental point of view, her conservation advocacy is, in Sara Ruddick's terms "an engaged vision of the world opposed to and superior to dominant ways of thinking" (Ruddick 1999, 406). Moreover, through conservation advocacy, Sharon Butala's triple subjectivities of environmentalist, wife, and artist come together. In such texts as the chapter entitled "Old Man on his Back" in *Wild Stone Heart*, Butala gives witness to what is fundamentally her husband's vision. She thus presents a complex construction of herself whereby she functions simultaneously as writer, ecologist, and wife.

As a couple, then, Sharon and Peter Butala seemed clearly to share what Gary Fine has described as the "protectionist" vision. Here, "wild" nature is seen as a "special realm – authentic and uncontaminated, fundamentally distinct from the built environment" (Fine 1992, 158), a realm the Butalas protected by "restraining their activities." They have more than fulfilled this responsibility. That does not mean, however, that they saw eye to eye with all members of the environmental movement. Butala has more than once expressed scorn for what she calls "city-slicker" environmentalists, urban dwellers who hand out advice to farmers and ranchers without knowing anything about what it means to live on the land close to nature.[14]

Because Peter Butala was a lifelong rancher, one might suppose that an "imperialist" positioning tempered their protectionist vision. Certainly Peter Butala made business decisions about the use of his land and the management of herds of cattle, who are, after all, raised for slaughter. Probably, however, Peter Butala's vision of nature in regards to raising cattle more properly is seen as one manifestation of an organic view wherein killing for food is seen as a natural prerogative of the human species, as with other animals. And while he would not join any animal rights movement, there was certainly a strong lifelong bond between Peter Butala, the animals he managed, and the land they all shared. Sharon envied this bond, one that comes only from a lifetime of living on the land. The most paradisal real life moment in Sharon Butala's writing is the one, mentioned earlier, in which she describes coming unexpectedly upon Peter Butala asleep among his cattle, with his horse and the wild antelope grazing nearby:

All of them were oblivious of my presence and paying no attention to each other, as if they were all members of the same contented tribe on that still, hot afternoon under that magnificent dome of sky and in the midst of those thousands of acres of short, pale grass. (1994a, 27)

Fine's notion of the organic vision of nature asserts that human beings have separated themselves *from* nature and are not separate *by* nature (1992, 160). In Sharon's depiction of her husband, Peter Butala emerges as one who has lived in the natural harmony envisioned in this organic view. Sharon, herself, can only approximate that way of life, coming as she does to the land as an adult and seeing it with a writer's eye. Even, however, as a latecomer to this sense of union, Sharon Butala locates "Nature" both as a primary physical environment and an affective Presence – a dominant "other" in the construction of her subjectivity.

MARY PRATT

While Mary Pratt sees her environment with a painter's eye, her positioning of herself in relation to the natural world is similar to that of Sharon Butala in that they both come into closer contact with untamed nature through the agency of their husbands. Both were urban women who, after their marriages, moved to unfamiliar cultures and landscapes, experiencing what appears to have been an inescapable sense of alienation. Butala walked resolutely out of the house into this landscape in order to feel more at home in it. She did, after all, have memories of a childhood in the northern Saskatchewan bush country. Pratt, on the other hand, was shaped as a child by the ordered Fredericton surroundings of Waterloo Road and, through choice or necessity or both, remained for the most part securely in the domestic world. The world of nature now comes to her through the windows of the house, as it were, supplying her most importantly with the natural light that acts both as her muse and the source of her aesthetic. Pratt's spiritual reaction to the presence of light reflects an almost animistic view of the immanent power of nature.

The natural world came to her also through the presence of her husband, a figure representing to her both the male "artist as hero" and the rugged Newfoundland lifestyle and landscape. As she says in her diary, they lived in Salmonier "on the edge of the Newfoundland wilderness" (Pratt 2000,

39) and one senses that she fought to keep that wilderness at bay, as did generations of Canadian women before her.

For Christopher Pratt, however, the presence of that wilderness and the equivalent Newfoundland sense of place are essential, both personally and as an artist. In *Christopher Pratt: Personal Reflections on a Life in Art* (1995), he makes countless entries referring to the Newfoundland masculine experiences of nature – fishing, hunting, sailing – and much of his art records the interaction between Newfoundland culture and the natural environment. His "reflections" serve to illuminate the Pratt family's Salmonier environment, the environment in which Mary Pratt first defined herself as artist, and while she does not embrace her husband's view of the culture and the landscape from which it springs, these supply her with the "wildness" her psyche needs to become an artist. Christopher Pratt may not be the embodiment of the masculine "Lord of the Wild," Butala's archetypal dream figure, but he and the Newfoundland spirit function in much the same way – that is, as a spur to feminine artistic creativity. Pratt says as much to friend Sandra Gwyn: "I don't think I'd have been a painter at all if I hadn't come here. This is an abrupt, dramatic, light and dark kind of society" (Gwyn and Moray 1989, 11) and Pratt contrasts it with the more sheltered and conventional Fredericton society in which she grew up. In the same vein, Pratt muses in her diary on the comfortable and conventionally feminine domesticity of her sister, who now lives in their mother's Waterloo Road home:

> April 1, 1997. I love her life. *But I never could live like that* … [emphasis added]. The dark preference for. the exotic – the unacceptable – drives the blood through me. I embrace it without a backward glance, rushing to it as surely as iron to a magnet…. And though I live on the edge of the sea and look with fascinated longing at the spray, I am still like a ribbon of fire that flares and glows and calms and flares again along the wet sand of the beach. (Pratt 2000, 40)

The fire simile in this passage cannot help but bring to mind Pratt's series of fire paintings, her most compelling landscapes. As I indicated earlier in Chapter Two, these paintings can be read as symbolic of the emergence from domesticity of Pratt's artistic self, of her throwing off of emotional restraint or of both. In this diary excerpt written in 1997, "the exotic" and "the unacceptable" are shown to be essential to Pratt's artistic subjectivity and are connected to the concept of "the wild." I would argue that Pratt's notion of the "exotic," the element that she needs to be an artist, is an expression of the untamed quality to be found both in Christopher Pratt, "the most masculine of men" (Reid 1996a, 45) and in the Newfoundland wilderness just outside her door. In the latter perception, Pratt confirms John Ralston Saul's understanding that "Canadian sensibility is of the edge, the unknown, the uncontrolled" (1997, 204).

Accordingly, I find it noteworthy that, from the earliest years of her career, fish paintings have formed a significant part of her artistic output. These still lifes are her way of bringing something of this masculine territory into her female domain. Certainly, fish have been a staple in the Pratt family diet; Christopher was an ardent angler and brought his catches home for Mary to clean and cook. So it was to be expected that, in an art practice taking its subject matter from domestic realities, a basic family food would make an appearance on the canvas. However, as various critics of Pratt's work have observed, the fish paintings can be read as richly symbolic. Sandra Gwyn sees them as "icons of a local identity and of a state of mind" as well as containing echoes of Biblical symbolism (Gwyn and Moray 1989, 31–32). Tom Smart sees the more mutilated fish images as sexual metaphors, with overtones of carnality and violation (Smart 1995, 85).

At a more immediate level there is, however, a lyric quality to many of the earlier fish paintings that can best be read as a tribute to the beauty and wonder of nature in the wild, and it is Christopher who routinely brings this emblem into Mary's kitchen. Here is Christopher writing in 1965: "It was one of those June days when the sun burned through a mist that seemed to be a ghost.... We caught a lot of strong silver trout – flawless, dappled, iridescent, mimicking the sky, living ice" (C. Pratt 1995, 22). The flavour of the wild and the beauty of the "flawless" fish still persist in paintings such as *Trout in a Bucket* (Gwyn and Moray 1989, 64) and *Two Trout* (ibid., 157) or any of a dozen or so other fish paintings that depict the whole fish. In *Herring on a Salt Bag* (Fig. 26), the fish are presented as Newfoundland icons, representing, as Pratt tells us, "the first unspoiled catch to be seen since the bay had been polluted the year before" (ibid., 46–47). In rejoicing, Pratt displays her awareness of the environmental problems plaguing Newfoundland's fishing industry. Other paintings that depict filleted fish (fish in or ready for the pan) allow Pratt the opportunity to depict the play of light on flesh and so can be read on another level to be about the aesthetics of painting.

Increasingly in such paintings as *Summer Fish*, however, filleted fish are presented as what Pratt herself calls "mutilated offerings" (ibid., 103). This portrayal of mutilation culminates in *Another Province of Canada* (Fig. 21), described earlier. As has been established, both sexual violation of women and the violation of nature exist in this painting as a subtext. The "other province" is clearly male-occupied territory. As noted earlier, critic Tom Smart couples *Another Province of Canada* with *The Service Station* (Fig. 20), the portrait of the gutted moose, and reads the intent in both as "call[ing] forward images of murder and rape" (Smart 1995, 85). In *The Service Station*, Pratt's notion of "mutilated offerings" is extended to the practice of hunting and the killing of wild land animals, another aspect of the male Newfoundlander's territorializing the out of doors. The theme of violation in the killing of animals is part of what Pratt calls "the dark side" of human interaction with nature (Reid 1996a, 14–15), a side she observed as a child in Fredericton, accompanying her grandmother into Mr. Sweed's butcher shop. Pratt insists that the shop "was not a tragic place" (Pratt 2000, 73), but the images of the hanging carcasses have nevertheless been engraved on her memory along with the smells:

> Their forelegs hung down. They had no heads and no insides. Their ribs could be seen, shimmering behind casings of pink flesh. There was sawdust on the floor, its fresh sweetness almost overriding the thick smell of fat and flesh. (ibid.)

In terms of their dynamics, Pratt's raw meat/poultry paintings function as extensions of her fish paintings, with the same combination of aesthetic pleasure in light and texture but with a darker subtext of violation and death.

The vision of nature implicit in this series of fish and meat paintings is ambiguous, perhaps conflicted. Certainly, Pratt is not a candidate for the animal rights movement even though she is fully aware of animal slaughtering procedures. As a practical homemaker, she knows what is required to put meat on the table and she accepts the darker side of the process. However, these are processes to be equated with male power; even in the butcher shop, it is Mr. Swede who is in charge of the animal carcasses. Towards the exercise of male power she is less accepting. The paintings with strong overtones of violence and violation can be read as equating the exploitation of animals with the subjugation of women. In this she takes an eco-feminist position, one that views both the ravaging of natural resources and the subjugation of women as manifestations of the masculine/patriarchal domination of culture (Diamond and Orenstein 1990, passim). However, Sherry Ortner's warning that identifying with nature makes women vulnerable to societal subordination, and her recommendation that women choose instead to identify with culture, is only partly congenial to Pratt's outlook.

In Gary Fine's terms, Pratt challenges the imperialist view of nature and takes up a protectionist position through her fish paintings and through voicing her distress at the effects of over-fishing and pollution of Newfoundland's offshore waters. There is, moreover, a level at which Pratt aligns the female self with the rhythms and dictates of nature, seeming thereby to go against Sherry Ortner. Like Butala, Pratt considers women's reproductive capacity as one of the primary elements determining female subjectivity and she associates this capacity with a kind of erotic sensibility peculiar to women. As she explained to me, "My analogy of Eve giving Adam the apple, that is what it is to me." Eve engages Adam erotically in the world (Reid 1996a, 21). In her art practice, this characterization of femininity is a subtext in her fruit paintings, one that co-exists, and is associated with, the image of fruit as celebration of nature's bounty. The manner in which Pratt paints fruit – presented in containers as if they were ceremonial offerings – makes the viewer understand that juicy, round apples, oranges, plums, pears, watermelon, cantaloupe or pomegranates have reference to what Smart calls "nature's abundance and fertility." In this, there is a clear representation of female sexuality as a manifestation of nature, a perception basic to women's self-identity.

As with the fish paintings, however, Smart observes the presence also of "metaphors of domestic aggression" in "the images of the cutting and preparation of fruit" (1995, 131), and here Pratt appears to exemplify Mary Kelly's theory that victimization is inherent in representations of female sensibility in painting by women. The suggestion of sexual violence is heightened through Pratt's use of images in which the flesh of the cut fruit is red (pomegranates or watermelon), in which seed spill out of the cut fruit, or in which the paring knife is still in the fruit.[15] Paintings that use these devices suggest again that Pratt equates society's subjugation of nature with the patriarchal subordination of women and is another indication that Pratt contests aspects of the imperialist view of nature as described by Gary Fine.

Landscape paintings as such do not form a major part of Pratt's body of work. The ones she has produced have a distinct sense of place – the crashing of waves on the Newfoundland coast, a snowstorm, the floating icebergs offshore – all are familiar east coast scenes. These suggest a power in nature beyond human control. The iceberg and snow paintings are often considered companion pieces to Pratt's series of fire drawings, depicting, as Smart suggests, the extremes of hot and cold and the two primary sources of natural light intensity (1995, 123). The fire drawings are a major series in Pratt's overall production of work but are not exactly pieces about landscape. They are more studies of a natural phenomenon to be read in some instances as records of a family ritual or, later, as metaphors for Pratt's emotional or psychological state.

Despite the metaphorical associations between female sexuality and animal and fruit images to be found everywhere in her work, Pratt cannot be seen as aligning herself unilaterally with nature over culture. For Pratt, nature in the wild is still male territory; the domestic realm remains the quintessential female domain. The form of nature that she does embrace wholeheartedly is the garden, and while the garden is seldom a central subject of her painting, it often forms the background, the site in which domestic objects connect with the organic world, an external source of beauty and light as glimpsed through a window. As such, the garden is presented by Pratt as the middle ground between the domestic space of the house and the rough terrain of the Newfoundland wilderness. It is part of nature but only as shaped by human hands. Hence, the garden is shown as the place in which nature and culture interact.

Pratt's positioning of the garden is one that finds echoes in the comments of ecocritic Frederick Turner. In searching for a model of how human beings can properly relate to nature, Turner holds up the act of gardening as the optimal prototype because it maintains a balance between scientific left-brain activity and right brain aesthetic and artistic sensibility. It is this kind of balance that Turner would wish to bring into play in all mediations between nature and human culture (Turner 1996, 49–51). Mary Pratt makes a plea for a similar equilibrium in a convocation address at Mount St. Vincent University, revealing again her protectionist vision. She acknowledges that "the greatest battle of all is the battle to save the planet," and she laments "the now-terrifying rate at which species are disappearing" (Pratt 2000, 126). She commends to her audience the values inherent in artistic creativity, the same right-brain activity prized by Turner, as showing the way to the survival of the planet.

In the creation of her gardens, Pratt clearly brings into play this marriage of nature with culture or, in Turner's terms, of right-brain and left-brain activity. She explains that, as children, she and her sister were taught the scientific basis of gardening, whereby "fertilizers and poisons and soil conditioners were not just whims … they had to be applied at exactly the right time and for exactly the right reasons." She grew up knowing about mildew and garden pests, and "what was necessary to grow fat, firm vegetables" (ibid., 77).

Her sister's report that the old Waterloo Road spruce tree had been blown down prompts these reminiscences; its demise gives Pratt a jolt (ibid., 75). Their childhood garden was the first of the three gardens in Pratt's life, the other two being an acre of garden surrounding the house at Salmonier, and the garden Pratt designed for the property around her St. John's house. The Fredericton garden has not been a painting subject, but Pratt paints a vivid word picture for her readers, envisaging the long perennial border planted with specific varieties of delphiniums and iris, the wide expanse of lawn, the rose trellis, the vegetable garden, and the play area in the shade (ibid.). The notion of paradise as a garden is as old as literature, one familiar to Pratt from her Christian upbringing, and there are paradisal overtones in Pratt's description, especially when associated with the long ago childhood for which one yearns in old age.

In her work, Pratt affords only limited views of the Salmonier garden. However, Pratt's friend, Sandra Gwyn, describes it evocatively as an anomaly in the surrounding Newfoundland barrens, as was Pratt herself:

> … some quirk of topography has created a kind of micro-climate: rhododendrons bloom in the garden as they do no where else on the island and the lawns that sweep down to the river's edge suggest, reeds and all, a gentle English water meadow. (Gwyn and Moray 1989, 3)

The Salmonier garden must have been as consoling an element for Pratt as the prairie grasslands were for Butala, both women feeling the effects of being transplanted to an alien culture. In Pratt's painting, this garden appears in a truncated fashion as a setting for still lifes such as *Trifle in the Garden* (ibid., 77), and for her wedding series, *Aspects of a Ceremony*, both of which similarly juxtapose nature and culture. In the latter paintings, the garden setting serves to enhance the bridal mood, rather than give any clear sense of the scope of the garden. The most romantic of the series is one of Pratt's rare landscapes entitled *Morning* (ibid., 148). As primarily a study of the effect of early morning light on fields and trees, this image serves to conceptualize the garden as paradisal once more.

In general, however, gardens exist for Pratt not primarily as subjects to be painted but rather as creative stimuli, physical settings conducive for her work as artist. When she moved to the St. John's house, there was only a scraggly lawn:

> What I missed when I moved here was the dappled light and movement and grass tumbled curves of the river outside my window in Salmonier. The garden was my first priority. I need to see some beauty, some energy and life when I paint. (Weiler 1998, 82)

This comment is contained in an article devoted to Pratt's St. John's garden in a Canadian home decorating periodical. The article is complete with photographs and a detailed description of its landscaping in which the basic concept is a river of rock running diagonally across the property. The photographs reveal a showplace garden with masses of flowers edging the "make believe brook" and a shady grove of trees at the rear (ibid., 87). Author Merike Weiler makes it clear that in planning the garden Pratt has utilized the same understanding of composition, movement, and colour employed in her art practice, and that the garden, while built and maintained by others, is as much a product of her artistic sensibility as are her paintings. In constructing her subjectivity, Pratt reveals that she named herself as gardener (Pratt 2000, 118) before she named herself as artist, one action being the harbinger of the other.

Only one painting reproduced in *A Personal Calligraphy* takes the garden as its subject, *Yellow Bench in Garden* (ibid., 77), and it again blends manufactured objects – the bench and fence – with the natural plant products. The main point of the piece, however, is as a study of afternoon light, light being Pratt's major preoccupation as a painter. Accordingly, the diary entries are full of references to this garden as it appears in the circle of the seasons. Both her painter's eye and her command of language are apparent in these descriptions as she notes the precise shadows the leaves make and the somewhat neglected summer garden. Similarly, the next entry describes the northern lights, as seen from the front yard by the river: "through the peach-leafed willow, the sky was pale yellow to green, and the sheets and curves of shooting lights came and went – almost pulsing in and out of view" (ibid., 89). Many of the journal entries record seasonal change, including the springtime return of the songbirds as seen through her studio window.

Pratt is always very aware of the weather outside as she works in her studio: Windows to the out of doors are essential to her process of art-making.

The most dramatic entry, however, tells of her leaving the studio after dark and being lured down the gravel path and into the front garden by the warmth of the night and the smell of growing things. Then Pratt becomes aware of the moon "still low in the sky and blurred by the haze and not silver but yellow – peach yellow" (ibid., 92). She tells of venturing out alone in the dark, listening, as she says, for moose. She walks unsteadily, assisted by a cane, irresistibly drawn to the river, hoping to see in it the reflection of the moon and the stars:

> I felt alien and alone. Well, I was alien and alone. I don't walk out at night. I never do. It doesn't occur to me. I was forbidden as a young girl and rightly so.... But there I was, quite insecure in my own garden. (ibid.)

Pratt persists and reaches the river:

> I knelt down, using my cane to steady myself, and put one hand in the water, sending arcs of light into the centre of the river, shivering the moon. (ibid., 93)

Pratt's description of her fleeting late night adventure is reminiscent of Butala's experience of struggling through the flooded countryside and then feeling the beneficence of the moon. Both women reveal a subjectivity that is emotionally open to the world of nature, and both feel a special enchantment in the presence of the moon, the ancient symbol of female power.

MARY MEIGS

Mary Meigs demonstrated a similar awareness of nature through her various and recurring descriptions of place. In the first instance, her life writing concentrated on her "coming out" narrative. Invariably, however, her descriptions of evolving relationships, sexual and otherwise, are combined with, and are partially the product of, an awareness of place. As with Pratt, this awareness centres most typically around a house, starting with the houses of Meigs' childhood and extending through a variety of homes up to and including her residence in Montreal and her summer home, "La Sucerie," in the Eastern Townships of Quebec. Again, like Pratt, Meigs extends the territory of the house through its windows out into the garden, always a necessary adjunct, in which nature and culture are joined. When, in *The Medusa Head*, she recounts her farewell to her beloved Cape Cod house, she presents the house and garden as a unit, referring to "the house and what lay outside it – the dappling of the light and shade on the locust trees and the birds in their marvelous Cape Cod variety" (1983, 38). Similarly, in describing "The Peak," her favourite childhood house, she recalls it as being permeated with the fragrance of the garden, "the perfume of box, lilac, roses and peonies" (1981, 40). In her happy dreams, this joining of house and garden appears as "sunlit rooms, radiant landscapes and birds" (ibid.), a paradisal vision. Meigs was a lifelong gardener and she was prone to retreat to this avocation after battling on behalf of her societal concerns: "And I am back again cultivating my garden" (ibid., 99).

With Pratt, the paradise stops at the edge of the garden where the Newfoundland wilderness takes over. Meigs extends the paradisal borders by locating house and garden in a felicitous landscape or, as she puts it, in "the surrounding peace that I choose by imperious necessity" (1981, 40). She wished to experience the natural world, as part of her daily life and her financial resources and, earlier, those of her family were such that it was usually possible to locate the various homes, especially the summer homes, in sought-after natural settings. Of course, from time to time other considerations dictated the location of the Meigs' domiciles; for example, during World War II, Mr. Meigs' career took him and his family to Washington, D.C., and no amount of horticultural effort could produce a garden or even a respectable lawn in the sun-baked backyard clay of their Georgetown mansion. Similarly, other priorities (one of which was her relationship with Marie-Claire Blais) influenced Meigs to buy a home in Montreal. Even in this urban setting, however, she evidently kept a garden, was visited by bobolinks and song sparrows, and looked out her window towards the modest Montreal "mountain." In describing these settings, she displays an ingrained sensitivity to the earth and to changes in climate and seasons that find echoes in her own mood changes:

> During those long periods of hot weather without rain, I feel the thirst of the trees and flowers and of the wilting lettuce in my own heart and I am unloving and cranky. When it rains or the wind changes it is as though a fresh spring bubbles up inside me. (Meigs 1981, 204)

Even during the disappointing Canadian visit of her Australian lover when she is immobilized by this visitor's anger, Meigs becomes momentarily revived by the sight of an eagle and by Salt Spring Island's landscape with its "dancing blue water" and the "blood red" arbutus trees shimmering in the strong sunshine (Meigs 1997, 111).

Meigs' description of her psychic responses to the natural world seem often to participate in a romantic perception of nature whereby one escapes horrific aspects of civilization into the more innocent non-human world. For example, sometime during the Vietnam War, she and Marie-Claire Blais were ensconced in a cottage in the Gaspe where Meigs found her "perfect peace in one of the oases where I have been able to work happily" (1983, 16). She describes her diary entries of the time as twofold: one page records the daily events of "fog, calm, rain … and of birds seen," while the facing page contains pasted cut-outs from the newspaper reports and photographs of the war. These diary pages were published subsequently by the War Resister's League, one of the many pacifist organizations supported by Meigs. Physically removed from a country at war, Meigs depicts her life at this Gaspe oasis as almost Utopian, set as it was in one of the remoter regions of Canada. In this, Meigs is expressing a more American sensibility in the tradition of Thoreau than a typically Canadian view of nature. As John Ralston Saul argues, Canada's northern positioning does not lend itself to a pastoral view of nature, nor, as he comments on an essay on Canada's lack of heroes, does its political history lend itself to Utopian aspirations (Saul 1997, 140).

This version of the romantic perception of nature (along with the pastoral view and what Gary Fine terms the "imperial view") normally presents the human and the non-human as separate orders of being. However, Meigs rejected this separation overall, perceiving "that all living creatures have a soul" (Meigs 1981, 147). Emotionally, Meigs identified so strongly with landscapes, plants, and animals that her subjectivity takes on permeable borders, so that the line between self and place becomes blurred. This is especially true of her childhood experience of nature, particularly her summers at Wood's Hole, Cape Cod. Here, in "dazzling sunshine," close to the ocean, she roamed the fields, discovering for the first time the multitude of wild plants and the immense variety of birds. Even as a child of nine, she reinforced her sense of ownership by listing precisely the names of thirty-four plants that grow in the Woods Hole area (1987, 176). The use of precise nomenclature for the various "flora and fauna" became a lifetime habit, a manifestation of her love of natural history (ibid., 21). Accordingly, texts of all five of her books are punctuated with the scientifically accurate names of plants, animals, and birds. Sixty-one years after the compiling of the plant list, Meigs' memories of Woods' Hole are ones of pure joy, and, as with Pratt, they centre around a house in which inside and outside blend much as nature and culture blend in Meigs herself:

> Memories as fragile as seashells wash up, memories of pure joy carried in with the rising tide and gently scattered above the tide line. Woods' Hole sounds: a song sparrow singing in the morning stillness, a bird running over the roof without insulation.... The house breathed fog and the perfume of rosa rugosa and bay bushes; its ears were open to the faint slapping of the waves below it or the sudden roar when a northeast gale struck it broadside. (Meigs 1987, 171)

This passage is remarkable, not only for its ability to evoke a sense of place and connection to place, but as a demonstration of Meigs' metaphoric cast of mind. The first sentence contains both simile and metaphor, likening the evanescence of memory to the fragility of seashells and paralleling a rush of memory with the action of an incoming tide. Then she extends the interplay of images, personifying the house and bringing it alive through interaction with elements of wind and water. This tendency towards metaphoric play is not confined to the manipulation of language but is fundamental to the way Meigs sees the world and to the construction of herself as artist. The same tendency, of course, is detected in the work of the other three artists under discussion but, in interpreting Meigs' work, no detection is necessary; metaphoric play is linguistically overt and everywhere.

Bob Samples, in an analysis of creative consciousness called *The Metaphoric Mind*, identifies four modes of metaphoric thinking, two of which – the synergic-comparative mode and the integrative metaphoric mode – have application to the present discussion.[16] The synergic-comparative mode corresponds to the comparative process at work in literary metaphor and simile; Samples makes the point that, unlike rational comparison, synergic comparison forms a unity of disparate elements that becomes more "than either one alone because of the comparison" (Samples 1976, 89). He suggests that symbolically this could be represented by $2 + 2 = 5$, an idea that would have delighted Meigs. She turns to this mode extensively when trying to convey in words the essence of a person or experience.

The second mode, the integrative mode comes close to what Northrop Frye has called "the motive for metaphor" (N.Frye 1963, 11), the human urge to identity with the non-human world, a characteristic Meigs amply displays in her writing. Samples claims that infants and children are deeply involved in this mode of thought nearly all the time; in adults it can be a form of what he calls "sensory nostalgia" (Samples 1976, 93). Meigs employed this mode both in recalling her memories of childhood experience (as in her descriptions of the "joy" of Woods Hole) and through immersing herself in the various landscapes she knew throughout her life. Speaking as a landscape painter, she speculates that it is visual artists in particular who display the capacity to identify with a landscape, whereas fiction writers, such as her erstwhile friend and lover, Andrée, perceive landscape only as a backdrop for human relationships:

> My memories of that year and a half ... zig back and forth, sharpening now on landscapes, on the way one takes landscapes into oneself little by little until they become extensions of one's body. Perhaps painters do this more than writers, perhaps they demand nourishment from certain landscapes and they consume them slowly, patiently. (1983, 49)

Meigs constructed her identity for most of her adult life primarily as a visual artist, and while the present discussion is concerned with her as a writer, evidence of her visual artist self is present in almost every page of her various books, in that (as is the case with Pratt's published diaries) Meigs allows the reader to see the world through her painterly eyes. In the discussion of the role of landscape, not only does she describe the integrative mode of the mind in action – that is, as taking "landscapes into oneself little by little" – but also, she provides an example of the synergic mode by perceiving "certain landscapes" metaphorically as "nourishing food" for the artistic temperament.

Meigs' ability to identify with nature, moreover, extends beyond a sensibility to landscape to include an intense fellow feeling for all animals that she perceives, like herself, as possessing a soul. She refers with horror to the use of animals as experimental subjects even though it is likely that her father's research into milk production included this kind of research (1987, 26). In Paris, she yells at a peddler for beating his horse (1983, 11) and while the entire spectacle of the Vietnam War causes her mental anguish, she is most horrified at the suffering of the animals because they seem to her the most innocent of the victims (1981, 96). Similarly, the practice by the French of stunning larks in the sky with a mirror so that they dropped to the ground fills Meigs with furious indignation, as did the hunting of wild geese and ducks. She queries, "How could people shoot geese after hearing them honking overhead?" (ibid., 185).

Meigs reacts particularly strongly to any harming of birds because of the central place birds occupy in her mind, imagination, and spirit. Birds are her ultimate consolation and she writes a virtual hymn of praise to them in *Lily Briscoe*:

> For me, birds are the embodiment of colour, joy, music and freedom. I have learned their songs, their arrivals and their departures and I mourn their disappearance. It is obvious to me that both birds and animals are able to identify so totally with human beings that there is an interchange of souls and that this interchange is irreversible, unlike the interchange of human love. (ibid.)

The idea of interaction between bird and humans is one that has been long embodied in story, where birds are given mythic powers. Meigs makes reference to one legendary power assigned to mythical birds that parallels her own experience: "like the birds of Rhiannon ... whose effect on human beings was that they lost their sense of time and their memory of pain. Birds have this effect on me. They make me lose my memory of pain" (ibid.).

Thus, even more than with landscape, Meigs' experience of birds energizes the integrative comparative mode of her psyche, involving the whole self in a process of identification so intense that she, as human being, joins what Samples calls "the mainstream of nature" (1976, 92). Meigs marks her days by bird sightings: red-winged blackbirds, bluebirds, brown thrashers, hummingbirds, orioles, bobolinks, towhees, quail, mourning doves, peregrine falcons, and, in Australia, parrots, rosellas, bellbirds, and currawongs. She knows them both through sight and by their song. One song in particular she loves best, that of the song sparrow. It is her emblem bird, the one that, at the age of ten, first spoke to her of joy (1997, 71) and, sixty-three years later, becomes the bittersweet symbol of life and loss in the film, *The Company of Strangers*.

It is no wonder, then, that Meigs, in employing what is for her a basic tool in writing – that is, the use of simile and metaphor – turns to bird imagery to convey the personality of the individuals who have shaped her subjectivity and the narrative pattern of her life. Accordingly, her grand-mother is "loquacious as a guinea hen" (1981, 29), her father is like "a swan brought up in captivity" (ibid., 215), and writing about her family feels "as though I were holding a wounded bird in my hands" (1987, 221). Similarly, her impressions of her friends are conveyed in bird images: Kate/Ruth is "like a weaver bird" (1997, 90), Marie-Claire at Wellfleet is "caged like a bird" (1981, 117), Bessie Poor "looked like a quail" (1981, 207), and Andrée is "both a bird of prey and gentle as a turtle dove" (1983, 101). Animal metaphors and similes, while not as frequent, are also used by Meigs to good effect. For example, Catherine in *In the Company of Strangers* is likened to an octopus in her ability to avoid unwanted questioning: "They emit inky clouds to confuse the enemy" (1991b, 134). Similarly, Meigs says of herself, "I was no more awake to life than a dormouse" (1981, 167) and of Ma-rie-Claire Blais, "She assimilates everything like a goat" (1983, 90). Meigs' imagination draws constantly upon the world of non-human creatures when seeking to communicate her personal vision. It is a measure of how signifi-cant the world of birds and animals is for her.

Bob Samples has a similar vision of the role of nature. So convinced was Samples of the connection between experience of nature and creative consciousness in humans that he reportedly went before a United States congressional committee to argue that wilderness areas be set aside "as res-ervoirs of metaphor" and "cathedrals of creativity" (Samples 1976, 111). It must be said, however, that much of the theoretical support that Samples presents is anecdotal, statistically limited, or both. His argument at heart is a plea for a restored equilibrium so as to give the poetic, imaginative per-spective a place in a culture devoted to science and rationalism. His theories, as he himself suggests (ibid., 2), are best regarded as speculative.

However, in their approach to their work as artists, Butala, Dyck, Pratt, and Meigs bear out Samples' contentions to a marked degree. Butala, for example, has rooted her life writing in her experience of the landscape of southwestern Saskatchewan. Similarly, Dyck's present practice is essentially a response to nature via her study of the honeybee. Pratt's art practice focuses on domestic subjects set in and around the house. As a painter, she considers access to nature via a window on the garden as a prime necessity for creative stimulus (Weiler 1998, 82). In their work, all four artists draw on nature as a primary source of metaphor. As for Meigs, Samples' work on metaphor underscores how profoundly her life, her subjectivity, and her life writing were shaped by her contact with the natural world, and most especially with birds. In invoking the legends and myths in which birds and humans take each other's forms (1981, 185), she indicated that the same degree of intense reciprocal identification, expressed through metaphor, was operative in her life. Overall, Samples' work is significant in the present context because it provides a critical basis, however tentative, for the perception of permeability existing between the construction of self and the experience of the natural world in the work of all four artists under study.

Certainly, Mary Meigs would have been supportive of Samples' representation to Congress concerning government protection of wilderness areas. Unlike Samples, however, she would be likely to have supported these projects for their own sake and not just for the benefit such wilderness areas afford to the psyche of human beings. In her strong identification with birds and other animals, Meigs demonstrated that she takes an organic view of nature, as defined by Gary Fine.

This view must, however, been a source of conflict for her because, as she makes clear in almost all of her life writing, she was a member of the privileged class of those whose income comes from the investment of inherited wealth. As David Suzuki has documented (1994, passim), those who stand to profit by the imperialist view of nature relinquish it reluctantly.

Over the course of a very long life, however, Meigs moved ideologically a great distance from the beliefs held by her family over sixty years ago. Moreover, it became clear to me in our discussions together that she supported financially many socially aware projects and causes, including ones involving the protection of the environment and the advancement of the arts. In old age, she achieved a perspective on contemporary society afforded only through long-term memory, perceiving clearly the increasing cost of multinational business and industry in terms of damage to the planet and its inhabitants. As with Butala and Pratt, Meigs often articulates a poignant sense of "paradise lost," not only as regards her beloved birds, but planet-wide, lamenting the loss of whole natural ecosystems ("Memories of Age," 1988, 59). Like Pratt, Meigs likens environmental damage to the oppression of women (in her case, particularly lesbian women) and attributes the cause of both kinds of oppression to the worldwide patriarchal domination of society and culture by the Western capitalist interests, an eco-feminist position. Further, she refers to "the brutalization of the world" and voices her distress through images and language that are both savage and evocative in a description of our post-natural world:

The enemies of life have practiced genocide on a global scale; they have wiped out entire races and countries, set fire to the earth and its vegetation and forced whole populations into exile. They are all those human beings who make inhuman decisions – sometimes in the name of conquest, sometimes in the name of development, that word with its cruel irony. Their victims are other human beings, the animals, fish, birds, forests that stand in their way. (1988, 58)

Here Meigs links the victimization of animals and forests equally with the victimization of human beings; again, this is characteristic of the organic view of nature. Nevertheless, she understood that it is humans who have agency over the fate of our planet, and in this she shared a protectionist view. She assigns a special role to old women: "our power does not lie in hope (we can live without it) but in our invincible power to remember and warn" (ibid., 57).

Undertaken after the age of sixty, all of Meigs' written work expresses an enduring sense of loss, a powerful component in her perception of the natural world. Part of this sense of loss is the inescapable result of aging that brings with it nostalgia for the scenes of one's childhood, these being, in Meigs' case, the landscape of Cape Cod and the houses and gardens of her childhood. Pratt expresses a similar longing for her mother's home and garden in Fredericton, while Butala, long an urban woman, is drawn to the Butala ranch initially because it awakens memories of a rural childhood. Dyck eschews nostalgia in any form but nevertheless attributes her penchant for organic "shapes, textures and materials" to her early experience of nature on the Manitoba family farm (Dahle 1990, 37). So, for all four artists, childhood exposure to nature was a crucial factor in shaping both their perception of the natural world and their devotion to it, personally and as artists.

SUMMARY

The adult life of all four artists has, however, been set in a world in which technological expansion has impacted upon nature. For these artists, the result has been for all four to position themselves as ecological advocates. Theologian Sallie McFague notes a shift in consciousness in the work of Sharon Butala and attributes it to a journey from self-absorption to awareness of her physical and psychic environment (McFague 1997, 139). The work of Dyck, Pratt, and Meigs contain similar shifts so that all four position nature as a crucial "other" in their constructions of self.

READING AS DAUGHTER, SISTER, AND MOTHER TO THE TEXTS

Of the four, it is Aganetha Dyck who communicates the most intimate perception of the physical world. For Dyck, bee study is an intellectual adventure, almost equal to an astronaut setting off into space, except that the world she seeks is best explored through a microscope (she covets a new one) and through chemical analysis. In my white bee suit, looking not unlike an astronaut, I was able to share this world for a few hours with Aganetha, learning first-hand the degree of knowledge, vigilance, and aesthetic sensibility this aspect of her art practice requires. I returned to a review of her work with a deeper understanding of this interactive process, one in which she tutored me as daughter. I retain to this day the excitement of being "mothered" into investigating a new arena of nature.

Similarly, my visit to the home of Sharon and Peter Butala in July of 1996 introduced me both to the ranching aspect of rural life and to an unfamiliar landscape – the rolling grasslands of southwestern Saskatchewan. My husband, Craig, accompanied me to Eastend that weekend and to the Butala ranch, where, over the period of two days, I talked to Sharon about her work and life while Craig followed Peter on his round of ranch duties. These duties took place in and around the Hay Farm, home to Sharon and Peter during their married life.[17]

After I finished the interview, Craig and I ventured further afield, driving some thirty miles to the original log cabin, and to the ranchland proper surrounding the ridge of hills known as "Old Man on His Back." I was excited to visit the site of *The Perfection of the Morning*, but I was not quite prepared for the impact of that landscape. The West I knew as a child was centred around the tiny settlement of Seven Sisters on the edge of the Winnipeg River, near Seven Sisters Falls, Manitoba, where my father and uncle were helping to build the hydroelectric plant. The prairie that I remember consisted of rough fields filled with clover and edged with pine and aspen trees. It was quite unlike the uninhabited expanse of wind-swept, rolling, treeless grassland below the brooding hills of *Old Man on His Back*. That day, the sun was warm, the grassland plants sweet-smelling, and we were afforded a glimpse of antelope springing away. Walking a little way down the road and over the fields, we better understood Butala's use of the word "perfection." As Butala has said, there is something very elemental about a landscape consisting wholly of earth and sky, and I came away reluctantly, wanting more of that contact with what Butala has labeled "Presence." Again, as an offshoot of my scholarly pursuits, I had been "mothered" into exploring a heretofore-unknown realm of nature, one affording again a sense of privileged contact. Short as that July interval was, it profoundly informed my reading of Butala's texts, especially *Wild Stone Heart*.

Previously, I had limited but intense periods of exposure to the untouched Canadian wilderness. This exposure allowed me to respond in a sisterly fashion to notions of the wild found in the work of Butala and Pratt. As with them, my mentor in the wild was a man. From 1937 to 1951, my father, John MacKay, was a partner or on-the-job supervisor in various construction companies that built many sections of the Trans-Canada Highway running along the north shore of Lake Superior between Thunder Bay and Sault St. Marie. It was a difficult job to reconcile with a settled family life, but, while my mother sometimes left me home in Winnipeg or Toronto with a housekeeper, we both joined Dad "on construction" during the summer months. Whenever he let me, I tagged along through the bush after my father.

The Canadian bush was an environment well known to my father. A Nova Scotian, he came "out west" at sixteen to join his brothers in the building of the CNR west of Edmonton and spent the 1920s in the British Columbia lumber business. He knew the ways of moose and bear, could run twenty miles on snowshoes, and navigated the muskeg of Northern Ontario wearing only soft moccasins. He hired men from many countries – Finland, Slovakia, Ukraine – as well as many Canadians who came out west to find work. In her early marriage, my mother occupied a position not unlike that of Susanna Moodie. Like Moodie, Mom's territory consisted of the houses provided for her in this wilderness and they varied from rough log cabins to tar-paper company shacks, to the more sumptuous structures erected in the wilderness by Dad's workmen. She went outside to socialize with other wives or, in some summers, to wash clothes in a nearby river (keeping an eye out for bears) but she never, to my knowledge, really came to terms with the surrounding bush. All exploration of this wilderness I did as a child was in company with my father. It is not surprising, therefore, that I feel a profound sisterhood with Sharon Butala and Mary Pratt in their perception of the

Canadian wild both as masculine territory and as possessing a masculine spirit.

During his career, my father bulldozed his way through probably millions of trees and dynamited tons and tons of the Canadian Shield rock, thereby changing the face of the wilderness forever. Yet, he had a profound respect and understanding of what Frye has called the "bush garden." When work permitted, he would, as I say, take me on excursions into this wild "garden," teaching me how to back off when a bull moose was crashing around in the undergrowth, how to judge the freshness of bear droppings, how to pull trout out of the backcountry rivers, and, his special delight, how to find and name the small outcroppings of wildflowers. Outside of fishing, my father never killed an animal, just shooing away, for example, the pesky black bears that hung around the construction camp meat house.

Consequently, in terms of Fine's classification of man's views of Nature, my father's position would resemble that of Peter Butala. As with Butala, my father's way of making a living took an imperialist view of nature for granted; yet there was a strong organic bond between himself and the wilderness that was part of his daily life. His older brother, Jim, was my father's closest friend and Jim knew the bush even better than John did. Jim often went prospecting for gold and even owned part of a now-defunct gold mine. Before he died, Uncle Jim told me that his happiest times were in the bush sitting around an open fire with the tea pail suspended between two forked sticks. To my mind it is a romantic and distinctly Canadian image, epitomizing a part of my heritage. In my personal mythology, my family has an imaginative claim on the bush of northern Canada because of the MacKay brothers' pioneering struggles to make a living out of the wilderness, thereby opening up the West.

Now, however, I come to the wilderness experience as an urban dweller, one who escapes to the wild "to get away." It is precious for me to have access to nature in this way as a refreshment and source of peace. Being brought up in northern Ontario, my husband finds this true as well. When our children were small, our weekends were spent tenting in the Rocky Mountains. Then, campsites were rustic and easy to come by. Since 1974, we have had a little cabin in the Kananaskis area east of Banff and this small property, like the campsites, is becoming threatened with overcrowding and urbanization. I join my four subjects in sisterhood to take an environmental protectionist view of Nature as I see the traditional grounds of the grizzly bear, elk, and moose being threatened.[18]

Nevertheless, like my mother, I take a cautious view of the wild. One of my mother's stories of my babyhood tells of her sitting me in my black overalls on a blanket near the back fence of a cabin yard in what was then British Columbia wilderness country. She left briefly to get wet clothes to hang on the line and when she returned, she saw a bear peering at me over the fence. I, of course, have no memory of this but the scene is still vivid for me because of the photograph in an old album of me in those overalls sitting on that self-same blanket. Margaret Atwood's phrase "fears hairy as bears" resonates strongly with me. Still, I like to hike in bear country, taking great care to make a noise and check bear droppings. As with Sharon Butala, the act of walking miles in wilderness landscape brings about a sense of unity with nature and gives my life an adventurous edge.

However, my greatest sense of connection with nature comes from another type of interaction – that of sketching on location out of doors. I returned to landscape painting during the 1980s and was lucky have access to workshops by such Alberta artists as Illingsworth Kerr, Ted Godwin, and Laurel Cormack. They emphasized, as did the Group of Seven artists before them, that direct immediate experience of the Canadian landscape in particular and of the natural world in general was necessary before the artist could hope to convey any sense of emotional possession and understanding of his/her subject. I have accordingly carried a small easel and a backpack of brushes and paints up mountain trails, into the foothills and prairie fields, along jungle paths, and onto shifting sands along the ocean shore. I have done so in order to pursue that existential moment that comes only for me in trying to transfer what I see and feel in nature onto paper or canvas. Sometimes I content myself with pencil sketches, sometimes I struggle with watercolour to catch a fleeting moment of light, but most often I use acrylic paints, the medium that gives me the luxury of a quick underpainting and allows a degree of reworking. It is the act of painting that allows me to enter fully into the scene before me. Pratt's comment "I have always tried to be what I paint" translates for me into "I become what I see through painting."

Consequently, painting out of doors allows me the chance of experiencing most fully "the here and now" and of attaining that heightened sense of awareness that Csikszentmihalyi calls "flow." These are some of my happiest times. I often take aesthetic pleasure in the product, but mostly my paintings act as a reminder of the process and of a particular experience in nature. Only a few times in my limited career as an artist has one of my paintings began to approach being what Lawren Harris called "a highway between a particular thing and a universal feeling" (Harris and Colgrove 1969). These I treasure. Yet the long-term benefit of this painterly interaction with nature has been my heightened awareness of the natural world. Painting has taught me to see.

Over a lifetime, however, my most long-term interaction with nature has been through gardening. Like Mary Pratt, I was a gardener before I was a painter, but unlike Pratt, my painting has never outstripped my gardening in terms of expertise. At this time of my life, I have more time for my garden and await with pleasure the yearly arrival of my roses, peonies, delphinium, and lilacs and the first taste of raspberries late in July. Also, for me as for Mary Meigs, the garden is not complete without birds, and I watch each year with maternal satisfaction as a family of adolescent robins strips my loaded Saskatoon bush of every one of its berries. I put out feeders and have a heated birdbath in our below-zero Calgary winters. I was thrilled at my one and only sighting of a pileated woodpecker; I feel privileged when the blue jays screech, when a nuthatch darts out from the spruce tree, when a flock of redpolls descend on the ground beneath the feeding stand. The birds provide me with an ongoing sense of union with nature, as do the blossoming of the annuals I plant and the vegetables I pull from our little patch.

Yet, while I join Meigs in the sisterhood of bird watchers, I do not bestow on these welcome bird visitors the magical significance that Meigs accords them. She sees bird life through eyes different from mine, just as people over the centuries have perceived the various landscapes of this planet differently. Susanna Moodie, for example, saw the Canadian wilderness through romantic eyes and found it desolate, while Lawren Harris and the Group of Seven experienced it as spiritually invigorating. Robert MacFarlane, a fanatical mountaineer, applies this idea to the perception of mountain terrain. In *Mountains of the Mind*, MacFarlane traces the ways in which the view of mountains in European culture has changed over the centuries. He presents such changes as a typical example of how emotional associations can affect our perception of our natural surroundings:

> So drastic was this revolution that to contemplate it now is to be reminded of a truth about landscapes: that our responses to them are for the most part culturally determined. That is to say, when we look at a landscape, we do not see what is there but largely what we think is there. We attribute qualities to a landscape that it does not intrinsically possess, – savageness, for

example, or bleakness – and we value it accordingly. We *read* landscape, in other words, we interpret their forms in the light of our own experience and memory, and that of our shared cultural memory. Although people have traditionally gone into wild places in some way to escape culture or convention, they have, in fact, perceived that wilderness, as just about everything else is perceived, through a filter of associations. (MacFarlane 2003, 18)

In the present context, MacFarlane's analysis presents one with a paradox. For artists such as Sharon Butala, Lawren Harris, and Emily Carr, to experience nature is to contact an ultimate reality. MacFarlane, on the other hand, points out that "we *read* landscape," reading being an act of interpretation, not simple perception. My painting experience leads me to side with Butala, Harris, and Carr, and yet I can see that association colours my emotional reaction to some scenes. The landscape that I irrationally long for, but rarely paint successfully, always features water, most particularly a river, and I attribute this to associations formed in the past. As a four-year-old, I fell asleep to the sound of the Winnipeg River and its waterfalls. I grew to adolescence near the broad Assiniboine River in Winnipeg and now live a few blocks from Calgary's more modest Elbow River and walk most days along its river paths. A river's flowing water not only affords me serenity and refreshment but also provides a comforting continuity with the little girl who was me.

This, I believe, is the source of the particular imaginative significance I bestow on this facet of nature. Consequently, two of my favourite books are still *Huckleberry Finn* and *The Wind in the Willows*, and I remember the thrill of my first sighting of the fabled Mississippi and the historic Thames. Similarly, I feel a profound sense of sisterhood with Mary Pratt as I picture her creeping down to her nearby river at night to place her hand in the reflected moonlight. It would be my way, too, of honouring the spiritual mystery that we five women perceive as embodied in the natural world.

4

Alive in the Spirit:
Growing Old

Age is a time of great wonder – a time when we have to hold, with a fine balance, contradictory truths in our heads and give them equal weight: old is scary but very exciting, chaotic but self-integrating, narrowing yet wider, weaker yet stronger than ever before. It is we who must name the processes of our own aging. – Barbara Macdonald, *Look Me in the Eye: Old Women, Aging and Ageism*

I began by describing how, in the 1980s, I was inspired by Judy Chicago's *The Dinner Party*, an installation that catalogued the accomplishments of women throughout the ages. *The Dinner Party* still inspires me, but now, twenty years later, in the midst of old age, I require additional female models, women of my generation who have lived substantially longer than their grandmothers and so have decades more of being "old." More specifically, I need to access examples of women who disregard the limits set by society's ageist attitudes and who continue to grow emotionally and spiritually despite the toll on the body that old age brings. In studying the autobiographical practices of Butala, Dyck, Meigs, and Pratt, I soon realized that I already possessed my models in these four women, each of whom deals with the phenomenon of aging in a way that enhances their spiritual maturity.

Growing old is no guarantee of spiritual maturity. In almost all religious or spiritual systems of belief, one's capacity for altruism is the outward manifestation of spiritual health. However, the coming of old age, with its physical challenges and losses, tests one's ability to think beyond oneself; all four artists have been tested in just this way, striving to find devices that help them to counteract isolation and to interact positively with the world around them. For example, just as Sharon Butala found consolation in mid-life through contact with the natural world, so now, approaching old age, she directs her attention outwards towards problems in the natural environment. Accordingly, theologian Sallie McFague describes Butala's spiritual journey as consisting of "small shifts in practice and imagination that move her from an isolated to an ecological self" (1997, 138). This shift in awareness is one demonstration of a heightening moral sensibility.

While Sallie McFague writes from a Christian point of view, she does not identify Butala as specifically Christian. Similarly, in my interviews with all four, it was apparent, in varying degrees, that the Christian church did not figure extensively as a factor in their adult life. By and large, the patriarchal basis of organized religion caused them to look elsewhere in their search for a spiritual dimension in their lives. Butala sees this search as a journey, one that she calls "soul"-building:

> I take my own life experiences, my dreams, my small visions
> and the insights I've gained from Nature as the material out of
> which I can build my soul, for I have come to believe that this
> is our purpose here on earth, in this bodily life which is often so
> painful and yet so very beautiful. (Butala 1995a, 2)

Nonetheless, all four were brought up in the Christian church: Butala, Roman Catholic; Dyck, Mennonite; Meigs, Episcopalian, and Pratt, United Church, and while these four referred to their childhood church attendance only in passing, there is evidence that early exposure to the Bible influenced their vision of life. For example, while Butala's soul-building is an activity with many facets, the most basic is the search for a moral code by which to live. Loving one's neighbour as oneself is a Christian ideal that she and the other three embraced, but they came to the enactment of this imperative only, as Barbara MacDonald says, by holding "with a fine balance, contradictory truths in [their] heads and giv[ing] them equal weight." Being mature women, all four of necessity struggled for moral "balance" and the struggle heightened their spiritual awareness. Both the struggle and the awareness shaped their work.

Moral sensibility has, however, been only one of the contributing factors to the presence of a spiritual element in the construction of self in this work. Those who espouse the traditional church view of the opposition between mind and body may find it surprising that bodily response has played a significant part in their spiritual growth of Butala, Dyck, Meigs, and Pratt.

For these artists, spirit and body are two sides of the same coin, and spiritual experience comes from an extension of bodily experience rather than as a denial of body. Nor do they support a view of the world of nature as being in opposition to the human world. For them, the experience of transcendence – the perception of union with a larger spiritual entity – results most often from interacting with the world of nature rather than withdrawing from this world. Similarly, they have not isolated themselves as artists and women from the larger social community. In their search for an authentic moral code, they have discovered a genuine and reciprocal sense of community, one energized by the power of love, the most potent element in spiritual awareness. Most importantly, however, for these women, as for most artists, creativity and spirituality are intimately connected: life and art interact.

This depth, therefore, emerges both a function of their maturity as persons and of their creativity as artists, one aspect of their subjectivity feeding the other. In considering the role of spiritual awareness in the writing of autobiography, Harvard critic Georg Misch similarly suggests that awareness of the "unconscious," that is "the transcendent or mystical," adds profundity to the text: "Autobiographies in which there is no trace of this hidden, unexpressed knowledge seem to us superficial or intellectually attenuated."[1] Misch is referring to literary autobiography, but, by extrapolation, one can apply his criteria to visual art practices in which there is an autobiographical dimension. Accordingly, I argue that the spiritual awareness that Misch seeks in autobiography informs the art practices of all four artists and gives their work the required depth and intellectual rigour. I recognize also that, simultaneously, the act of art-making, whether literary or visual, energizes this awareness; it is hard-won, the result of a lifetime of experience. I will argue further, therefore, that these women can rightly be regarded as female elders in our society and their work as a spiritual resource.[2]

Defining what is meant by spirit can be controversial; one's beliefs tend to dictate one's understanding of the meaning of the word "spirit." It can refer to the animating principle in consciousness, to the immaterial soul, or as Professor Adam Morton has it, "to the kind of emotion we might have towards God or some other factor beyond one's material life."[3] Pratt and Meigs, in particular, name that kind of emotion as "joy," and Butala and Dyck would likely agree with them. Spirituality could then be understood in this context as that elevating aspect of experience characterized by a consciousness of joy. In examining the relationship between creativity and spirituality, critic Deborah Haynes says of spirituality:

It is a vague term. It conjures up the ineffable and mysterious.... It transcends denomination and religious tradition, for there are many diverse expressions of spirituality in different traditions and cultures. Through spiritual disciplines, we reach into the greater world and into ourselves. (Haynes 1997, 26–27)

Haynes says further that she uses visual art as a spiritual vehicle, and she links the sacred and the divine with the ongoing universal process of creativity, a process in which human beings participate in a variety of ways:

This creativity happens, and is expressed, in the matrices of relationship, in interconnected networks of people loving and engaging with each other. Artistic creativity is a special case of the ongoing creativity in the world and I believe artists have a vocation to take their work seriously as this sacred dimension of existence. (ibid., 27)

While Butala, Dyck, Meigs, and Pratt might hesitate to elevate their practice of art by naming it as "sacred," their spiritual actualization does centre on their vocations as artists. For all four, the practice of art – literary or visual or both – can be seen as the primary spiritual discipline. However, I believe all four would agree with Mary Pratt when she says, "the art is only as successful as the life" (Pratt 2000, 23). Part of that success is achieved by coming to terms with the life processes of aging and with mortality.

The practice of art acts both to consolidate the sense of self and to bring into being new aspects of self. Old age, on the other hand, attended as it is by the gradual deterioration of the body, brings with it a diminishing sense of self. One feels betrayed by one's body, and one's world becomes smaller as one's range of activity becomes more limited. The resultant loss of the sense of self is exacerbated by the rampant ageism in our society, an ageism that is especially virulent in the case of aging females.[4]

Mary Meigs and Mary Pratt have dealt with the limitations of living alone without a significant companion. Fortunately, both have had long-time connections to a supportive community. In Pratt's case, support came both from an extended family – sister, children, and grandchildren – and from the wider community of the Maritimes where, as a longtime artist and resident, she is a known and revered figure. However, somewhat to her surprise, Pratt was to find companionship in a new relationship; in June of 2007, she married American artist and art historian James Rosen. After reading *A Personal Calligraphy*, Rosen had called on Pratt while vacationing in Newfoundland and their friendship flourished right away. Meigs' emotional base was a circle of intimate friends (centring mainly on Marie-Claire Blais) and a respected place in the lesbian community. She also had a secure role as aunt to her siblings' children, an even more important role after the death of her twin sister. Moreover, her work as writer, visual artist, and film personality gave her worldwide contacts and brought renown both inside and outside of lesbian circles. As the two oldest of our four subjects, Meigs (age 85 at the time of her death in 2002) and Pratt (age 73 in 2008) experienced first hand the body's betrayals: Meigs suffered a stroke in 1999 and struggled fairly successfully to recover speech and movement; Pratt endures a form of arthritis that, intermittently, makes travel difficult and confines her to her home base in St. John's.

Aganetha Dyck and Sharon Butala, now officially "seniors," have also had their share of health problems and, like Meigs and Pratt, have suffered the death of family and friends, eventualities that are part of the last third of life. For Butala, the biggest blow was likely the death of husband Peter in August, 2007. All four continued, nevertheless, to practice their art into old age and to hold at bay, thereby, their sense of diminution. As senior practitioners, these four women have displayed, through their work, a grace and wisdom that comes from accepting life on its own terms. Their art-making has given them a continuing sense of self, the actualization they have desired. While one's specification of "old" might vary, it is clear to me that old women artists in general, and these four artists in particular, offer an alternative female role model that is based on spiritual growth, one that acts to offset the stereotyping of old women as useless to society. Shelagh Wilkinson reiterates this point: "old women who use their age to tap into sources of their own creativity remain vital and visible. They are like beacons showing us all new stories and new symbols to live by."[5]

Each of the four artists under discussion casts her life narrative in a particular way. Mary Pratt, of course, works within the parameters of the female domestic life, even now when she constructs herself primarily as artist.[6] She embodies the concept of spirit in her art practice through her elevation of the notion of light and through expressing her feminine experience of family. Similarly, Aganetha Dyck locates herself initially in the feminine world of domesticity but transforms that arena as she, too, goes on to construct herself almost entirely as artist. Because she explores the nature of what she calls "the life force" in her work and sees the vocation of the artist as an expression of "spirit," one might regard her artistic practice as a spiritual undertaking. Essentially though, it is Dyck's proclivity for seeking and promoting community that establishes her spiritual presence.

In *Lily Briscoe: A Self-Portrait*, Meigs also presents herself as an artist figure, dedicated to establishing herself as a visual artist. With the publication of *Lily Briscoe*, however, Meigs, the writer, begins to overshadow Meigs, the visual artist. The writer self accomplishes what the painter self has not – an in-depth "self-portrait." She is able finally to fashion herself as lesbian, "coming out" in print. This act of honesty enhances the spiritual dimension in her life writings, a dimension nourished throughout her life by her artistic vocation and by contact with her beloved birds. Meigs' most powerful expression of spirit, however, is to be found in her capacity for love, one that flowers most bountifully in old age. Meigs, herself, did not categorize her autobiographical telling as "spiritual." Of the four women, Sharon Butala alone specifically casts the narrative of her life experience as a spiritual journey. Accordingly, Butala's life writing can be categorized as spiritual autobiography.

In order for such a categorization to be appropriate, however, the traditional understanding of this genre of life writing must undergo revision. Earlier definitive forms of spiritual autobiography find their sources in St. Augustine's *Confessions* and in the writings of such Christian mystics as Teresa of Avila and Julian of Norwich. Their narratives, and subsequent ones in this tradition, are concerned with their personal struggles to know God through prayer, fasting, and meditation and to discern and to do His will. The quest is for a meaningful relationship with God, as understood within the traditions of the Christian church. While Butala was raised as a Roman Catholic, she rejects the notion of an authoritative God or of religious dogma of any kind because they no longer have meaning for her (1994a, 180). She sees both as constructs of a patriarchal mentality that have little application to her female experience (1999, 13). Nevertheless, Butala, like the Christian mystics, is energized by a spiritual quest. Her quest, however, is not for a personal God but for a sense of the sacred in ordinary experience. Such an awareness restores to her an authentic sense of self, a sense lost in the vicissitudes of a lonely childhood and a painful divorce. Butala finds this awareness of the sacred ultimately through contact with nature whose rhythms are in harmony with those of her female self.

The question is whether the non-religious context of Butala's spiritual quest positions her life writings outside the parameters of spiritual autobiography. In his survey of the genre, John Barbour observes that the substitution of the spiritual realm for the religious one is part of a legitimate trend in contemporary life writing, one exemplified by American female writers Kathleen Norris, Nancy Mairs, Patricia Hampl, and Terry Williams. While he sees these writers as still sharing "religious" commonalities, the characteristics he assigns to their life writing have application to that of Butala:

> In contrast to many earlier spiritual autobiographies, these writers do not propose a single model of belief or affiliation ... they seem to share the view that every individual must find his or her own spiritual path.... No single normative path is proposed for readers. These writers are open-minded in this pluralistic sense, and their works are open-ended, leaving the impression that the author's search is not completed. If Norris, Mairs, Hampl and Tempest are exemplars for their readers in any way it is primarily as exemplars of searching and striving for further experience of what is truly ultimate, holy and worthy of commitment. (Barbour 2001, 837a)

Butala can rightfully be regarded as another exemplar.

As I have indicated, Pratt, Dyck and Meigs (during her lifetime), tend to share Sharon Butala's rejection of Christian orthodoxy. In the case of Butala, Meigs, and Dyck, this can be seen as an extension of their rejection of patriarchal authority, a tenet of radical feminism (see Mandell 1998, 10–11). Mary Meigs is at least as vociferous as Butala in rejecting any form of religious belief, although she is very clear in insisting on personal spiritual experience (Reid 1997, 13). Mary Pratt was raised within the United Church, but over the years church attendance has lapsed, and in her meditations about death and old age throughout *A Personal Calligraphy*, she tends to stray from Christian orthodoxy. Still, Christopher Pratt says of Mary, "She is the most Christian person I know" (1995, 208). Aganetha Dyck maintains strong connections to the Mennonite culture but attends church only sporadically. In our conversations together, she shied away from discussing her religious beliefs; however, when questioned specifically, she did voice her discomfort with the patriarchy "not only of the Mennonite church but with that of any church" (Reid 1996c, 8). Undeniably, however, the religious education of their childhoods, with its emphasis on Biblical narrative, shaped the imagination of all four artists and left its mark, as I have said, on their moral sensibilities.

My four subjects are not the only Canadian or American creative artists troubled by religious orthodoxy; such unease may even be considered the norm. A survey done by Douglas Todd, the religious writer for the *Vancouver Sun*, bears this out. He interviewed, as he says, "twenty-eight of North America's most creative souls" concerning their spiritual experience and belief (1996, 1). These are writers, visual artists, film directors, and performers of various kinds who, because of their vocation, could be seen as articulating the views of the larger societies from which they come. Todd found that, without exception, the spiritual exploration of the whole twenty-eight led them outside the confines of institutional religion. Some were avowedly atheistic but that did not mitigate against their seeking spiritual experience. Even the most determinedly skeptical towards any kind of mysticism, such as Jane Rule and Mordecai Richler, found meaning by searching for a moral code by which to live. For them, ethical conduct was the means of spirit-building.

At the other end of the spectrum were Sylvia Fraser and Carol Shields, who reported experience of the paranormal – precognition, emanations at the passing of a loved one, feelings of foreboding before a disaster. They tended to see such experiences as indicative of the existence of a spiritual realm external to the mind, or of mental powers exceeding what is considered normal.[7] While experience of the paranormal was comparatively rare, more than a third of the artists in Todd's study reported having mystical experiences, and, most often, these came about as a response to nature. This was to be expected in the case of Farley Mowat and Barry Lopez, both well-known Canadian nature writers and two of Todd's subjects. However, journalist Peter Newman discovers the spiritual when sailing off British Columbia, Douglas Coupland, of *Generation X* fame, when walking the Capilano forest, and both writer Timothy Findley and Inuit performer Susan Aglukark when exploring the solitudes of the Arctic tundra.

Consequently, when Sharon Butala rejects organized religion and claims Nature as a primary spiritual resource for human beings, she shares a common perception. Butala, however, offers her readers an extended meditation on the implications of this perception – one being, for example, the acceptance of nature itself as mystical – and she is able to do so because of the candidly confessional quality of her autobiographical writing. As Helen Buss explains (1995), Butala's bravery in confiding her more extraordinary experiences in nature transports the reader into new territory for, as Butala tells us, she does not merely sense "Presence" in Nature, she is led into more numinous realms where visions and dreams are interjected into her ordinary life.

Buss sees Butala's juxtaposition of bodily, material, everyday life with her narrative of the mystical and paranormal as the device that permits her to skirt the "other worldly" excesses of "New Age" writing. Butala can write convincingly of the "feminine soul," Buss says, "because she is not caught in a single narrative or single self" (1995, 173). The practical housewife and the experienced academic are always evaluating the experience of the visionary Butala, caught up in the mysteries of nature. And while Pratt, Dyck, and Meigs also experience the mysteries of nature, each in her own way, they do not embrace the mystical. As visual artists, Pratt and Dyck discover the spiritual in the material rather differently. For her part, Meigs claims no interest in the visionary, expressing an extreme distrust and dislike of all things mystical: "There is no mysticism in me" (Reid 1997, 11).

THEORETICAL CONTEXTS OF MYSTICISM

Definitions of Mysticism

Their autobiographical practices reveal, then, an important spiritual dimension in the constructions of the self and, for Butala at least, this dimension includes mystical experience. However, as William James observed, "the words 'mysticism' and 'mystical' are often used as terms of mere reproach, to throw at any opinion which we regard as vague and sentimental, and without basis in either facts or logic."[8] Further, in a similar vein, James made the point that mystical experience is "authoritative" for those who have it, but not for others.[9] This questioning of the validity of mystical experience is based on the conviction in Western society that the scientific method and scientific findings are the only reliable sources of knowledge. The autobiographical act, whereby Butala positions incidents of mystical experience on an equal footing with the external events of ordinary life, serves as a device to legitimize the mystical – that is, to place it as having objective, as well as subjective, reality. If one does accept mystical experience as authoritative, the questions remain as how best to describe or define this experience. In considering the role of mystical experience in spiritual autobiography, literary critic Carole Slade offers a useful definition of mysticism from psychologist James Leuba (1929) that is broad enough to accommodate many mystical traditions:

Any experience taken by the experiencer to be a contact (not through the senses but "immediate" "intuitive") or union of the self with a larger-than-self, be it called World Spirit, God, the Absolute or otherwise. (Slade 1991, 154)

Some in the Christian tradition believe that religious mystics receive from God an intuitive sense of his presence; others (for example, those in Eastern religious traditions) attribute the intuitive faculty of mystics to a variety of spiritual practices including prayer, fasting, and meditation. Explanations outside religious tradition vary. One of the more persuasive psychological models has been formulated by Elisabeth Kübler-Ross (1985),[10] the founder of the hospice movement, who envisages the human personality as having four quadrants: the physical, the emotional, the intellectual, and the spiritual – the spiritual being the most highly developed faculty, encompassing the intuitive and dependent for its operation on the successful interplay of the other three. Exercise of the spiritual faculty is all but impossible if physical, emotional, or intellectual needs are not fulfilled.[11] According to Kübler-Ross, the spiritual faculty potentially exists in all human beings, to be actualized as a result of psychological health. On the basis of her clinical experience, moreover, Kübler-Ross accepts without reservation the many varieties of mystical experience that often accompany the development of spiritual awareness.

Psychiatrist and best-selling author M. Scott Peck,[12] who has written extensively about the development of human spirituality, also views psychological well-being as a precondition of such development. In acknowledging the existence of both the unconscious and conscious mind, Peck sees spiritual growth as an evolution of consciousness that makes free and informed ethical choice possible (1997, 67–68). Sharon Butala's narrative of her spiritual journey conforms to a considerable extent to Kübler-Ross's model and demonstrates Peck's notion of the evolution of consciousness. In Butala's case, it is the act of shaping her own story that brings about this evolution.

Mysticism and Geography

It took, however, exposure to a particular geographic environment to spark Butala's spiritual awareness. In his book *Landscape of the Sacred*, humanities professor Belden Lane has made the relationship between spirituality and geography in North American experience his special area of study. His findings have considerable application to the life writing of Butala. As a result of his investigations, he stresses the importance of place and landscape in the development of human spirituality. He comments, "Landscape is a connector of the Soul with Being" (2002, 20) and explains further "not every place seems equally adept at communicating the fullness of being." As the result of comparative cultural investigation, Lane embraces the idea of the existence of "sacred" places and enunciates four axioms that apply to such places.

Firstly, he declares, "sacred places are not chosen, they choose. Ultimately the holy exists entirely apart from any human control" (ibid.). This is an enunciation that "place" *per se* can have its own power and life. Butala will call this "the genius loci" (Butala 1995a, 21). The second axiom is that the sacred place is very often a quite ordinary place, not necessarily pastoral or rural, becoming extraordinary only when human experience elevates it. The third axiom declares that being on location in a sacred place does not guarantee entry into the life and spirit of that place. One can take up residence in a landscape and not be on its spiritual "wavelength." In some sense, it is necessary to undergo an epiphany, to be "born anew." Finally, the fourth axiom concerns the tension between the local and the universal. There is a marked tendency in the spiritually aware both to locate themselves psychically at the centre of the sacred space and to move away from it so as to extend its influence.

These axioms reflect and affirm Lane's theoretical understanding of the reality of the sacred in the geographical. This understanding has its source in phenomenologist Maurice Merleau-Ponty's theory that perception is more than cognitive and involves parts of the body besides the brain. Lane conceives of the process of knowing as a reciprocal and participatory process involving the "vitality" of the person and is best described as "intersubjective." Consequently, for Lane, experiencing the material environment as sacred is conditional upon participation in the "particularities," these being found in the "visual, auditory, olfactory and kinesthetic qualities" of the geographical features, be they trees, rocks, or rivers (ibid., 57). The meaning of place is supplied not only by the human being but also by the place itself. Lane's theories have particular application to Butala's narrative of her spiritual journey in that the terms by which she locates herself in the landscape of the Saskatchewan grassland – her acute awareness of and interaction with "particularities" – are strongly suggestive of the intersubjective model of perception.

There are various ways, then, of conceptualizing the source of mystical experience. Firstly, religious tradition may see mystical contact with God as a divinely inspired gift or as a faculty fostered by traditional spiritual practices. Secondly, spiritual counsellors such as Kübler-Ross and Peck, working outside of the boundaries of traditional dogmatic religion, view spiritual and mystical experience as conditional upon, and a by-product of, emotional and ethical maturity. Finally, in phenomenological recognition of the experience of legions of people who are awakened to spirituality through contact with nature, theorists such as Belden Lane see spiritual awareness as a product of human interaction with a numinous physical environment.

Those who have had a mystical experience of nature tend to have what Douglas Todd calls a "panentheistic" view of the universe (Todd 1996, 146), in which the "larger than self," or God, is coextensive with the created universe, God being in all things, and all things being in God. This view is to be distinguished from pantheism, which holds that everything *is* God. Similarly, animism – a theory by which all things, including inanimate objects, are seen as having a spirit – is to be distinguished from the philosophy of animism, "a doctrine which holds that the principle of life called 'the vital force' cannot be reduced to the mechanistic laws of physics and chemistry but is separate and distinct from matter."[13]

Evelyn Underhill, a much-quoted authority on mysticism, embraces "vitalism," a system of beliefs that resembles in many respects the philosophy of animism.[14] For Underhill, reality cannot be perceived by the intellect, its domain being the mechanistic world of the senses. Underlying the latter is a realm of aliveness, of change and becoming, what the philosopher Henri Bergson calls the "*élan vital*," Bergson being one of Underhill's early influences.[15] The universe is the product of Life, a ceaseless, surging force of change, Underhill's "beating heart of God." She explains:

> If we accept this theory, we then must impute to life in its fullness – the huge, many levelled, many coloured life, the innumerable worlds which escape the rhythm of our senses; not merely that patch of physical life which our senses perceive (Underhill 1990, 29).

It is the mystic whose intuitive abilities reach these "innumerable worlds."[16] None of the four artists under discussion would subscribe totally to vitalism as Underhill presents it, but there are certainly echoes of the philosophy of vitalism or animism or both, in Butala's notion of the "creative flow," in

Dyck's concept of a "life force," and in Mary Pratt's psychic response to light.[17] Only Butala, however, has a mystical response to the "élan vital" found in nature.

Mysticism and Ethics

Sharon Butala has read carefully the books of Evelyn Underhill. Underhill sees the attainment of mystical vision as a developmental process, part of which consists of "the purification of the will" (Underhill 1990, 199). By this, she means a move away from egocentricity into a disinterested view of life. Here Underhill is expressing a view held by atheists and religious believers alike that, barring a moment of conversion, spiritual growth is dependent initially on the development of a moral code and on the implementation of ethical conduct in one's personal behaviour. The rule of good conduct has always been the same: "do unto others as you would have them do unto you."[18]

In her psychiatric practice, Elisabeth Kübler-Ross has observed similarly that even to begin to put the "Golden Rule" into practice requires a considerable degree of spiritual maturity, and that the precondition of such maturity is that one rids oneself of the inherited or accumulated burdens of guilt, shame, anger, pride, prejudice, hate, resentment – a burden of emotional negativity which Kübler-Ross calls "unfinished business" (1985, side one). To attain any degree of emotional health and spiritual growth, she stresses the necessity of first dealing with "unfinished business," whether through introspection, spiritual counselling, or psychotherapy. Scott Peck similarly puts emphasis on the necessity of facing one's evil proclivities as a precondition of spiritual growth. He calls the process "emptying" (1987, 94), an openhearted renunciation both of preconceived notions and prejudices and of the need to convert and control. Only then does implementing the "Golden Rule" become a real possibility.

Peck, like Evelyn Underhill, places mystical awareness as the most advanced stage of spiritual development, the stage marked by the greatest degree of the awareness of unity. However, while Peck does not rule out the mystic experiencing of a sense of union being with the divine (Slade's "larger than self"), Peck's emphasis is on another kind of union, the union experienced in human community:

Mystics throughout the ages have not only spoken of emptiness but also extolled its virtues. I have labelled Stage IV [the highest stage] communal as well as mystical, not because all mystics or even a majority of them live in communes but because among human beings they are the ones most aware that the whole world is a community and realize that what divides us into warring camps is precisely the *lack* of this kind of awareness ... they *know* this to be one world. (1987, 193)

While only Butala concerns herself with mysticism *per se*, all four artists are conscious of the spiritual necessity of ridding themselves of emotional negativity – of "emptying" themselves. Most often, the autobiographical nature of their art-making is a tool in the emptying process. Moreover, all four find some of their most profound spiritual experiences in union with others, in "community." To varying degrees, this sense of community is manifest in a variety of ways in their art. In this, they reflect an aspect of postmodernism.

Scott Peck embraces community-building as the primary way to achieve a just and more peaceful society and to effect the spiritual evolution of humankind.[19] In a similar vein, Suzi Gablik calls for a greater sense of community in the conception of the artist's role (1991). She is responding to the traditions of modernism in which visual artists have divorced themselves from the concerns of society and have adopted a confrontational mode of thought, setting the individual against society. In *The Vocation of the Artist*, art professor Deborah Haynes echoes Gablik's plea for a more socially connected art. Haynes calls for a visionary and prophetic role for artists whereby the artist is elevated to a position of spiritual leadership. Moreover, critics such as Haynes and Gablik make a plea, in this postmodern world, for art that connects with the actual particularities of human life as experienced in society. Such a connection is a by-product of autobiographically based art.

Haynes observes also that the creative act of art-making, when not connected to the production of art as a commodity, can be a spiritual experience even for those artists who are resolutely secular (1997, 97). Artistic creativity, when divorced from ego-gratification, can bring about a union that some writers might term "mystical." Evelyn Underhill calls it a moment of illumination (1990, 243). For Haynes, the mark of such a spiritual experience is the absorption of the self into the creative act – an inner dimension of attentiveness similar to what Csikszentmihalyi has described as "flow" (1997). All four artists experience this kind of creative absorption, and it is likely, therefore, that the practice of their art in itself is a tool in their spiritual development.

SHARON BUTALA

Aside from her practice of writing, Butala's spiritual experience over the years has included other phenomena – powerful dreams, states of altered consciousness, visions – and experiences one can only classify as paranormal – precognition, noisy hauntings, ghostly apparitions, and the like. Butala reports on these types of occurrences in the three earliest of her autobiographical texts, such reports being the thematic keynote in *Coyote's Morning Cry*. If one is a student of Jung, as Butala is, much of this dream and visionary experience can be accounted for through Jung's dream theory, whereby dreams and other devices (such as projections) are seen as tools of the unconscious, used to communicate necessary but hidden material to the conscious mind (Jung 1965, 301). While Butala accepts the Jungian methods of dream interpretation, she is not open to the idea that waking visions were, in her case, subjective projections. In our conversations, Butala made this clear, and insisted, despite Jung, that her visionary experience is as objectively real as the ordinary events of her daily life: "I think all of it was real and not self-generated as a psychoanalyst would say it was" (Reid 1996b, 13). Butala makes a similar claim of objectivity for her experience of the paranormal. She might, however, quarrel with the term "paranormal" because it is her observation that a far greater percentage of the population have experienced these mysterious events than is generally realized, so that precognition, hauntings, telepathy, and the like could almost be regarded as "normal" events, a routine part of ordinary human experience.[20]

One's beliefs about one's experiences of mysticism and the paranormal determine how one sees oneself. If such a person considers these experiences to be exceptional or abnormal, then that person must construct herself as different, that is, as having extraordinary gifts. Even if one feels oneself to be spiritually gifted, making such experiences public can expose one to ridicule in a society in which science invariably turns a skeptical eye. That is one reason why many hesitate to reveal these experiences to others and, as a result, experience a sense of isolation. Similarly, if one accepts the estimate of others, that these experiences are self-induced or hallucinatory even though they appear very real, then one's confidence in one's own perceptions and judgment is undermined.

Emily Carr is an example of an artist whose mystical view of nature, as expressed in her work, did not find early acceptance and whose sense of isolation and marginalization caused her to give up painting. It was her meeting with Lawren Harris that reassured her and led her back to painting.[21] His sense of the mystical in nature, which equalled or surpassed her own, restored her faith in her own perception of reality and energized her as an artist. Butala's mystical view of nature has much in common with Carr's, and she, like Carr, has had to come to terms with the threat of alienation that comes in Western society when one embraces a mystical view of reality. That is the reason both Carr and Butala were attracted to the spiritual beliefs of Canada's aboriginal people who perceive experience of the mystical as an integral part of human experience.

To accommodate the complex aspects of her spiritual journey, Butala has experimented with the various autobiographical forms. In a review article of *The Perfection of the Morning*, Helen Buss comments on Butala's experimentation, likening it to that of such writers as Margaret Laurence and Maxine Hong Kingston. Buss suggests that Butala

> ... brings together a series of writing strategies borrowed from other genres and formats and shapes and joins these forms through the vehicle of an autobiographical voice, which, while using the devices of fiction, guarantees its source in the real life of the writer.... [This allows] a true expression of the multiplicity of their lives in relationship to other lives, the environment and the world of dreams and fantasy. (1995a, 171)

Such experimentation of form allows Butala to trace several narrative strands in her spiritual journey, not only in *The Perfection of the Morning*, but also in the companion pieces of life writing, *Coyote's Morning Cry* and *The Wild Stone Heart*. Together with a variety of articles, these three works simultaneously tell of the events of her everyday life, trace the development of her mystical attachment to the land, detail a series of numinous dreams and visions, give accounts of a variety of paranormal occurrences, take a political stance on environmental issues, and comment on her inner life. She manages to combine storytelling, journalling, editorializing, and confession almost seamlessly. What energizes both this *métissage*[22] of forms and the journey it represents is, I submit, not a particular desire for union with a "higher force," or for numinous experience for its own sake; at heart, these are unsought experiences, by-products of a basic drive for moral integrity. What Butala seeks, a quest she shares with traditional spiritual autobiographers, is to live on a higher ethical plane and to begin the initial approach to moral perfection. Consequently, the basic narrative thrust of her life writing can be seen to be her struggle for goodness.

In conceptualizing the nature of goodness, the goal of her spiritual quest, Butala cites James Hillman, invoking his notion of "transparency":

> This is my concept of life: to reach a degree of clarity, of what James Hillman calls transparency, a transparent life, so that what I say, what I do, what I am, what I believe are all one and the same thing. And truth is the first step, the path itself and the last step. (Butala 1995a, 4)

Evil, then, has its source in a lack of unity between the inner and outer life. In defining the nature of evil, psychotherapist, Scott Peck, identifies its root as the inability to tolerate the truth of one's own wrongdoing; as Peck says: "We become evil by trying to hide from ourselves" (1983, 76), and he explains that a primary tool of effecting this self-deception is the technique of projecting the evil onto someone else, an action called "scapegoating." Evil, then, is "the exercise of political power – that is, the imposition of one's will upon others by overt or covert coercion – in order to avoid spiritual growth" (ibid., 74). In Jungian terms, this means the refusal to face up to one's "shadow." Similarly, Kübler-Ross explains evil as resulting from "emotional negativity," and the failure to deal with what she calls "unfinished business."

In an address for St. Stephen's College (1999) entitled "A Spiritual Journey,"[23] Butala condenses the material from her three earliest autobiographical books so as to highlight the one strand of the *métissage* that characterizes this part of her life writing. In so doing, she concentrates on the phenomena of her inner mental and spiritual states rather than on the character of the environment that has so affected her. Accordingly, she divides her spiritual development into a series of stages or steps that correspond roughly to the decades of her life. As she explains, she abandoned religious belief in her teens, had a spiritual epiphany in her twenties, dealt with spiritual despair in her thirties, found a belief in a higher power she calls the "creative flow" in her forties, and investigated the world of myth and dreams in her fifties. In turning sixty, and having dealt with what Kübler-Ross calls the "unfinished business" of her childhood and early adult life, she devotes herself in her personal life to causes that she perceives as promoting good in the world around her.

In her St. Stephen's address, she made it very clear, however, that she places the same premium on the danger of self-deception, as do Peck and Kübler-Ross, and that, like them, she now perceives the facing of the truth about oneself and dealing with the "unfinished business" to be the foundation of all spiritual growth. By the time she was in her thirties, her spiritual task was to seek out the truth about herself and her own life first of all, and then the truth about the world around her. Both kinds of truth are hard won. Her life writing has been both an instrument in these tasks and a progress report on them.

In an article entitled "Telling Lies" (1994b, 49), Butala recalls taking the first important step towards understanding the importance of truth when, as a schoolgirl of thirteen, she was caught in a lie by her schoolmates. Shamed and humiliated, she vowed never to lie again. Not telling lies, however, is not quite the same thing as facing up to the truth, and coming to know and to face the truth, especially about oneself, usually requires an experiential jolt or crisis. For Butala, such a crisis occurred in her mid-thirties with the break-up of her first marriage and, subsequently, with the abrupt shift in lifestyle that accompanied her marriage to Peter Butala and her move to the country. The two events sparked two kinds of responses. The marriage break-up made her realize that she had been living according to other people's agendas – first her mother's and then her husband's – and that these agendas truly had warped her psychological development. As a result she vowed, "from that moment on I would never again allow anyone else to tell me what I thought" (1999, 6). Butala here was questioning both the positioning of women as propagated by mother and husband and the constructions of organized religion that reinforce patriarchal values. Like Scott Peck, Butala sees skepticism and doubt in matters of religion as psychologically healthy and a necessary step in spiritual growth; she would agree with Peck "the path to holiness lies in questioning everything" (Peck 1997, 261). This questioning paves the way to genuine spiritual discovery and a sense of connection "to the unseen order of things" (ibid., 247).

Similarly, following her second marriage, she experienced a period of alienation and despair sparked by the social isolation of life in the ranching community. This led her into lengthy self-examination, guided only by the careful study of relevant books. In reviewing this self-examination, Butala reports that she returned to the truth-telling vow of her adolescent self, "couched now in a new language, and with a new angle." Now it was "*Stop Kidding Yourself. Practice the most rigorous honesty, yes but primarily with yourself, about yourself*" (1999, 9).

Sharon Butala's commitment to the principles of truth-telling and independent thought is the result of her autonomous choice, and she is the sole agent in the enactment of these principles. However, while these principles may be the foundation of her spiritual life, they are very far from being the total sum of her spiritual experience. Other events in this experience apparently have a source completely outside of herself, while still others appear to result from the interaction of her psyche with a particular environment, either material or immaterial. Of the unprompted events Butala says this:

> But the odd thing about the spiritual life is that it will suddenly intrude out of nowhere to hit you on the head, so that you are forcibly reminded that there is a power or powers far greater than you are, quite able, in an instant, shake you out of any system of thought you might have devised, able to change your life utterly, in a flash. (ibid.)

Butala's life has been punctuated by these mystical events that seem "to come out of nowhere." The initial event occurred just after she made her first communion in the Roman Catholic Church. She was eight or nine, dressed in a white veil and dress and had just received the "Host" and walked to her place at the back of the church when she felt her chest fill with a cloud of white light: "It was both within me and bigger than me ... it was as if the Holy Ghost had come and filled me with its whiteness and purity" (1994a, 21). It has been a key event for Butala, one filled with wonder, over which she says she has puzzled most of her life (1999, 4). Butala constructs herself here as the beneficiary of a mysterious spiritual power. Peck would call such an event an act of grace (1997, 258), that is, an unasked-for conferral of goodness from a supernatural power (a power Peck would name as God). Paradoxically, while one cannot seek grace – it comes unasked – grace most often is given to those in a state of spiritual readiness.

One might conclude, then, that the little girl who was Sharon Butala, found the preparation for her first communion very meaningful and entered into the act in excited anticipation. She told her mother of this happening and, as she says in her St. Stephen's address, she might have felt singled out and special, she might even have gone on to become a nun, if her mother had not dismissed the event angrily and with disgust (1999, 25). As it was, the feeling of being special came much later while walking the Butala ranch. Remembering the white light, Butala, the writer, uses it in her fiction to denote the presence of the supernatural. In *The Gates of the Sun*, the light is a signal of impending death (1986, 112).

The second mystical event occurred with the birth of her first and only child. Butala describes it as the experience of Universal Oneness and of a heightened aliveness, "in which all living things were all made of the same material: the tree, the baby, the sky" (1999, 4). After giving birth, most women probably feel a kind of spiritual exaltation at the miracle of the baby. Mary Pratt, for example, expresses this emotion through the portrait of her grandchild (Fig. 4). In Butala's case, this exaltation takes the form of an important vision of the connectedness of all things. Like the white light she experienced as a child, the second vision informs her future moments of spiritual awareness. She remembers it during those numinous encounters with wild animals in which she experiences a kind of trans-species contact (1994a, 68), and she becomes motivated to write in order to contemplate further this vision of wholeness.

These two mystical experiences came to Sharon Butala unbidden and, like subsequent ones, they form part of her spiritual journey, serving to convince Butala of the existence on an alternate reality. She sees dreams as another kind of reality, associated with the world of myth. They act as guides on her spiritual journey, speaking to her not so much of the nature of the world but rather of that hidden part of herself she must discover if, as she vows, she is to know the full truth about herself. For Butala, dreams are tools in the task of self-discovery and are even more influential in that role than the numerous books she reads. Accordingly, she writes, "I take my dreams very seriously; I believe I should live my life based on them although practical matters keep intervening, not all of which are of my own making" (1995a, 72). For example, she tells of a dream about walking amongst a herd of wild stallions (ibid., 77). She becomes aware of five newly born foals and, realizing that one of the stallions intends to kill them, struggles frantically to head it off. The dream helps her to become fully aware of the conflict she is experiencing because of the success (the stallion) of her non-fiction. She realizes that the demand to continue with a commercially successfully form of writing is threatening to crowd out the more creatively satisfying writing of fiction (the foals). Butala makes the point that, however she deals with the conflict, "I am now, because of my dreams, fully aware of what I am doing" (ibid., 72).

In subscribing to the Jungian theory of dreams, Butala accepts that the subconscious uses dream imagery as a central method for communicating important information to the conscious mind.[24] Jung asserts that dreams are about the future and are concerned with recommending a psychic adjustment or a course of action to the dreamer. Dreams, however, must be decoded by the dreamer, not always an easy task when the means of unconscious communication is elliptical, using images and symbolic action. The subliminal content of the unconscious finds its source in material ignored, discarded, forgotten, or repressed by the conscious mind, and the unconscious collates, as it were, this material in order to pass along significant findings to the conscious mind (Jung 1965, 150–51).

However, some dream images do not have their source in personal experience, employing, rather, universally occurring motifs and symbols, which Jung calls "primordial images" or "archetypes." According to Jung, archetypes have their source in the "aboriginal, innate and inherited shape of the human mind" (ibid., 67). Dreams employing archetypal images are singularly powerful and beautiful. It was this kind of dream that Butala started to have when she moved to the Butala ranch and began to come under the influence of the landscape. Butala's dream life is exceptionally active; only a fraction of it is described in her life writings. However, certain dreams emerge as crucial to her construction of self. Chief among these are two dreams, which, like the stallion dream, feature animals.[25]

In the first of these dreams, described in *The Perfection of the Morning*, Butala, dressed only in a nightgown, steps outside into a winter night to see a white coyote passing within four feet of her, limping and holding up a wounded right paw (1994a, 19). Even in her dream, she realizes that this is a mythic creature, a spirit animal. Over the years, Butala comes to regard this white coyote as a talisman, representing both the mystery of the realm of spirit, and the wonder of the world of nature. The wound could be interpreted as referring specifically to Butala's psychic pain (one healed through contact with the natural world), or to the wounding of nature through environmental crises, or to the subjugation of the Amerindian people, or to all three. The coyote dream leads Butala to ponder these interpretations as well as the overall relationship between human beings and nature, a unifying theme in her life writing.

In the second dream, Butala is again looking out into the yard of the old ranch home when she is confronted by two out-sized but beautiful animals – one, a huge eagle whose wings almost shade the whole yard, and the other, a delicately coloured, six-foot owl, standing close by on the ranch-house porch. She senses that both are trying to enlist her allegiance. This was a life-changing dream that, in Butala's search to interpret it, "launched [her] on a journey through comparative religion, mythology, the study of dreams, psychoanalysis and finally into the study of the female" (1994a, 103). She comes to understand that the dream is about male power (the eagle) and female power (the owl) and that, having spent her life up to then following the eagle, it was time to "cleave to the owl" and "come to terms with her own feminine soul" (ibid.). As with most of her personal experience, this resolution finds expression in her writing – in the production of the novel, *Luna*, and the collection of short stories, *Fever*, both of which are concerned with honouring the "feminine souls" of ordinary women, rural or urban.

In Jungian terms, then, the active, vivid dream life of Sharon Butala is prompted by her subconscious. Seemingly, therefore, the dream content is self-generated, directed from one part of the mind/psyche to another part. For Butala, however, that is not the whole story. It is her view that the fervent activity of her dream life was only noticeable after her move to the Butala ranch and was undeniably prompted by the development of a close bonding with landscape of the prairie grassland. She explains:

> … significant dreaming is one way in which Nature influences and changes the individual, developing in him/her an awareness of Nature as more than mere locale, a context, more than beauty. (1994a, 104)

Butala experiences this "more" as Presence. It is a natural force that resembles Underhill's "beating heart of God," underlying all reality. In the same vein, Butala notes thoughtfully that Amerindians consider Nature to be "ensouled."

In studying the relationship between spirituality and geography, Belden Lane observes, "some parts of space are qualitatively different than others" (2002, 20). Lane asserts that these spaces possess a distinct mythic power and that the human psyche seeks a break or "fissure" in the reality of such spaces, one that might "afford entry to a numinal reality" that lies beneath the spaces' material surface. It is a subtle and elusive concept that finds echoes in Butala's conceptualization of nature as a spiritual resource. Butala observes that the dreams prompted by Nature take the dreamer to "an archetypal realm, a limitless, timeless world of pure wilderness" (1994a, 19). She describes it further as "another unknown world, a mythical world of great beauty where everything is imbued with intense and powerful meaning.… This is the world of visions" (2000a, 59–60). Archetypal dreaming is one such species of visions. However, Butala tells of experiencing visions while awake and observes that the frequency of their occurrence has increased as she grows older. She insists these are not self-generated nor forms of psychic projection but are objectively real. She prefers to class them as "mystical experiences," feeling uncomfortable with the kind of de-mythologizing that she sees as inherent in the term "altered state of consciousness" (ibid., 60). Nevertheless, the latter is an expression that creeps into subsequent texts.

Butala's visions come under the heading of paranormal phenomena and, as such, have no satisfactory scientific explanation. In keeping with Lane's analysis, they do have, however, an unmistakable connection to the environment in which they appear – to be, in fact, an expression of the "genius loci." One such vision appears to Butala while visiting Crete some years ago, and the vision seems to Butala to have been prefigured by a dream about a "big red cat, with a gold tipped tail, gold ears and gold feet" (1995a, 28). Butala declares Crete to "have a magical feel, for those who are sensitive to it" (ibid., 27): by this time it has become apparent to Butala that she is one of those who are peculiarly responsive to the numinous nuances of place. Crete, with its ancient ruins and storied sites, is seen by her to be the cradle of prehistoric mythology.

It is an appropriate place for visions. One night she awoke to see the figure of one of Crete's two ancient snake goddesses at the foot of her bed. Statuary replicas of these goddesses were discovered in the ruins of the palace of Knossos, just three kilometres from where Butala was staying, so that there existed a connection between the place and the vision. While Butala rejects any suggestion that visions such as these are self-produced, she does state that she awoke in a peculiar state of consciousness, a state that allowed her to accept with pleasure but no surprise the presence of the goddess. This little goddess, she discovers later, wears a headdress incorporating the figure of a seated cat, perhaps the cat in her dream. That night, the presence of the goddess floods the room with female power, a power that surrounds and invades Butala and fills her with joy.

In 1998, Sharon Butala experienced another marvellous vision, again with strong mythological associations. In keeping with Lane's theories, this time the setting was familiar and prosaic, the road between Eastend and Shaunavon as seen through the windshield of a Chevy Blazer. Butala was experiencing a respite from caring for a sister dying of lung cancer and was doing some routine errands. An antelope ran across the road in front of the car, and, slowing down, she saw him run down into a ditch and onto some farmland, where he stopped and looked at her. It wasn't until she started to drive on that she realized that something extraordinary had happened:

> *What was that?* I rehearsed what I had just seen; how the
> clouds had parted narrowly and beams of white light shone
> down the road in front of me and the antelope, how his body

turned slightly away from me, his head lifted, and a wide beam
of bluish light bathed him, in it his warm brown body turned a
hazy blue-white and – *he became a unicorn*. – (2000a, 67)

Butala's explanation of the unicorn vision echoes Lane's notion of the possibility of discovering a "fissure" in everyday reality, one that allows access
to an underlying numinous realm. Butala describes it as opening her eyes
to see *"what is always there"* (ibid.), allowing "a glimpse of a mythic world"
(ibid., 68). The visions of the goddess and the unicorn serve to reinforce
Butala's mystical view of the world; the goddess allows her to experience the
existence in the world of another dimension, that of feminine power. The
unicorn[26] confirms once again for Butala the palpable existence of another
dimension of reality expressed in and through the world of myth.

Butala is quite aware of the skepticism with which many of her readers
will greet her visions and other paranormal experiences.[27] However, review-
ers generally have accepted her accounts at face value. Her position is that
it is not that such experiences are so unusual, but that most persons having
similar encounters dread ridicule and will not speak of them. Her resolve
is to tell the truth about her life, whatever the consequences. That is not to
say that Butala does not find these events puzzling, even bizarre, or that she
does not have trouble fitting them into a coherent view of the universe. She
does, however, reject any conventional religious framework for these experiences, any notion that God has chosen her and is speaking to her directly.
Nevertheless, she feels that these experiences may come to her because she
is open to them, that they give meaning to her life, and that somehow she is
directed to them (2000a, 69).

This sense of being "directed" is particularly apparent in *Wild Stone
Heart*, an account of her devotion to the "field," a portion of land given to
the young Peter Butala by his father and left uncultivated. At this point in
her life, Butala had completed the difficult task of dealing with her personal
"unfinished business" and was turning her attention outward, the next phase
in her spiritual journey. In her walks in this particular field, she gradually
becomes aware that, for her, it has become a sacred place – that is, a place
filled with "a quiet sense of holiness" (2000a, 37) and a place where she
takes direction from "voiceless voices" (ibid., 28, 71, 74) whose source is
clearly outside of herself. Over the years, her walks in this field take on the
overtones of pilgrimage.

As indicated earlier, two of Belden Lane's axioms concerning the relationship between spiritual awareness and North American geography

have particular application to Butala's account of her devotional visits to the field. These specify that a "sacred place is not chosen, it chooses" and that a "sacred place can be tread upon without being entered" (Lane 2002, 19). In accordance with the former, it is clear from Butala's narrative that the sanctity of the field was not a quality projected upon it but something to be discovered over time. The first indication that the field had a special quality was the inexplicable exhaustion Butala often felt during her walks there. She is repeatedly alerted to spiritual dimensions in her environment by bodily sensations, but this feeling of exhaustion was the most persistent bodily response. It was as if something was being demanded of her. This gradually became accompanied by a special sense of peace and of Presence then by a series of serendipitous and mystical events for which she had no explanation. It was her determination to discover the meaning of these events, the source of the sacred power of the field that led to her discovery that the field was the sacred burial ground of unknown aboriginal people, part of the race of North American natives whom Butala calls the "Amerindians."[28]

Over the years Butala walked the field scores of times with her husband and occasionally shared the site with friends and relatives. Most marvelled at the beauty and quiet peace of the field, but only one other person, an Amerindian woman, sensed that they had entered a sacred place. This is in keeping with the other applicable axiom – that not all who "tread" can "enter." Evidently those who enter are to some extent "chosen" or "directed," but, as with receiving grace, being chosen comes to those in a state of spiritual readiness. As Lane explains, "the identification of a sacred place is … intimately related to states of consciousness" (2002, 19), and the precondition of a receptive state of consciousness is full participation in the particularities of the site. This kind of participation requires an interchange between the subject and the ensouled environment that Lane terms "intersubjectivity." In Chapter Two, it was noted that these four artists displayed a permeable sense of self that allows each artist to merge with her environment. This permeable sense of self (comparable to Lane's concept of intersubjectivity) allows Butala to devote herself to the field and to discover there what no one but the descendants of the original inhabitants could sense.

Butala's careful observation of all facets of the field culminates in a series of experiences both mundane and bizarre that serve to bring the past alive. She embarks on specific exploration after deciding that the seemingly random stones dotting the field must be tepee rings "just where they would be if people had passed this way" (Butala 2000a, 24). She discovers other signs of previous occupants – the remains of tools, and then a mysterious white quartz circle and cylinder, which on her next visit seem worn away as if by an enormous passage of time (ibid., 27–28). Similarly, she sees signs of human shapes on a rock in the field, but on revisiting the rock some months later, she observes with surprise that the signs have been obliterated. It is as if Butala, in an unusual state of "altered" consciousness, could enter a time warp and discover features of the field as it was hundreds or thousands of years before. These glimpses of the past include, more surprisingly, the ghostly appearance of a group of Amerindian women, apparently laughing at her rage when she trips and falls in a bed of sage (ibid., 76). The first contemporary Amerindian visitor communes silently with the Presence and subsequently sees a ghostly band of figures, (invisible to Butala) whom she calls "the people" (ibid., 155). Her visit reinforces Butala's conviction that this was indeed a sacred place. The discovery of a burial mound and much historical research lead Butala to understand that the field had been the scene of an Amerindian disaster and that the Presence that communicated with her in the field had its source not in Nature but in "the restless spirits of the dishonored dead" (ibid., 158).

In this way, Butala came to take another step in her spiritual journey. In her encounters in and with the field, Butala's attention became focused outside of herself and, as she explains in her St. Stephen's address (where she describes the steps in her spiritual development), "it led inevitably … to an acceptance of responsibility for more than my own life" (1999, 20). She realizes what it means to be the descendant of the settlers of Saskatchewan and of what their coming meant: "I began to feel in my heart instead of just my mind, the hideous injustice, the horror of what our ancestors did to the native people of this continent" (ibid.). Assuming responsibility on behalf of her antecedents develops into a moral imperative. The writing of *Wild Stone Heart* was one way of responding to this imperative. In responding as she does – that is extending her concern for the fate of one group of aboriginal people to that of "the native people of this continent" – she exemplifies another of Belden Lane's axioms, the tendency to universalize the significance of an experience of a particular sacred space. Lane's findings concerning sacred spaces in North America provide an important context for *Wild Stone Heart* by showing that Butala's experience of sacred space is really not as singular as she thought but is part of a phenomenon which is seldom named but which is, in fact, characteristic of North American experience of the landscape.

For Sharon Butala, the writing of non-fiction has been a tool both in her spiritual journey and in bringing attention to the causes she champions.

However, that kind of writing is not, in itself, a spiritual experience. It is as a fiction writer that she feels most inspired. She explains in *Coyote's Morning Cry*:

> When I am writing fiction, I feel myself dissolve into another world where things both are, and are not of my own making, where if I can be absolutely still and observant, I feel myself to be in touch with something I call the Creative Flow. (1995a, 73)

Apparently, then, Butala's fiction writing and her walking of the land are activities that prompt her mystical experience. Furthermore, it is also apparent that the fiction writing follows roughly the steps of her spiritual journey, focusing first on the perception of nature and Saskatchewan rural life and then turning to the investigation of female sensibility and what it means to be a woman. In her 1998 novel, *The Garden of Eden*, these themes persist. As with *Wild Stone Heart*, she begins also to turn her attention outward, placing the narrative against a Third World background and invoking the issues of world hunger. Butala has no reservations about using her fiction for political purposes. When I questioned her about this, she responded, "I think it is one of the great purposes of the novel, not just as a social document but further as a force for change" (Reid 1996b, 33). In using her fiction this way, Butala fulfills the prophetic and visionary function of the artist for which Haynes argues (Haynes 1997, 252).

In 2002, Butala published a collection of short stories entitled *Real Life* that reflected the most recent stage in her spiritual growth – that is, her awareness of moral responsibility and her attempt to come to terms with the fact of human and cosmic evil. In a key story entitled "Light," the female narrator, Lucia, is caring for a dying sister and in an effort to understand suffering, she begins to read true life accounts of the Holocaust. Lucia remembers seeing Elie Weisel's face on television with an expression she could not decipher. After reading Weisel's *Night*, the most harrowing of these accounts, Lucia comes to realize the significance of that look on his face:

> Since the camps, he has become a witness, determined never to look away from the terrible pictures he carries in his mind, or from the stories he's been told, the photographs he's seen. (2002, 157)

Butala presents Weisel's witnessing as an act of moral responsibility, a theme that links these stories together. *Real Life* is Sharon Butala's act of bearing witness to what she knows of human suffering and evil, either "from the terrible pictures in [her] mind or the stories [she's] been told." While her accounts are fictional, they are certainly drawn from "real life" and many, such as "Light" and "Saskatchewan," have clear autobiographical elements. Butala does not plumb the depths of human evil as Weisel does; nevertheless, these stories are harrowing enough, telling of petty meanness in private and public life, of the tragic results of casual adultery, of the male conspiracy of silence in the face of domestic violence, of rape, and of the various kinds of self-betrayal and personal shame. The affirming acts of love (the unfailing human source of "light") relieve this dark picture. Such an act forms the conclusion of "Light." Elaine, the dying sister, is close to death and cannot sit up to breathe. Lucia cannot raise her, so she eases her own body in behind that of her sister to support her through the night,

> ... until the heat of their two bodies has so melded that, awake now as the first pale rays of dawn seep around the drawn curtains, Lucia can no longer tell where her sister leaves off and she begins. (Butala 2002, 162)

These stories are the work of a mature and aware artist at the height of her powers. Moreover, they are the creation of a woman (age sixty plus) working in the full acknowledgment of growing old. She sees them as necessary for spiritual growth. As happens so often with Butala, this spiritual insight is prompted by a dream. In this case, she dreams about a dwarf woman with a shining face who welcomes her into her home (1994a, 17). It takes seven years before she is ready to accept the meaning of the dream, that is, to let go of youth:

> In fact, the numinous figure of the dwarf woman, who looked rather like my first mother-in-law, a truly wonderful woman, and whose apartment looked like my mother's house, was a figure representing maturity. She was telling me, Your youth is over, this is what is left, and I refused it, as most of us do. (1994a, 179)

In an essay on aging (1995a, 38–44), Butala reiterates that the soul can thrive only on truth and that, for herself, as for others, growing old is "the biggest truth in [one's] life" (ibid., 42). In her dreams, death is a "gentle black horse nuzzling me" (ibid., 44), and she voices the hope that she will greet death as a teacher and a friend.

The implication of this essay is that, if one ages well, one gains in wisdom and is therefore entitled to society's respect. Moreover, Butala allots a particular place in society for aging women. In another essay (in *Dropped Threads*, 2001), she observes that, throughout the ages, women between the ages of fifty and sixty-five have displayed particular psychic powers, described as

> ... an increasingly strong and accurate intuition, a more meaningful and richer dream life and the occasional mystic experience of one kind or another, from hearing a "voice" (usually soundless in the normal sense) to seeing a vision. Incidents of clairvoyance – clear vision, for example "seeing" something true that is beyond the range of normal vision – and having predictive dreams are also a part of this package of possibilities. (2001, 213)

This assertion fits as a description of Butala's own psychic powers. Here, however, she is presenting these powers, not as the outcome of sustained encounters with the natural world, but as a function of her age and gender.[29]

Although she understands that it is almost never overtly acknowledged, Butala observes that women over sixty-five occupy an even more important role in society. She sees the figure of the old woman as the repository of female power, the force behind creation of the world. In *Luna*, she investigates the truth about female lives and invests the old woman, Rhea, with the most power. Rhea is facing her own death and is slowly withdrawing from the life around her. Nevertheless, she wants to pass on the female knowledge accumulated over a lifetime to her daughters and granddaughters, and she does so symbolically through the making of bread and through supporting her grand daughter Phoebe in childbirth. Knowledge of life and its sustenance are Rhea's gift to her female descendants. Accordingly, Rhea tells her grandchildren a Creation story, a story which allows Butala to communicate clearly that she considers the feminine principle to be the activating force in the universe: "In the beginning.... There was Woman.... No one knows what there was before she came. Perhaps there was nothing" (1988b, 112–13). Similarly, in the face of all patriarchal tradition and power, which, she says, has trivialized and warped it, Butala asserts "there *is* a feminine soul" (1994, 180). Nevertheless, Butala resists the notion of any woman- or goddess-centred religion, just as she resists all other forms of organized religion (ibid.). She is content to know that women continue to be "the soul of the world," and that old women embody this notion "because they know women's mysteries" (2001, 212).[30]

MARY PRATT

While Mary Pratt may not see the role of old women in society in those precise terms, there are many parallels between Butala's perceptions of female power and those of Pratt. As with Butala, Mary Pratt comes to the spirit through the body and, like Butala, she is particularly sensitive to her physical environment. Pratt sees physical sensuality as more heightened in women than men – this being, therefore, the female's gift to the male. Pratt's sees it as a crucial gift because she perceives sensual awareness to be synonymous with life:

> Life is a sensual engagement of the body and the mind with the world. If you are dead you have no senses. You cannot be sensually engaged unless you are alive and you have five senses. They teach you, they delight you, they give you everything. The things that inform your intelligence. So I think to be sensually engaged is absolutely necessary – for me anyway. (Reid 1996a, 41)

Putting this another way, she explains, "They [women] are receptors; men are not" (Reid 1996a, 43). Mary Pratt's capacity as an acute visual receptor in the physical world leads her to become an artist. That is, her artistic inspiration is tied to her sensuously engagement, primarily through the sense of sight. And, just as Butala has her first mystical experience during girlhood, so Pratt's first fascination with the visual occurs during childhood when she becomes enraptured with the effects of coloured light streaming through a church's stain-glassed windows. And, while that first experience makes an indelible impression, it is not until she is a grown woman with children, trying to find her way as an artist, that the effects of light become truly galvanizing and become her primary area of investigation as an artist.

This occurs during a mundane domestic situation. Pratt is mopping the bedroom floor beside an unmade bed when she notices the sun spilling over the sheets and the red blanket and is astounded by her visceral reaction. It is an instant of revelation that Sandra Gwyn (echoing Underhill) calls "a moment of illumination" (Gwyn and Moray 1989, 12) and Tom Smart describes as an "epiphany" (Smart 1995, 54). A physical occurrence has suddenly become a spiritual experience, prompting intense engagement with her surroundings. This revelatory experience was prefaced by a curious event in which Pratt reportedly heard her grandmother MacMurray's voice telling her that the important quality in a painting "is the light, it's the light you know. That's what's important'" (Smart 1995, 53). Like Butala alone on the prairie, Pratt attributes her heightened state of awareness, her hearing of "voices," to the isolation of remote St. Mary's Bay: "It was really primitive out there" (Tousley 1995, C9). Both women give credit to "place" as a crucial factor in their coming to a self-definition as artist, "place" interacting with psyche.[31] Art critic John Berger calls this phenomenon "collaboration." He deems it to be at the heart of the art of painting.

In an essay for *Harper's* magazine, Berger argues that the art of painting ought properly to be a spiritual act verging on the mystical. The essay is written in response to the proliferation of electronic images in the contemporary world, images that he classes as being all spectacle and in which the virtual is substituted for the actual. Berger contends that such involvement with the virtual is against the intrinsic aims of painting, aims that historically have always been concerned with the actual. It is "an affirmation of the visible which surrounds us and which continually appears and disappears" (Berger 2002, 30). The impulse to paint comes thus from the urge to give permanence to the impermanent visible.

Certainly, the effects of light are the most ephemeral of all the qualities of the visible. Mary Pratt has said many times that what she therefore tries to do in her still-life paintings is to preserve the fleeting effects of changing light. Her use of photography is a tool in achieving this goal, and it is interesting to speculate whether or not Berger would consider this use an intrusion on the painting process. In any case, Berger enlarges further on the source of the impulse to paint and states that it comes not from observation nor from inspiration but from an "*encounter*" between painter and model. It is the result of collaboration between painter and the thing to be painted and this collaboration is to be achieved by striking a balance between over-identification with the subject and over-distancing from it: "To go in close means forgetting convention, reputation, reasoning, hierarchies and self" (ibid.). Through her choice of domestic subject and in her steadfast defiance of art trends, Pratt has demonstrated this kind of forgetting throughout her career. Pratt's affirmation (referred to earlier) that "I have always tried to be what I paint," and that it must be "so much a part of me that I am what it is" corresponds closely to Berger's concept of collaboration.

Berger makes it clear that not all painting is the result of authentic collaboration. Some painters stay at a "copying distance" while others succumb to stylistic tricks (Berger 2002, 32). Mary Pratt herself is aware that some of her paintings result from working at a copying distance and fall short of the standard of authenticity. She expresses her concern on CBC-TV:

I can paint almost anything. And when you can do that it is very dangerous, because you can make something very beautiful and there is nothing there.[32]

Pratt hopes to avoid triviality by showing the "darks" of experience as well as the "lights." Like acts of grace and mystical experience, however, genuine "encounters" with a subject often come about unbidden, as a gift. Berger says further that the experience of collaboration – these authentic encounters – "[are] seldom based on goodwill: more usually on desire, rage, fear, pity or longing" (2002, 31), and so it is with much of Pratt's work.

One of the clearest examples of the successful collaboration of artist and subject is her *Fire* series, especially *Burning the Rhododendron* (Fig. 7), a wall-size work that confronts (or "encounters") and involves the viewer as much as it did the artist. As explained earlier, Pratt's choice of fire as a subject coincided with the upheaval in her personal life that occurred when trouble in the Pratt marriage could no longer be glossed over (Reid 1996a, 54). The fire paintings emerged as the vehicle for expressing her rage and disappointment. It is not a simple matter of venting emotion in art, but rather of galvanizing the blend of emotion and subject so that the art becomes something beyond representation.

An earlier Pratt painting, *Child with Two Adults* (Fig. 4), is another work that conveys, and is prompted by, powerful emotions. The painting combines bodily sensibility with spiritual nuance. The figure of the baby is shown as supremely physical, yet with the intent gaze of a full-formed personality. The painting is about the act of giving birth as an expression of female soul, joining one generation of women to the next. It is as if mother and grandmother are baptizing baby Katherine into the spiritual community of women.

At the other end of the emotional spectrum is the 1978 painting, *The Service Station* (Fig. 20). It pictures a quartered moose carcass hanging hoisted on the back of a wrecking truck. When she first saw the carcass, the sight of it horrified Pratt because, as indicated earlier, it signified the male world of physical violence (a sharp contrast to the nurturing female world of birthing and babies). This aspect of the male world was not unknown to Pratt, living in Salmonier as she did, and immersed, therefore, in the male hunting and fishing culture of Newfoundland, a much harsher one than she had known growing up in Fredericton. Her decision to paint this subject was an act of moral responsibility that served to further her spiritual growth, not unlike Butala's decision to tell the harrowing stories in *Real Life*. Both artists use their art to attest to their personal knowledge of human suffering and evil. The protest inherent in Butala's story "Gravity" (2002, 112–29), which depicts male complicity in the face of domestic violence, is the same protest implicit in *The Service Station*, in *Another Province of Canada* (Fig. 21) and in Pratt's fish paintings.

Pratt also has discovered that her painting practice serves on occasion to alert her to the complex truth of relationships, the ability to face the truth about oneself and others being another condition for personal spiritual growth. The two clearest examples of this come from the roles played by *Aspects of a Ceremony* and the *Donna* series in alerting her to troubles in her marriage. In creating the former, purportedly celebrating the wedding ritual, she had to deal with true state of her marriage to Christopher and her feelings about marriage in general. Pratt explained that her preparations for the show coincided with a declaration from Christopher:

> This was the summer Christopher decided he wanted a life of his own. And I found this very, very difficult and my arthritis had got to a point where my life was in pain physically and it became painful psychologically and philosophically and I had to deal with all of this. So I suppose the show was heightened by that. (Reid 1996a, 45)

In the latter, the *Donna* series, she faced her mixed feelings about the female code of femininity and the complexities in the triangular relationship between herself, Christopher, and model, Donna Meany. Pratt said of these paintings: "They are supposed to be confrontational"(Reid 1996a, 25). Pratt communicates these feelings most powerfully in *Girl in My Dressing Gown* (Fig. 22), in which the figure of Donna is shown in terms of masquerade and feminine challenge. In the context of Pratt's personal life, it is a brave painting which confronts the truth and which embodies, on many levels, Berger's notion of painting as encounter.

Because Pratt's prime interest as a painter is in the visual effects of light, art historians David Burnett and Marilyn Schiff have classified her work in another way:

> Hers is a type of painting that has been called "pictorial phenomenalism." … Its essence lies pictorially in the emphasis of light on the surface of objects, an approach that recognizes reality in the immediate visual contact with objects. To paint that

is to represent the primacy of that contact and affirm its reality. The use of the photograph is a confirmation of that immediacy, a way to see objects not first in a conceptual sense – how we use them and how we understand their use – rather as they are in their visual immanence, that is, as the direct embodiments of our perceptions. (1983, 167)

However, in our discussions Pratt made it clear that the display of technical mastery evident in her depicting of objects in their "visual immanence" is not to be construed as an end in itself. At its height, Pratt's ability to capture the immediacy of perception through the painterly representation of light is a means of affirming a vital life force described by Bergson as the *élan vital* and by Underhill as vitalism. The erotic tingle that is Pratt's response to a particularly luminous moment of perception is the action of life greeting life. While there is little of the paranormal or supernatural in this response, it does resemble mystical experience in the desire for union of the self with what James Leuba describes as "the larger than self." The impetus comes from the senses, but the response comes from the soul or spirit. Pratt, borrowing from C.S. Lewis, calls it being "surprised by joy" (Reid 1996a, 23).

It is no coincidence that Pratt makes reference to one of Britain's leading Christian writers; she was raised firmly in the Protestant Christian tradition. She tells how, as a child, she sat every Sunday in Wilmot United Church gazing at that stained glass window, pondering the relationship between God and the light that fascinated her so much (M. Pratt 2000, 139). She surely became aware, during those multitude of Sundays, that Jesus is characterized by Christians as the "true light" sent by God to dispel "the darkness."[33] He is represented to be the true source of the moral (life) and spiritual (light) nature of man.[34] In Christian iconography, Christ, light, life, and goodness are joined imaginatively in opposition to Satan, darkness, evil, and death.

As we talked together about her art, Pratt made it clear that her painterly use of light and dark, while being a representational device, could also be read metaphorically as embodying the basic Christian symbolism, and that she expected it would be recognized as such by viewers of her work. As noted earlier, she comments to this effect while explaining to me why her still lifes have such "punch":

PRATT: But it won't stand without the darks. You have to have the darks there or the lights won't work.

REID: Are you talking metaphorically now?

PRATT: I'm talking both ways and that's true.

REID: It's true in terms of representational technique.

PRATT: Don't you think, though, there is a general truth about all men's experience whether it is actual hands-on creativity or whether it is metaphorically in your head, these truths are truths and they hold throughout the whole experience.... I am a person who has concentrated on the lights of my experience. (Reid 1996a, 15)

Pratt believes that the spiritual nature of human beings is self-evident. In keeping with her internalization of Christian symbolism, she expresses this truth metaphorically through her depiction of light. The light that floods over the Pratt supper table is like a benediction, paying tribute to the spiritual closeness of family. The light that emblazons the jars of red currant jelly (Fig. 1) commemorates the loving connection between Pratt and her mother. The same red light floods Mrs. West's dining room (Smart 1995, 27), an evocation of her childhood home and the spirit of her mother. The darks, which Pratt says one must have to balance the lights, have their source in Pratt's moral obligation to depict the truth, however unsettling, and to acknowledge personal pain and suffering (the darks) in a practice acknowledged to be autobiographical. These darks figure most strongly in her later works, with their pronounced shadows predicting the final darkness and with knives cutting into fruit to hint of violence or pain.

Her still lifes of fish have a particular place her spiritual expression. They, together with bread and apples, are the subjects that Pratt paints with full acknowledgment of their Biblical associations, as reflected in her childhood memories of the New Testament stories of the loaves and fishes, and those of the fisherman disciples of Jesus. In Pratt's rendering, fish such as trout, herring, and salmon – common catches around Salmonier – become sacred and sacrificial subjects, laid out dead in rows, reflecting the light off of iridescent scales. At the deepest associative level, the whole Christian iconography of beauty, death, violence, and victimization that arises from the story of Christ is summoned to mind by these fish paintings. She told me, "They are all Christian symbols" (Reid 1996a, 57). It is my view that Pratt's incorporation of these themes is prompted by her observation of Newfoundland culture and her anguish at the fate of the fishing industry, central to that culture. Further, they reflect Pratt's personal feelings of alienation and sacrifice at coming to live in a remote part of Newfoundland. Of course, on a more literal level, they appear simply as renderings of a foodstuff commonplace in the Pratt household, set forth as offerings from the animal world to the human one. However, in such paintings as *Another Province of Canada* (Fig. 21), the rendering of the gutted fish borders on the obscene so that any possibility of religious overtones is obliterated. Accordingly, Tom Smart observes that in Pratt's work (as in life), the line between the sacred and the profane is frequently blurred (1995, 105).

A comment in one of the entries in *A Personal Calligraphy* serves to spark further speculation about the spiritual significance of Christian imagery for Pratt. The journal entry concerned the place of Donna Meany in the Pratt household, and it described how the Pratt home was different from that which Donna was used to: "paintings on the wall ... wedding crystal and china" and in the living room, French doors, a geranium plants, a view of the river and *"a print of a Botticelli tondo of the Virgin and the Baby Jesus over the mantle"* (2000, 31) [emphasis added]. Perhaps the print was hung there solely because of its beauty. Nevertheless, it had the place of honour in the house. In an analysis of the use of religious art in the home, professor David Morgan states, "placing the image of Christ on the mantle identifies it as 'the center of the home'" (1998, 51). Morgan is referring here to a segment of the American middle class who, unlike Pratt, was more concerned with the subject of the artwork than its aesthetics. Still, Pratt did look at Botticelli's Baby Jesus every day, and I cannot but think that she felt her home was being sanctified by this image.

However, it is in another journal entry that Pratt displays her most imaginative involvement with the story of Jesus. It is Palm Sunday and she is musing about the particular odours that have come to symbolize for her the mystery of the Resurrection:

> I have always associated gingerbread with Easter. The cloves, cinnamon, the ginger – all redolent of mystery, the Middle East, Calvary. Golgotha. The horror of the crucifixion masked by the odour of spices. Surely the body was wound in linen soaked in cloves. Long strips of linen wound carefully around the body. Surely the vision of the angel at the sepulchre was perfumed with a mixture of cinnamon and lily. The empty cave, dark, mysterious, could not have smelled of wet rock and mould and decaying leaves. The smell of spice – the odour of sanctity – must surely have pervaded. (2000, 27)

This remarkably evocative passage builds a bridge between her personal experience (the gingerbread which she had just eaten "topped with sour cream and a sprinkle of chopped crystallized ginger") and the scene that is at the heart of the Christian religion. There is no mystical happening here for Pratt but there is an imaginative joining of the self with the mysterious "larger than self" that, for James Leuba, is the mark of the mystical.

This 1994 journal passage ends on an anxious note: "my mother doesn't sound well" (ibid., 28). The entry acts as a note of forewarning for the reader. In the mosaic of private musings and public addresses that forms *A Personal Calligraphy*, the death of her mother, Katherine West, emerges as the emotionally central event. Pratt allows the reader a glimpse of her last days with her mother, including her mother's gradual physical deterioration. However, Pratt's abiding love for her mother and the spiritual connection between the two render the deterioration irrelevant: "When I'm with her, it [our mutual forgetfulness] doesn't seem to matter" (ibid., 14); Pratt is content to sit by her side while they listen together to "The Lark in the Clear Air." The power of the mother-daughter relationship is evident once again as Pratt is struck with reminiscence, recalling her mother's particular style and beauty and the values that they embody. At her mother's death, she voices the universal lament: "After years of 'coming home,' there is now no longer 'home'" (ibid., 41).

Time, of course, has brought many other changes for Pratt: one of these is the degree of involvement with family. Her children are now grown with their own lives and families and she and first husband Christopher are divorced. Before her remarriage in 2006, Pratt was for many years alone and confessed to mixed feelings about her solitary state. Although often lonely, she realized that a degree of solitude was necessary for her work. Becoming older, she felt she could no longer afford the energy required to divide her time between work and an active social life. Both through choice and necessity, she was most often alone. Even now, she and husband James Rosen, although enjoying much travel abroad, spend time apart because of Rosen's teaching commitments in the United States. One cannot help but feel that this marital situation is a happy compromise for Pratt, offering her both companionship and time alone.

Nevertheless, she still endeavours to keep closely connected with the extended Pratt family. For example, for many years, her daughter-in-law, Sheila, took care of the office duties that accompany Mary's career. Similarly Ned, her photographer son, takes on the task of documenting her work. The whole family observes holiday rituals together and, in *A Personal Calligra-*

phy, Pratt shares her 1997 diary account of that year's Thanksgiving. She yearns for "those long ago Thanksgivings" when the children were small, then describes in detail the amazing food of the present-day dinner, each family household contributing what Mary would call a "yummy" dish – a ham, "brown sugar crusted," a "potato scallop, all the slices layered perfectly," turkey, sauerkraut, pumpkin pies, and a partridgeberry pudding, "a great treat" (2000, 44–45).

In this description, Mary Pratt's domestic self joins with her artist self to exclaim over the sensual appeal of the dinner. Her depiction echoes her whole still-life *oeuvre*, the sense of celebration being embodied in the written description of light: "Sun streams in through the reaching, opening buds of the geraniums." Just as in *Supper Table* (Fig. 2), the light acts as a benediction, revealing family life, as seen even through the eyes of old age, to be "interconnected network[s] of people loving and engaging with each other" (Haynes 1997, 27) As Deborah Haynes argues, such acts of connection are a form of creative expression, one which she equates with spiritual experience. And yet, as Pratt always insists, "you have to have the darks" to give an accurate representation in life as in art. Accordingly, this Thanksgiving entry ends with a note of confusion and uncertainty regarding Christopher's motive for confiding his plans for a new studio (Pratt 2000, 46).

In her references to her personal life, both in her work as a visual artist and in her writing, one can observe Pratt striving for the ethical authenticity that Scott Peck and Elisabeth Kübler-Ross establish as the precondition of spiritual growth. In terms of her marriage to Christopher, for example, not only did Pratt face the truth about marriage problems through the medium of painting, she was candid about their relationship both in her lectures on her retrospective show *The Substance of Light*,[35] and in such CBC-TV series as *Adrienne Clarkson Presents* and *Life and Times*. In the latter series, the careers of Mary and Christopher are presented jointly, interspersed with material about their life together and apart. It was not easy for Mary to do this show, but she did not flinch from truth-telling, even if it had to be subtly presented.

Nor does she flinch from truth-telling when writing about her beloved Fredericton. In the 1998 piece for *The New Brunswick Reader* (reproduced in *A Personal Calligraphy*, 47–54), she describes the joys of growing up in Fredericton, a prosperous, cultured, and safe community – the "lights." Again, she does not hesitate to name the "darks" – that is, the existence of a rigid class system of privilege, "the Fredericton gentility." The gentility excluded the Wests from the inner circle but treated them politely. As Pratt explains, "We knew when to leave" (ibid., 54). Personally, Pratt felt freed to be herself by this exclusion so that, at this distance in time, she exhibits no obligation to varnish over the truth. Pratt is equally forthright in examining her own conscience, and acknowledging her feelings, even if she thinks they do her no particular credit.

Mary Pratt was sixty-five when she painted *Burning the Rhododendron* (Fig. 7) and was by her own admission beginning to use her work to come to terms with issues in life: "I'm facing the last part of my life now, and I've gotten this kind of anxiety to solve things" (Smith-Strom, CBC-TV, 1996). As established in our discussion of Sharon Butala's spiritual journey, this introspection is the precondition of spiritual growth and tends to be undertaken later in life. Earlier, her work was the means of saving evanescent sensual experience; now the work is a means of "understanding things." Perhaps that is why, as some critics have noted, her paintings since 1995 have a particularly darker edge. For example, Brayshaw calls *Dinner for One* (Smart 1995, 133) and *Breakfast Last Summer* (Fig. 6) "dark and brooding pieces which speak of the artist alone" (Brayshaw 1995, 32). Another reviewer notes the recurrence of the image of a knife cutting into the flesh of a piece of fruit, saying, "There is recent violence here." It is my view that in works such as these, Pratt is working out her understanding of old age – that is, coming to terms with spending many of her days alone, dealing with the constant pain of arthritis, the knife in the flesh. "It takes me now, because of the arthritis, an hour and a half to get ready for the day" (Reid 1996a, 17).

Part of one's spiritual growth in old age is the acknowledgment of the fact of death. One senses that Pratt's paintings of the empty rooms of her childhood home (circa 1995) act to prepare her for the inevitable death of her mother. In 1997, when Katherine West was terminally ill, Pratt experienced a heightened awareness of her own mortality. As she remarked on CBC's *Life and Times* (Gregg 1997), she hears "the rumbling of the falls" before going over the precipice. In her journals of the same year, she muses about the nature of death, asking, "Does our soul run free when the body is broken?" and answering, "Our faith says it does." She imagines heaven and wonders poignantly, "Have my dead found each other?" as she thinks of her stillborn twins (2000, 42). This is five months before her mother's death. Earlier, however, in a 1991 journal entry she appears to reject the notion of an afterlife: "When we die, nothing of the living part of us will remain" (ibid., 93). Perhaps she means "here on earth." In any case, she sees her art as the only assurance of a kind of immortality, art "which in itself has no life" but can embody "an idea," part of the essence of self. Philosopher Hannah Arendt sees creativity as the one legitimate avenue of immortality, and Haynes cites Arendt in discussing the vocation of the artist: "Arendt believed that the task of human beings is to produce things that transcend human mortality. In short, we create in order not to die" (Haynes 1997, 44).

In contemplating the likelihood of life after death, Pratt does not consult Biblical scripture. The Easter story is vivid in her imagination but does not seem to offer any reassurance of life after death or any comfort when grieving for her mother, if her published journal entries can be taken as typical. The one image of a kind of resurrection is in her 1996 painting, *Lupins in Christopher's Burned Out Studio* (Pratt 2000, 46), and, while the flowers serve as a metaphor for hope, it is likely they have specific reference to Christopher's recovery from the destruction of his studio, a personal catastrophe. Similarly, despite her affection for Wilmot United Church, she questions the phenomenon of building churches as places of worship. As with Butala, in a 1993 journal entry Pratt equates spiritual experience with being in nature:

> Very funny to imagine thousands of humans running around making elaborate cages for gods.... Better to imagine them standing on cliff beside the sea, praising the rising sun, looking to the horizon with their hearts full of the pleasure of the air. (ibid., 102)

Pratt would call herself Christian, yet in this passage, and in her sensuous response to the world, there is something of the pantheistic view of the universe.

It is clear, therefore, that in her diary entries, Pratt reveals a liminal positioning as regards Christianity. On the one hand, Biblical images and stories have shaped both her imagination and her view that human experience is necessarily made up of "lights" and "darks" – joy and suffering. And yet, she is far from whole-hearted in her acceptance of Christian orthodoxy, musing and trying to fit her knowledge of the particular into some theory of the general[36] (Reid 1996a, 37). Perhaps Pratt's liminal positioning in the area of religion is an indication of her spiritual maturity. In a video designed for parish use,[37] Father Richard Rohr recommends the study of the parables of Jesus as an example of experiencing "liminal space," the space that challenges unthinking orthodoxy and a rigid view of the nature of salvation. Rohr says "All [spiritual] transformation takes place in liminal space." For

Scott Peck, the germinative liminal space is between the conscious and unconscious mind, and spiritual transformation takes place when the unconscious is made conscious through the act of reflection (1997, 76–85). Mary Pratt occupies this liminal space both in her practice of art and in her daily journal writing, the realms in which spiritual transformation takes place.

Pratt does not see the drive to create as lessening in old age. On *Life and Times* (Gregg 1997), she observes, "As you become physically weaker, the flame at the end becomes brighter and you go for it, more than you did and with more concentration." Elsewhere, she comments with equanimity on the psychic growth both in herself and in friends such as Gordon Pinsent, who are contemporaries. They greet and celebrate their "larger selves" while remembering with affection the "lesser selves" of the past (Pratt 2000, 64). It is reassuring to contemplate this notion of "larger selves" when our ageist society so often conceives of old age in terms of loss and the diminution of self. Pratt demonstrates an heroic conception of the aging, a perception she reinforces by quoting Tennyson's "Ulysses," her father's favorite poem: "To strive, to seek, to find and not to yield" (ibid., 65).

MARY MEIGS

In her handling of a disabling stroke at the age of eighty-five, Mary Meigs similarly offers a strong example of spiritual strength. She was hospitalized for some time and then underwent extensive therapy, struggling to regain movement in the left side of her body. Physical infirmity of this kind affects not only one's body, but also one's whole sense of self. Meigs' response was to mobilize her artist/writer self in order to turn the experience into art through the medium of life writing. She calls the pieces "Hospital Notes," some of which appeared initially in periodicals.[38] In these "Notes," she documents not only her physical and mental struggle but also her interaction (via a wheelchair) with the hospital community. Here is an example of the struggles:

> September 25. A dialogue between mind and index finger.
> Mind: "Lie down flat." Left finger: "I don't hear you. I'm tired."
> Mind (angrily): "Lie down, *flat*." (Meigs 2001, 72)

and an example of the interaction:

The men, much less talkative than the women, can be silent through an entire meal. At lunch I was between the two. "Coffee shop will be open at 12.30" said an announcement. "Have you been to the coffee shop?" "No I haven't" left man said in what I interpreted to be a surly voice. Right man's stomach is squeezed under table top with difficulty; he has had a stroke and has trouble with his speech but has a sunny disposition and laughs gently (at group therapy sessions). (ibid.)

Here, Mary Meigs is insisting on the essential humanity of all persons, including the old and infirm, and, by publishing accounts of her struggles and encounters in the hospital, she is drawing aside the curtain of fear and revulsion that often marginalizes people suffering severe physical trauma. What is extraordinary is that her spirit remains vital: "There is no use being scared." She adds:

"Working Note" Hospital life (2 months of it) ... gave me a strange joy, since I wasn't in pain and fascinated by the activities around me and the details of care. (ibid.)

In another journal, the text is reproduced exactly as she typed it so that her difficulty in operating the keyboard with her weakened hand is apparent: "wall of snowv isi bly cars because bright diamonds of sunlight ..." (Meigs 2002, 30). In her introduction explaining the source of the text, she again uses the word 'joy': "In occupational therapy, it was a great joy to use the old Underwood electric typewriter to strengthen the finger of my left hand." Being able to look out the window at the "tree-clad face of the mountain, leafless then completely green, which rose at the back of the hospital" adds to the joy. For Meigs, as for Butala, the natural world is a reliable source of spiritual consolation.

In "Hospital Notes," Meigs makes it apparent that one's spiritual development shows in the connections one makes with other people. Meigs had come to be mindful of others, even when in physical distress herself, or when the contacts are fleeting (as in the hospital's coffee shop and therapy room). Spiritual mindfulness consists in being truly present for another person. In *Lily Briscoe: A Self-Portrait*, Meigs voices her awareness of the need for connection when she says, "a real flowing of attention into another being is like a transfusion of life" (1981, 189). She quotes Martin Buber, the existentialist theologian, as the writer who describes best this aspect of subjectivity:

If I am not really here then I am guilty. When I answer the call of present being "where art thou?" with "I am here" but am not really there, that is not with the truth of my whole life, then I am guilty. Original guilt consists in remaining with oneself. (ibid.)

While interaction with others can (as it does with Meigs) last until one's death, facing one's immanent death is a task that can only be accomplished alone. Here Meigs' ability to write serves her once again. In the free-writing sections of *Beyond Recall*, the reader is allowed intimate access to her thought and emotions as she works through her grief at the gradual loss of bodily functions and the knowledge that the end of life is not far away. There is no forced cheerfulness: "How I've struggled to feel joy but lo and behold I'm in a joyless state" (2005, 141). There is something cathartic in Meigs' use of death imagery to express her feelings. She writes repeatedly about the language of silence, of turning to stone, and the rolling forth of shadows. She would "rather be a cicada singing my life's end" (ibid., 145), but she dreams of "twelve pairs of coal-black horses" drawing a carriage along a railway track (ibid., 151). Just a month before her death, she responds again to the train image, a train going

> ... in another direction. The feeling of being headed towards doom. The feeling of being scared, of being herded by an ignorant madman, of being helpless. But I don't want to go in that direction. (ibid., 148)

In her diary entry for the same day, she writes of a "huge tiredness and ineptness," but the images are of the garden roses, "pink-white" on their upright stems (ibid., 123). Her thoughts are of Marie-Claire Blais, still her most intimate friend to whom she plans to give a perfect rosebud. Despite her fully articulated fear of death, Meigs reaches out to life and to other people right to the end. As editor Lisa Weil explains (ibid., 125), three hours before she died, Meigs was consulting publisher Karl Seigler of Talonbooks about the publishing of *Beyond Recall*.

Much of the material in Meigs' first five books deals with the act of "coming out." However, read in the present context, these texts reveal themselves also as accounts of Meigs' struggle to be present to other people, even at the last when she is so ill. Earlier, however, Meigs found redemption through her writing because she discovered that significant relationships took on deeper nuances, and people were perceived more clearly in art than they were in life. For example, Meigs and her mother often failed in life to give and receive the attention each craved; however, in *The Box Closet*, Margaret Meigs is fully present in her letters (left for her children to find) and, for her part, Mary, in writing the book, devotes her attention single-mindedly to the young Margaret she meets on the handwritten page. Similarly, Meigs perceives the relationship with her Australian lover in a more rounded fashion when re-lived (thinly veiled as fiction) in *The Time Being*.

According to the paradigm of spiritual maturity set out by Scott Peck, and encapsulated in another form by Martin Buber and Elisabeth Kübler-Ross, the awareness of community and the ability to attend to that awareness is the mark of spiritual maturity. The precondition of attaining such maturity is the process of facing one's moral imperfections, attending to "the mote in one's own eye" as the Bible would have it. One can trace Meigs' ethical stocktaking in all of her life writing but primarily in *Lily Briscoe: A Self-Portrait*, *The Medusa's Head*, and *The Time Being*, all of which are concerned with lesbian relationships. In *The Box Closet* and *In the Company of Strangers* Meigs focuses more on other people and is therefore less intense in her self-scrutiny.

Otherwise, Meigs' self-scrutiny *is* intense. However, she is wholly concerned with commonplace relationships and not with God, as in traditional spiritual autobiographies. In her description of these relationships, one can observe a pendulum swing between (in Buber's terms) striving to be truly present to another and setting one's attention firmly on oneself. Meigs is fully aware of these swings between generosity and self-interest and, like Mary Pratt, she experiences conflict in balancing the demands of life and art:

> One is perpetually walking the tightrope between selfishness and generosity, the generosity that comes from a state of awareness of others, and an artist's selfishness – the holding together of the conditions necessary to be an artist.... I need chunks of visible time and hours everyday of total silence in which I can attempt to see and to learn. (1983, 103)

Deborah Haynes adds to the complexity of the ethics of "attention" by positing that the "matrices of relationship" and "artistic creativity" are both manifestations of "the ongoing creativity of the world" and "sacred dimensions of existence" (1997, 27). The question, then, is whether choosing the creativity of art-making above the creativity of relationship is valid. I would think that Martin Buber would say "no," and Deborah Haynes, a tentative "yes." It is this conundrum with which Mary Meigs wrestles, especially when in a love relationship. However, by aligning herself with Lily Briscoe rather than with Mrs. Ramsay in Woolf's *To the Lighthouse*, Meigs sides with Haynes. She declares as much as a preface to examining her intimate friendship with Barbara Deming and Marie-Claire Blaise:

> ... at last I feel free to speak about the place of love in my own life. To begin with, I should say that love has always taken a secondary position in my life, secondary that is to my work as an artist. (1981, 69)

When lovers become demanding, asking more attention than she is willing to give, Meigs quickly falls out of love: "Why? I couldn't explain.... The more she loved and needed me, the more cranky and sullen I became" (ibid., 70). It is a phenomenon that, I suspect, Pratt and Butala also would understand, being able in their mature years and in most instances, to put art first. Pratt and Butala, however, display less ambivalence, possibly because of their longtime service as wives and mothers. Dyck, with her skill in creating community, manages to align family relationships with the practice of art, her husband and one son becoming collaborators in her practice.

Through writing, then, Meigs attempts arrive at the truth about herself in relationship. However, of the four artists, Meigs is the one who articulates most clearly the notion that her version of truth is contingent and that a relationship can look quite different from the friend's point of view or, for that matter, from her own point of view at a different time and in a different mood. Morality, then, is a matter of judgment, operating in an ambiguous grey area. In an interview with feminist writer, Betsy Warland, Meigs agrees that autobiography as a genre similarly operates in the grey area, in a liminal space beyond or behind the facts. In an article for *Inversions*, an anthology of lesbian writing, she makes the point that lesbian writers of autobiography, in particular, must develop an instinct for the grey areas in genre and in language in order to be circumvent the positioning of a homophobic readership (1991a, 114).

There are circumstances, however, in which the creating and occupying of a grey area constitutes an evasion of moral responsibility: those circumstances concern the recognition and naming of evil. Any evasion is toxic to spiritual growth. One, however, does not always recognize evil and, in the textual pursuit of the truth about herself, Meigs realizes that she was often slow to identify the social and personal evils she perpetrated or encountered. In *The Medusa Head*, she says, "Andrée had no sense of oppression; she swam in her racism like a fish in the sea" (1983, 33). In the same way, the Meigs family of pre-war Philadelphia accepted racism as part of the social code that befitted their class and social status. Meigs recalls with shame the subservient position of black servants in their household and of black people in general: "My mother held to the belief that you did not entertain black people in your drawing room or consider them as possible friends" (1983, 47). Similarly, in reading the letters stored in the box closet, Meigs is dismayed to learn of the habitual and unthinking anti-Semitism of her youthful mother and father. This discovery assumes such proportions that she devotes a chapter in *The Box Closet* to a discussion of its ramifications. She faces the dilemma of all autobiographers of how much to tell – about oneself, and more importantly, about others:

> To quote them is to commit a kind of disloyalty to my family and to expose them to retroactive accusations. Their only defense would be the same one that is used so often to defend the indefensible, that they were victims of their culture and class. (1987, 178)

Ashamed and angry, Meigs is tempted not to mention her parents' telltale comments in her book. Moreover, she confesses that she is in no position to judge, having been in "a moral fog until I was shaken out of it by events outside of me and by people who saw more clearly than I did" (ibid., 179). It is to Meigs' credit that she informs on both on her parents and herself, acting as a witness to an evil that poisons not only the victims of the prejudice but also the psyche of its perpetrators. Homophobia is part of the pattern of prejudice to which Meigs is reacting, a form of discrimination that affected Meigs personally. It has motivated her to denounce both the oppression of lesbians and the patriarchal construction of the female that has penalized generations of women. It is her *testimonio*, her act of witness.

The evil that Meigs denounces in *The Box Closet* and in *Lily Briscoe* is a cultural phenomenon; the evil in *The Medusa Head* comes in the form of a personality aberration. In this text, she examines a period in her life when she and Marie-Claire Blais were held in thrall by a French novelist she names simply as Andrée. Meigs tells of a love triangle that begins when Meigs follows Blais to France, eventually replacing Blais as Andrée's lover.

Meigs and Blais seem to believe that a love triangle without jealousy and pain is feasible and so remain closely connected. Andrée's motives eventually are revealed to be mercenary; she hopes that she can permanently separate Meigs from Blais and have access to Meigs' considerable wealth. The plot, when outlined thusly, is banal but, in *The Medusa Head*, Meigs is less concerned with plot than with investigating the psychological dynamics of Andrée's control and manipulation.

Meigs creates an unforgettable portrait of a woman who delights in living a lie, in deceiving and exploiting others. Throughout, Meigs uses the language of Satanic possession: Andrée is "the Medusa head who turns us to stone all too often" (1983, 75). Andrée is also "my succubus" (ibid., 51), while Meigs is "less a zombie" than Blais (75). Meigs develops a sexual coldness and monitoring of money that allow her eventually to escape:

> … instinct had always told me that sexual possession gives absolute power, the power to say you are mine. To be Andrée's, I realized, was to be in mortal danger, to lose not only my body but my soul, and to live, not my life but hers. At the time she was in control of my guilty psyche, I took back my body, and with the same parsimony began to ration my gifts of money. (ibid., 55)

Scott Peck states that one of the characteristics of the evil personality is "scapegoating," the projection of one's own evil onto the world (Peck 1983, 75–76). Andrée writes her own account of the love triangle, and, in Andrée's version, Meigs identifies a perfect example of scapegoating:

> Andrée's book is an almost diagrammatic lesson in the art of how to escape judgment by transferring it to someone else, a shifting of positive and negative poles (1983, 148).

Earlier, Meigs identifies the same phenomenon from a different perspective, pinpointing even more precisely how evil people are more than merely sinful:

> Both [she and Blais] of us know when we become our worst selves; we have a sense of shadow ("Get thee behind me, Satan!") which has to be kept in its place or it will invade one's inmost being. Andrée's shadow was internalized then bleached by some burning substance like Clorox, so that looking in her magician's mirror, she saw a person who was shadowless and blameless. (ibid., 132)

Even after the ties to Andrée have been broken, Meigs' fear of her remains for some time. However, as Scott Peck says, "To name something correctly gives us a certain amount of power over it" (Peck 1983, 68). Meigs' courage in naming Andrée as evil allows her to move on, to recoup, and to continue to grow spiritually.

That is not to say that the reader of *The Medusa Head* comes away with unmitigated admiration for Meigs. In dealing with her "unfinished business," as she surely does in this particular text, Meigs does not hesitate put herself in a poor light. In a direct address to the reader, she voices the reader's unspoken question, "Why did I hang on?" but provides no real answer: "An autobiographer can only answer whys like this with further stern moral scrutiny and the plaintive wish that people would not insist on reasonable explanations" (87). The only explanation Meigs gives for her inaction is inertia, a vain hope that everything would work out, and an ingrained reluctance to do anything "not nice." This leaves the reader impatient but not censorious. The reader is more likely to judge Meigs as culpable because of her reluctance to acknowledge that the love triangle was going to cause somebody pain. Moreover, the ordinary reader is apt to fault Meigs for being rich. People of ordinary means probably feel that they could not possibly afford to relocate to a house in France in order to pursue a liaison, no matter how swept up by infatuation.

Generally, however, Meigs disarms the reader by being candid and self-deprecating about her financial independence. She raises the issue up front in the opening lines of her first book: "I belong to an endangered species which in the eyes of many ought to be extinct: the gently born, the monies, the sheltered" (1981, 7). In the early chapters of *Lily Briscoe*, Meigs details the many ways she has been sheltered; she calls it "the baggage of her inheritance" (ibid.) and voices her regret that wealth and position initially cut her off from the mainstream of life. She informs the reader of her adolescent insensitivity by telling of her distaste for the poor children she had volunteered to teach:

> I remember only my distaste for these strange clamouring little girls whose clothes smelled of stale cooking oil.... It was a long time before I learned that we were as handicapped by our wealth as they were by their poverty. They, at least, had an accurate idea of what life was like; ours was restricted by the blinders we wore. (1981, 49)

In all the accounts of her life, Meigs demonstrates that she is shaped by relationship, despite her insistence on autonomy. Relationships helped to remove Meigs' "blinders." For example, her association with American writer and social activist Barbara Deming is shown to be instrumental in raising Meigs awareness of social inequities and all forms of oppression. In Meigs' narrative, Barbara and Andrée serve as reverse images of each other. If, as Meigs' French housekeeper says, Andrée was "an emissary of the devil" (1983, 122), Barbara was Meigs' good angel. In fact, Meigs reports that she heard others describe Barbara as a "saint." In the same vein, she observes that Barbara's influence activates one's conscience:

> By her faith, Barbara is able to make people change in good ways. Something in her, says Jane Gapen, who lives with her now, 'tugs at one's devil / Unmistakably one's devil wants to fly out / and throw itself at one's feet.' (1981, 82)

Meigs herself is reluctant to let some of her devils go, saying that conscience is more superego than an intrinsic God-given faculty. Nevertheless, as a pacifist, Barbara enlists Meigs in protesting against the Vietnam War and, while Meigs cannot bring herself to be militant, she does become a heavy financial contributor to pacifist organizations. Moreover, it is Barbara's example and encouragement that gives Meigs the courage to declare her sexual identity by writing *Lily Briscoe*, the primary act that nurtured Meigs' spiritual growth. It is Barbara, also, who sees the fight for lesbian rights as part of the larger feminist cause and is instrumental in raising Meigs' awareness of the insidiousness of the patriarchal oppression of women. In an article for *Language in her Eye*, a Canadian anthology about writing and gender, Meigs traces the evolution of her feminist consciousness, giving credit both to Barbara Deming's example and to the thinking process necessitated by the act of writing autobiographically. Of the latter, she says:

> For me, it [writing] is a study of the kinds of oppression that are a part of my own life, suffocation by upper class principles and squeamishness, the blindness of privilege, the abuse of power by friends and lovers, the oppression of enforced heterosexuality. (1990, 196)

Her writing does not protect her from raging at the "invisibility and powerlessness of women" (ibid., 195), but to name evil is one way to fight it, and is a powerful stimulus to spiritual growth.

In the area of religious belief, however, even Barbara Deming was not able to bring Meigs around to accepting any form of Christian orthodoxy. All discussion affirming the existence of God did nothing but enrage Meigs, particularly when Barbara insisted that Meigs believed in God without knowing it. Years after these discussions, Meigs tempers her reactions enough to affirm a belief "in the miracle of creation, however it came about, in the oneness of time, and in destiny, as opposed to pure chance, somehow allowing for a tiny exercise of free will" (1981, 83). Still, she confesses to a "resistance to all things mystical" (1983, 42).

However, Meigs' account of a dream about her deceased mother, and her penchant for referring to Biblical incidents and characters suggest that she wavers in this resistance to faith. In the dream, the mother gives her a message that is eerily like Pratt's message from her mother: "Don't worry about the light," says the elder Meigs to her daughter. "You'll always have enough to see your way" (1981, 49). Meigs reaction is revealing: "I took these words spoken in a dream six years after she died as having come *directly from* her" [emphasis added]. Meigs does not elaborate, other than to say that perhaps the memory of her mother's remark: "There is something light about you – like a butterfly wing" prompted the dream. Meigs immediate and intuitive reaction, however, is that the spirit of her mother has spoken to her, indicating, at the very least, a yearning to believe in the survival of the spirit.

Similarly, Meigs' passing references to Biblical stories and figures indicate an easy familiarity. For example, she describes Andrée's outbursts as having "the force of Joshua trumpeting down the walls of Jericho" (1983, 23). Similarly, she identifies herself with the rich young man in the New Testament (Mark 10: 17–22), who cannot give up his worldly goods, even to be saved: "I am still the reluctant and gloomy young man who turns away when it is a matter of relinquishing all his possessions" (1981, 232). In the same vein, Meigs ponders over which of her rich friends has successfully "passed through the eye of the needle." It is, however, the story of Mary and Martha (Luke 10: 38–42) that is the most meaningful for Meigs. She sees these New Testament figures as prototypes of two kinds of women, the practical woman and the spiritual woman, or as two sides of the female personality. Wanting to be Mary, "to be praised by Jesus" (1981, 85), she fears she is mostly Martha. In a wonderful passage of spiritual longing, she connects this Bible story with a painting by Rembrandt, linking Mary's rapt attentiveness to Jesus with Rembrandt's philosopher, who sits lost in thought in the late afternoon light, while behind him a staircase spirals up into darkness (1981, 86–87). Meigs longs for the spiritual attentiveness (a species of grace) that she finds embodied both in Rembrandt's painting and in Biblical story.

I find it significant that Meigs internalized Biblical narrative (that is, Biblical myth) so thoroughly that it acted to shape her imagination, influencing her reading of both literature and visual art. Northrop Frye has written extensively on the importance of the Bible as literature, making a case for the Bible as the most complete myth, myth being an imaginative vision of humankind's place in the universe, a vision of the universe as humanity's home. Accordingly, Frye asserts:

> It [the Bible] should be taught so early and so thoroughly that it sinks straight to the bottom of the mind, where everything that comes along later can settle on it. (1963, 46)

For me, Frye's injunction accounts for the dominant place of the Bible in Meigs' imagination; it has settled on "the bottom of [her] mind." Paradoxically, however, she abhors many features of Christianity as a religion – what she sees as its patriarchal sexism, its emphasis on conformity and "proper behaviour," and the seemingly harsh cast of mind found both in the Ten Commandments and in Jesus' parables (1981, 190). Still, one senses that the person of Jesus and his emphasis on loving your neighbour as yourself is at the heart of Meigs' ethical sensibility.

Meigs would have said that such a sensibility makes attentiveness, moments of grace, and genuine love of oneself and others possible. This kind of spiritual awareness often takes place in authentic community and is accompanied by the consciousness of joy. It is in the making of *The Company of Strangers* and in the writing of the accompanying book that Meigs communicates joy most unequivocally. By the time of the making of the film, Meigs had made public her sexual orientation through the writing of *Lily Briscoe* and had worked through her feelings about her family and the significant women in her life. In other words, she had dealt with her personal unfinished business and was free to turn her attention outward, a mark of spiritual maturity. The making of *The Company of Strangers* brings her into relationship with a group of older women of differing backgrounds, and Meigs, feeling safe in the structure provided by the director, Cynthia Scott, opens herself up to them. Her habitually careful delineation of personal space seems to have been relaxed in this setting; she says, "On the set we seemed never to have stopped laughing" (1991b, 104), and, like children, these old women frolic and splash in the water, irrepressible because "we had discovered that we were happy in each other company" (ibid., 108). Meeting later, they exclaim, "Wasn't it beautiful? Wasn't it wonderful?" (ibid.).

What was wonderful and what allowed them to form close bonds with each other was the fact that they were in a culture that fostered the authenticity of self of old women. Such an environment is rare in our society, rife as it is with ageism. In an article in the anthology, *Look Me in the Eye*, Barbara MacDonald and Cynthia Rich, self-identified aging lesbians, speak out against ageism and against the cult of female beauty, which renders old women ugly and therefore without social value. They also reject all attempts by health professionals to analyze what old people need, and they refuse to fit any old woman image.

Like McDonald and Rich, *The Company of Strangers* also refutes ageism. It does so in two ways. First, it makes older women not only the subject of the film – thereby declaring older women as worthy of attention – but also the actors in the film, despite the fact that none of the seven are professions. This gives these women a new way of defining themselves – that is, as actors – and bestows on them a sense that they are important enough to warrant a film, even though most had lived their lives out of the public eye. Secondly, Scott does not force the actors into role-playing or a set script but allows them, not only to act themselves on film, but also to define which aspects of self they will perform. As a result, all grow in confidence as the process unfolds, permitting "the central truth of each to appear" (Meigs 1991b, 148). Their many differences in experience and background fade into insignificance, and they take joy in being older women coming together in community.

Nevertheless, there is an elegiac tone to both the film and Meigs' book. The film ends with them flying out by bi-plane, destination unknown, shouting "Goodbye house." Similarly, the actual filming comes to an end and the friends go their own way. The sadness of these partings is a reflection of the larger sadness that accompanies aging – the loss of one's youth, illness, death of friends and one's own impending death. Both the book and the film suggest that what sweetens this sadness is memory – as, for example, Constance's memory of the song of the white-throated sparrow, the notes of which she can still whistle even though she can no longer hear them. Meigs perpetuated the film experience by writing her memories of it and of the women who shared it. She told me in our conversation together that, despite her wavering after the dream of her mother, memory is the only form of immortality she can believe in:

MEIGS: When people die, in a real sense they are more precious to me after-wards but not in any faraway place, just in my own mind. And that's where I think people live.

REID: So "ashes to ashes, dust to dust"?

MEIGS: Yes.

REID: You've always thought that?

MEIGS: It doesn't disappoint me or make me regret my future life. It is just something I believe deeply. That it doesn't make sense. Afterlife. (Reid 1997, 12)

In tracing the movement toward death by two of the women in the film (Cissy and Constance), Meigs notes their withdrawal into a realm removed from the everyday world (1991, 166–69), just as in Butala's *Luna*, Rhea withdraws into the world of dream and myth. While Meigs rejects mysticism, she does divulge the details of an active dream life. She speaks of the world of dreams and hallucinations in tones that echo Butala's description of the realm of archetypal dreams as an alternate reality, "a limitless and timeless world" (Butala 1994a, 19). Like Butala, Meigs accepts the Jungian theory of dreams, takes her dreams seriously, and uses them as a guide to self-understanding. Again like Butala, bird dreams are the ones with special power and meaning. "And birds have always occupied first place in my hierarchy of dream images and have played a visionary and prophetic role in my life" (1981, 174). Therefore, her interpretation of a dream of bluebirds, flying away and disappearing on the wind, must carry special weight:

> This dream deals, I think, with my joys and beliefs … my horror of inattention that poisons my own life, my longing to believe in the transparent relation between life and death, and with birds as messengers of freedom, flying in a sky empty of even the impalpable barrier of clouds. (1981, 174–75)

For me, this is a dream about Meigs' spiritual positioning and, despite her dismissal of the possibility of an afterlife, the dream and her interpretation indicate a liminal spiritual state where hope affirms, in the face of common sense, "a transparent relation" between this world and the next.

Meigs feels spiritual anguish when witnessing another kind of death, the death of basic elements in nature. She says, "I have lived the slow process of deprivation which has spread over the earth, the gradual reduction of all the elements essential to life" (1988, 17), and she lists the losses – forests, a multiplicity of animal species, pure air and water, and arable land. In the face of these losses that threaten to deprive humanity of hope of a future, Meigs ascribes a special power to older women – that is, their power to remember and warn. Art critic Deborah Haynes voices the same kind of anguish, seeing death everywhere in the man-made destruction of the natural world: "Life – all of life, species, forests – is threatened with death" (1997, 28). Haynes, however, invokes the creative power of art and of artists to participate in witnessing for life and in giving the kind of prophetic warning that Meigs sees as the special contribution of old women.

AGANETHA DYCK

Like Haynes, Aganetha Dyck connects creativity and the artistic vocation with visionary spirituality. Dyck's spirituality is "part and parcel" of her art practice, an endeavour expressive both of the life force inherent in the natural world and of humanity's social possibilities. Aside from a metaphoric book in *The Library: Inner/Outer* (Fig. 14) dedicated to her Mennonite grandmother, Dyck's work contains no overt reference to the Mennonite faith in which she was raised, to religion (either for or against), to mysticism, Christianity, or the Bible, although she did tell me that the books in her childhood home were "fairy tales, books on the Bible, religious little story books and lots of books on German because we were studying German" (Reid 1996c, 56). Moreover, she did say, when questioned, that she did not like the patriarchal nature of churches, Mennonite or not (ibid., 8).

However, as we have seen, a part of what she did inherit spiritually from her Mennonite upbringing was a deep affinity for community. In describing for Robert Enright her move to Winnipeg and into appropriate studio space, it is significant that she sought affiliation as well as a place to work: "I was frantic to meet these people [other artists]. I wanted to know what was going on in the community and I wanted to be in it" (Walsh and Enright 2000, 52). Entering into community and realizing her artistic vocation are Dyck's two primary avenues of spiritual expression and growth. In actual implementation, the line between the two is often blurred, creating community being part of the art practice. To put it another way, she becomes inspired creatively in the liminal space where self and community meet.

The merging of the two in this liminal space was apparent in my 1996 interviews with Dyck. In talking about her ideas and the impetus behind the production of her various works, Dyck invariably mentioned a conversation or dialogue with other persons – beekeepers, scientists, her grandmother, her son Richard, her teachers and mentors in Prince Albert, her Prince Albert girl friends (Winona Senner and Annabel Taylor), fellow artists Wanda Koop and Reva Stone, photographer William Eakin, curator Sigrid Dahle, visiting artist Mary Scott, various critics of her work and others. It is not just that she talks about art with her friends; it is that interaction is a necessary and spontaneous part of Dyck's artistic process.

These conversations have much in common with the aforementioned intersubjective dialoguing as described by phenomenologist Peter Spader. He defines a true dialogue as "a co-acting, a co-discovery, a co-thinking – a thinking together" in which the emerging ideas cannot be ascribed to either participant alone (1983, 9–10). Spader takes this kind of dialogue as an indication that there is such a thing as co-consciousness and that human beings are essentially a communal species. This is at variance, on the one hand, with the "artist as hero" construction of modernism, in which the artist insists on his (usually "his") individuality and autonomy and is, on the other hand, in keeping with Haynes' notion that, in the present-day global crises, artists must initiate a dialogue with society and take a visionary role in its shaping and healing.

An example of how a simple conversation can spark Dyck's creativity is found in Dyck's description of the origin of *Hand Held: Between Index and Middle Finger* (Fig. 17). As Dyck tells it, a young couple was explaining that they would have nothing to hold in their hands if they quit smoking. As noted earlier (chapter 2), Dyck improvised a decorated surrogate cigarette for each to hold: "So I ran to the store and got some glue and stuff and did it for them" (Reid 1996c, 44). Subsequently Dyck created a whole community of non-smokers by asking people to send her their "last cigarette." This interactive process culminated in her extensive *Hand Held* and *Altered Cigarette* series. Similarly, a colleague's accidental shrinking of a fleece she was preparing for Dyck, led to the *Close Knit* series (Fig. 8), while a gift of a honeycomb sculpture from a Winnipeg beekeeper led her to see the possibilities of bees as collaborators. However, one of the most influential series of dialogues was with artist Mary Scott,[39] who introduced her to reading as a source of input for her art. In particular, Scott shared books about the oppression of women and the lives of those otherwise marginalized by society:

She gave me lots and lots of titles and a lot of them I read and most of them were from women all over the world – white black, anything and also the physically challenged and it got me into reading about people that they used to put into asylums. That was the scariest part for me. It probably happens today.... It got me to all those darknesses of people and it got me also to read of the boredom in some people's work spaces. I was reading of house work and of not being paid for it and not being acknowledged or honoured.... These books lead me to all these different human conditions. That's what happened with Mary basically and then the library was like my home away from home. (Reid 1996c, 74)

It would be difficult to overestimate the significance of her meeting with Scott, or the role of her heightened awareness of "all those darknesses of people" in both Dyck's spiritual growth and the direction of her art practice. Even before meeting Scott, Dyck was examining through her art what it means to be human, or female, or both. Dyck does not deal overtly in her work with the "unfinished business" in her life in the way that Butala, Pratt, and Meigs do. Nevertheless, there is much in her work that speaks of the societal oppression she has observed or experienced and that serves, in Peck's terms, as a kind of "emptying."

For example, her use of repetitive form in such installations as *Cabbages* (Madill 1995, 19), *Close Knit* (Fig. 8), and *The Large Cupboard* (Fig. 10) are read as indicating community, but where the forms are presented with no variation, the suggestion is that the individual is caught in the prison of convention. As Dyck realizes, too often the price of membership in a community is conformity, and, for Dyck, the price has become too high. She reveals her frustration with conventional expectations in a conversation with Robert Enright. In speaking of her arrival in Prince Albert, Dyck said that the community's expectations of a corporate wife (Peter Dyck was Eaton's store manager) left her feeling alienated: "I was just this appendage.... I didn't fit in" (Walsh and Enright 2000, 48). In particular, the installation entitled *Cabbages* (rows of cabbage-like objects made out of shoulder pads) suggests women's mindless response to the demands of convention. The complex installation, *The Extended Wedding Party* (Fig. 12), through the metaphor of the queen bee, has reference again to the restrictive role assigned to women in the conventions of marriage and motherhood. Some of the "darknesses" uncovered by Dyck in her own experience and in Mary

Scott's recommended reading find expression in this, her largest installation. As with Butala, Pratt, and Meigs, art gives Dyck both an avenue of self-examination and a voice. She explains this to Enright:

> I wouldn't have survived without art. They'd have to put me away. I couldn't survive in a world where I couldn't speak. It's a way of saying something, it's communication, and I couldn't have done it at home [that is, in the position of homemaker]. (Walsh and Enright 2000, 53)

As I have indicated, her realization that she was indeed part of the Manitoba art community helped Dyck to find her artist's voice. In finding that voice, she followed the same pattern as that of Butala and Meigs in that she gradually moved away from self- examination to an identification with the larger world.

As part of her movement away from self, Butala tells in *Wild Stone Heart* of the development of her intense devotion to a sacred field and of the passionate attention she pays to all its aspects. Dyck has come to display a similar devotion to two phenomena, and both are for Dyck the site of spiritual experience: these are, firstly, the practice of art in general and, secondly, her own art practice as related to the life and world of the honey bee. The practice of art is for Dyck at once the site of freedom and, in an indirect way, a tool for the redemption of society. Disliking so ardently the confinement of social convention, Dyck rates freedom as art's most precious handmaid. As described earlier, she expressed this to me in two separate responses. The first was in reference to George Glenn; Dyck emphasized that Glenn's talent as a teacher came from his ability to impart in the studio a sense of creative freedom (Reid 1996c, 17). That is, Glenn facilitated Dyck's total ownership of her own work, beginning with the dictum "Do what you know." The second came in response to my query about her dislike of false stereotyping; she replied to the effect that any kind of stereotyping, false or otherwise, limited one's personal freedom (ibid., 35). Dyck here is describing the condition that makes possible the actualization of self.

Having both an immigrant father and an immigrant husband, Aganetha Dyck does not take freedom for granted, especially political freedom. Members of her own family and her husband's family experienced the Mennonite version of the Holocaust at the hands of both the Russians after World War I and the Germans in World War II. That is perhaps one reason why the work of German artist Joseph Beuys is of such interest to Dyck.

Beuys was an artist in post-war Germany who was passionately devoted to freedom and to the creation of a truly democratic state, despite, or perhaps because of, his past history as a member of Hitler Youth and his service as a soldier in World War II. Beuys regarded art as the most potent tool with which to achieve social revolution. Consequently, he always spoke of art in terms of its healing effects on society. He offered an expanded definition of art, equating it with creativity in action so that, for example, scientists, engineers, doctors, or teachers should be regarded as artists to the degree that their work is creative. Dr. Stachelhaus, a German professor and colleague of Beuys explains, "Creativity, to him, was the science of freedom" (1987, 64). Beuys coined the term "social sculpture" to refer to the creative reshaping of the state by its citizens.

As a visual artist, Beuys saw himself as a modern-day shaman, a spiritual figure who, through his art, performed magic by offering a curative vision of society in its authentic democratic form, having first of all healed himself. To communicate and reinforce his shamanic role, Beuys always appeared in costume – a fishing vest and felt hat. In keeping with his notion of shamanism, Beuys allocated a mythic and totemic role to animals. He identified with the vulnerability of animals and assigned to them a heroic lineage in view of their place in evolution as forerunners of humanity: "The animals," he said, "have sacrificed themselves to make humanity possible" (Stachelhaus 1987, 60). Animal motifs are everywhere in his work, which incorporated animal by-products, such as fat and horn, as well as actual animals, dead and alive. The ability to converse with animals is part of the shaman's powers (ibid., 75), and in his New York happening entitled *Coyote*, Beuys succeeded in establishing a form of communication with a live coyote who, for an entire week, shared gallery space with him. A wide variety of installations, performances, and happenings, including *Coyote*, are reviewed by Caroline Tisdall in her definitive book, *Joseph Beuys*, and in it, she refers to Beuys' atavistic descent into the darkness's of psychic wounding, the area proper to shamanistic action. Beuys expresses a profound identification with the marginalized sections of society, and displays the avant-garde artist's contempt for what he saw as the narrow, materialistic work-oriented values of the middle class.

Loath as she is to be pigeonholed, Aganetha Dyck would not classify herself as an avant-garde artist, nor would she likely claim for herself shamanic status. Nevertheless, there is much in Aganetha Dyck's approach to, and practice of, art that suggests Joseph Beuys; undoubtedly that is the reason why he is mentioned so often in critical discussion of her work. As artists, they come together dramatically in two ways: firstly, in their acute sensitivity to the material they use in their art, and, secondly, in their appropriation of animals into their art practices. Tisdall sees Beuys' shamanism as expressing a need to connect with the metamorphosis, transformation, and regeneration that is characteristic of the material world (not to be confused with static bourgeois materialism):

> At a serious level, it [shamanism] is a reminder of a human constant without which we would be all drastically impoverished: the need to come into intense physical and psychological contact with the material world, to understand and feel its energetic substance rather than skim over the surface of experience. (Tisdall 1979, 23)

Dyck displays a similar responsiveness to the existential possibilities of material. It is this intuitive sensibility that led her to shrink hundreds of woolen sweaters, to gather thousands of buttons, to work with other people's cigarettes, and to succumb artistically to the architectural perfection of honeycomb. As with Beuys, Dyck displays an awareness of the characteristic mutability of the material world and can accept with equanimity, therefore, not only the instability of much of her own work, but also the fact of her own mortality.

And, as with Beuys, Dyck displays a passionate reverence for animals, especially *apis mellifera*. She understands this species of bees to be an expression of a basic life force, just as the hare and the coyote are for Beuys. In fact, a study of Beuys' 1974 New York gallery encounter with his coyote can act as a remarkably illuminating explication of Dyck's latest bee work. In *Coyote*, Beuys addresses the psychic wounding that he sees as implicit in the capitalist society of North America. He does so through presence of a live coyote, the coyote being a powerful totem figure in American aboriginal societies, but persecuted as a scavenger in modern day America. Here is Tisdall description:

> The man [Beuys] brought objects and elements from his world to place in this space, silent representations of his ideas and beliefs.... The coyote responded in coyote-style by claiming them with his gesture of possession. One by one as they were presented he pissed on them slowly and deliberately: felt, walking stick, gloves, flashlight and the Wall Street Journal, but above all

the Wall Street Journal.... The man had also brought a repertoire of movements with him and a notion of time. These two were then subject to the coyote's responses, and were modulated and conditioned by them. (1979, 228–30)

Photographs of the "happening" show Beuys taking on the persona of a shepherd, a benign figure, and playing tug of war with the coyote as if he were a dog. What emerges is an exchange of energy brought about by allowing the coyote access to the material and by a kind of responsive dance between Beuys and the coyote. Both the exchange of material and the reciprocal dancing expand the notion of dialogue and give freedom to the coyote as an equal partner in the happening. In its conceptualization of dialogue and of the freeing of the marginalized, Beuys intended *Coyote* to be a paradigm for the enactment of freedom in the body politic. Beuys' aim is always the transformation of society through art: that is, through "the transformation of verbal dialogue to energy dialogue" (Tisdall 1979, 235).

There are clear parallels between Beuys' shamanic work in *Coyote* and the bee work of Aganetha Dyck. Both artists are in close contact with an animal presence in the course of art-making, and both allow the animal access to material. Both artists choose animals with mythic significance, the coyote being a powerful totem figure for Amerindians, the bee and its honey serving in the Bible as a metaphor for abundance. Both artists take the animal(s)' deposits on the material as a form of communication in a non-verbal language signifying possession. Just as the coyote claims the *Wall Street Journal* by urinating on it, so Dyck's bees take over the material placed in the hive either by chewing it up or depositing honeycombs on it.

What is different is the degree of permanence. *Coyote* was a "happening" lasting a week; only a photographic record remains. In Dyck's bee work, the honeycomb structures deposited on the objects are a stable construction by the bee artists, likely to last indefinitely. With the work of both Beuys and Dyck, the viewer understands that the actions of the animals are free from human control. There is a sense of mystery in their response as collaborators, a perception that the artist has entered a mysterious and ancient realm. Accordingly, Dyck says of honey, "In a single drop of honey is the history of all bee kind" (Enright 2001, V8). Dyck's collaboration with the bees has ritualistic overtones in that her interaction with the bees follows a strict protocol as worked out by experienced beekeepers. With the beekeepers' guidance, she performs a dance around the bees much like Beuys' dance with the coyote. Photographs of Dyck in beekeepers' protective clothing show a shaman-like figure, whose clothing allows her entrance into an alternate world. Dyck herself feels the magic of this entrance – "going somewhere where very few people go" (Walsh and Enright 2000, 57).

All of Dyck's discussion of her bee work points to the fact that she is engaged in an inter-species dialogue, physical material being the language. There is a new possibility of an even more direct communication with the bees using chemical substances called the pheromones secreted by the bees as a means of communication: "I'm hoping that if I put a line down the bees will add another line" (Enright 2001, V8). Whether or not she and the scientists can interpret the added line is a moot point. Dyck is ready to accept any outcome. Two exhibitions prefigure this current project that involves biologist Mark Winston of Simon Fraser University, a worldwide authority on bees. One show is specifically entitled *Inter Species Communication Attempt*. In it she displays, set out on tables, a selection of bee-related pieces, ones which represent a variety of ways of entering the bee world: honey pots, encrusted shoes, hive or bee fragments, drawings of bee parts and beekeeping tools. These are all coated in sweet-smelling wax and accompanied by a hive soundscape recorded by Richard Dyck, the artist's son. French art critic Estelle Pagés comments that examining the installation was like "discovering the vestiges of a lost civilization" (Pagés 2001, 27). Accordingly, the vocabulary Pagés uses to describe the power of Dyck's work comes from the language of myth. She suggests that the work transfixes us like the Medusa's gaze, "numbing our senses and points of orientation" (ibid.). As with Joseph Beuys, the artist is characterized as shaman, one whose spiritual power allows us to experience mysterious and possibly forbidden territory. Moreover, Dyck assigns to the bees and their territory a status equal to that of humans and their society. This community of insects is judged to be fully worthy of the passionate attention Dyck devotes to them. Her attentiveness is a reminder that, as Mary Meigs asserts (quoting Buber), "the flowing of attention into another being feeds the spirit" (Meigs 1981, 189).

The inherent mystery of bee territory is reflected in the title of a second installation, *Working in the Dark* (Fig. 25). As described earlier, this work is an intensely collaborative piece created through the bees' transformation of Braille tablets inscribed with a poem specially written by Di Brandt for that purpose. The bees' ornamentations are as delicate as embroidery or lace, but the remaining fragments of Braille are virtually indecipherable even to the touch of a blind reader.

In *Working in the Dark*, shaman Dyck simulates for the viewer two darknesses, the organic darkness of the hive, and the physical condition of blindness. Similarly, she identifies at least two aids to communicating in the dark: the bees' post-visual sensory equipment and the fingertip language of Braille. In a call to me, Dyck explained, "This work is about language, comprehension, collaboration" (September 2002). As Estelle Pagés suggests, the serious viewer of Dyck's two latest works becomes involved imaginatively in the possibility of reading the re-ordered visual language – part Dyck, part Brandt, part bee – and thus becomes Dyck's final collaborator, the designated shamanic subject.

This is not to suggest, however, that viewer collaboration is the only goal. The modern artist as shaman is concerned with society as a whole and intercedes on its behalf. Just as Beuys interacted with a live coyote to point to the dark trauma of the treatment of North America's native peoples and to suggest a remedy, so Dyck incorporates the community of the blind as an equal collaborator in order to model in her work the inclusion of the physically handicapped into the mainstream of society. Accordingly, arrangements were made with the Canadian Institute for the Blind (November 2000) for the visit of fifteen blind persons to an exhibition of Dyck's bee works at the University of Manitoba. These are the acts of a spiritually aware artist working, not in solipsistic isolation, but fully within the context of society.

SUMMARY

This chapter examines the modes of experience expressed in the art of Butala, Pratt, Meigs, and Dyck as they approach old age. These four artists model a different scenario from that ordinarily assigned in our society to older women because, instead of playing a diminished social role as expected, they continued to pursue a vital art practice into the sixth, seventh, and, in Meigs' case, eighth decades of their lives. In these practices, a spiritual component persisted and grew, so that I was able to trace the development of spirituality in their work to almost the present moment. Many cultures have typically viewed old women as spiritual resources and, despite the persistence of ageism in our society, Butala insists that many Canadian communities still recognize the special wisdom of old women. I argue that these four artists display such wisdom.

However, despite the strong spiritual elements in the work of all four, only Sharon Butala expressly casts the narrative of her life experience as a spiritual journey, and it is only she whose life writing can be categorized therefore as a species of spiritual autobiography. It is only Butala as well who specifically positions the experience of the mystical and paranormal as powerful parts of that journey but who refuses, nevertheless, any construction of self as psychically exceptional, claiming that such experiences are so common as to be normal. Meigs and Dyck make no specific claims to similar experience and Meigs, in particular, voices her distaste "for all things mystical." Pratt reports premonitions and the one-time guidance of an inner voice but draws no conclusions as to their source. Nevertheless, it became evident in the analysis of the art practices of all four, and of their relevant comments, that they specify a particular spiritual dimension in their construction of self, having experienced transcendence and a sense of union, mystical or otherwise, with a power greater than themselves. With Butala, this sense of union is genuinely mystical; with Pratt, it verges on the mystical. In the case of Meigs and Dyck, this sense of union is the product of coming together with others in the spirit of community and love.

In their construction of themselves as spiritual, all four artists do agree in four particular respects: in their attitude to organized religion; in their notion of the relation of body and spirit; in their response to nature; and in their positioning of art-making as a spiritual undertaking. As regards organized religion, all four occupy a liminal positioning. They each describe a traditional upbringing within the Christian church. However, as with many women of this post-World War II generation, they became alerted to the patriarchal domination of the Christian church; that awareness and their discomfort with much of the church's dogma has led them to distance themselves from formal religious observation. On the other hand, they are far from being thoroughly secularized as is typical of many in our postmodern society. Biblical narrative shapes their imaginations and New Testament ethical standards fashion their moral principles.

In their view of the connection of body and spirit, these artists again part company with Christianity, all four rejecting its traditional body-spirit duality. Not only do they construct themselves equally as body and spirit, they find that their espousal of bodily experience is a conduit to spirituality. Contact with nature emerges as paramount in this regard. Butala's bodily devotion to her field, Dyck's to her bees, Pratt to the sensual apprehension of light, and Meigs to birds, those mythic emissaries of spirit, lead to the sense of joy mixed with the perception of union that all four understand as a primary manifestation of spirit. Part of what contributes to this joy is a sense of life rising to greet life, a characteristic of vitalism as described by Evelyn

Underhill. Similarly, all four describe the creative process of their practice of art as nourishing to the spirit and as essential to an authentic sense of self.

However, beneath this euphoria that marks the peak spiritual experiences is the life-long work of honest self-scrutiny that is apparent in the work of all four. By dealing with emotional unfinished business – by casting out the anger at past wrongs, by recognizing their own proclivity for evil, and by the naming of the evil they encounter – they facilitate their spiritual development. The autobiographical nature of their art is a tool in this task, and their honesty in this regard elevates their work. It is their construction of themselves as spiritual, and the honesty that is a precondition of this construction, that lends to their work the perception of transcendence that Georg Misch sees as essential to serious autobiography.

Being well into their senior years, Butala, Dyck, and Pratt have had to face illness in their own lives and the death of family and friends. Each, in her own way, has come to terms with mortality, as did Mary Meigs before she died. In *Beyond Recall* (2005), published after Meigs' death in 2002, Meigs shares with the reader the details of her gallant struggle to retain her sense of self in the face of a debilitating stroke. She was helped in this by the fact that, like the other three, she came into old age as an artist and found, like them, that the practice of art creates a construction of self that works against the psychic diminution that ageism and illness forces on old women.

In a 1992 article about the perception of older women in literature by Canadian and American female writers, Shelagh Wilkenson refers to *The Trojan Women*, a poetic drama by Gwendolyn MacEwan. She comments:

> MacEwan shows that it is the figure of the crone who is the freeing agent. The old woman (who knows all of the past and is willing to call the present into account) is able to accomplish this because she moves beyond patriarchal rules. And because she is more free than most of us, it is the old women who is "righting" our stories, providing us with a future that is kinder and open-ended. (Wilkenson 1992, 107)

As members of a liminal female generation, all four women struggled to gain the freedom that is ascribed to old women by MacEwan. It is the vision of this freedom, a necessity for individual spiritual growth that these four artists bequeath to their female readers and viewers through their autobiographical practice of literary and visual art.

PERSONAL REFLECTIONS AS TEXTUAL SISTER, MOTHER, AND DAUGHTER

As the fifth member of this small intertextual community, I am encouraged by Wilkenson's view that it is old women who are "freeing agents," able to move "beyond patriarchal rules." Paradoxically, my early education within the canon afforded me a portion of the kind of freedom that I, as an old woman, now possess. When, at age eighteen, I first walked through the front door of Victoria College, I passed beneath the arch bearing the words "The truth shall make you free." That portion of John's gospel (John 8: 32) refers to the freedom to be found as a follower of Jesus. The founders of the college saw this promise also as being the chief benefit of an authentically liberal education, producing what Northrop Frye called "an educated imagination." Frye regarded the Christian promise and this central role of education as part of the same vision. Much of my spiritual development has come from trying to incorporate Frye's creative view of education into my own teaching practice. In so doing, I gained a large measure of the freedom that the practice of art has brought to Sharon Butala, Aganetha Dyck, Mary Meigs, and Mary Pratt and so feel a sisterly comradeship.

Moreover, as I became more able to pass on to my own students a sense of the power of story, (a prime way of educating the imagination), the experience of being part of an intellectual/spiritual community that I felt in Northrop Frye's classes very gradually came to emerge in classes that I taught. Still living in Calgary as I do, I meet many ex-students and quite often we rejoice together as we recall together the mysterious alchemy that took place in such classrooms. Occasionally I hear the words, "That class changed my life." I take very little credit for this: I know that there is a force larger than myself at work in such instances, a force that wiser people than myself name as "grace." I can take credit only for showing up faithfully in Frye's classes as a student and, as a teacher, persisting steadily in following Frye's example. As Woody Allen once observed "Eighty percent of success is showing up."

I have been able to venture this far by myself in discerning my own spiritual journey, still a work in progress. In addition, I do know that, as with Butala, spiritual awareness is sometimes a function of place. Water, especially that of rivers, but water in any form whether that of oceans, lakes, or streams, uplifts me and affords peace. Being a "prairie girl" and living in Calgary, I similarly seem to need an open sky. In recent years, I have been grateful for my doctors' skill employed in the surgical repair of both my hip and back. During recovery, I was confined indoors more than usual and discovered that what I missed most was being able to see the full sweep of the sky. I had not consciously realized that my first habitual act in the morning is to inspect the sky and breathe the morning air. Over the years, it has been my way of connecting at the start of the day to the larger world, both physical and spiritual.

The love of my husband and his actual physical presence and touch are likewise necessary to my spiritual well-being, more so as time goes by. Family surrounds me: three children, their spouses, six grandchildren, and, at the time of writing, two great-grandchildren, as well as extended family living throughout Canada. While our connection with family members can be intermittent and occasionally fractious, we know that a spiritual bond exists through the grace of what I name as the Holy Spirit. This family connection extends back in time; relationships do not end with death, a fact evident both in my own experience and in that reported in such texts as Meigs' *The Box Closet* and Pratt's *A Personal Calligraphy*. Again through the action of grace, there will be family connections in the same way into the future. Much of grandparents' planning, imperfect as it may be, is with this future in mind. On special occasions when we can all gather, we sometimes sing the Doxology, a song of praise that comes from everyone's heart. These things I know; the universality underlying this knowledge connects me spiritually to women and families of every culture and has allowed me to act as mother in co-joining the bodies of work of these four artists.

I have been mothered in turn. Mary Meigs' example of bestowing loving attention on others, whether strangers or not, has inspired me, usually very task-oriented, to try to reach out more to others. Similarly, the truthfulness evident in the autobiographical practices of these four female artists has led me to delve further into discerning patterns in my own spiritual construction of self and has mothered me into a heightened spiritual awareness. Accordingly, I embarked on a more careful self-examination in order to deal with my own personal "unfinished business." As a result, I have come finally to recognize that it is past time to relinquish my carefully complied list of wrongs perpetrated against both members of my family and myself. I have found it harder to forgive the former – for example, the dealings of the Canadian Navy with my brother after World War II, or the betrayal of my father by a partner he trusted. However, I am working on it, understanding that many circumstances came into play. Meanwhile, I am learning also to forgive myself for my many mistakes as a wife, mother, daughter, and friend. As I grow older, I find it more difficult to live in the present moment; the past, happy or sad, keeps intruding. As many before me, I have learned that forgiving others is the path to forgiving myself and to living productively in the present, all the while retaining whatever wisdom I have gained in living a long life.

Also, the texts of Sharon Butala have mothered me into seeing the mystical and paranormal as part of my life experience, and into honouring my dreams. The mystical is defined as that intuitive sense of "union of the self with the larger than self" that is commonly called "God," or "the Holy Spirit" or by the non-doctrinaire term "the Higher Power." I seek such union in prayer both in church and outside of it. Most usually though, such an intuitive sense of the presence of the Holy Spirit comes to me unbidden.

Sometimes it is expressed through a special energy I feel in the presence of another person. In the late fifties, for example, we were living in Ajax, Ontario, when my husband was hospitalized with pneumonia. He seemed to me to be desperately ill and fretful. I was visiting anxiously one day when our clergyman, Hanley Perkins, entered the sick room and immediately the power of his presence changed the whole atmosphere of the sickroom. Both my husband and I could feel the therapeutic power and peace emanating from Hanley's bodily presence. My husband and I agree that his recuperation began at that moment. Similarly, when I had occasion to be physically within arm's length of Elisabeth Kübler-Ross, I could sense her aura of energy revitalizing me. I did not want to leave her side. Reading Butala's witness to mystical events reinforced my belief that these experiences are not self-induced but part of an external reality that I sense but do not understand.

I felt a profound sense of Presence some years back when visiting the Roman Catholic Martyr's Shrine at Midland, Ontario, a cathedral honouring the martyrdom of priests Jean de Brébeuf, Lallemant, and Daniel, among others. As an Anglican and therefore Protestant, I was not entering a church I might regularly attend. Although I do say a brief prayer when entering any site of worship, I visit shrines such as this essentially as a tourist. Furthermore, this visit was the last stop in a sightseeing tour escorted by friends in the area, so I did not expect to linger. As it happened, I did linger because I was not prepared for the impact of the church's interior. Immediately upon entering, a sense of spiritual power struck me like a blow. I was drawn to the candle-lit altar containing the reliquary of Brébeuf and knelt instinctively. I was flooded with an intense sense of connection similar to that described by Butala, alone with the moon in a water-logged field: "a kind of warmth one feels when someone loving is near, like a child basking in the warmth of its mother's love" (2000a, 167). For Butala, the beaming of the moon prompted the feeling of warmth; for me, the warmth came from a candle-lit altar. In both cases, the source was outside of oneself, an unexpected gift of grace. Even the presence of the church's many visitors did not break the spell of the Brébeuf altar. Again, I did not want to leave.

My experience of the paranormal is much more limited but to me even more mysterious. The most striking was my seeing, in a dream, an event in progress some two thousand miles way. In the dream, I saw my mother lying very still on a gurney and, alarmed, I thought "My mother's dead." I paused and looked more closely: "No, no" – I thought in the dream – "she's not dead, but merely unconscious." In the early morning I received a phone call from my daughter in Toronto telling me that she had found Grandma unconscious in bed and had called an ambulance. The time of that discovery corresponded to the time of my dream some half a continent away. I had been called to the phone at 7 a.m. and knew right away what the call would be about. Similarly, at the age of twelve, I was in the back seat of an automobile, an unconcerned passenger, when suddenly I felt an overpowering feeling of foreboding several minutes before a truck headed right for us out of a small patch of fog. The driver, a friend of my mother's, swung the steering wheel hard and the truck sideswiped us, shearing off the door handle on the side where I was sitting. I emerged trembling and furious and had to be cautioned for shouting at the truck driver. I usually keep such experiences to myself; I find them distressing. But, with Butala, I can acknowledge that there are dimensions to human experience that demonstrate levels of connection to a reality not customarily acknowledged or talked about.

As for my ordinary dream life, I pay more attention to dreams and remember them more easily as I grow older. Most often they can be seen as reflecting my daily anxieties and problems. Occasionally there are intense erotic dreams that leave me with the pleasant recognition that, despite my age, my sexual proclivities are still intact. I have had, however, one dream that seems to contain a different order of significance. My reading of Butala's totemic animal dreams of the owl and eagle and of the wounded coyote brought this particular dream again to mind and allowed me to realize that it belonged in the same category and deserved my thoughtful attention.

Like those of Butala, my dream had as its focus a luminous animal presence, that of a rather wonderful rabbit. It was not like Alice's rabbit – a human in disguise – but was truly a creature of the woods with a non-human magic and wisdom. In the dream I had gone to visit my mother and grandmother in a small house set in a little clearing in the woods, a place that was apparently familiar to me. The house had two rooms with front and back doors. I went through the front door expecting to see them both, happy at being together and happy to see me. The rooms were full of a sense of their presence but there was no sign of them. I had just missed them – they had gone out by the back and I knew instinctively in the dream that they were not coming back. I was struck by a feeling of acute disappointment but decided to stay anyway. I went out into the back yard and there was a large greyish brown rabbit with his attention fixed expectantly upon me. He began to talk in a language I did not understand. Nevertheless, it was very clear to me that this rabbit had been well known to my mother and grandmother and that they had understood his form of speech. I thought to myself "Mom and Nannie have been feeding this rabbit. I guess it is my job to take over now." I felt a strong sense of female continuity at this realization and with that the dream ended.

I have attempted to paint this dream and have written a poem about it, trying in both mediums to capture its compelling mood but with little success. It is a dream that offers a strange comfort through the image of my mother and grandmother being happy together. Imaginatively, I draw close, wanting wistfully to be in their company. I recognize also that any kind of joining requires a commitment from me, a commitment to feed that talking rabbit whose language I do not understand. I have come to realize that my rabbit, like Butala's owl, likely represents the feminine side of the psyche for which traditionally there has been little expression in our culture. My investigation into the art and lives of these four artists is an attempt to decode this psychic language expressive of unspoken feminine experience for the sake of all of our daughters and granddaughters. In this way, perhaps I come again into the company of my mother and grandmother.

Conclusion:
"A Reading Space of their Own"

> Perhaps that is why I like reading their stories so much. They
> remind me of my own story. – Helen Buss, *Mapping Ourselves.*

In the above passage (1993, 205), Helen Buss is explaining the validation
she felt after discovering parallels between Canadian pioneer women's accounts of childhood and her memories of her early days in Newfoundland,
so different from the experience of urban children. Discovering reflections
of their own female experience allows women to make intimate connections
with their textual sisters and constitutes one of the chief pleasures offered
by all forms of autobiography. For example, while women are drawn to the
art of Pratt and Dyck for a variety of reasons, I found that they usually respond first of all to the accurate depiction of female domesticity, still a vital
part of most contemporary women's adult life. And, while lesbian readers
can identify easily with Meigs' accounts of "coming out," almost all women
find that her frank portrayals of bodily experience strike a chord. Similarly,
Butala's life writing directs women towards the consolation women can find
in nature when they are feeling alienated, as women often do, in a male-
oriented society.

As I have said previously, I, too, was drawn initially to the study of the
autobiographical art of Butala, Dyck, Meigs, and Pratt because their stories
reminded me of my own. Like them, I am a member of the first generation
whose lifespan has extended decades beyond a woman's child-bearing years,
and who therefore has had the opportunity of redefining herself in later life.
I have characterized ours as a liminal generation, one which occupies the
threshold between the home-centred world of our mothers and the career-ori-
ented world of our daughters in which women, in addition to their domestic

duties, are routinely expected to be employed outside of the home. Women of this liminal generation are now the present-day "seniors" and many of them, like my four subjects who came into the prime of their careers after the age of fifty, are extending the parameters of female old age.

In the conclusion of *Mapping Ourselves*, Buss writes of Canadian women needing "a reading space of their own" and of extending Canadian women's autobiography in order to shape a tradition that nourishes and gives voice to their sense of themselves (1993, 207). In studying the autobiographical art practices of my four subjects, I have co-joined them in each chapter, thereby allowing the *oeuvre* of each to illuminate that of the other three. In this way I have sought to test the boundaries and emerging traditions of Canadian female autobiography by crossing the border between literature and visual art. I will review the four chapters now in order to illustrate how each confirms or reshapes different aspects of this tradition, ending in the final chapter with the refiguring of the notions of female old age.

TOWARDS A NEW TRADITION IN CANADIAN AUTOBIOGRAPHICAL ART

In Chapter One

The honouring of domesticity, the most compelling feature of the art of Mary Pratt, is the element in Chapter One that I see as particularly freeing for women, allowing us to feel good about a routine part of our daily lives as women. In this chapter, the study of Pratt's painterly use of her domestic experience served to highlight the penchant for domesticity (apparent but not obvious) in the work of the other three. Like Pratt, Aganetha Dyck, long a wife and mother, also valorizes domesticity by importing household objects and techniques directly into her multimedia installations. On the other hand, Sharon Butala describes the details of her domestic life only in passing. In both marriages, she takes it for granted that it is her job to look after the house and make the meals, even though she has always worked professionally, first as a teacher, then as a writer. As for Mary Meigs, one might have thought that, as a single lesbian woman of independent means, she would have delegated all domestic tasks and, undoubtedly, she had help with everyday chores, especially as she grew older. However, her autobiographical texts reveal her aesthetic sensibility and her precise need for order. The arrangement of her domestic surroundings was very important to her. Personal choice was everything to her, and she devoted a great deal of thought to where and how she lived. In the work of all four, then, I found that domestic activity is an integral part of their daily life as women.

Consequently, as we have seen, Meigs describes in careful detail "the Peak," the most loved house of her childhood. She incorporates its characteristics – "sunlit rooms … bright with polished silver and blue and white chintz" (1981, 40) – into all her subsequent homes. Similarly, an intimate knowledge of household routine informs Pratt's detailed paintings of household paraphernalia and interiors. For her part, Butala presides over a secure ranchland home that offers refuge from the vagaries of nature, while Dyck imports "homey" tables, chairs, radiators, refrigerators, and so on, creating a house for such domestic artifacts within gallery space. I submit that, in any Canadian tradition of female autobiographical art, the concept of the house as a predominantly female space must continue to play a part: the female sense of self is still closely bound to this notion. Mary Pratt has said that "When I dream I dream of houses." Likewise, Mary Meigs tells of dreaming happily of a Georgian house in which sunlight streams through French windows. Such a house is a reflection of her best and happiest self.

Most of Mary Pratt's still life paintings, however, take a point of view from within the house. They usually focus on a single domestic object – a bowl of fruit, a casserole freshly out of the oven, a tray filled with china. Always they are presented to the viewer as important and worthy of notice because they are sparkling with light and luscious with colour. They communicate the message that this world of objects has a special connection with personal lives of women, a message that emerges also from the study of the work of Dyck, Meigs, and Butala. For example, in her bee practice, Dyck elevates familiar feminine objects – purses, shoes, articles of clothing – by coating them with beeswax or honeycomb. Similarly, Meigs' writing contains many descriptions of beloved objects, perhaps precious not only in themselves but also because of their associations. It is her mother's little cabinet of curios, described in *The Box Closet*, which comes closest to encapsulating the significance of objects in women's lives. Meigs realized right away that these little keepsakes revealed a side of her mother not apparent in her letters. They were a result of her mother's personal choice, and represent of kind of feminine language through which to express the self. For Butala, too, such objects signal "home." In her article in *Western Living*, it is clear that, for both the Butalas, re-doing the living room is a feminine priority, of concern mostly to Sharon. However, Sharon's attempts at achieving a completely new decor are undermined by the emotional associations she connects with long-familiar objects – the cat's chair, Peter's old lounger, a cloth elephant given to her by her son, the drawing of a chuchwagon race. Sharon feels no choice but to leave these in the same locations they have always been; they speak of the love that binds the family. The language of objects, then, forms a part of a Canadian tradition of female autobiographical art.

Nevertheless, Chapter One suggests also that there is a darker side to women's experience, to be reflected also in this tradition. Pratt, for example, insists that in her painting, depiction of darkness plays as important a role as that of sparkling light and, as she told me, this is to be taken metaphorically as well as literally. Accordingly, dark shadows balance the light in her portrayal of house interiors. Similarly, some of her still lifes suggest hidden or enclosed spaces because the true subject of the painting (a turkey, a pudding, groceries in a box) is shown covered in tinfoil or encased in paper bags. Rather than being a celebration of domesticity, I felt that such paintings indicated the loss of status and the sense of constraint women experienced when their whole lives were centred on domesticity and the upkeep of the home. In view of the initial celebration, I argue that negative perceptions of domesticity come, not from the inherent value of homemaking, but from the subordinate positioning assigned to it by a predominantly patriarchal society.

Therefore, as Mary Kelly's theories suggest, the notion of victimization is an inescapable part of art about women's domestic experience. In the art of Mary Pratt, this notion of victimization extends into the paintings purportedly celebrating traditional marriage. As Pratt explained to me, she had intended that her wedding paintings be celebratory but she unconsciously subverts her own intentions so that two of them turned out quite differently. An anxious expression is the chief feature of *Barby in her Wedding Dress*; similarly *Wedding Dress*, in which the dress is shown outside hanging on a tree, reminds Pratt right away of the Crucifixion. The Pratt marriage was dissolving just as Pratt was preparing these paintings and her sense of victimization is clear. Aganetha Dyck's marriage is a secure enough partnership that she and husband Peter were easily able to accommodate her art practice in their life together. However, it is evident in *The Extended Wedding Party* that Dyck, like Pratt, views the subordinate positioning of women in traditional marriage as prejudicial to the wife's well-being. Likening the bride's future to that of the queen bee encased for life in the hive is a strong statement about the inherent potential for victimization.

Mary Meigs takes the same view of traditional marriage, and uses much the same imagery, likening society to "an immense queen bee" whose reproductive function is overseen by "mindless drones." Meigs never married but she gets a privileged view of her parents' marriage through reading the box of letters left by her mother after her death. As with Pratt, the basic image in the letters is one of constraint. In fact, Margaret Meigs coped with two forms of constriction – those inherent in traditional marriage in a patriarchal society and those imposed by upper-class propriety. Meigs mourns the unfulfilled potential of her mother's life – Margaret was permitted to exercise little of the rebellious spirit typical of her daughter.

On the face of it, Sharon and Peter Butala had a traditional marriage that followed the marriage pattern common to ranching communities in which the demands of the husband's occupation are the ones around which the household revolves. However, as Sharon's writing practice developed, the Butalas found ways to accommodate two careers. On the other hand, Sharon has earlier memories of a first marriage in which her artistic aspirations were so little recognized (she then wanted to be a painter) that, in packing for a move, her husband thoughtlessly put her precious paintings in the garbage. Butala does not comment directly on the institution of marriage in her life writing, but often in her autobiographically based novels and short stories, she gives a picture of the effects of the subordination of women that traditional marriage often fosters. Like Meigs, she is influenced in her view of marriage by the example of her parents' marriage and she grieves for her mother's unfulfilled potential. However, Butala realizes that her mother's life was circumscribed not only by her position as wife but also by the strictures of poverty.

The work of all four women reveals the strong influence their mothers' lives had on their own. In Chapter One, I discussed the overall power of alterity on these artists' perception of self. Relationships with husbands, lovers, friends, extended family, colleagues, and so on, all went to influence how they saw themselves. However, no relationship was shown to be more powerful than the one each had with her mother. In many fundamental ways, each woman is her mother's daughter. Yet, in naming herself as artist, each has repudiated the pattern of her mother's life. To quote Heilbrun once again, "The key to liberation is an act of denial of the mother's life" and, by putting art at the centre of their lives, all four performed this denial. Nevertheless, as daughters, all four wish to remain close to their mothers. Paradoxically, such closeness is necessary to their sense of self, and so they return again and again to their mothers' example as a model of femininity.

That is one reason why they embrace so many vestiges of domesticity. In any case, their work demonstrates that the power of the mother is an enduring part of Canadian female autobiographical tradition.

However, as we have seen, these four view traditional marriage, the usual site of women's domesticity and the focus of their mother's lives, as potentially detrimental to women's well-being in that it facilitates subordination or even oppression. Contemporary Canadian society, however, still glorifies the trappings of marriage ritual. Despite the high divorce rate, and the increase in common law unions, weddings continue to be celebrated as a high point in a woman's life. Wedding dress stores do good business, and wedding television programs have a high rating. Nevertheless, with women routinely holding down careers after marriage and with mixed families being common after divorce, patterns of relationship are changing. Households in which there are two incomes are more likely to see a sharing of power or even a switching of roles between husband and wife. The conventional unalloyed marriage plot cannot be accepted as an unquestioned part of a Canadian tradition of female autobiographical art. The life and work of these four artists, while honouring women's longtime domesticity, point the way towards a new concept of marriage, a tradition that would give women the opportunity to pursue their full potential.

In Chapter Two

In its treatment of perceptions of the female body, Chapter Two points to the primacy of bodily experience in women's lives. In particular, its study of the work of Mary Meigs reveals how important it can be for women to construct themselves as sexual subjects whatever their sexual orientation and to contest the demands of what Brownmiller has called "the code of femininity," a widely accepted cultural code that sees women primarily as sexual objects whose worth is determined by their conformance to the agreed-upon standards of feminine beauty.

Meigs counters the code's sexual positioning of women as objects through graphic descriptions of her bodily responses as an active sexual subject and, while she writes as a lesbian, her sexual responses will be familiar to most women. Two things are noteworthy about her descriptions. First, by showing herself as sexually active well into her seventh decade, she contests the stereotyping found both in the code of femininity and in the constructions of ageism, both of which consider overt sexuality distasteful in older women: only younger women are permitted to be sexually active. Secondly, in her erotic descriptions, Meigs shows that feminine sexual arousal involves all parts of the female body and is not strictly centred, as is the masculine, on the genital area. Moreover, in writing of "mouths," "nipples," and so on, Meigs locates sexual pleasure more through the sense of touch than of sight, thereby differing again from stereotypical male sexual experience.

French feminists confirm Meigs' representations of female sexual pleasure as typical for women in general. Chapter Two introduces the notion of *jouissance*, a Lacanian term adopted by Luce Irigaray to indicate female gratification beyond the phallus. She declares: "Woman has sex organs everywhere ... the geography of her pleasure is much more diversified, more multiple in its differences, more subtle than is imagined" (Irigaray 1981, 10). To be true, therefore, to female experience, Canadian autobiographical art should reflect *jouissance*. Whether visual or literary, art forms with erotic content have, however, routinely represented male sexual experience as the norm. In order to form a new tradition, ways must be found to use what Meigs has called "the spaces between" the genres.

Accordingly, *jouissance* has only indirect expression in the work of Pratt, Dyck, and Butala. Mary Pratt's most direct representation of the female body comes in her *Donna* series. However, based as the series is on photography by Christopher Pratt, the figure of Donna is portrayed as the object of male scrutiny, embodying most aspects of the code of femininity. It is Pratt's still lifes of food, especially those of lusciously modelled fruit, which suggest female eroticism. In the same way, Aganetha Dyck suggests women's sexuality through her gallery use of honey seen dripping off the female form. But then, most of Dyck's work exploits the sense of touch through her voluptuous use of material.

Sharon Butala portrays women as experiencing sexual subjects only through Phoebe, a character in her autobiographically based novel, *Luna*, and through various female short story characters. Otherwise, in our talks together, she made it clear that she considers women's ability to bear children (that is, their gender) to be the defining bodily fact in their perceptions of self, making them irrevocably different from men. Again, this is touched on, not in her life writing, but in her various novels, especially *Luna*, which climaxes in a graphic birth scene. Similarly, in my discussions with Mary Pratt, I discovered that she, too, felt that women's reproductive capacity was crucial to their sense of identity. She celebrates this perception in her painting of her baby grandchild being bathed. And, while both Mary Meigs and

Aganetha Dyck might celebrate with her, they would more likely perceive differences between men and women as the result of social construction rather than of the biology of gender. Accordingly, both take issue with what theorists have called "essentialism," feeling that such a position lends itself to the subordination of women. It is my view that, while the mothers of the present generation of women routinely accepted the essentialist position, their daughters are less likely to see differences between the sexes as radical. Therefore, it is likely that essentialism will not always be a fixed part of the Canadian female autobiographical tradition.

Nevertheless, the work of all four artists contains a profound sense of the vulnerability of the female body – to acts of violence, to the toll taken by childbirth, and to the effects of disease and aging. Mary Meigs' last writings are a witness to her experience of the latter. Aganetha Dyck's art contains references both to the bodily effects of addiction and environmental poisoning and to the frequent occurrence of violence against women in what continues to be a predominantly patriarchal society. As for Pratt, I, together with other critics, have argued that Pratt's paintings of flayed meat and fish also refer, at least metaphorically, to the various kinds of bodily violence experienced by women. Similarly, Butala's fiction contains several scenes of domestic violence against women, including wife-battering and rape. In Canadian society at large, the conspiracy of silence concerning spousal violence is being broken; this is reflected now in Canadian female autobiographical art.

Then again, Chapter Two shows that, on the whole, Sharon Butala's life writing figures the female body somewhat differently. In describing her life as a rancher's wife, Butala comes across as a physically vigorous woman who could help out of doors as well as run the house. Becoming familiar with the ranch shortgrass landscape was part of Butala's new life and she walked it daily. She discovered that walking affected not only her body but also her mind and spirit. This interdependency of body and mind is one of the major themes of *The Perfection of the Morning* and *Wild Stone Heart*. Based on Butala's experience, bodily sensations are shown to be a clear indication of one's mental state. Butala alerts women to the necessity of being bodily aware, an important idea to include in any female autobiographical tradition.

That is not to say that the more frivolous preoccupation with feminine adornment would be banished from such a tradition. That would not be in keeping with present social attitudes. North American women experience enormous pressure to spend time and effort on their appearance. Television "make-over" programs draw top numbers of female viewers and would-be participants because they assume (correctly) that they will be judged in the marketplace on the basis of their appearance. Women's efforts to comply can have pernicious effects. At the very least they experience an ongoing anxiety about their looks. Mary Pratt reflects this chronic anxiety in *Cold Cream*, which shows the marks made by a woman unhappily dragging her fingers through the cream on her face. Similarly, Aganetha Dyck's *Anorexic Dress* dramatizes the pernicious effects of the fad for thinness.

Yet, in *Pocketbooks for the Queen*, Dyck accepts the accoutrements of femininity as part of being a woman; her three fellow artists would do the same. Even Mary Meigs insists that many lesbians are very feminine in dress and deportment. In Chapter Two, I attribute the continuing power of the code of femininity at least partially to what Brownmiller calls "a brilliant, subtle esthetic," one that satisfies many women's need for self-expression. Just as houses are closely tied to women's construction of self, so are her clothes. As long as women take pleasure in "dressing up," the less damaging aspects of society's notions of femininity will likely remain as part of a Canadian tradition of female autobiography, despite the objectification that is an ingrained part of the code of femininity.

In Chapter Three

John Ralston Saul has said that Canada's northern location is a central factor affecting the Canadian view of nature. It conditions us Canadians to think of nature in an animistic way, perceiving the natural world, not as a backdrop, but as an actor in the Canadian human drama. Furthermore, because of the rigours of the climate and the vast wilderness areas, Canadians have also traditionally portrayed interacting with nature as a masculine pursuit, and the natural world as masculine territory. For example, it is men who predominate in the oil industry, wresting the "black gold" from the earth, and men who do the hard work of farming, ranching, and fishing the ocean. In Gary Alan Fine's terms, such men have routinely taken an imperialist view of nature, seeing it as a resource for human use, or as a force to be controlled.

While conceding that the natural world has, in this way, functioned as masculine territory, Chapter Three begins to shape a new autobiographical tradition, one in which women inhabit the natural world as fully as men.

In so doing, women are more likely to seek a cooperative relationship with nature, seeing it as both nurturing and in the need of safeguarding. Rather than taking an imperialist view, they view nature from (in Fine's terms) a protectionist or organic point of view, perceiving it as a precious realm of which they are an integral part. In their art, Dyck, Butala, Pratt, and Meigs indicate the nurturing roles they assume in their contacts with the natural world.

Chapter Three focuses first of all on the work of Aganetha Dyck because, of the four, it is Dyck who has developed the most single-minded relationship with nature through her connection with the honeybee. Not many women, however, work with honeybees in the way that Aganetha Dyck does. Nevertheless, her experience demonstrates that an intimate knowledge of a tiny segment of the natural world can illuminate the whole. From her investigation into the bee world, Dyck has learned first hand that nature is both mysterious and intelligible. The bee instinct for community, for example, is a phenomenon that has yet to be explained, other than to say that it seems to be both inborn and socially taught. However, bee scientists such as Mark Winston have learned that the hive's survival depends on the bees' ability to communicate, either through the chemistry of pheromones or through the physical movement of the bee dance. In working with Winston, Dyck has delighted in her acquisition of bee science, and through her participation in various experiments, has become something of a scientist herself.

However Dyck's chief joy in working with the bees has come from her relationship to them as collaborators in the creation of her art. She now regards them as fellow artists, whose skill in honeycomb design rivals that of human architects. In no sense does she perceive human beings as "lords" over the honeybees. Rather, she embraces them as fellow creatures that inhabit a world far removed from her own. Nevertheless, her growing understanding of their world has helped her to understand her own, especially her experience of community. Her dealings with the buzzing bodies in the hive engage her fully and give her a sense of what she calls the "life force" of nature.

Yet, among our four artists, Sharon Butala is the most insistent in declaring that contact with the natural world is essential for the psychic health of human beings. She sees this as being particularly true for women, whose reproductive rhythms resonate with the cycles of nature. Moreover, as Chapter Three shows, she sets an example that even urban Canadian women will likely find easy to follow in that she interacts with nature simply by walking alone, day after day, in the fields surrounding her home. Physically exploring the untouched grassland landscape, she gradually encounters its indigenous animals and learns the names of the prairie plants. She also finds traces of the aboriginal people, whose land it first was, and becomes aware that, eons, ago, this was the territory of dinosaurs. Butala's interaction with the land produces an animistic sense of what she calls "Presence," an imminent quality resembling Dyck's "life force." Butala experiences a sense union or engagement with the land, a "flow" that gives her peace and a sense of belonging. Nature becomes an important "other" in the shaping of her sense of self.

Still, she never loses the awareness that ranching country is, in occupational terms, male territory and that ranchers have knowledge of the land that comes only from a lifetime of dealing with its exigencies. She acknowledged that, as a rancher, husband Peter Butala's understanding of the prairie environment always outstripped her own, and she envied his ease and comfort with the land and its occupants. In her dreams, the spirit of the untamed part of nature is personified by a powerful male figure called "The Lord of the Wild," onto whom she projects the unknowable and mysterious aspects of the natural world.

Chapter Three shows that Mary Pratt's first husband, Christopher, acted also as a primary influence, not only in his wife's return to painting after their marriage, but also in introducing Mary to the wilderness areas of Newfoundland that surrounded their Salmonier home. Just as ranching country is essentially male territory, so the streams and forests of Newfoundland are viewed generally as male territory, one that yields up prime opportunities for fishing and hunting, Christopher's chief avocations. Certainly Mary, with all Newfoundlanders, took it for granted that the Newfoundland's fishing industry was staffed entirely by men. Christopher was not a fisherman in the professional sense; nevertheless, his "catches of the day" brought something of the wild into Mary's kitchen, and her fish paintings are her tribute to their beauty and their sacrifice. Mary never really claims the Newfoundland wilderness for herself, but her few ocean landscapes show that she thrills to nature's wildness. She credits this quality in the Newfoundland landscape with sparking her creativity; she muses that she might never have become an artist without it.

However, over the long term, Mary Pratt's main contact with nature has been through gardening. Pratt was an avid gardener long before she became an artist, the one being the precursor of the other. Unlike the rough Newfoundland landscape, the garden can easily be part of the female domain; accordingly, in her diary writings, Pratt describes the Fredericton garden of her childhood as intimately connected to her mother's house. She learned the skills of gardening as a child, and applied these in designing and caring for the two primary gardens of her adult life – one at Salmonier and the other surrounding her home in St. John's. Journalist Merike Weiler describes the design of the St. John's garden in a feature article for a decorating periodical (*Style at Home*). In the article, Weiler makes it clear that, because of its artful design, she sees this garden as an extension of Pratt's art practice.

Although this is undoubtedly true, Pratt's chief purpose in creating gardens is to provide herself with access to nature thorough her studio windows. As she tells Weiler, "I need to see some beauty, some energy and life when I paint." However, she seldom uses gardens as a primary subject of her paintings. They appear as backdrops for her still life subjects, or to provide a bridal atmosphere in her *Aspects of a Ceremony* series. Her one garden painting (*Morning*), seen in the mist of early morning, is paradisal in its mood.

Certainly, Pratt found her gardens far more welcoming than Newfoundland's hunting-fishing countryside. They have been her delight and solace for most of her life. Chapter Three makes reference to Frederick Turner, who cites gardening as the prime example of how human beings should enhance nature through culture. Grounded as they are in domesticity, women are particularly suited to bring about such a happy conjunction. However, while gardens are still part of Canadian suburban life, it is debatable whether the large number of urban women living in condominiums or apartments, or forming part of a two-career family, will wish or have the opportunity to have gardens. Although their main interest in nature lies elsewhere, both Dyck and Butala keep gardens. They, with Pratt, would feel a sense of loss if, as seems likely, gardens were no longer part of the ordinary Canadian women's lives. They would wish that this ancient symbol of paradise would still form part of the Canadian female autobiographical tradition.

Like Pratt, Mary Meigs loved gardens from childhood and saw them always as part of any house she chose. To her very last days, her first act in the morning was to look through her window to the garden, noting the weather, and the effects of the changing light and seasons on the trees and plants. In *Lily Briscoe*, she comments that painters such as herself were most likely, because of their visual awareness, to connect closely to the landscape. According to the notes accompanying her 2005 retrospective show at the Bombardier gallery, Meigs' red canvas painting chair was routinely set up so she could paint out of doors. Many of these landscapes, particularly the ones depicting the scenes of the Eastern Townships of Quebec, were exhibited in that show. Her love for that part of Canada was readily apparent in this part of her art.

Meigs sometimes revealed a romantic, Thoreau-like perception of nature and liked to escape from the complexities of society into what she saw as a more innocent world. On the whole, though, she took an organic view of nature, seeing human beings, animals, and plants as equally part of the natural order. She identified closely with all aspects of nature, but particularly with birds, whom she took as talismans, embodiments of joy and freedom. It is hard to overestimate her ability to identify with all animals, especially birds. Consequently, her writing is punctuated with animal metaphors, used mostly to summon up vivid mental pictures of he friends.

However, Meigs' writing about nature has undertones of loss. She mourns the vanishing of bird habitat and the diminished bird sightings in eastern Quebec. This sense of loss, and an awareness of the various threats to the environment, marks the work of all four of these artists, who uniformly take up a protectionist attitude towards the natural world. For example, Dyck has sounded warnings about dangers to the bee population from loss of natural habitat and the importing of infected bees. She pleads the cause of the bees with even more fervour nowadays since the advent of a mysterious disease called "total colony collapse disease" for which there is no known cure. She sees the bees as the "canaries" of nature, creatures whose fate warns of general disaster. Butala has written of her concern over the loss of the family farm, feeling that these farmers possessed knowledge of the ways of nature that is difficult to acquire in any other way. For her part, Pratt shares concern with all Newfoundlanders concerning the vanishing fish populations. She has spoken publicly in support of the threatened fishing industry. Her fears are well founded. A Canadian-led research team has predicted that, if present trends continue, the world's fisheries will collapse by 2050 because of over-fishing and the growing pollution of the world's oceans.[1]

While the art of these four women points to the sense of well-being that intimate contact with nature offers to women, the effects of industrialization, urbanization, and technology may make it difficult for future women to duplicate their experience. Ecologist Dana Phillips has warned that there well may be a post-natural world in which human culture fully manipulates nature. To mitigate against such an eventuality, I dare to hope that any female Canadian autobiographical tradition will be marked by an organic and protectionist perception of nature in order to preserve at least some elements of the wild.

In Chapter Four

While North American ageist attitudes tend to marginalize both older men and women, women are particularly affected because of the value society places on vigour and on youthful, female beauty. The discussion in Chapter Four offers women an alternate tradition, one that opens them up to the spiritual and emotional possibilities of old age, without attempting to deny the ravages visited on the body by the passage of time. The works of Butala, Meigs, Dyck, and Pratt offer examples of the ways in which growing older can be a vehicle for spiritual growth, thereby restoring old women to a valued place in society as contributing and inspiring members. Also, because all four continue[d] to practice as artists well past their sixty-fifth birthday, their life and art testify to the fact that, as Barbara Macdonald has said, women are able "to name the processes of our own aging." These four never relinquish their basic identity as artists.

I make the case that their longtime work as artists furthers their spirituality in two ways, spirituality in this context meaning an awareness of a transcendent reality. First, as Deborah Haynes contends, all truly creative endeavours are a form of spiritual discipline that "help us to reach into ourselves and into the world" and deepen our spiritual experience. Authentic creativity and spirituality go hand-in-hand. Secondly, because their art practices have a strong autobiographical component, these four artists become necessarily more adept at "reaching into themselves" as they deal with life issues in and through their art. Both Elisabeth Kübler-Ross and Scott Peck, well-known psychological theorists referred to in Chapter Four, stress the importance of practising unflinching self-scrutiny and see it as a precondition of spiritual growth. Both insist that one must deal with one's "unfinished business" before one can usefully begin "to reach into the world." According to Peck, all evil has its source in self-deception, in the inability to face the truth about oneself.

Both Sharon Butala and Mary Meigs incorporate self-scrutiny into the texts of their life writing, providing readers with examples of a developing moral sensibility. In a college address, Butala tells of her teenage experience of being caught telling a lie. She goes on to explain that, in her thirties, she rededicated herself to truth-telling after realizing that she was living according to the agendas of others, primarily those of her mother and first husband. She vowed then to be true to her own convictions. Moreover, Butala does not varnish over the alienation she felt when first moving to the

Butala ranch. Her hard-won spiritual struggles are shared openly with the reader.

Mary Meigs' life writing centres on her acknowledgment of her lesbianism. Her "coming out" in print is her central act of truth-telling, but she dos not hesitate to inform on herself on other matters. She admits regretfully that she realized only as a grown woman that her family and her younger self were racist in their attitudes towards their black servants and other minorities. Similarly, she confesses to her foolishness in being duped into an obsessive relationship with the manipulative Andrée. In fact, she devotes a whole book to careful examination of her behaviour and that of Andrée, a woman she came finally to realize to be evil because of her habits of lying, self-justification, and projection. This kind of process is what Scott Peck calls "emptying," and it made possible the capacity for altruism and concern for issues beyond the self that marks the work of Butala and Meigs in their later years. For example, Sharon and Peter Butala won several awards for their work in saving the original grasslands of southern Saskatchewan, while Mary Meigs, long a patron of other writers and of women's causes, displayed in her final years an unusual capacity for the attentiveness to others that theologian Martin Buber has placed at heart of spiritual maturity.

Chapter Four traces a similar change in the artistic focus of Mary Pratt and Aganetha Dyck, who treat personal issues first before turning their attention to the wider world. As with Butala and Meigs, both artists display through their work a forthright honesty about their personal life that helps them to deal with any "unfinished business." In my interviews with Pratt and in public discussions about her work, Pratt was always candid about her life and in particular about the failure of her marriage to Christopher, and about the fact that her distress in this regard formed a subtext in many of her paintings. In the same way, her sorrow about the miscarriage of twins and her discomfort about her parents' marriage find honest expression in her painting. In later life, she has to a great extent come to terms with past sorrows and mistakes, and, for the years before her second marriage, she built a life alone. She is now a public figure who gives generously to the Maritime community through her support of the arts and of environmental causes. It is apparent from the writings in *A Personal Calligraphy* that she continues in her honest self-scrutiny and that, for her extended family and the public at large, she has become a source of inspiration, both as a woman and as a practising artist.

Aganetha Dyck, too, has displayed, both in her work and life, a rigorous honesty. That is not to say, however, that there are not personal issues – such as the evolution of her religious beliefs – which she wishes, as she told me, to keep private. Still, her early work reveals much about her concerns as an individual – her intense misgivings about any form of social regimentation, her horror at the results of addiction, including those she herself experienced as a smoker, and her suffering as a victim of an auto-immune disease. In various interviews, she has also been very candid about her need to find self-expression beyond the roles wife and mother and about her decision to name herself primarily as artist. Since the early 1990s, however, her collaboration with honeybees has drawn her out of herself into an investigation of the wider world of nature of which the honeybee is a part. This in turn has allowed her to view human culture with critical eyes. Her latest work investigates the plight of those on the margins of society, while her worry over environmental threats to her beloved bees has led her to express concern over the fate of the planet as a whole. Both are forms of *testimonio*. As with Butala, Meigs, and Pratt, the evolution of subject matter in Dyck's art is derived from a life pattern that demonstrates the possibilities in the lives of older women for new meaning and service. As greater numbers of older women choose to express themselves autobiographically in literature and art, their contributions to society will become more apparent. Such contributions will shape anew the perceptions of older women in female Canadian autobiographical tradition.

In talking with them, I learned that the moral sensibilities that these four artists have developed over the years are rooted in their childhood Christian education. From their work, it is apparent also that the stories of the Bible still inform their imaginations. However, as Chapter Four points out, Butala, Meigs, Pratt, and Dyck have all voiced, as adults, their discomfort with basic Christian dogma. While Pratt and Dyck retain tentative ties to the churches of their childhood, Butala has not been a church attendee as an adult and rejects assumptions of an all-powerful deity. The same was true of Meigs. The spiritual inspiration of all four comes primarily from other sources – from contact with nature, from their work as artists and from an abiding sense of community with other people. All mention a sense of joy that occurs unbidden and is accompanied by a feeling of connection to a larger-than-self whole, whether it be nature, a human community, or a "presence" or "life force," intuitively felt.

Sharon Butala accepts such experiences as mystical; Pratt and Dyck are less specific, while Meigs rejects all notions of mysticism. Mysticism is part of all religions and Christians name this presence as God or the Holy Spirit and see its action as a species of grace. Also, perhaps as a result of their discomfort with institutionalized religion and in seeking spiritual experience outside its confines, Butala and Meigs have voiced discomfort also with the notion of an all-powerful deity. In this, they reflect the sentiments of a significant proportion of the Canadian population. As journalist Douglas Todd discovered in a North American survey, the majority of artists, writers, and performers of various kinds do not connect spiritual experience with religiosity and find spiritual inspiration most often through contact with nature. In view of this trend, and of the multicultural nature of our society, I cannot argue (in spite of my personal inclinations) that Christian orthodoxy must be a part of the spiritual exploration that properly forms part of this new autobiographical tradition.

Despite the fact that all four artists view spirituality as part of their sense of self, only Sharon Butala describes her life pattern as a spiritual journey, during which she has sensed the existence of an realm beyond the ordinary world of the senses. As she explains in her life writings texts, her life since early adolescence has been marked by a series of occurrences that could be classified as mystical, paranormal, and/or supernatural, depending on one's frame of reference. Included in these is the unbidden sense of union with a larger realm that occurred during her first communion and the birth of her son and paranormal visions of an ancient Cretan goddess, of a deer on the side of the road turning into a unicorn for a magical split second, and of ghostly apparitions of Amerindian women, past inhabitants of her special field. She also reports her significant dream life, which she has come to believe is the result of her soulful contact with the powerful landscape of the prairies. Butala would contest classifying these events as paranormal or supernatural because she considers such events to be part of ordinary life, experienced by a far larger percentage of the population than is generally realized. Nevertheless, in this scientific age, popular opinion tends to cast doubt on the objective reality of events not scientifically explainable. Because Butala places such events on the same footing as those of everyday life, and because the perceptions of the visionary co-exist in her texts along side of those of the practical housewife and the experienced academic, her insistence on their objective reality is convincing. In this regard and in keeping with her personal commitment to truth-telling, Butala has made a valuable contribution to a new female Canadian autobiographical tradition by creating a space in this tradition in which other women can feel safe in confiding the "mystical" or "paranormal" events in their lives.

Butala does not theorize about the precipitating cause of the earlier mystical events. That is, she does not assume the existence of a divine being in order to explain them; for Butala and for the reader, they remain mysterious. Once, however, her exploration of the world of the prairie grasslands becomes habitual, she sees her continued experience of the mystical as a function of place and landscape. She attributes not only her sense of presence and her totemic dreams but also the apparition of the aboriginal women and her vision of the Cretan goddess to her interaction with various landscapes. Chapter Four offers theoretical support for affirming a connection between spiritual experience and geographical location by introducing the findings of Professor Belden Lane. Lane stresses the importance of geography in the development of human spirituality and investigates North American sites in particular. He maintains that there are "sacred" places that are especially spiritually alive, having a particular spirit and life. Lane would conclude from Butala's descriptions of her mystical experiences that she was spiritually ready and so could attune herself to the sacred quality of these prairie environments.

In a different way, Aganetha Dyck and Mary Meigs also are spiritually inspired by nature. For these two, it is not contact solely with landscape that prompts the joy that is the hallmark of spiritual elevation but intimate contact with animals. For example, Dyck's prolonged interaction with honeybees allows her to sense the life force that connects all things. For Meigs, it is the presence of her beloved birds that, as we have seen, inspires her spirit and gives her the sense of elevating joy. As for Mary Pratt, her spiritual touchstone acts also as her muse; it is the presence of light, a gift to her from the natural world that inspires her artistically and spiritually. Chapter Four builds on the conclusions offered in Chapter Three because it offers evidence that contact with nature is not only necessary for women's emotional health but also for their creative inspiration and spiritual growth. All the more reason, then, for any Canadian female autobiographical tradition to bear witness to the necessity of preserving a vibrant natural world for all succeeding generations.

Spiritual growth is, however, not the same thing as spiritual maturity. The latter is a goal of most spiritual journeys and the precious commodity that old women can come to offer society. The mark of such maturity is not mystical awareness (although that often accompanies it) but an ability to connect lovingly and in a perceptive way with other people. As Chapter Four points out, Martin Buber set the standard when he asked that all of us answer "Here am I" to the existential question "Where art thou?" Buber is referring the quality of attentiveness necessary to be truly present to another person. Such awareness requires that one move beyond one's ingrained self-centredness. The best that most of us likely can do is to attain this attentiveness intermittently, in what Buber calls "the grace of everyday." It is a gift that most grandmothers are familiar with, the one that they most easily can give to their grandchildren. As mature women and artists, Meigs, Dyck, Pratt, and Butala model the grace of attentiveness, each in her own way.

Of the four, Mary Meigs is the most explicit in revealing both her struggles for this grace and her achievement of it. Her loving outpouring of attention is evident first in *The Box Closet*, the book about her mother written after her mother's death. It allows Meigs to deal, as Kübler-Ross suggests, with "unfinished business," but it goes beyond that; in this text, Meigs achieves a spiritual bonding with her mother not possible while the latter was alive, and this frees her, I believe, to reach out more easily in love to other people. Four years later, she writes *In the Company of Strangers* about the NFB film in which she appeared. Here she turns her attention to her film companions to create a series of loving word portraits of the nine women – seven cast members, the director, and her assistant – with whom she shared this adventure. Apparent in both Meigs' book and in the film itself is the loving community these women achieved. ("Wasn't it wonderful," says Constance.) Scott Peck rates community-building of this kind as perhaps the most profound manifestation of spiritual maturity. In *Beyond Recall*, it is evident that Meigs was the centre of a loving community of friends who organized a roster of care so that strangers would not surround her during her last months. Moreover, in the article *Hospital Notes*, Meigs demonstrates that even in the midst of her stroke rehabilitation, a time when she had to concentrate fiercely on the responses of her body, she was able reach out warmly to casual hospital acquaintances.

Community-building has been part of Aganetha Dyck's life since childhood when she and her family were enthusiastic members both of their rural community and of the Reform Mennonite church. Much of Dyck's work examines both the negative and positive sides of being part of a close-knit group. For Dyck, freedom is a primary value, and she reveals that she has been loath to sacrifice any part of that freedom to the demands of the group. Nevertheless, the concept of community is of prime importance to her both as a woman and as an artist, and her instinct is always to involve others in what she is doing. As an artist, her work with the bees is a way of studying community in nature and, to do so, she had, of necessity, to become part of the beekeeping community. This involvement has been a joy for her, both because of the access it gave her to the world of nature and because of her interaction with like-minded people. I do not think it is an overstatement to say that this involvement has been a spiritual experience for Dyck and that her ability to build relationships is a demonstration of her spiritual maturity. Both her joy and her maturity are evident in *The Nature of Things* television program (2006) entitled *Bee Talker; The Secret World of Bees*, in which the work of bee scientist Mark Winston and his collaboration with Aganetha Dyck is explored. Here, the collaboration between scientist and artist seems as magical as the complex interaction typical of the world of the honeybee.

The collection of diary entries and public speeches found in Mary Pratt's *A Personal Calligraphy* shows the development of Pratt's community awareness and of her spiritual maturity. As time goes by, Pratt has increasingly taken an active role in the cultural life of the Maritimes and of Canada and, at some cost to her time in her studio, has agreed over the years to serve on the board of such bodies as the Canada Council for the Arts and the Provincial Art Gallery of Newfoundland. Moreover, she has been a steadfast advocate both for the arts community as a whole and for the environment, and she has demonstrated he ability to work with others in pursuit of those goals. Similarly, in later years, Sharon Butala has turned her attention to two of her major concerns, the preservation of the environment and the plight of the aboriginal people of Saskatchewan and, with her husband Peter, was the recipient of many awards for the work to preserve the original Saskatchewan grasslands. For both Pratt and Butala, these involvements constitute a form of *testimonio*.

My goal here is not exactly to recommend volunteerism to senior citizens, although that is an important venue for their talents. Rather, I wish to draw attention to the fact that the spiritual maturity of older women is an important societal resource and to recommend that any female autobiographical tradition inspire women to value their wisdom in old age and to recognize the important role they can continue to play in their communities.

Finally, of course, each woman must deal with old age in her own way. The goal of such a tradition is to open up the autobiographical canon so that all present-day female experience becomes acceptable. As the accounts of these four artists have shown, women are living longer so that there are far more opportunities for a productive and spiritually mature old age, and that does not preclude being sexually active. Similarly, contact with nature emerges as important for women, but such contact is being threatened by an urban way of life and by changes in the environment. Women's erotic experience, both heterosexual and lesbian, is shown to be more global than men's, and they are increasingly seeing themselves as active sexual subjects, feeling desire as well as inspiring it. And, despite the fact that women now have a long work life outside the home and that it is not unusual for their male spouses to cook and even clean, the domestic realm by and large remains a female domain and women respond with joy to seeing this honoured. The autobiographical work of Butala, Dyck, Meigs, and Pratt suggests that these four elements should rightly be part of a new autobiographical tradition. The important thing is that such a tradition challenge preconceived notions of what a woman's life should be and that autobiographical work offer Canadian women a space of their own.

Apart from the content of their own work, these four artists add a new dimension to female autobiographical tradition in that they continue[d] to be working artists well past the traditional age of retirement. For example, in 2002, Mary Meigs was consulting her publisher about a new manuscript three hours before her death. In 2007, Mary Pratt ventured into new territory by completing a portrait drawing of long-time friend and former governor general, Adrienne Clarkson, which was installed in Rideau Hall on February 15 of that year. Similarly, Sharon Butala broke new ground in a 2008 book about the 1962 unsolved murder in Saskatoon of a high school girlfriend entitled *The Girl in Saskatoon: A Meditation on Friendship, Memory, and Murder*. It describes Butala's investigation into the circumstances surrounding her friend's terrible death and the ways in which this investigation changed Butala's view of the world and of herself. Also Aganetha Dyck has been energized in her practice by her collaboration with bee scientist Mark Winston, one that has informed most of her exhibitions in Canada and the United States since 2001. In their patterns of productivity in their senior years, these artists reflect a new trend in Canadian society and refigure the stereotypes of female old age.

Epilogue:
"Do You Think You'll Ever Go Back?"

I have been dreaming of my father recently – dreams in which he assures me that he is busily employed and happy, but ones in which my mother is nowhere in evidence. These dreams have rekindled in me a sense of the presence of my dad, a person I was closest to and knew best in early childhood, before war and the resultant job opportunities took him away for most of the year.

During those early years we had certain rituals that we both found enjoyable. Each morning I would watch him shave, waiting with giggles for the moment during lathering when he would take his shaving brush and dab me with a bit of the shaving cream. Similarly, in late afternoon, I would loiter on the sidewalk in front of our west Winnipeg house, waiting to run to meet him as he came home from work, swinging his tool box and lunch pail, cap on the side of his head. Around home, he would often sing a phrase or two from one particular Gaelic song, accompanied sometimes by a quick step dance, like the ones I saw later at Nova Scotian community concerts. When he wanted to quiet someone down, usually my mother or myself, he would say something that sounded like a breathy "wisht," a sound I learned later was part of the Gaelic.

The puzzling part of these rituals was that they included an oft-repeated question that always came out of the blue, seemingly *a propos* of nothing: "Do you think you'll ever go back?" he would say, as if talking to his older brother, Jim, who came West with him before World War I. Jim was my grandmother's second husband, my father's best friend and my beloved uncle/grandfather. In its ritual repetition, the question became more of a family saying than an actual query. Addressed by my father to the child that was I, it served to elevate my status to that of an adult, even though no response was ever expected or given. It conveyed to me that there was an earlier "back" in his life that he wanted me to know about so that I might realize that it somehow had a connection to me. That question and vestiges of the Gaelic that I absorbed were my father's way of communicating this unknown part of his life to me, his daughter. They were his form of auto-biographical telling. The question was a wistful one, humorous yet full of a sense of loss. In retrospect, it seems that it expressed the loneliness of being away from the community that formed him and of fulfilling his need to establish a sense of a living connection to the past. That also was what my Aunt Martha must have meant when she would say to me, a Westerner, on my infrequent visits to Nova Scotia: "Ah, so you've come home." If one was a MacKay in Canada, "home" must forever be Nova Scotia.

I surmise that these memories and dreams of my father are prompted by old age, a period in one's life when an imaginative return to childhood scenes is not uncommon. I, like other women of my age, find comfort in establishing continuity with an earlier childhood self and an earlier commu-nity – my birth family. Mostly, however, I suspect that the specific memory of my father's recurrent rhetorical question comes most precisely from my immersion in the present project where I serve as "hostess" at this textual "dinner party," the result of which is my becoming the fifth strand in the total *métissage*. As this "fifth," I, too, have become involved in an autobio-graphical review parallel to that of the other four, working as critic "close to the bone." Consequently, I have been searching, in Meigs' terms, for my own "inscape." Claiming inclusion in my father's Nova Scotian heritage is part of that inscape.

In the present context, however, the query, "Do you think you'll ever go back?" emerges out of my past to evoke more universal associations. It has come to represent an essential autobiographical positioning in which the "I" in the text speaks inextricably from the "here and now" of the present, yet is often catapulted back to the "there and then" of the past. For example, the sight of the orange on Peter Butala's table brings to Sharon's mind the im-age of another dessert orange from her rural past. Dyck's present penchant for community has its source in her Mennonite roots. Meigs' memory of the sunlit rooms of her grandmother's house, "The Peak," dictates her adult choice of all subsequent houses. Similarly, Pratt's painted domestic images, epitomized by the shining jars in *Red Currant Jelly*, hold her Fredericton past like a fly caught in amber. The result is a note of bittersweet wistful-ness that recalls my father's understanding that, while elements of the past persist in some form within the present, he could effectively go "back" only in memory.

The act of aligning my personal family history with elements in the work of these four artists is possible because autobiographical art practices are exercises in intimacy and disclosure. Because of these attributes, I have been able to share their lives through their art and to connect them with each other and with myself. Critic Evelyn Hinz attributes the abundance and popularity of life narratives to this communal quality:

> ... and perhaps the reason auto/biographical documents are so abundant in the Western tradition has to do with the extent to which they provide a sense of the communal that we lack.... The appeal of auto/biography today, I would argue, is best understood through an awareness of its ritual nature in terms of how it answers to spiritual needs: the need of role models who inspire feelings of "pity" and "fear" by reason of the limited stage on which they perform, the need to face mortality, and the need to establish a living connection with the past. Instead of serving to reinforce a sense of the unique individual, auto/biography appeals because it counters such "loneliness." (Hinz 1992, 208–9)

Hinz is arguing that life narratives serve as substitutes for the group identity provided to individuals by ritual activity in more indigenous societies. This holds true for me. The autobiographical texts under study, both literary and visual, have allowed me entrance into the lives, value systems, emotions, thoughts, and dream life of four women in a fashion intimate enough to confer on me a sense of belonging. This sense was, of course, heightened by the series of dialogic interviews that took place with the four subjects and were marked by a collaborative equality. The act of reading in all its aspects has been, of course, an intersubjective process through which my own construction of self has acted as a screening device for issues emerging from these texts. To borrow Helen Buss's description when analyzing her own feminist reading practices (1993, 29), "I have constructed frameworks, named priorities, assumed particular readings."

This kind of feminist reading could be considered as "mothering" the text, to use once more the metaphor that Buss refigured from the phenomenology of reading. I embarked on three central acts of mothering. The first was to create a textual community in a cross-disciplinary framing that illuminated communal elements in the artists' constructions of self, despite the difference in art forms. The second was the thematic organization of the chapters by which the shaping force of the self-perception of each artist provided the context for the relevant chapter. The third and most important act of mothering came from my identification of the liminal positioning that was so significant in the autobiographical practices of all four artists. It was this positioning that allowed them to occupy multiple subjectivities, changing and growing as they explored the threshold between the modernist and postmodernist worlds.

Most involving for me, however, was the first act, that of forming the art practices of these four artists into a community. Being placed in a textual community allowed me to trace how they could serve as textual sisters, daughters, and mothers to each other, the work of each illuminating the more obscure aspects in that of the other three. So it was that Mary Pratt's still lifes cast a spotlight on the basic domesticity of her sister artists, that Mary Meigs' investigation into the truth of her bodily experience revealed how rooted in body were the perceptions of those other three, that Aganetha Dyck's adventurous explorations of a microcosmic aspect of nature revealed not only her reverence for all forms of life but placed in a new context the crucial role of nature in each of the others' work. Finally, Butala's fearless revelations of the mystic aspects of her spirituality cast a light on the differing spiritual components in the autobiographical practices of the remaining three. What joins them in firm sisterhood is their core identity as artists and their adventures in occupying the threshold between the world of their mothers and the world of their daughters, whether actual or virtual. While they all cast their eyes sometimes to that world they left behind and perhaps ask metaphorically "Do you think you'll ever go back?" they have stepped firmly over that threshold and have set a new course for themselves and for other women.

Apart from the act of mothering inherent in setting up the initial reading framework, I most routinely gave the texts a sisterly reading. In sisterhood with real life mothers, I joined Mary Pratt in her celebration of her countless motherly birthday performances as invoked by her *Chocolate Birthday Cake* (Fig. 27). I wept with Mary Meigs as she read the belated gift of her mother's letters and grieved over the reshaping of the young woman in those letters into the convention-bound mother whom she knew. I, too, have a box of my mother's letters in which, as a younger woman, she pours out her hopes and fears. Similarly, I joined Mary Pratt as she sat in the nursing home with her mother listening to "The Lark in a Clear Air." I, too, remember my mother's last days during which she gamely dressed and left her apartment to attend her granddaughter's wedding. Most poignantly, I sat with two-year-old Sharon Butala, plopped down under a tree, feeling abandoned and alone. All women know in some way or another, the desolation of being absent, physically or psychologically, from their mothers. I joined with all four artists in finding the power of the mother a characteristic of my own lifelong experience. Similarly, I connected with Pratt and Aganetha Dyck in positioning the domestic role as basic in my life, yet, with them, I often longed to transcend it. On a lighter note, I had to admit, as do all four artists, that I found the appeal of the feminine aesthetic – clothes, makeup, feminine adornment – to be, in a mild way, irresistible.

Most basically, however, I joined them also in any contesting of the subordination or oppression of women and in any expression of feminist positioning. The first took me into acknowledgment of the darker areas of female experience seemingly inherent in a patriarchal society. For example, I made common cause with Mary Pratt as her celebration of her domestic subjectivity was undercut by hints of victimization and violence. In particular, *The Service Station* (Fig. 20) articulated for me, in a powerful and metaphorical way, our shared sense of female bodily vulnerability to the predatory violence seemingly intrinsic in a male-dominated culture. Similarly, Aganetha Dyck's *The Extended Wedding Party* (Fig. 12) dramatized for me Dyck's obvious ambivalence about the institution of marriage. I joined her in her construction of herself as profoundly uneasy at the spectacle of this elaborate ritual that valorized the bride, only to leave her open to the possibilities of future subjugation. For the same reason, I found Sharon Butala's autobiographically based novel, *Luna*, to be involving in the way that the author presented the plight of the traditional woman, subordinate yet burdened with responsibility, a subjectivity Butala claimed for herself in her first marriage. As for Mary Meigs, I shared in her struggle against the bodily shame that tainted her self-esteem. Most women, myself among them, have been made to feel shame as sexual subjects (whatever their orientation) in a culture that values them still as sexual objects.

There are countless other ways in which I gave a sisterly reading to the representations of self in these texts, bringing into consciousness, for example, my identification with Aganetha Dyck's construction of herself as thinker, and my delight at her adventurer subjectivity, which surfaced as she investigated the world of *apis mellifera*. I also felt a tug of recognition as Butala related how necessary to her female sense of self was the continuing contact with the world of nature as found in the prairie landscape of western Canada. As she tells us in *Lilac Moon* (2005), her book on perceptions of Western Canada, Butala did succeed in going "back," at least to the open sky vistas of the prairies.

But I have pushed the sisterly reading metaphor far enough to illustrate how I wove my reader/critic self into these literary and visual texts. I wish now only to pay tribute to the ways in which I became a textual daughter, or in Hinz's terms, the ways in which these texts supplied me with role models and helped me to face mortality. In the fourth chapter, my joining with Butala, Dyck, Meigs, and Pratt in their shaping of themselves as spiritual subjects was a profound experience. I was instructed by all four in the role of ethical conduct in making a spiritual subjectivity possible. In her down-to-earth affirmation of herself as a spiritual sojourner, Sharon Butala opened my mind to the mystical dimensions of everyday reality. In her artistic identity as shaman, Aganetha Dyck taught me about the social and collaborative possibilities of art as she opened her practice up to blind people in her innovative *Working in the Dark* (Fig. 25). From Mary Pratt, I learned gallantry from her construction of herself growing older, facing illness with affirmation and hope and insisting that the creative fire burns more brightly as physical energy diminishes. It was Mary Meigs, however, who, in her perception of self in old age and facing death, modelled most clearly for me and for all readers the power of love. Even when hospitalized and disabled by a stroke, she could answer Martin Buber's symbolic call of "Where art Thou?" with a cheerful "Here I am" and be fully present to other people.

As older women, all four subjects present a narrative of identity as artists that contests ageism and allows women in the later stages of life a vision of selfhood that allows for self-determination. I submit that being on the threshold is a psychically healthy place to be, allowing mature women to construct themselves as adventurers and trail blazers. At times, of course, they cast they eyes to a world left behind and, with my father, yearning for aspects of that world, ask metaphorically, "Do you think you'll ever go back?" Aganetha Dyck sees this "back" as a foundation for the future and honours her female predecessors by asking a different question: "Who made the path for where I am?" (Reid 1996c, 4). Dyck, together with Sharon Butala, Mary Meigs, and Mary Pratt, likewise have made, through the construction of themselves in their art, a clear path for younger women to follow.

Notes

PROLOGUE: "TO TEACH IS TO LEARN"

1   While Mary Meigs considered herself to be primarily a visual artist, she is best known in Canada for her book of autobiography and, while some reference will be made to her painting and drawing, I will be focusing my discussion mostly on her work as a writer.

2   A comparison of the art and cultural roles of these three female artists was the organizing principle of a gallery show entitled *Carr, O'Keefe, Kahlo: A Place of Their Own*, which I viewed at the Vancouver Art Gallery in 2002.

3   In her description of the inspiration for *The Dinner Party*, Chicago remarks that she began to see the piece as a reinterpretation of the Last Supper from "the point of view of the women who had, throughout history, prepared the meals and set the table. In my 'Last Supper' however, the women would be the honored guests" (Garden City, NY: Doubleday, 1979), 11.

4   Accordingly, her first book, *Lily Briscoe: A Self-Portrait* was named after the artist character, Lily Briscoe, in Virginia Woolf's novel *To the Lighthouse*.

5   The retrospective (June 21 to December 4, 2005) was called *Mary Meigs Peindre, Ecrit-elle....* It was held at the *Centre Culturel Yvonne l. Bombardier*, Valcourt, Quebec. The curator was Annie Boudin, assisted by Marie-Claire Blais.

6   See Betty Friedan, *The Fountains of Age* (New York: Simon & Schuster, 1993), 158–64. See also Nancy Gibbs, "Midlife Crisis, Bring It On," *Time* (June 6, 2005): 30–39.

INTRODUCTION– WORKING CLOSE TO THE BONE

1   Verna Reid, "Emily, Laurie and Me: An Academic's Adventures in Studioland," *Proceedings: National Conference on the Liberal Arts and the Education of the Artist* (New York: School of Visual Arts, 1993).

2   In 1967, I resumed my teaching career as an instructor in a career-based educational institution. Nine persons were hired that year for academic positions, four of whom were women. Previously, the only female instructors were in the sewing department. My first day I was called to the office of the vice-president and told that if I did not "work out" they would not be hiring any more women. After a year's probationary period, when a male instructor would have been awarded a permanent position, we women were given a "continuing" appointment. It was not until a year later that we, after protesting, were given permanent status and were permitted to enroll for pension benefits.

3   During the 1990s, I taught, among others, a course entitled *The Uses of*

Autobiography in Canadian Literature Written by Women at the Alberta College of Art and Design and, later, *Women's Studies 309* at the University of Calgary. During my studies for my PhD, I was enrolled in courses in autobiographical and biographical theory in which the issues of myths about women were raised.

4   A fuller account of how the interviews were arranged and how each subject received me is as follows:

I had met Sharon Butala previously as a guest juror for the Alberta Foundation for the Literary Arts on which I served as a board member. I had been struck at that time by her good sense and sound literary taste and knowledge. I met her again when she was asked to read in support of the preservation of the grasslands on Nose Hill Park in Calgary. I had read *The Perfection of the Morning* and her novels, and I knew that she was a potential subject for my PhD dissertation. At that meeting, I was impressed at how she publically integrated her life and her work, and I was elated when she agreed to have me visit the Butala ranch near Eastend, Saskatchewan, for the purpose of an extended interview.

I approached Aganetha Dyck as she entered the Glenbow Museum in Calgary on the occasion of the opening of her retrospective show. I had already seen this show in Vancouver and had been very impressed by her sensuous use of materials. At the Glenbow, she responded immediately to my last-minute request for a short interview, and we sat together on a bench and discussed the sources of he art and the possible feminist slants it contained. She agreed to an extended interview in Winnipeg, and when the time came, she insisted that I stay in her home for the weekend so we wouldn't waste time. What impressed me the most, aside from her hospitality, was the way she saw her art and her life as part of the same continuum.

I contacted Mary Meigs by letter on the advice of her publisher. I had been enchanted by the persona in the NFB film and by her artful autobiography, *Lily Briscoe*. Meigs responded to the letter immediately by phone and seemed thrilled that I would travel to Montreal to interview her. Part of the reason she agreed to see me was that I broached the subject of her lesbianism right away and made this issue a part of the reason for my interest in her work. As with the others, I was impressed by her good sense and no-nonsense attitude.

I met Mary Pratt when she visited Calgary in connection with her retrospective show *The Substance of Light*. I knew her work and was aware of its autobiographical content. She was giving a lecture on the show, and I chanced to arrive at the venue early. Pratt came early as well and, at my request, gave me an on-the-spot interview. It wasn't until after her talk, which lasted over an hour, that I knew she was a key candidate for my project. She gave one of the most candid explanations of the autobiographical source of art that I had heard any artist give publicly.

5   Throughout this text, I use the term "artist" to refer both to writers and visual artists, and the term art-making to refer to the production of literary texts as well as to the making of visual art.

6   Langellier and Hall, Interviewing women: A phenomenological approach to feminist communication. In *Doing Research on Women's Communication: Perspectives and Methods* (1989), 201.

7   Sadly, Peter Butala died of cancer on Thursday, August 9, 2007.

8   "Life writing" is the inclusive classification of which "autobiography" is now a sub-genre, one among many,

as indicated. For an extended commentary on Canadian life writing, see Shirley Neuman, "Life Writing," in *A Literary History of Canada: Canadian Literature in English*, 2nd ed., Vol. 4, ed. W.H. New (Toronto: University of Toronto Press, 1990), 333–70.

9 Three examples of critical articles examining autobiographical practices in the visual arts are: Erika Billeter, "The World of Frida Kahlo: The Self-portrait as Autobiography," *Southwest Art* 23 (1993), 94–96, Gabriel Weisberg, "Painting as Autobiography: Cezanne's Early Work," *Arts Magazine* 63 (1989): 54–57, and Ora Lerman, "An Autobiographical Journey: Can Art Transform Personal and Cultural Loss?" *Art Magazine* 59 (May, 1985): 103–7.

10 There is, of course, much feminist theory that takes as its subject the work of female visual artists and while some commentary deals with the female personal in art, it is my observation that it deals with it only in a fragmentary manner. One exception is the 1987 article by Mary Kelly I refer to in chapter 1.

11 For example, this conflicted subjectivity is a basic feature in both *The Perfection of the Morning* by Sharon Butala, and *Lily Briscoe: A Self-Portrait* by Mary Meigs. Pratt makes reference to being "a woman first and then an artist" (Reid 1996a, 37). Only late in life does Pratt come to see her true identity as being that of an artist (ibid., 53). She made a similar declaration in her opening statement on the CBC television program *Adrienne Clarkson Presents: Infused with Light, A Journey with Mary Pratt*. Dyck took another tack; her domestic self was transformed into her artist self because her work in the studio started as an extension of her work in the home.

12 Meigs told me in our interview, "I love Jung" (Reid 1997c, 20). Similarly, Butala lists Carl Jung, *Memories, Dreams and Reflections* (New York: Random House, 1961), 204, in the "Sources" at the "Endnotes" of *Wild Stone Heart*, and her method of analyzing her dreams reveals a Jungian influence. She uses the 1961 edition.

13 These four texts are *Revelations* or *Showings*, by Julian of Norwich, *The Book of Margery Kempe*, *True Relations*, by Margaret Cavendish, and "To My Dear Children," by Anne Bradstreet.

14 Bella Brodzki, in defining this branch of life writing, comments, "In the 1980s within autobiographical studies, testimony and *testimonio* [the singular form of the term, the plural being '*testimonios*'] were practically interchangeable terms since Latin American narratives served as the prototype for first person accounts of collective trauma, crisis, loss, struggle and survival, a personal story raised to the level of history" (2001, 870).

CHAPTER 1– HOUSE, HOME, AND MOTHER: FULFILLING EXPECTATIONS

1 For example, in tracing the history of women's needlework, Judy Chicago learned that "Women have been associated with the textile arts since the beginning of time" (1980, 24).

2 In postmodern theory, the line between fiction and non-fiction is, in any case, blurred. As Marlene Kadar comments (1992, 10): "The postmodern vision … enjoys contesting the boundaries between fiction and autobiography." She cites Linda Hutcheon (*The Canadian Postmodern*, 1982): "To write anyone's history is to order, to give form to disparate facts; in short to fictionalize." It also works the other way. At a conference on Canadian Studies (ACSUS, Calgary, 2000, September 15–16), Lyall Powers, a biographer of Margaret Laurence, affirmed the autobiographical basis of Laurence's novels in a paper

"Alien Hearts: Laurence and the Lords of the Prairies." Knowing Laurence since childhood, Powers asserts that Laurence's true subjectivity was more in evidence in fiction such as *The Diviners* or *A Bird in the House* than in her avowed autobiography, *A Dance on the Earth*. For an economical examination of the blurred line between fictive autobiography and autobiographical fiction, see Gayla Diment, "*The Autobiographical Novel of Co-consciousness*," 52–54.

3   Butala made this point several times in the 1996 interview. Here are two further examples:

I did not have to make things up. I didn't have to write out of an invented world, but out of the world around me, the world that I had seen and known. Not necessarily my own experience, obviously who would have enough experiences of that. But out of what I had seen and heard and read and felt and thought. (Reid 1996b, 24) And:

The one story I have to tell is how a woman comes to find herself and for me that has been the story of my life and everything feeds into it and comes out of it. (ibid., 1996b, 5)

4   Her short stories, especially those in *Fever*, turn at times from a rural to an urban setting and tend to examine the inner world of relationships more than the workings of a community. Here, too, autobiographical influences can be detected in plot, theme, and setting, if not directly in creation of character.

5   For an in-depth analysis of how the code of femininity shapes women's perceptions of their bodies, see Susan Brownmiller, *Femininity* (New York: Ballantine, 1984). In her final chapter, she observes that, with the rise of the middle class, the code of femininity came to include the notion that the proper place for female endeavour was in the home. Chapter 2 offers a full discussion of Brownmiller and the code of femininity as regards the female body.

6   I am relying here on Kelly's restatement of Lacanian theory in "On Sexual Politics and Art," in *Framing Feminism: Art and the Women's Movement, 1970–1985*, R. Parker and G. Pollock, eds. New York: Pandora, 303–4.

7   For images for which there is no corresponding figure in the present text, the reader will be referred to reproductions in an easily available text. In the case of Mary Pratt, that text is Tom Smart, *The Art of Mary Pratt: The Substance of Light* (Fredericton: Goose Lane and the Beaverbrook Art Gallery, 1995). See also Sandra Gwyn and Gerta Moray, *Mary Pratt* (Toronto: McGraw-Hill, 1989), and Mary Pratt, *A Personal Calligraphy* (Fredericton, NB: Goose Lane, 2000). For reference to images of the work of Aganetha Dyck, the main source cited is Shirley Madill, ed., *Aganetha Dyck* (Winnipeg: Winnipeg Art Gallery, 1995).

8   Rosen is professor emeritus at the Pennsylvania Academy of Fine Arts in Philadelphia.

9   Reid/Pratt phone call, June 30, 2007.

10   Images of Mary Pratt's prints of 1995–2002 can be found in Patricia Deadman, *Simple Bliss: The Paintings and Prints of Mary Pratt* (Regina: MacKenzie Art Gallery, 2004).

11   In Betsy Warland's 1995 interview with Meigs, Warland asks Meigs how long she worked as a visual artist. She replies, "From post-war, when I went to art school until 1979 or so when I started writing my first book" (5). Meigs is one of five Quebec visual artists featured in the 1979 National Film Board of Canada's film, *La Toile d'araignée*.

12   See Luke 10: 38–42.

13   This interplay between the younger self and the older self is observable also in the organization and the text of Mary Pratt's *A Personal Calligraphy* (2000).

CHAPTER 2– ALIVE AS A WOMAN: EMPOWERING THE BODY

1 For a description of the history of the "coming out story," what Jolly calls a characteristic genre of life writing, see Margaretta Jolly, "Lesbian and Gay Writing," in *Encyclopedia of Life Writing: Autobiographical and Biographical Forms*, vol. 2, Margaretta Jolly, ed. (London: Fitzroy Dearborn, 2001), 547–50. The three books by Mary Meigs that have "coming out" as a major theme are *Lily Briscoe: A Self-portrait*, *The Medusa Head* and *The Time Being*. It is a minor theme in *The Box Closet* and in *In the Company of Strangers*.

2 Lisa Weil describes freewriting as follows: "The cardinal rule of freewriting is that you keep your pen moving. You don't stop to edit or correct" (2005, xi).

3 In a concise analysis of the work of Jacques Lacan, Madan Sarup explains that Lacan's term *jouissance* signifies "the ecstatic – or orgasmic enjoyment – and exquisite pain – of someone or something" (1992, 99). "Jouissance is unconscious, it is unconscious pleasure which becomes pain, as in listening to music which is so beautiful it brings tears to one's eyes." As I understand it, the French feminists make the point that women are not "monolithically unified" around a single organ as are men. Rather "her sexual organs are composed of many different elements (lips, vagina, clitoris, cervix, uterus, breasts), and her jouissance is therefore multiple, non-unified, endless" (Sarup 1992, 138). It is in the latter modification that I use the term *jouissance* in reference to the work of Butala et al.

4 For a discussion of painting as a male-dominated visual art genre, see Mary Kelly, "On Sexual Politics and Art," in *Framing Feminism*, Roszika Parker and Griselda Pollock, eds. (New York: Pandora, 1987), 303–12. For a discus-sion of women's place in language, see Margaret Homan, *Bearing the Word: Language and Female Experience in 19th Century Women's Writing* (Chicago: University of Chicago Press, 1986), 1–39.

5 See, for example, a comment made by Pratt in Reid 1996a, 27. When speaking of painting nude models, she said: "I wanted to look at naked men far less than I wanted to look at naked women."

6 Judith Butler would view all expressions of gender as comparable to Meigs using fashion to "pass," all gender behaviour being species of performance. Sidonie Smith cites Butler in her article on perfomativity and extends the notion to include "heterogeneous recitations of gender" by a multiple and interactive subject. (Sidonie Smith, "Performativity, Autobiographical Practice, Resistance," *a/b: Auto/biography Studies* 10, no. 1: 17–33).

7 Meigs' paintings are on the cover of *Lily Briscoe*, *In the Company of Strangers*, *The Time Being*, and *Beyond Recall*.

8 The extent to which the *Hand Held between Index and Middle Finger* installation expresses Dyck's personal perceptions of the vulnerability of the human body is demonstrated by the fact that the lighting of the installation must always be arranged to throw a shadow on the gallery wall. As Dyck explained to me (Reid 1996c, 47), the gallery shadow is a direct correlative of the shadow she observed on the lung X-ray taken during the diagnosis procedures relating to her auto-immune disorder.

9 See Donald Kuspit, "Joseph Beuys: The Body of the Artist," in *Joseph Beuys: Diverging Critiques*, D. Thistlewood, ed. (Liverpool: Liverpool University Press, 1995), 100–101. Here, Kuspit examines the concept of damage, both physical and psychic, in the work of

Joseph Beuys. As a central motif in his work, Beuys conceptualized material as transmitting the experience of warmth, a basic component in the process of bodily healing. Dyck's use of honey and beeswax are seen as having the same healing dimensions.

10   See earlier comments in Chapter One.

11   In the months following Peter's death, Sharon has responded positively to speaking offers, etc., spending, for example, the month of February, 2008, at the home of a writer friend in Vancouver.

12   For an analysis of the role of the body in learning and of the connection between body and mind, see Carla Hannaford, *Smart Moves: Why Learning is Not All in Your Head* (Arlington, VA: Great Ocean, 1995). She says, "Thinking is a response to our physical world. In studying the brain, we can only understand it in the context of a physical reality, an action reality. Movement is an integral part of all mental processing."

13   Reid (1996a), 15, and Smith-Strom, CBC-TV (1996).

14   See David Garneau, "Remodelling the Gaze," *Border Crossings* 78 (2001): 126–27. In this article Garneau reviews a recent showing of the work of Elizabeth Coop and Iris Hauser and cites their paintings as two examples of women painting women who work "through the tradition to recover the female body from the male gaze" (126).

15   See Sandra Gwyn, "Introduction," in *Mary Pratt*, Sandra Gwyn and Gerta Moray, eds. (Toronto: McGraw-Hill Ryerson, 1989), 14. Here, Gwyn comments, "Mary herself has always been ambivalent about being constructed into a feminist heroine." She quotes Pratt: "I think of myself as a woman painter and I have quite strong feelings

about the women's movement without being really a part of it."

16   It is fitting that writer Audrey Andrews chose *Cold Cream* for the cover of *Be Good, Sweet Maid* (1999), the story of Dorothy Joudrie, a Calgary socialite convicted of attempting to murder her husband. Andrews explains in the Preface that the Joudrie story is illustrative of the damage done to upper-class women like Dorothy who become lost to themselves because of their responding to society's "unrealistic and unreasonable" demands.

17   For commentary of the significance on the advent of the "pill," see Nora Underwood, "Female Liberation," a review of *The Pill: A Biography of the Drug that Changed the World* by Bernard Asbell, *MacLean's*, 108, no. 33 (1995): 53. See also Margaret Wente, "Reproductive Freedom: The Pill Changed Everything," *The Globe and Mail* (April 10, 2004): A19.

18   For me, the most evocative references to the bodily relationship between baby and mother comes in the excerpts from Margaret Meigs' (Mary's mother) letters to her husband, which contain day-by-day accounts of nursing and bowel movements and the possibility of supplementary bottle feedings and the fact that baby routine is "rather like a life sentence on a treadmill" (Meigs 1987, 119–21).

19   I did not see the actual installation presented in London, England, in 1977 but gathered my impressions of that installation from Mary Kelly, *Post-partum Document* (Boston: Routlege and Kegan Paul, 1982).

CHAPTER 3– ALIVE IN THE WORLD: CONNECTING TO NATURE

1   Again, for critical commentary on the proclivity of female autobiographers to construct themselves in relationship to

others, see Mary Mason, "The Other Voice; Autobiographies of Women Writers," in *Life/Lines: Theorizing Women's Autobiography*, Bella Brodzki and Celeste Schenck, eds. (Ithaca, NY: Cornell University Press, 1988), 19–44.

2 An example of a critic linking of Butala's work with these American writers came at an *Association for Canadian Studies in the United States* conference entitled "Western Mindscapes" (Sept. 15–16, 2000). Here Linda Spalding gave a paper entitled "Spirituality and Ranching on the Great Plains: Sharon Butala and Kathleen Norris." During the question period, the work of both writers was compared with that of Anne Dillard.

3 In the *Random House Dictionary of the English Language* (New York: Random House, 1967), "usufruct" is defined as "Roman and Civil Law, the right of enjoying something which belongs to another as far as is compatible with the substance of the thing not being destroyed or injured."

4 A basic source for this branch of literary criticism is Cheryll Glotfelty and Harold Fromm, eds. *The Ecocriticism Reader: Landmarks in Literary Ecology* (Athens, GA: University of Georgia Press, 1996). Glotfelty describes ecocriticism as follows: "Ecocriticism is the study of the relationships between literature and the physical environment. Just as feminist criticism examines language and literature from a gender conscious perspective ... ecocriticism takes an earth-centred approach to literary studies" (xviii).

5 For accounts of animal-human bonding, including that experienced by Jane Goodall, see Linda Hogan, Deena Metsger, and Brenda Peterson, eds., *Intimate Nature: The Bond between Women and Animals* (New York: Fawcett Columbine, 1998).

6 This is a phrase invented by John Ruskin. Shelley's *Adonais* and Tennyson's *In Memoriam* use the pathetic fallacy to good effect. In fiction, one example of this device can be found in Hemingway's *A Farewell to Arms* in which the constant rain is used to foreshadow and accompany the death of the heroine, Catherine.

7 Two examples of the process being discernible in the product are, first, the *Shrunken Sweaters* series, in which the process of washing and shrinking is clearly implied, and, secondly, in the initial installation of *The Extended Wedding Party* at the Winnipeg Art Gallery, in which live bees were part of the installation.

8 At the *Language and Texts Conference* sponsored jointly by University of Leeds and University of Calgary, in Leeds, England, July 2–6, 1997, I gave a paper on the work of Aganetha Dyck entitled "The Vocabulary of an Art Practice." As I indicated earlier, Dyck was a visiting artist at the Scarborough Sculpture Gardens outside of Leeds, where she was working with local beekeepers. She invited me to an opening of the hives, and, as I recall it, the bees swarmed when some bee-feeding mixture was spilled.

9 Meeka Walsh and Robert Enright, "The Incredible Lightness of Bee-ing: An Interview with Aganetha Dyck." *Border Crossings* 19, no. 2 (May 2000): 55.

10 In her interview in Troyes with Estelle Pagés, Aganetha Dyck refers to her meeting with Dr. Mark Winston of Simon Fraser University and her plans to talk to Winston's French colleague Dr. Yves Leconte of Avignon. See Estelle Pagés, *Passages* (Paris: Services culturels de l'Ambassade du Canada, 2001), 79–80.

11 See "Bee World All Abuzz over Smuggling," *The Calgary Herald*, June 3,

2002, A1–A2, concerning the illegality of importing bees from the United States because of concern over the Varroa mites. The article describes the allegations of widespread smuggling of bees across the Alberta border: "Mites and other diseases are already in Canada," said a Peace River beekeeper.

12 See also Sallie McFague, *Super Natural Christians*, 128. Here Mcfague sees Butala's journey as moving from a romantic generalized view of nature to one focusing on the particular actualities of nature.

13 For an announcement of the Butala conservancy, see *The Maple Creek News* 95, no. 48 (July 23, 1996): 1. For an account of how the Conservancy came about, see *Wild Stone Heart*, 101–4. For a tribute to the Conservancy see Sharon Butala and Courtney Milne, *Old Man on His Back: Portrait of a Prairie Landscape* (Toronto: HarperCollins and the Nature Conservancy of Canada, 2002).

14 For example, Butala takes urban environmentalists to task in *Wild Stone Heart*, 108, and in *The Globe and Mail* (July 6, 1996): C2 and *The Globe and Mail* (March 4, 2000): A24.

15 See *Water, Spout and Cut Melon* (Pratt 2000, 87), *Pomegranates in Glass on Glass* (Smart 1995, 139), and *Pomegranates with a Knife* (Pratt 2000, 39).

16 The first mode is the symbolic metaphoric mode which has two versions, the abstract and the visual. Examples of the abstract would be writing and mathematical symbols. Examples of the visual would be trademarks, logos, maps, and road signs. The fourth mode is the inventive metaphoric mode. The latter will be referred to in the discussion of the vocation of the artist, a vocation that constitutes part of the spiritual experience of the four subjects.

17 In 2008, the Hay Farm continued to be home for Sharon while she pondered her future after Peter's death.

18 I have become environmentally aware that, in 1974, we were part of the first wave of cabin owners in this wilderness and, as such, were intruders in the traditional wildlife preserves, Moreover, I now can see that in our travels, we have added to the burden placed on such places as Venice and Maui. In our defence, I can say that my husband, in particular, has worked very hard politically in the Kananaskis area of Alberta to protect the wildlife and to address environmental issues, and that we, as a family, disturb the plants on our little plot as little as possible.

CHAPTER 4– ALIVE IN THE SPIRIT: GROWING OLD

1 Cited in Carole Slade, "Introduction: Autobiography and Mysticism," *a/b: Auto/biography Studies* 6, no. 2 (Fall 1991): 154.

2 For a commentary on the archetypal role of old women as a spiritual resource for society, see Shelagh Wilkinson, "Old Woman 'Bearer of Keys to Unknown Doorways,'" *Canadian Woman Studies* 12, no. 2 (1992): 103–7.

3 See Adam Morton, "Spirit," *The Oxford Companion to Philosophy* (New York: Oxford University Press, 1995), 848.

4 See Barbara Macdonald and Cynthia Rich, *Look Me in the Eye: Old Women, Aging and Ageism* (San Francisco: Spinsters Book Company, 1991).

5 Again, see Shelagh Wilkinson as above. This article analyzes the changes in how post-menopausal women are represented in Canadian and American literature towards the end the twentieth century, and it posits the figure of the crone as a freeing agent in contemporary society.

6   See Mary Pratt, *A Personal Calligraphy* (Fredericton, NB: Goose Lane, 2000), 110. Pratt's Vancouver sojourn seemed instrumental is consolidating her primary identity as artist: "Just living for myself and the painting." Even so, she speaks of veal shanks for dinner.

7   It is useful to draw a distinction between paranormal experience and mystical experience. The former denotes the direct perception of a distinct and seemingly supernatural event; the latter, while it may or may not be based on such a perception, refers primarily to an inner response to, or an intuitive apprehension of, a numinous quality in the environment.

8   Cited in Carol Slade, "Introduction: Autobiography and Mysticism," 154. She quotes from William James (1985) *Varieties of Religious Experience* (Cambridge: Cambridge University Press, 1985).

9   Cited by George I. Mavrodes, "Mysticism," in Ted Honderich, ed. *The Oxford Companion to Philosophy* (New York: Oxford University Press, 1995), 599.

10 She was born in 1926 and died in 2004.

11 Kübler-Ross's analysis owes much to Maslow's theory of the hierarchy of needs. See Abraham H. Maslow, *The Psychology of Being* (New York: D. Van Nostrand, 1962).

12 I have had occasion to meet both Kübler-Ross and Scott Peck and have attended seminars given by both. In both instances, I was impressed by their sanity, intelligence, and spiritual depth. For myself and many others in Western society, they are figures of spiritual authority.

13 W. Bridgewater and S. Kurtz, eds., *The Columbia Encyclopedia*, 3rd ed. (New York: Columbia University Press, 1968), 78.

14 In John Ralston Saul's concept of animism, "it is *everything* in nature that is seen to be alive" (emphasis added; 1997, 185). According to Saul, that is the view of nature that Canadians, being a northern people, must inevitably espouse. He does not discuss directly any mystical implications of Canadian animism, although such implications are implicit.

15 In "Note to the Twelfth Edition" (1990, 43), Underhill acknowledges that, because Bergson is no longer so highly regarded, she would "choose other philosophers" if she were now writing the chapter on vitalism. She, however, asserts that she still endorses the basic ideas of this chapter.

16 In *The Logic of Ecstasy: Canadian Mystical Painting* (1992), Ann Davis explains Underhill's notion of the Real: "But this Real seems to have two contradictory orders. Metaphysicians call these great pair of opposites Being and Becoming, Eternity and Time, Unity and Multiplicity: others speak of the spiritual and natural world s as the two extreme forms under which the universe can be realized. Those whose consciousness is extended full span can live in both, be aware of both" (4). There is a third order, Ultimate Reality, that unites the other two. Vitalism is concerned with the union of the natural and spiritual, and it is that concept which has particular application to the work of the four artists being studied.

17 See Butala (1999, 6), Reid (1996c, 8), and Smart (1995, 82, 88, 132).

18 See Matthew 7:12. The exact wording is "So whatever you wish that men would do to you, do so to them; for this is the law and the prophets." (*Revised Standard Edition*).

19 Indeed, in Peck's vision of the "hereafter" in his novel, *In Heaven as on Earth, A Vision of the After-life*, those who have attained a considerable degree

of spiritual development on earth are assigned to committees to work with others on behalf of those still alive.

20 A careful report on investigation into the high incidence of paranormal experience is in H.J. Irwin, *An Introduction to Parapsychology*, 3rd ed. (Jefferson, NC: McFarland, 1999).

21 See Emily Carr, *Hundreds and Thousands: The Journals of an Artist* (Toronto: Irwin, 1966), 14–16.

22 Lionnet (1989) uses this term metaphorically to refer to the "braiding" of various strands of identity. Cited in Buss (1993), 15, 25.

23 I was present when Sharon Butala gave this address, April 14, 1999, in Calgary under the auspices of St. Stephen's College, University of Alberta. Dr. Butala gave me the printed text of the speech and the references noted are to this printed unpublished text.

24 For a concise statement of Jung's theory of dreams, see Carl G. Jung, "Approaching the Unconscious," *Man and his Symbols* (Garden City, NY: Doubleday, 1964), 20–193.

25 For a discussion of the totemic use of animal imagery in Butala's work, see W.W. Finlaw, *The Word Made Animal Flesh: Totemic Archetypes in Five Western North American Writers* (doctoral dissertation, University of Nebraska, Lincoln, 1993), in *Dissertation Abstracts International* 54, No. 07: 2573. For a Jungian interpretation of Butala's *Wild Stone Heart*, see Craig Stephenson, "Finding Words for Wonder" *Ottawa Citizen* (August 26, 2001): C11–12.

26 Thomas Bulfinch's *The Age of Fable* (1942) posits the unicorn as a symbol of innocence and purity. In medieval iconography, the unicorn is associated with the figure of Christ and the Virgin Mary. Butala herself does not overtly make the connection, but it is likely that the imminent death of her handicapped sister inspired the vision of the unicorn.

27 One writer, Maureen Garvie, reviewing *Wild Stone Heart* for *Quill & Quire* (August 2000) does confide: "one might wish she had held back on that unicorn" (24).

28 See "Author's note" at the end of *Wild Stone Heart* (201). Butala explains "I have chosen to use the term 'Amerindian' used by Olive Dickason, who wrote *Canada's First Nations: A History of Founding People's from Earliest Times*, to refer to the people we grew up to call … 'Indians'."

29 Butala reports finding support for this observation in an unpublished doctoral thesis: Linda Smith Stowell, *Subjective Religious Experience among Unitarian Universalists: A Generationalist Study* (1995) in Sharon Butala, "Seeing," *Dropped Threads: What We Aren't Told*, ed. C. Shields and M. Anderson, 207–8 (Toronto: Random House, 2001).

30 In *The Perfection of the Morning*, Butala recalls attending the funeral of an old woman "who was born here and who died here well into her old age" (213). She had lived the life of an ordinary rural woman, and Butala was struck by the fact that the church was full to overflowing at the funeral. She concludes: "Why else I thought, but because … we all know, we all understand in our hearts that women are the soul of the world."

31 In an interview with Sandra Gwyn, Pratt says "I don't think I would have been a painter at all if I hadn't come here. This is an abrupt, dramatic light-and-dark kind of society" (Gwyn and Moray, 1989, 11–12).

32 On *Adrienne Clarkson Presents* (Smith-Strom, Producer). Similarly, in our conversations together, Pratt explained, for example, that *Venus from a Northern Pond* (Smart 1995, 122) "did not say anything that [she] wanted it

to say," and I could sense that she really never connected with the model. Further, in *A Personal Calligraphy*, she expresses doubts about how much she contributes in her collaboration with printmaker Masato "anybody can do an image" (115). Also, she ponders whether the arts are merely "decorative" (ibid., 120), and she asks herself, after the mounting of her retrospective show, "why have I thrown out just about everything I have tried to paint this year?" (ibid., 117).

33 *The Gospel according to John*, 1: 1–9.

34 See Herbert G. May and Bruce M. Metzger, "The Introduction to John," in *The Oxford Annotated Bible* (New York: Oxford University Press, 1989), 1286.

35 I attended one such lecture in September 1995 at Sandpiper bookstore in Calgary. The frank nature of her discussion on that occasion made it clear to me that her work had an explicit autobiographical dimension. Her talk that night, our meeting then, and the subsequent interview in February 1996 were crucial in my choice of Pratt as a woman whose art and life I wished to investigate.

36 Professor Maurice Yacowar, in contrasting the work of Mary and Christopher Pratt, says that Mary's area of interest is the particular while "Christopher's agenda subordinates the particular to the general" (388). See M. Yacowar, "The Paintings of Mary (vs. Christopher) Pratt," *Dalhousie Review* 68, no. 4 (1988): 385–99.

37 Richard Rohr, "What Does It Mean to Be Sent?" (videotape, 2001). *National Association of Diacnate Directors*, 921 State Street, Rockford, IL, 61102.

38 Published subsequently by Talonbooks in *Beyond Recall*.

39 See also the earlier reference to Mary Scott's influence in chapter 1. In that chapter, I was commenting on the place of reading in Dyck's practice. Here I am commenting on the content of that reading.

CONCLUSION– "A READING SPACE OF THEIR OWN"

1 *Calgary Herald*, November 3, 2006, A19.

Bibliography

Adam, Ian. 1998. Iconicity, space and the place of Sharon Butala's "The Prize" (Prairie literature). *Studies in Canadian Literature* 23, no.1: 178–89.

Andrews, Audrey. 1999. *Be Good Sweet Maid: The Trials of Dorothy Joudrie*. Waterloo, ON: Wilfrid Laurier University Press.

Atwood, Margaret. 1972. *Survival*. Toronto: Anansi.

———. 1985. *The Handmaid's Tale*. Toronto: McClelland & Stewart.

Bachelard, Gaston. 1994. *The Poetics of Space*. Marie Jolas, trans. Boston: Beacon.

Baert, Renée. 1996. *Trames de mémoire*. St. Hyacinthe, Québec: Expression Centre, d'Exposition de Saint-Hyacinthe.

Barbour, John D. 2001. Spiritual autobiography. In *Encyclopedia of Life Writing: Autobiographical and Biographical Forms*, Margaretta Jolly, ed., 2:835–37. London: Fitzroy Dearborn.

Beaudet, Marc, Jean-Marc Garand, and Jacques Giraldeau, producers, and Jacques Giraldeau, director. 1979. *La toile d'araignée*, film. Toronto: National Film Board of Canada.

Benstock, Shari, ed. 1988. *The Private Self: Theory and Practice of Women's Autobiographical Writings*. Chapel Hill: University of North Carolina Press.

Berger, John. 1997. *Ways of Seeing*. Toronto: Penguin.

———. 2002. Another way of seeing. *Harpers* 304, no. 1822: 29–32.

Beverley, John. 1992. The margin at the center: On *testimonio* (testimonia narrative). In *Decolonizing the Subject: The Politics of Gender in Women's Autobiography*, 91–114, Sidonie Smith and Julia Watson, eds. Minneapolis: University of Minnesota Press.

Billeter, Erika. 1993. The world of Frida Kahlo: The self-portrait as autobiography, *Southwest Art* 23: 94–96.

Brayshaw, Christopher. 1995. Mary Pratt: Vision to see. *Artichoke* 7, no. 1: 32–33.

Brodzki, Bella. 2001. Testimony. In *The Encyclopedia of Life Writing: Autobiographical and Biographical Forms*, ed. Margaretta Jolly, 2:870–72. London: Fitzroy Dearborn.

Brodzki, Bella, and Celeste Schenck. 1988. *Life/Lines: Theorizing Women's Autobiography*. Ithaca, NY: Cornell University Press.

Brownmiller, Susan. 1984. *Femininity*. New York. Ballantine.

Bryson, Norman. 1990. *Looking at the Overlooked: Four Essays on Still Life Painting*. Cambridge, MA: Harvard University Press.

Bulfinch, Thomas. 1942. *The Age of Fable*. New York: Heritage Press.

Burnett, David, and Marilyn Schiff. 1983. *Contemporary Canadian Art*. Edmonton: Hurtig.

Buss, Helen. M. 1986. Canadian women's autobiography: Some critical directions. In *Amazing Space: Writing Canadian Women Writing*, eds. Shirley Neuman and Smaro Kamboureli, 154–64. Edmonton: Longspoon/Newest.

———. 1991a. *Canadian Women's Autobiography in English: Introductory Guide for Researchers and Teachers*. The CRIAW papers, 24. Ottawa: Canadian Research Institute for the Advancement of Women.

———. 1991b. Reading for the doubled discourse of American women's autobiography. *a/b: Auto/Biography Studies* 6, no. 1: 97–107.

———. 1993. *Mapping Ourselves: Canadian Women's Autobiography in English*. Montreal and Kingston: McGill-Queen's University Press.

———. 1995. Correcting/perfecting the self in nature. Review of *The Perfection of the Morning: An Apprenticeship in Nature. Prairie Fire* 16, no. 3: 170–74.

———. 2001. Memoirs. In *Encyclopedia of Life Writing: Autobiographical and Biographical Forms*, Margaretta Jolly, ed., 2:597–98. London: Fitzroy Dearborn.

Buss, Helen M./Margaret Clarke. 1999. *Memoirs from Away: A New Found Land Girlhood*. Waterloo, ON: Wilfrid Laurier University Press.

Butala, Sharon. 1984. *Country of the Heart*. Saskatoon: Fifth House.

———. 1985. *Queen of the Headaches*. Regina: Coteau Books.

———. 1986. *The Gates of the Sun*. Saskatoon: Fifth House.

———. 1988a. Time, space and light: Discovering the Saskatchewan soul. *NeWest Review* 13, no. 5: 4–7.

———. 1988b. *Luna*. Toronto: Fifth House.

———. 1990. *Fever*. Toronto: HarperCollins.

———. 1991a. A hero to his people. *NeWest Review* 16, no. 5: 21–24.

———. 1991b. *Upstream: "le pays d'en haut."* Saskatoon: Fifth House.

———. 1992. *The Fourth Archangel*. Toronto: HarperCollins.

———. 1993. The night Wallace Stegner died. *Brick* 46 (Summer): 21–25.

———. 1994a. *The Perfection of the Morning: An Apprenticeship in Nature*. Toronto: HarperCollins.

———. 1994b. Telling lies. *Brick* 49 (Summer): 49–52.

———. 1995a. *Coyote's Morning Cry: Meditations and Dreams from a Life in Nature*. Toronto: HarperCollins.

———. 1995b. Young woman powdering her face. *Brick* 50 (Fall): 83–86.

———. 1996a. A pair of shoes. *Brick* 54 (Spring): 67–69.

———. 1996b. True west: Writer in residence: Sharon Butala, Eastend, Sask. *Western Living* 21, no. 1: 13–21.

———. 1998. *The Garden of Eden*. Toronto: HarperCollins.

———. 1999. A spiritual journey. Lecture presented at Knox United Church, Calgary, April 13, for the *Keeping the Spirit Alive* series, St. Stephen's College.

———. 2000a. *Wild Stone Heart: An Apprentice in the Fields*. Toronto: HarperCollins.

———. 2000b. Writing a memoir: The perfection of the morning. *Canadian Woman Studies* 20, no. 1: 104–8.

———. 2001. Seeing. In *Dropped Threads: What We Aren't Told*, eds. C. Shields and M. Anderson, 209–18. Toronto: Random House.

———. 2002. *Real Life*. Toronto: HarperCollins.

———. 2005. *Lilac Moon: Dreaming of the Real West.* Toronto: HarperCollins.

———. 2008. *The Girl in Saskatoon: A Meditation on Friendship, Memory, and Murder.* Toronto: HarperCollins.

Butala, Sharon, and Courtney Milne. 2002. *Old Man on His Back: Portrait of a Prairie Landscape.* Toronto: HarperCollins and the Nature Conservancy of Canada.

Butler, Judith. 1993. *Bodies That Matter: On the Discursive Limits of "Sex."* New York: Routledge.

Carter, K., and C. Spitzack. 1989. *Doing Research on Women's Communication: Perspectives on Theory and Method.* Norwood, NJ: Ablex.

Calvert, Ann E. 1996. An art curriculum model for gender equity. In *Gender Issues in Art Education,* 154–64, Georgia Collins and Renne Sandell, eds. Reston, VA: National Art Education Association.

Cheeseman, Josephine. 1981. Mary Pratt dislikes image as 'martyr.' *Daily News,* St. John's, 19, August 8.

Chicago, Judy. 1979. *The Dinner Party: A Symbol of Our Heritage.* Garden City, NY: Anchor Press/Doubleday.

———. 1980. *Embroidering Our Heritage: The Dinner Party Needlework.* Garden City, NY: Anchor Press/Doubleday.

Chicago, Judy, and Edward Lucie-Smith. 1999. *Women and Art: Contested Territory.* Vancouver: Raincoast Books.

Chodorow, Nancy. 1978. *The Reproduction of Mothering: Psychoanalysis and Sociology of Gender.* Berkeley: University of California Press.

Commoner, Barry. 1971. *The Closing Circle.* New York: Alfred A. Knopf.

Conway, Jill Ker. 1994. *True North.* New York: Alfred A. Knopf.

———. 1998. *When Memory Speaks: Reflections on Autobiography.* New York: Alfred A. Knopf.

Csikszentmihalyi, Mihalyi. 1997. *Finding Flow: The Psychology of Engagement in Everyday Life.* New York: HarperCollins.

Dahle, Sigrid. 1990. *Aganetha Dyck.* Vancouver: Lateral Gallery.

———. 1995. Talking with Aganetha Dyck: A ten year conversation. In *Aganetha Dyck,* 16–27, ed. Shirley Madill. Winnipeg: Winnipeg Art Gallery.

Dallery, Arleen B. 1989. The politics of writing (the) body: Ecriture feminine. *Gender/Body/Knowledge: Femininst Reconstructions of Being and Knowing.* Eds. Alison M. Jagger and Susan R. Bordo. New Brunswick, NJ: Rutgers University Press, 52–67.

Davies, Bronwyn. 1992. Women's subjectivity and feminist stories. In *Investigating Subjectivity: Research on Lived Experience,* 53–75, Carolyn Ellis and Michael Flaherty, eds. London: Sage.

de Beauvoir, Simone. 1952. *The Second Sex,* H.M. Parshley, trans. New York: Knopf.

de Lauretis, Teresa. 1987. *Technologies of Gender: Essays on Theory, Film and Fiction.* Indianapolis: Indiana University Press.

de Oliviera, Nicolas, Nicola Oxley, and Michael Petry. 1993. On installation. *Art and Design* 18, no. 5&6 (March and April): 4–5.

Diamond, Irene, and Gloria Feman Orenstein, eds. 1990. *Reweaving the World: The Emergence of Eco-Feminism.* San Francisco: Sierra Club Books.

Diment, Galya. 1994. *The Autobiographical Novel of Co-Consciousness; Goncharov, Woolf and Joyce.* Gainsville/Tallahassee, FL: University of Florida Press.

Dogan, Mattei, and Robert Pahre. 1990. *Creative Marginality: Innovation at the Intersection of the Social Sciences*. Boulder, CO: Westview Press.

Dufrenne, Mikel. 1993. *The Phenomenology of Aesthetic Experience*. Evanston, IL: Northwestern University Press.

Dyck, Aganetha. 1982. Artist's statement. In *Under Construction: Six Manitoba Sculptors*, 12–15, Shirley Madill, ed. Winnipeg: Winnipeg Art Gallery.

———. 1993. Artist's statement. In *Cultural Commentary: New Work from Manitoba*, 12, Cindy Richmond and Timothy Long, eds. Regina: Mackenzie Art Gallery.

———. 1999. Working in the dark [Artist's statement]. *De Leon White News* 4, no. 20 (Fall): 4–5.

Egan, Susan. 1991. From the inside out: *Lily Briscoe: A Self-Portrait*. An autobiography by Mary Meigs. Review of *Lily Briscoe: A Self-Portrait*. In *Autobiography and Questions of Gender*, 37–55, Shirley Neuman, ed. London: Frank Cass.

Ellis, Carolyn, and Michael G. Flaherty, eds. 1992. *Investigating Subjectivity: Research on Lived Experience*. London: Sage.

Enright, Robert. 2001. Angels and insects. *Globe and Mail*, Saturday, November 3, V8.

Fine, Gary Alan. 1992. Wild life: Authenticity and the human experience of "natural" places. In *Investigating Subjectivity: Research on Lived Experience*, 125–37, Carolyn Ellis and Michael G. Flaherty, eds. London: Sage.

Finlaw, W. W. 1993/1994. The word made animal flesh: Totemic archetypes in five western North American writers. PhD diss., University of Nebraska, 1993. In *Dissertation Abstracts International* 54, no. 7: 2573.

Friedan, Betty. 1993. *The Fountain of Age*. New York and Toronto: Simon and Schuster.

Friedman, Susan Stanford. 1988. Women's autobiographical selves: Theory and practice. In *The Private Self: Theory and Practice of Women's Autobiographical Writings*, 34–62. Shari Benstock, ed. Chapel Hill: University of North Carolina Press.

Frye, Marilyn. 1992. *The Willful Virgin*. Trumansburg, NY: Crossing Press.

Frye, Northrop. 1963. *The Educated Imagination*. The Massey lectures, second series. Toronto: Canadian Broadcasting Company.

———. 1967a. The baccalaureate sermon. In *Victoria Reports*, 3–10, F.C. Stokes, ed. Toronto: Board of Regents, Victoria University.

———. 1967b. *Anatomy of Criticism: Four Essays*. Toronto: McClelland & Stewart.

Fuss, Diana. 1989. *Essentially Speaking: Feminism, Nature and Difference*. New York: Routledge.

Gablik, Suzi. 1991. *The Reenchantment of Art*. New York: Thames and Hudson.

Garneau, David. 2001. Remodelling the gaze, *Border Crossings* 78: 126–27.

Garvie, Maureen. 2000. Prairie songs. Review of *Wild Stone Heart: An Apprentice in the Fields* by Sharon Butala, *Quill & Quire*, 24, August.

Gilmore, Leigh. 1994. *Autobiographics: A Feminist Theory of Women's Self-Representation*. Ithaca, NY and London: Cornell University Press.

Glotfelty, Cheryll, and Harold Fromm, eds. 1996. *The Ecocriticism Reader: Landmarks in Literary Ecology*. Athens, GA: University of Georgia Press.

Gould, Stephen Jay. 1989. *Wonderful Life: The Burgess Shale and the Nature of History*. New York: Norton.

———. 1998. The golden rule: A proper scale for our environmental crisis.

In *Land and Environmental Art*, 270–71, Jeffrey Kastner, ed. London: Phaedron.

Graham, Mayo. 1975. *Some Canadian Women Artists*. Ottawa: National Gallery of Canada.

Gregg, Andrew, producer; director. 1997. The life and times of Christopher and Mary Pratt. *Life and Times*. CBC-TV, February 8. Toronto: 90th Parallel Production Company.

Grenville, Bruce. 1995. Chance, abstraction expression: Aganetha Dyck's shrunken clothing. In *Aganetha Dyck*, 28–31 (February 8). Winnipeg: Winnipeg Art Gallery.

Griggs, Claudine. 1998. *S/HE: Changing Sex and Changing Clothes*. New York and London: Berg.

Grimshaw, Jean. 1992. Autonomy. In *Feminism and Psychoanalysis: A Critical Dictionary*, Elizabeth Wright, ed., 196–19. Oxford: Blackwell.

Gusdorf, George. 1980. Conditions and limits of autobiography. In *Autobiography: Essays Theoretical and Critical*, James Olney, ed., 28–48. Princeton: Princeton University Press.

Gwyn, Sandra, and Gerta Moray. 1989. *Mary Pratt*. Toronto: McGraw-Hill.

Hannaford, Carla. 1995. *Smart Moves: Why Learning Is Not All in Your Head*. Arlington, VA: Great Ocean.

Harris, Bess, and R.G.P Colgrove, eds. 1969. *Lawren Harris*. Toronto: Macmillan.

Haynes, Deborah J. 1997. *The Vocation of the Artist*. Cambridge: Cambridge University Press.

Heilbrun, Carolyn. 1988. *Writing a Woman's Life*. New York: Ballantine.

———. 1991. *The World According to Women*. Interview on *Ideas*, CBC radio, June 24–28. Transcript available.

———. 1997. Interview on *Ideas*, CBC radio, January 30. Based on the Alexander Lectures: *Women's Written Lives: View from the Threshold*. Transcript available.

———. 1999. *Women's Lives: The View from the Threshold*. Toronto: University of Toronto Press.

Hinz, Evelyn. 1992. Mimesis: Drama as a touchstone for a "poetics" of life writing. In *Essays on Life Writing: From Genre to Critical Practice*, Marlene Kadar, ed., 195–212. Toronto: University of Toronto Press.

Hogan, Linda, Deena Metsger, and Brenda Peterson, eds., 1998. *Intimate Nature: The Bond between Women and Animals*. New York: Fawcett Columbine.

Homans, Margaret. 1989. *Bearing the Word: Language and Female Experience in Nineteenth Century Women's Writing*. Chicago: University of Chicago Press.

Irigaray, Luce. 1981. This sex which is not one. In *New French Feminisms*, 99–106, C. Reeder, trans., Marks and I. de Courtivron, eds. New York: Schocken.

Irwin, H.J. 1999. *An Introduction to Parapsychology*, 3rd ed. Jefferson, NC: McFarland.

Isle, Walter. 1999. History and nature: Representations of the Great Plains in the work of Sharon Butala and Wallace Stegner. *Great Plains Quarterly* 19, no. 2: 89–95.

Jaggar, Alison M., and Susan R. Bordo, ed. 1989. *Gender/Body/Knowledge: Feminist Reconstruction of Being and Knowing*. New Brunswick, NJ: Rutgers University Press.

Jansen, H. W. 1977. *A History of Art: A Survey of the Major Visual Arts from the Dawn of History to the Present Day*. New York: Abrams.

Jolly, Margaretta, ed. 2001. *The Encyclopedia of Life Writing: Autobiographical and Biographical Forms*. London: Fitzroy Dearborn.

Jordan, Betty Ann. 1995. Is it serendipity or brilliant planning? *Canadian Art* 12, no. 4 (Winter): 20.

Jung, C. G. 1965. *Memories, Dreams, Reflections*. New York: Random House.

Kadar, Marlene, ed. 1992. *Essays on Life Writing: From Genre to Critical Practice*: Toronto: University of Toronto Press.

Kelly, Mary. 1985. *Post-Partum Document*. Boston: Routledge & Kegan Paul.

———. 1987. On sexual politics and art. In *Framing Feminism*, Roszika Parker and Griselda Pollock, eds., 303–12. New York: Pandora.

Knudson, Peter, and David Suzuki, eds. 1992. *Wisdom of the Elders*. Toronto: Stoddart.

Korol, Todd, and Sharon Butala. 1992. *Harvest: A Celebration of Harvest on the Canadian Prairies*. Saskatoon: Fifth House.

Kristeva, Julia. 1977. *Desire in Language: A Semiotic Approach to Language and Art*. New York: Columbia University Press.

Kübler-Ross, Elisabeth. 1985. Working with terminally ill children. Cassette Recording No. 7. *Proceedings, 12th Annual Human Unity Conference*. Kaneohe, HI: Human Unity Institute.

Kuspit, Donald. 1995. Joseph Beuys: The body of the artist. In *Joseph Beuys: Diverging Critiques*, D. Thistlewood, ed., 95–105. Liverpool: Liverpool University Press and Tate Gallery, Liverpool.

Lane, Belden C. 2002. *Landscapes of the Sacred: Geography and Narrative in American Spirituality*. Baltimore: Johns Hopkins University Press.

Langellier, Kristin M., and Deanna L. Hall. 1989. Interviewing women: A phenomenological approach to feminist communication. In *Doing Research on Women's Communication: Perspectives and Methods*, Kathryn Carter and Carole Spivak, eds., 193–222. Norwood, NJ: Ablex.

Laurence, Robin. 1994. The radiant way. *Border Crossings* 11, no. 2: 26–35.

———. 1996. Prattfalls. *Border Crossings* 15, no. 2, 12–17.

Lerman, Ora. 1985. An autobiographical journey: Can art transform personal and cultural loss? *Art Magazine* 59 (May): 103–7.

Lind, Jane. 1989. *Mary and Christopher Pratt*. Vancouver: Douglas & McIntyre.

Lionnet, Francoise. 1989. *Autobiographical Voices: Race, Gender, Self-Portraiture*. Ithaca, NY: Cornell University Press.

Lippard, Lucy. 1976. *From the Centre: Feminist Essays on Women's Art*. New York: Dutton.

———. 1990. *Mixed Blessings: New Art in Multicultural America*. New York: Pantheon.

Liss, Andrea. 1994. The body in question: Rethinking motherhood, alterity and desire. In *New Feminist Criticism: Art, Identity, Action*, J. Fruch, C.L. Langer, and A. Raven, eds., 80–96. New York: HarperCollins.

Lodge, David, ed. 1988. *Modern Criticism and Theory: A Reader*. London and New York: Longmans.

Loewen, Harry. 1984. Canadian-Mennonite literature: Longing for a lost homeland. In *The Old World and the New*, Walter E. Reidel, ed., 73–93. Toronto: University of Toronto Press.

Long, Timothy. 1996. Beyond the facade. *Cultural Commentary: New Work from Manitoba*. Regina: Mackenzie Art Gallery, 4–5.

Macdonald, Barbara, and Cynthia Rich. 1991. *Look Me in the Eye: Old Women, Aging and Ageism*, expanded ed. San Francisco: Spinsters Book Company.

MacEwen, Gwendolyn. 1994. The Trojan women. In *Trojan Women*, Gwendolyn MacEwen and Nikos Tsingos, eds., 31–89. Toronto: Exile Editions.

MacFarlane, Robert. 2003. *Mountains of the Mind*. New York: Pantheon.

Madill, Shirley, ed. 1995. *Aganetha Dyck*. Winnipeg: Winnipeg Art Gallery.

Mandel, Barrett J. 1980. Full of life now. In *Autobiography: Essays Theoretical and Critical*, James Olney, ed., 47–83. Princeton: Princeton University Press.

Mandell, Nancy, ed. 1998. *Feminist Issues: Race, Class and Sexuality*, 2nd ed. Scarborough, ON: Prentice Hall.

Mark, Lisa Gabrielle. 1999. *Aganetha Dyck: Given to the Bees*. Published in conjunction with the exhibition, *Aganetha Dyck: Working in the Dark*. Toronto: De Leon White Gallery.

Mason, Mary G. 1988. The other voice: Autobiographies of women writers. In *Life/Lines: Theorizing Women's Autobiography*, Bella Brodski and Celeste Schenk, eds., 19–44. Ithaca, NY: Cornell University Press.

McArthur, Tom. 1992. Metaphor. In *The Oxford Companion to the English Language*, Tom McArthur, ed., 653–55. Oxford: Oxford University Press.

McFague, Sallie. 1997. *Super, Natural Christians: How We Should Love Nature*. Minneapolis: Fortress Press.

Meigs, Mary. 1981. *Lily Briscoe: A Self Portrait*. Vancouver: Talonbooks.

———. 1983. *The Medusa Head*. Vancouver: Talonbooks.

———. 1987. *The Box Closet*. Vancouver: Talonbooks.

———. 1988. Memories of age. *Trivia* 12, 57–65.

———. 1990. My evolution as a lesbian writer. In *Language in Her Eye: Views on Writing and Gender by Canadian Women Writing in English*, Libby Scheier, Sarah Sheard and Eleanor Wachtel, eds., 194–96. Toronto: Coach House Press.

———. 1991a. Falling between the cracks. In *InVersions: Writing by Dykes, Queers & Lesbians*, Betsy Warland, ed., 105–16. Vancouver: Press Gang.

———. 1991b. *In the Company of Strangers*. Vancouver: Talonbooks.

———. 1992a. After reading *Look Me in the Eye: Old Women, Aging and Ageism*. *Trivia* 19: 96–101.

———. 1992b. Self-portraits in time. In *Forbidden Subjects: Self-Portraits by Lesbian Artists*, C. Kelley, ed., 53–56. Vancouver: Gallerie.

———. 1997. *The Time Being*. Vancouver: Talonbooks.

———. 2000. Writing-my-self-body. *Journal of Lesbian Studies* 4, no. 4: 97–100.

———. 2001. Excerpts from *Hospital Notes*. *Capilano Review* 2, no. 33: 72–73.

———. 2002. Keystroke. *Geist* 11, no. 44: 30–31.

———. 2005. *Beyond Recall*, Lisa Weil, ed. Vancouver: Talonbooks.

Merleau-Ponty, Maurice. 1962. *Phenomenology of Perception*. C. Smith, trans., F. Williams, trans., rev. London: Routledge and Kegan Paul.

Misch, Georg. 1951. *A History of Autobiography in Antiquity*, 2 vols., 3rd ed. Cambridge: Harvard University Press.

Morgan, David. 1998. Domestic devotion and ritual: Visual piety in the modern American home. *Art Journal*, 57, no. 1: 45–54.

Moss, John. 1999. Critical readings: Urquhart, Butala, Gibson, Wiebe, Marlatt, and Michaels. In *The Paradox of Meaning: Cultural Poetics and Critical Fictions*, John Moss, ed., 155–74. Winnipeg: Turnstone Press.

Nelson, Jenny L.1989. Phenomenology as feminist methodology: Explicating interviews. In *Doing Research on Women's Communication: Perspectives on Theory and Method*, K. Carter and C. Spitzack, eds., 221–41. Norwood, NJ: Ablex.

Neuman, Shirley. 1990. Life writing. In *A Literary History of Canada: Canadian Literature in English*, 2nd ed., W.H. New, ed., 4:33–30. Toronto: University of Toronto Press.

———. 1991. Autobiography and questions of gender: An introduction. In *Autobiography and Questions of Gender*, Shirley Neuman, ed., 1–11. London: Frank Cass.

———. 1992a. Autobiography: From different poetics to a poetics of difference. In *Essays on Life Writing*, Marlene Kadar, ed., 213–30. Toronto: University of Toronto Press.

———. 1992b. "Your past … your future." Autobiography and mother's bodies. In *Genre, Trope and Gender*, Barry Rutland, ed., 53–86. Ottawa: Carleton University Press.

Newell, William H. 1990. Interdisciplinary curriculum development. *Issues in Integrative Studies*, 8: 69–86.

Nochlin, Linda. 1988. Some women realists. *Women, Art, and Power and Other Essays*. Toronto: Harper & Row.

Norwood, Vera L. 1996. Heroines of nature: Four women respond to the American landscape. In *The Ecocriticism Reader: Landmarks in Literary Ecology*, Cheryll Glofelty and Harold Fromm, eds., 323–50.

Athens, GA: University of Georgia Press.

Nussbaum, Jon F., Loretta L. Pecchioni, James D. Robinson, and Teresa L. Thompson. 2000. *Communication and Aging*, 2nd ed. Mahwah, NJ: Lawrence Erlbaum Associates.

Olney, James. 1980. Autobiography and the cultural moment: A thematic, historical and bibliographical introduction. In *Autobiography: Essays Theoretical and Critical*, James Olney, ed., 3–27. Princeton, NJ: Princeton University Press.

Ortner, Sherry B. 1974. Is female to male as nature is to culture? In *Woman, Culture and Society*, M. Rosaldo and L. Lamphere, eds., 67–87. Stanford: Stanford University Press.

Pagés, Estelle. 2001. *Passages*. Paris: Services culturels de l'Ambassade du Canada.

Parker, Rozsika, and Griselda Pollock. 1981. *Old Mistresses: Women, Art and Ideology*. London: Routledge.

———. 1987. *Framing Feminism: Art and the Women's Movement, 1970–1985*. New York: Pandora.

Peck, M. Scott. 1983. *People of the Lie: The Hope for Healing Human Evil*. New York: Simon & Schuster.

———. 1987. *The Different Drum: Community Making and Peace*. New York: Simon & Schuster.

———. 1996. *In Heaven as on Earth: A Vision of the After-Life*. New York: Hyperion.

———. 1997. *The Road Less Travelled and Beyond: Spiritual Growth in an Age of Anxiety*. New York: Simon & Schuster.

Pell, Barbara. 1993. Deliberate ordinariness. Review of *The Invention of the Truth* and *Fever*. *Canadian Literature* 136: 157–58.

Perreault, Jeanne. 1995. *Writing Lives: Contemporary Feminist Autography*. Minneapolis: University of Minnesota Press.

Peterson, Linda H. 1988. Gender and autobiographical form: The case of spiritual autobiography. In *Studies in Autobiography*, James Olney, ed., 211–22. New York: Oxford University Press.

Phillips, Dana. 1996. Is nature necessary? In *The Ecocriticism Reader: Landmarks in Literary Ecology*, Cheryll Glofelty and Harold Fromm, eds., 204–22. Athens, GA: University of Georgia Press.

Pike, Bev. 1989. Women of vision: Portraits within the mentor tradition in Winnipeg's visual arts. *NeWest Review* 14, no. 2: 15–17.

Pitts, Mary Ellen. 2001. Nature writing, American. In *The Encyclopedia of Life Writing: Autobiographical and Biographical Forms*, Margaretta Jolly, ed., 2:641–44. London: Fitzroy Dearborn.

Pollock, Griselda. 1988. *Vision and Difference: Femininity, Feminism and Histories of Art*. London: Routledge.

———. 1999. *Differencing the Canon: Feminist Desire and the Writing of Art Histories*. London: Routledge.

Powers, Lyall. 2000. Alien hearts: Laurence and the lord of the prairies. Paper presented at *Western Mindscapes: 3rd Biennial ACSUS-in-Canada Colloquium*, September 15–16. Association for Canadian Studies in the United States (ACSUS).

Pratt, Christopher. 1995. *Christopher Pratt: Personal Reflections on a Life in Art*. Toronto: Key Porter.

Pratt, Mary. 1998. Another time, another place, another me. *Globe and Mail*, August 19, C12–10.

———. 2000. *A Personal Calligraphy*. Fredericton, NB: Goose Lane.

Rafelman, Rachel. 1995. Mary's not-so still life. *Globe and Mail*, October 14, C4–5.

Rasporich, Beverly. 1990. *Dance of the Sexes: Art and Gender in the Fiction of Alice Munro*. Winnipeg: University of Manitoba Press.

———. 1993. Locating the artist's muse: The paradox of femininity in Mary Pratt and Alice Munro. In *Woman as Artist: Papers in Honour of Marsha Hanen*, Christine Mason Sutherland and Beverly Matson Rasporich, eds., 121–43. Calgary: University of Calgary Press.

Reid, Verna. 1992. There are very few female birds who sing. In *Proceedings: National Conference on Liberal Arts and the Education of the Artist*, 145–53. New York: School of Visual Arts.

———. 1993. Emily, Laurie, and me: An academic's adventures in studio-land. In *Proceedings: National Conference on the Liberal Arts and the Education of the Artist*, 173–76. New York: School of Visual Arts.

———. 1996a. Transcript of interview with Mary Pratt. Vancouver, February 9–11, unpublished.

———. 1996b. Transcript of interview with Sharon Butala. Eastend, July 25–26, unpublished.

———. 1996c. Transcript of interview with Aganetha Dyck. Winnipeg, August 10–12, unpublished.

———. 1997. Transcript of interview with Mary Meigs. Montreal, April.4–5, unpublished.

———. 2001. Carr, Emily (1871–1945). Canadian painter, autobiographer and diarist. In *The Encyclopedia of Life Writing: Autobiographical and Biographical Forms*, Margaretta Jolly, ed., 1:183–84. London: Fitzroy Dearborn.

———. 2002. Review of *Simple Things: The Story of a Friendship* and *A Personal Calligraphy*. *Canadian Literature* 174: 163–66.

Rich, Adrienne. 1979. *On Lies, Secrets and Silence: Selected Prose, 1976–1978*. New York: Norton.

———. 1986a. *Blood, Bread, and Poetry: Selected Prose, 1979–1985*. New York: Norton.

———. 1986b. *Of Woman Born: Motherhood as Experience and Institution*. New York: Norton.

Root, A.I. 1966. *The ABC and XYZ of Bee Culture*. Medina, OH: A.I. Root.

Ross, Cecily. 2000. Sharon's stones. Interview with Sharon Butala. *Globe and Mail*, July 1, D10–11.

Ruddick, Sara. 1999. Maternal thinking as a feminist standpoint. In *Feminist Philosophies: Problems, Theories and Applications*, Janet A. Kourany, James P. Sterba, and Rosemarie Tong, eds., 404–15. Upper Saddle River, NJ: Prentice Hall.

Samples, Bob. 1976. *The Metaphoric Mind: A Celebration of Creative Consciousness*. Don Mills, ON: Addison-Wesley.

Sarup, Madan. 1992. *Jacques Lacan*. Toronto: University of Toronto Press.

Saul, John Ralston. 1997. *Reflections of a Siamese Twin: Canada at the End of the Twentieth Century*. Toronto: Penguin.

Sceats, Sarah. 2000. *Food Consumption and the Body in Contemporary Women's Literature*. Cambridge: Cambridge University Press.

Schissel, Wendy, L. 1991. *The Keepers of Memory: Canadian Mythopoeic Poets and Magic Realist Painters (James Reaney, Ken Danby, Margaret Atwood, Mary Pratt: Poets, Painters)*. PhD dissertation, University of Calgary. In *Dissertation Abstracts International* 53, no. 10: 3520.

Scott, Mary. 1986. Artist's statement. In *Songs of Experience*, Jessica Bradley and Diana Nemiroff, eds., 132–34. Ottawa: National Gallery of Canada.

Sharp, Robert. 1995. Metaphor. In *The Oxford Companion to Philosophy*, Ted Honderich, ed., 555–56. New York: Oxford University Press.

Sielke, Sabine. 1997. *Fashioning the Female Subject: The Intertextual Networking of Dickerson, Moore and Rich*. Ann Arbor: University of Michigan Press.

Slade, Carole. 1991. Autobiography and mysticism. In *a/b: Auto/Biography Studies* 6, no. 2: 153–56.

Smart, Tom. 1995. *The Art of Mary Pratt: The Substance of Light*. St. John's: Beaverbrook Art Gallery.

Smith, Sidonie. 1987. *A Poetics of Women's Autobiography: Marginality and the Fictions of Self Representation*. Bloomington: Indiana University Press.

———. 1993. *Subjectivity, Identity, and the Body: Women's Autobiographical Practices in the Twentieth Century*. Bloomington: Indiana University Press.

———. 1995. Performativity, autobiographical practice, resistance. *a/b: Auto/Biography Studies* 10, no. 1: 17–33.

———. 1999. Virtually modern Amelia: Mobility, flight and the discontents of identity. In *Virtual Gender: Fantasies of Subjectivity and Embodiment*, Mary Ann O'Farrell and Lynne Vallone, eds., 11–36. Ann Arbor: University of Michigan Press.

Smith, Sidonie, and Julia Watson, eds. 1992. *De/colonizing the Subject: The Politics of Gender in Women's Autobiography*. Minneapolis: University of Minnesota Press.

Smith-Strom, Patricia, producer; director. 1996. Infused with light: A journey with Mary Pratt. In *Adrienne Clarkson Presents*, Jan. 31, Adrienne Clarkson, executive producer. Toronto: A CBC-TV Production.

Sommer, Doris. 1988. Not just a personal story: Women's testimonios and the plural self. In *Life/Lines: Theorizing Women's Autobiography*, Bella Brodski and Celeste Schenk, eds., 107–130. Ithaca, NY, and London: Cornell University Press.

Spader, Peter H. 1983. Scheler, Schutz and intersubjectivity. *Reflections: Essays in Phenomenology* 4 (Summer/ Fall): 5–13.

Stachelhaus, Heiner. 1987. *Joseph Beuys*, David Britt, trans. New York: Abbeville Press.

Stanley, Liz. 1992. *The Auto/Biographical I: The Theory and Practice of Feminist Auto/Biography*. Manchester: Manchester University Press.

Stanton, Domna C., ed. 1987. *The Female Autograph: Theory and Practice of Female Autobiography from the Tenth to Twentieth Century*. Chicago: University of Chicago Press.

Stephenson, Craig. 2001. Finding the words for wonder. Review *Wild Stone Heart*. *Ottawa Citizen*, August 26, C11–12.

Suzuki, David. 1994. *Time to Change: Essays*. Toronto: Stoddard.

———. 2006. Bee talker: The secret world of bees. *The Nature of Things*, July 23. Toronto: A CBC-TV Production. Also on DVD.

Tavris, Carol. 1992. *The Mismeasure of Woman: Why Women Are Not the Better Sex, the Inferior Sex or the Opposite Sex*. New York: Simon & Schuster.

Taylor, Peter A. 1995. Living in nature. Review of *The Perfection of the Morning*. *Canadian Literature* 147 (Winter): 201–2.

Tippett, Maria. 1992. *By a Lady: Celebrating Three Centuries of Canadian Art by Women*. Toronto: Penguin.

Tisdall, Caroline. 1979. *Joseph Beuys*. New York: Solomon R. Guggenheim Museum.

Todd, Douglas. 1996. *Brave Souls: Writers and Artists Wrestle with God, Love, Death and the Things that Matter*. Toronto: Stoddard.

Tong, Rosemarie. 1989. *Feminist Thought: A Comprehensive Introduction*. Boulder, CO, Westview Press.

Tousley, Nancy. 1992. Aganetha Dyck. *Canadian Art* 9, no. 3: 60–65.

———. 1995. No more apologies, says Mary Pratt. *Calgary Herald*, Oct. 1, C1, C9.

Travis, Molly Abel. 1998. *Reading Cultures: The Construction of Readers in the Twentieth Century*. Carbondale: Southern Illinois University Press.

Turner, Frederick. 1996. Cultivating the American garden. In *The Ecocriticism Reader: Landmarks in Literary Ecology*, Cheryll Glofelty, and Harold Fromm, eds., 40–51. Athens, GA: University of Georgia Press.

Turner, Victor, and Edith Turner. 1978. *Images and Pilgrimage in Christian Culture*. New York: Columbia University Press.

Underhill, Evelyn. 1990. *Mysticism*. New York: Doubleday.

Underwood, Nora. 1995. Female liberation. Review of *The Pill: A Biography of the Drug That Changed the World*. *Maclean's* 108, no. 33 (Aug. 14): 53.

Valone, James. 1992. The problem of intersubjectivity in transcendental and mundane phenomenology. In *The Annals of the Phenomenological Society*, Myrtle Korenbaum, ed., 1:63–86. Dayton, OH: Wright State University Press.

Visser, Margaret. 1991. *The Rituals of Dinner: The Origins, Evolution, Eccentricities and Meaning of Table Manners*. Toronto: HarperCollins.

Walsh, Meeka, and Robert Enright. 2000. The incredible lightness of bee-ing: An interview with Aganetha Dyck. *Border Crossings* 19, no. 1: 48–57.

Warland, Betsy. 1995. Beyond the facts: An interview with Mary Meigs. *West Coast Line* 29, no. 1: 42–63.

Weiler, Merike. 1998. A river runs through. *Style at Home* 25, no. 4 (Summer): 82–86.

Weir, Alison. 1996. *Sacrificial Logics: Feminist Theory and the Critique of Identity*. New York: Routledge.

Weisberg, Gabriel. 1989. Painting as autobiography: Cezanne's early work, *Arts Magazine* 63: 54–57.

Wente, Margaret. 2004. Reproductive freedom. The pill changed everything. *Globe and Mail*, April 10, A19.

Wilkenson, Shelagh. 1992. Old woman, "bearer of keys to unknown doorways." *Canadian Woman Studies* 12, no. 2: 103–13.

Wilson, David, producer, and Cynthia Scott, director. 1990. Per. Alice Diablo, Constance Garneau, Winnifred Holden, Cissy Meddings, Mary Meigs, Catherine Roche, Michelle Sweeney, Beth Webber. *The Company of Strangers*, film. Toronto: National Film Board of Canada.

Wolf, Naomi. 1990. *The Beauty Myth*, Toronto: Random House.

Woolf, Virginia. 1978. *A Room of One's Own*. London: HarperCollins.

Wright, Elizabeth, ed. 1992. *Feminism and Psychoanalysis: A Critical Dictionary*. Oxford: Blackwell.

Yacowar, Maurice. 1988. The paintings of Mary (vs. Christopher) Pratt. *Dalhousie Review* 68, no. 4: 385–99.

Yeo, Marion. 1987. Sharron Zenith Crone, Aganetha Dyck, Esther Warkov: Three Manitoba artists. *Woman's Art Journal* 8, no. 1: 33–39.

Young, James E. 2000. *At Memory's Edge: After Images of the Holocaust in Contemporary Art and Architecture*. New Haven, CT: Yale University Press.

Colour Plates

FIG. 1
Mary Pratt, *Red Currant Jelly*, 1972 • oil on masonite, 45.9 cm x 45.6 cm
Collection of the National Gallery of Canada • Photograph by Tom Moore

FIG. 2
Mary Pratt, *Supper Table*, 1969 • oil on canvas, 61.0 cm x 92.4 cm
Collection of the artist • Photograph by Ned Pratt

FIG. 3
Mary Pratt, *Salmon on Saran*, 1974 • oil on panel, 45.7 cm x 50.8 cm
Collection of Angus and Jean Bruneau • Photograph by Ned Pratt

FIG. 4
Mary Pratt, *Child with Two Adults*, 1983 • oil on board, 54.5 cm x 54.5 cm
Private collection • Photograph by Tom Moore

FIG. 5
Mary Pratt, *Wedding Dress*, 1986 • oil on panel, 74.3 cm x 57.2 cm
Private collection • Photograph by Rob Johnson

FIG. 6
Mary Pratt, *Breakfast Last Summer*, 1994 • oil on canvas, 91.4 cm x 121.9 cm
Private collection • Photograph by Ned Pratt

FIG. 7
Mary Pratt, *Burning the Rhododendron*, 1990 • watercolour and pastel on paper, 127.6 cm x 239.4 cm
Collection of Sun Life Assurance Company of Canada • Photograph by Ned Pratt

FIG. 8
Aganetha Dyck, *Close Knit*, 1976–81 • felting, shrinking of 65 off white, woolen sweaters,
20 ft. x 3 ft. x 14 in. (variable) • Collection of the Canada Council Art Bank, Ottawa, Canada
Photograph by Sheila Spence (courtesy of the Winnipeg Art Gallery)

FIG. 9
Aganetha Dyck, *Canned Buttons*, from a series of 620 jars from *The Large Cupboard*, 1984
mixed media, buttons, toothpicks, water, canning, frying, baking, cooking, quart jars
Private and public collections in Canada • Photograph by William Eakin

FIG. 10
Aganetha Dyck, *The Large Cupboard*, 1983–86 • mixed media, buttons, found objects, water, glue, canning, frying, baking, cooking in various jars in 10 wooden cupboards, 6 ft. x 2 1/2 ft. x 1 1/2 ft. each
Private and public collections in Canada • Photograph: Ernest Meyer (courtesy of the Winnipeg Art Gallery)

FIG. 11
Aganetha Dyck, *The Glass Dress; Lady in Waiting*, 1990–99
glass, pearls, honeycomb, bee work, woman's size 7, weight is 300 lbs.
Collection of the National Gallery of Canada, Ottawa, Canada • Photograph: Peter Dyck

FIG. 12
Aganetha Dyck, *The Extended Wedding Party*, 1995
canvas embroidered by the honeybees, bee altered shoes, metal queen excluders, various men's suit and shoe sizes.
garment bags: 64 in. high, 20 in. wide, 20 in. deep
Collection of the Art Gallery of Hamilton, Hamilton, Ontario
Photograph: Sheila Spence (courtesy of the Winnipeg Art Gallery)

FIG. 13
Aganetha Dyck, *The Groom and Groomsmen* from *The Extended Wedding Party*, 1995
canvas embroidered by the honeybees, bee altered shoes, metal queen excluders, various men's suit and shoe sizes.
garment bags: 64 in. high, 20 in. wide, 20 in. deep
Collection of the Art Gallery of Hamilton, Hamilton, Ontario
Photograph: Sheila Spence (courtesy of the Winnipeg Art Gallery)

FIG. 14
Aganetha Dyck, *The Library: Inner/Outer*, 1990 • mixed media including beeswax. Installation varies
Collection of the Winnipeg Art Gallery, Winnipeg, Manitoba
Photograph: Daniel Smith (courtesy of the Art Gallery of Lethbridge, Lethbridge, Alberta)

FIG. 15
Aganetha Dyck, *Pocketbooks for the Queen Bee*, 1995
wood, evening bags, beeswax, approximate 5 ft. in diameter (variable)
Collection of the Winnipeg Art Gallery, Winnipeg, Manitoba.
Photograph: Sheila Spence (courtesy of the Winnipeg Art Gallery)

FIG. 16
Aganetha Dyck, *Pocketbook for the Queen Bee*, 1991 • evening bag, found objects, beeswax, 6 in. x 12 in. x 3 in. wide
Collection of the Winnipeg Art Gallery, Winnipeg, Manitoba • Photograph by William Eakin

FIG. 17
Aganetha Dyck, *Hand Held: Between Index and Middle Finger*, 1987–88
cigarettes, cigars, pipes, found objects. 4 in. to 10 in. (variable)
Collection of the Canada Council Art Bank and in private and public collections in Canada
Photograph by A. Talbot, University of Manitoba

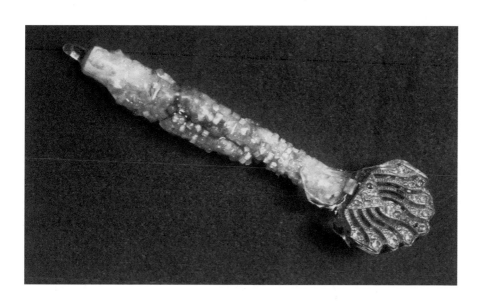

FIG. 18
Aganetha Dyck, *Altered Cigarettes* from *Brain is not Enough*, 1987
cigarette, jewellery, glue, mixed media, 8 in. long
Private collection, Canada • Photograph by William Eakin

FIG. 19
Mary Pratt, *Eviscerated Chickens*, 1971 • oil on panel, 47.5 cm x 62.2 cm
Collection of Memorial University of Newfoundland, St. John's • Photograph by Ned Pratt

FIG. 20
Mary Pratt, *The Service Station*, 1978 • oil on masonite, 101.5 cm x 76.5 cm
Collection of the Art Gallery of Ontario • Photograph by Ned Pratt

FIG. 21
Mary Pratt, *Another Province of Canada*, 1978 • oil on panel, 91.4 cm x 70.0 cm
Collection of Memorial University of Newfoundland, St. John's • Photograph by Ned Pratt

FIG. 22
Mary Pratt, *Girl in My Dressing Gown*, 1981 • oil on panel, 153.6 cm x 77.5 cm
Private collection, Vancouver • Photograph by Tom Moore

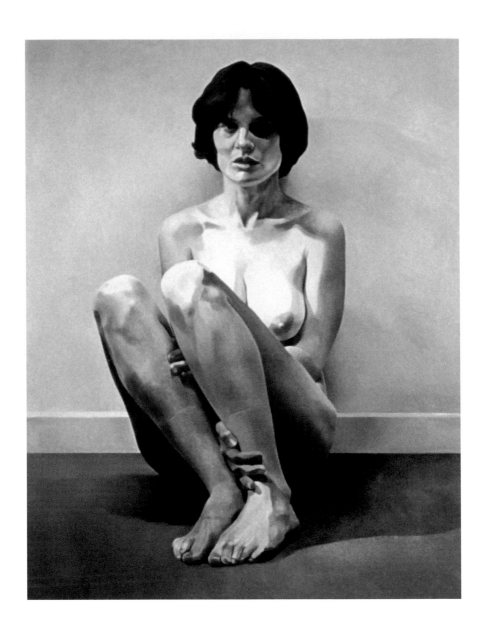

FIG. 23
Mary Pratt, *Donna*, 1986 • oil on panel, 89.9 cm x 70.5 cm
Collection of Memorial University of Newfoundland, St. John's • Photograph by Ned Pratt

FIG. 24
Mary Pratt, *Cold Cream*, 1983 • pencil on oil on gesso on masonite, 48.3 cm x 41.9 cm
Collection of the Canada Council Art Bank, Ottawa

FIG. 25
Aganetha Dyck, *Poem to the Bees* (detail of one line from 61 lines),
poem by Di Brandt and the bees, from *Working in the Dark*, 1999
wooden tile, braille text, pen and ink, bee work, 19 in. x 6 in. x 1 in. (variable)
In private and artist collections • Photograph by William Eakin

FIG. 26
Mary Pratt, *Herring on a Salt Bag*, 1969 • oil on panel, 76.2 cm x 53.3 cm
Private collection, New Brunswick • Photograph by Ned Pratt

FIG. 27
Mary Pratt, *Chocolate Birthday Cake*, 1997 • oil on canvas, 61 cm x 76.2 cm
Private collection • Photograph by Ned Pratt

Index

spiritual awareness and, 197, 278, 280
  as spiritual undertaking, 198, 208, 257
art/science collaboration, 160–61
"artist as hero," 171, 249
artist as shaman, 12, 119, 255–56
Atwood, Margaret, 3, 152
  The Handmaid's Tale, 66, 159
  "Nature as Monster," 167
autobiographical art, xviii, 3, 17, 31, 33, 208, 258, 289
autobiographical telling, 287–88, 292
autobiography, 17, 21–22, 28, 119, 265
  Canadian female autobiography, 267–68, 270–73, 276–77, 280–85
  female memoirs written in the 1990's, 42
  liminal space, 239
  relation to ritual, 24
  role models, 28
"autography," 32, 58, 157

B

Bachelard, Gaston, 45, 54, 108
  Poetics of Space, 51
Barbie doll, 120, 145
Barbour, John, 200
"the beauty myth," 117. *See also* Wolf, Naomi
Beauvoir, Simone de, 20, 93
Beaverbrook Art Gallery, xviii
bee/human connections, 161–62
bee art. *See under* Dyck, Aganetha
bee communication, 163–64
bee science, xv, 7, 160, 274
"Bee Talker" (TV program), xv, 284

bees, xv, 7, 53, 145, 147, 168
  Biblical metaphors, 254
  bodily activity, 91
  "canaries" of nature, 162, 277
  hive soundscape, 255
  instinct for community, 274
  "life force," 7, 120, 207, 253, 274–75, 280, 282
  as magic creatures, 161
  as "other," 25, 157
  power of, 148, 160
  "TTC" ("total colony collapse disease"), 161, 277
Berger, John, 12, 225–27
Bergson, Henri, 206, 228
Beuys, Joseph, 116, 161, 163, 251, 256
  Coyote, 252–54
  shamanism, 12, 253
  "social sculpture," 252
Beverley, John, 169
Bible, 196, 201, 238, 244–45
  Biblical narratives, 257, 280
  Biblical symbolism, 173, 254
  imaginative centrality of, 3
  New Testament ethical standards, 257
bird imagery, 184–85, 277
birds, 8, 150, 153, 156, 181, 184–86, 192, 257, 277, 282
birth control pill, 141, 298n17
birthing (childbirth), 90, 142–44, 213, 271
  expression of female soul, 226
Blais, Marie-Claire, xvi, 50, 55, 104, 180–81, 185, 199, 237, 240–41, 293n5
body (bodily experience), 7, 10, 70, 270
  aging (*See* aging and mortality)
  art-making about the female body (*See* female body)
  Barbie doll, 120, 145

C

Dillard, Anne, 149

dinner party on the page, xiii, 7, 288

dinner table as organizing motif, xii, 87, 129

"disengagement" theory of aging, 109–10

Dogan, Mattei, 18

domestic violence. *See* violence against women

domesticity, 7–8, 43, 58, 129, 199, 291
    domestic images, xvii, 6, 8, 31–33
    domestic materials and method in art, 7–8, 34, 60–61, 63–64
    embraced as part of maternal inheritance, 84
    facilitating subordination and oppression, 270
    male painters' treatment of, 21
    quintessential female domain, 176
    rural women, 35
    subversion of, 36
    toxic psychic effects, 116
    valorization, 9, 35–36, 82, 266
    victimization (*See* victimization)

dreams, 262, 281, 287–88
    archetypes, 215
    bluebirds, 247
    coyote, 215, 262
    eagle and owl, 215, 262
    guides on spiritual journey, 214
    honouring, 261
    houses, 51
    "the Lord of the Wild," 165
    mother, 244
    rabbit dream, 262–63

Driver, Tom, 19

Dyck, Aganetha, xiii, 3, 6, 61
    About Prayer, 69
    acceptance of mortality, 253
    advocate for bees, 161–62, 277
    alterity, 157
    Anorexic Dress, 117, 273

artist's voice, 251
"autography," 58, 157
"autotelic" personality, 159
awards, xv
bee art, 7, 91, 147–49, 157–58, 254
Bee Work series, 72
bodily engagement with bees, 120, 157, 257
Brain is not Enough, 114
Cabbages, 250
Canned Buttons, xv, 62–64, 72, 115, 117
Close Knit, 27, 61, 63, 113, 249–50
collaboration in art practice, 25, 34, 67, 112, 239
collaboration with bees, 65, 119, 157, 160, 163, 249, 254, 274, 280
community, 24, 64, 200, 248, 251, 257, 283
comparison to Joseph Beuys, 252–54
construction of self as artist, beekeeper and scientific technician, 120
construction of self as thinking person, 67, 70, 116, 120, 291
contact with another species, 120, 156–57, 257, 282
cosmopolitan sensibility, 149, 251
dislike of stereotyping, 58, 67, 97, 250–51
domestic materials and methods, 7–8, 25, 34, 60–61, 63
emotional connection to "house, home, and mother," 71
environmental awareness, 149, 162, 272
essentialism, 10
exploration (*See* Dyck, Aganetha, bee art)
The Extended Wedding Party, xv, 10, 65–67, 118–19, 140, 250, 268, 291
father's influence, 68
feminist gestures, 70
found objects, 34, 62, 162

E

environmental damage linked to oppression of women, 186

environmental poisoning, 272

epiphanies, 50, 128, 205, 224

essentialism, 10, 83, 95–97, 99, 103, 126, 143
subordination of women and, 11, 272

"essentialism with a difference," 10, 99, 103

essentialist versus social construction theories, 97, 143

ethical conduct, 202, 206. *See also* moral responsibility

evil, 211, 222, 239–40, 242, 258, 278

F

family farm, 26, 72–73, 150, 186
extinction of, 81–82, 169, 277

farming and ranching
male territory, 167, 275

female anatomy (body art), 36

female as "other," 20–21

female body, 6, 91, 131, 133–34, 271
recovering from male gaze, 133, 298n15
vulnerability of, 272, 291

"female culture/mother art," 36, 45, 58, 64, 82, 133

female elders. *See* old women

female eroticism, 6, 96. *See also* female sexuality; jouissance

female experience (ego art), 36

female nude. *See* female body

"the female problematic," 37, 95

female sexual pleasure. *See* jouissance

female sexuality, 10
insufficiency in language, 95
as a manifestation of nature, 175

feminine aesthetic, 291. *See also* clothing
"a brilliant, subtle esthetic," 106, 145, 273

"feminine" behaviour. *See* code of femininity

feminine discourse, 36

feminine "ego art," 137, 140

feminine experience as area of hidden knowledge, 69

feminine love of objects, 54, 268

feminine principle. *See under* women's reproductive power

feminine sensibility, 38, 75, 221

feminine soul, 216, 223

feminism(s), 2–6, 68–69
feminist as "undomesticated woman," 49
French feminists, 6, 68, 95, 135, 271
post-structural feminists, 41, 71
psychoanalytic feminism, 5
radical feminism, 5, 127, 201
"standpoint" feminists, 26, 72

"feminist problematic," 134

Findley, Timothy, 202

Fine, Gary Alan, 12, 151, 153, 170–71, 175, 186, 273

Fleming, Donald, 1

"flow," 158–59, 191, 208, 275

Fossey, Diane, 156, 158

Foucault, Michel, 94, 116, 129

Fraser, Sylvia, 202

Fredericton, 45, 48, 130, 133, 232

Fredericton garden, 276

freedom, 3, 57, 67, 116, 251–52, 258–59

Freud, Sigmund, 95

Freudian-Jungian unconscious, 23

Freudian-Lacanian position on unconscious, 36

Frye, Marilyn, 49, 97
Frye, Northrop, 3, 14, 156, 245
   "educated imagination," 4, 156, 259
   "the motive for metaphor," 183
Fuss, Diana, 10, 97, 105
   Essentially Speaking, 98

G

Gablik, Suzi, 208
garden, 180, 192, 275–76
   "bush garden," 190
   grounded in domesticity, 276
   nature and culture joined, 176, 180
   paradise as, 177
gendering, 27, 32
   assumption of difference, 93
   contingency of, 144
   as a function of language, 98
   gender stereotypes, 67
   inborn or socially constructed, 10,
      95, 98
   social construction, 93, 144
Glenn, George, 59–60, 251
Glotfelty, Cheryll, 153, 165
God, 25, 197, 204, 206, 244, 280
Godwin, Ted, 191
going "back," 291
   "Do you think you'll ever go back?",
      287–88, 292
"Golden Rule," 207
Goodall, Jane, 156, 158
grace, 213, 245, 259, 262
Grenville, Bruce, 61
Grimshaw, Jean, 41, 52
Group of Seven, 2, 191–92
Gwyn, Sandra, 37–38, 40, 172–73, 177,
   224

H

Hampl, Patricia, 201
Harris, Lawren, 191–93, 209
Haynes, Deborah, 12, 197, 221, 232,
   234, 238–39, 248–49, 278
   The Vocation of the Artist, 208
Heilbrun, Carolyn, 21, 42–43, 46, 52,
   70–71, 112, 145, 269
   theory of liminality, 19
Hillman, James, 211
Hinz, Evelyn, 23–24, 28, 119, 289, 292
Holy Spirit, 260–61, 280
homemaking. *See* domesticity
honesty. *See* truth
honey, 118, 161, 163
   Biblical imagery, 163, 254
   ideas of jouissance, 119
   mythological significance, 163
honeybee. *See* bees
Hooper, Gary, 65
Hopkins, Gerard Manley, 50
house, 34, 49, 179, 182
   Breton farmhouse, 107
   dreams of, 33
   female domain, 87, 152, 267
   image of childhood houses, 42, 45,
      51, 75
   in Mary Meigs' work, 33, 49, 51, 107
   maternality and, 108
   mothers' and grandmothers', 33–34,
      45–46, 48, 52, 75
   "the Peak," 51–52, 180, 267
   La Sucerie, 179
   Waterloo Road house, 48, 64, 172,
      177
household objects. *See* domesticity
human contact with other species, 183,
   252, 254, 282. *See also* animal-
   human bonding

inter-species dialogue, xv, 156, 163, 255, 282

personal satisfaction, 156, 158–59

I

immortality, 233–34, 246. *See also* aging and mortality; death

imperial view of nature, 151–53, 155, 175, 186, 273

Indigenous people. *See* Aboriginal people

"individual dissent," 10, 19–20

individual in community theme, 24

individual/society relationship, 65, 112

integrative metaphoric mode, 182–84

inter-species dialogue, 156, 255, 282. *See also* human contact with other species

intersubjective model of perception, 205, 219, 249

Inversion, 239

Irigaray, Luce, 97, 99, 101, 134, 271

J

James, William, 12, 203

Jesus, 228–30, 245

jouissance, 10, 95–96, 99–101, 131–32, 135, 138, 140, 146, 271

Jungians, 23, 211

Jung's dream theory, 209, 214–16, 247

K

Kelly, Mary, 9, 21, 36–37, 45, 58, 64, 82, 95, 133, 136–37, 175, 268
  Post-Partum Document, 143

Kerr, Illingsworth, 191

Kingston, Maxine Hong, 210

Kollwitz, Käthe, 103

Koop, Wanda, 113, 249

Kristeva, Julia, 6

Kübler-Ross, Elisabeth, 12, 204, 206–7, 211, 232, 238, 261, 278, 283

L

Lacan, Jacques, 10, 36–37, 95

Lane, Belden, 12, 205–6, 216–20, 282
  Landscape of the Sacred, 204

language, 3, 98, 256
  "id-liberated female discourse," 54
  language of female liberation (1970s), 27
  language of objects, 267–68
  male dominated, 142
  marks separation from mother, 36

Language in her Eye, 243

Laurence, Margaret, 210

Le Blanc, Amy, 76

lesbian communities, 199

lesbian writing community, 100–102

lesbianism, xvi, 7, 16, 55, 98–99, 135, 238
  degrees of, 103, 105
  "passing," 105–6

Leuba, James, 203, 228, 231

Lewis, C.S., 228

libido, 141–42. *See also* female sexuality; jouissance

Life and Times (TV segment), 47, 232–33, 235

"life force," 7, 207, 274–75, 280, 282

life writing, 3–4, 26, 48, 150, 235, 289, 294n8. *See also* autobiography

light, 191, 224, 244. *See also* darkness
    in Christian iconography, 228
    "lights" and "darks," 46, 232, 234
    Pratt's use of, xvii, 33, 38, 92, 128, 135, 144, 171, 177–78, 199, 224–25, 227–29, 282

liminal cultural positioning, 139

liminal generation, 9, 28, 71, 84, 144, 258
    careers after age of fifty, xi, 1, 266
    extending parameters of female old age, 266
    between modernist and postmodernist worlds, 19, 42, 87, 141, 290
    redefining self in later life, 265
    between two-career family and traditional one, 87

liminal space, 140, 234
    between conscious and unconscious, 235
    between self and community, 248

liminal spiritual state, 247

liminality, 46, 71, 86, 152, 257
    theory of, 19–20, 28
    typical of female memoirs written in 1990s, 42

Lippard, Lucy, 6, 21

Liss, Andrea, 10, 99

literary ecology, 153

loneliness, 24, 231, 288

Long, Tomothy, 62

Lopez, Barry, 202

"The Lord of the Wild," 165, 168, 275
    masculine power of, 166

loss, sense of, 186–87, 288. *See also* aging and mortality
    demise of family farm, 82, 277
    environmental damage, 155, 248, 277

love, 222, 245, 257, 260, 292

love triangles, 55, 100, 136, 227, 240–42

M

Macdonald, Barbara, 196, 278
    Look Me in the Eye, 195, 246

MacEwan, Gwendolyn, *The Trojan Women*, 258

MacFarlane, Robert, *Mountains of the Mind*, 192

MacKay, Jim, 190, 287

MacKay, John, 189–90, 287–88

Madill, Shirley, 34, 62

Mairs, Nancy, 201

male "artist as hero," 21, 171, 249

male complicity in domestic violence, 222, 227

Marlatt, Daphne, 122

marriage plot, 42–43, 48–49, 52–53, 270

masculine/patriarchal domination of culture. *See* patriarchal culture

Mason, Mary, 10, 24–25, 41, 78

McCarthy, Mary, 70

McFague, Sallie, 187, 196

Meany, Donna, 133, 227, 230

Meigs, Margaret, 52, 269
    personal collection of treasures, 54

Meigs, Mary, 6, 197, 235
    act of "coming out," 90, 245, 279 (*See also* lesbianism)
    alterity, 55, 107

veneer of gentility, 95, 99
as visual artist, xvi, xvii, 183
as witness to evil, 240–42

Mennonite holocaust, 27, 113–14, 251

Mennonite sense of community, 64–65, 248, 283

Mennonites, xv, 13, 15, 34, 50, 58–59

Merleau-Ponty, Maurice, 205

middle class, 26–27, 31, 33, 38, 95, 230, 252

Misch, Georg, 12, 196–97, 258

modernism, 10, 19–20, 56, 171, 208, 249

Moodie, Susanna, 152, 189–90, 192

moon, 166–67, 178, 261

moral code, 197, 207

moral integrity (sense of goodness), 210

moral responsibility, 226, 239. *See also* ethical conduct

moral sensibility, 196, 278, 280

Moray, Gerta, 37–38, 40, 130

Morgan, David, 230

mortality. *See* aging and mortality; death

Morton, Adam, 197

mother, 34, 41, 48, 67, 143. *See also* domesticity
Butala's, 76
in Canadian female autobiographical tradition, 270
contradictory portraits of, 77
criticism or laments about the lives of, 35, 53–54, 269
denial of mother's life, 42, 52, 269
Mary Meigs', 53–54, 108, 238, 244, 267
maternal pretexts, 41–43
as "other," 25
power of, 9, 40–42, 85, 142, 269, 290–91
Pratt's, 40, 231

Reid's relationship to mother, 85–87, 141, 189, 262
role in transmitting traditions, 40

Mother Earth, 166

"Mother Nature," 152

Mowat, Farley, 202

Munro, Alice, 37–38, 54, 95

Murphy, Emily, 5

mystical awareness, 207, 261, 282

mystical experiences, 202, 206, 228, 231

mysticism, 203–4, 206–7, 209, 280

mysticism and ethics, 207–8

myth, 37, 95, 218, 245, 255
as organizing principle, 3
of the West, 5, 35, 80

N

narcissism, 93, 134, 138

nature (natural world), 7–8, 171, 257. *See also* bees; birds; garden
Aganetha Dyck, 147–49, 154, 156–64
artistic creativity and, 172
childhood exposure to, 187
connection to the rhythms of femininity, 148
culture as part of, 153, 162
distinct from built environment, 135, 154, 170
emotions and, 192
as feminine entity ("Mother Nature"), 152
imperial view of, 151–53
as leading character, 165, 273
Mary Meigs, 150, 179–87
Mary Pratt, 150, 171–79
organic view of, 151, 153, 162

as "other," 75, 149, 151, 165, 171, 188, 275

pastoral view of, 153

perceived as masculine territory, 148, 166, 169, 190, 273

protectionist view of, 151, 153, 163

ravishing of, 174–75 (*See also* environment)

as refreshment and source of peace, 190

rural women and, 127

sense of loss, 155, 248, 277

Sharon Butala, 25, 73, 121–23, 149–50, 165–71

spiritual inspiration, 202, 216, 280–82

spiritually enhancing, 149, 236

as ultimate reality, 193

ways of viewing (Fines), 12

"wild," 168, 170, 173, 191

wilderness, 173, 180, 189–90, 250, 265, 275

"Nature as Monster," 167

Nature "ensouled," 216

The Nature of Things (TV series), xv, 284

Neuman, Shirley, 27, 98, 103, 122

Newell, William H., 17

Newfoundland male hunting and fishing culture, 132, 226, 276

Newfoundland wilderness, 173, 180, 250, 265, 275

Newman, Peter, 202

Norris, Kathleen, 149, 201

Norwood, Vera, 152

O

objectification of the female. *See under* code of femininity

O'Keefe, Georgia, xii, 86

old lesbians, 108–9. *See also* old women

"Old Lesbians" (conference), 103

"Old Man on His Back," 188

"The Old Man on his Back Shortgrass and Priairie Preserve," 169

old women, 108–9, 199, 246

adventurers and trail blazers, 292

freedom and, 258–59, 300n5

in literature, 258

repository of female power, 223

as sexual beings, 101, 271

special role, 187, 248

as spiritual resources, 197, 256, 282, 300n2

organic view of nature, 151, 153–55, 162, 171

Ortner, Sherry, 11, 152, 167, 175

P

Pagés, Estelle, 255–56

Pahre, Robert, 18

"pantheistic" view of the universe, 206

paranormal, 202, 217, 261–62, 281, 301n7

"pathetic fallacy," 156

patriarchal culture, 4, 20, 32, 56, 66, 175, 186, 201, 240, 243, 245

in language usage, 6, 36

Northrop Frye and, 3

organized religion, 196, 257

ravishing natural resources, 174–75

women's internalization of, 5

Tong, Rosemarie, 58

traditional marriage, 44–46, 268–69. *See also* marriage plot

transcendence, 197, 258

transitional generation. *See* liminal generation

Trilling, Diana, 70

truth and truth-telling, 12, 212, 227, 229, 232, 278
    "coming out" in print, 279
    contradictory truths, 195–96

Turner, Frederick, 176, 276

Turner, Victor, 19

U

unconscious, 23, 36, 196–97, 209

Underhill, Evelyn, 12, 206–8, 228, 258

unfinished business, 207, 211–12, 242, 245, 258, 260, 278–79, 283. *See also* truth and truth-telling

unicorn vision, 218, 392n26

upper class, 45, 48, 53, 102, 269, 298n16

V

Veldhuis, Phil, 65

Vendler, Helen, 70

veneer of gentility, 95, 99

victimization, 9, 36, 43, 45, 132–33, 175, 268, 291
    inherent in patriarchal system, 58, 82
    in reproductive and sexual experience, 64

violence against women, 114–15, 173–74, 222, 227, 272

Visser, Margaret, 129
    The Rituals of Dinner, 128

vitalism, 206, 228, 257, 301n16

voyeurism, 93, 97, 136, 138

W

Walsh, Meeka, 114

Walshem, Margaret van, 59–60

Warland, Betsy, 239

Weil, Lisa, 90, 237

Weil, Simone, 121

Weiler, Merike, 276

West, Katherine, 33, 53, 231, 233

Wilkenson, Shelagh, 199, 258–59

Williams, Terry, 201

Wilson, Edmund, xvi, 33, 55–56, 104

Winston, Mark, xv, 255, 274, 284

Wolf, Naomi, 117. *See also* beauty myth

women. *See* old women

Women and Art (courses), 32

Women Studies courses, 5, 294n3

women's psychic benefits from contact with land, 167, 291

women's reproductive power, 127, 138, 140, 142, 153, 175
    feminine principle, 152, 223
    institutionalizing of, 65
    sense of identity and, 271

Woolf, Virginia, xii, 21, 86, 108
    To the Lighthouse, 48, 239

Wordsworth, William, 152, 167

Y

York Sculpture Gardens, 67, 147, 157